# GETTING HOOKED

The essays in this volume offer the most thorough and up-to-date discussion available of the relationship between addiction and rationality. This is the only book-length treatment of the subject and includes contributions from philosophers, psychiatrists, neurobiologists, sociologists, and economists.

Contrary to the widespread view that addicts are subject to overpowering and compulsive urges, the authors in this volume demonstrate that addicts are capable of making choices and responding to incentives. At the same time they disagree with Gary Becker's argument that addiction is the result of rational choice. The volume offers an up-to-date exposition of the neurophysiology of addiction, a critical examination of the Becker theory of rational addiction, an argument for a "visceral theory of addiction," a discussion of compulsive gambling as a form of addiction, several discussions of George Ainslie's theory of hyperbolic discounting, analyses of social causes and policy implications, and an investigation of the problem of relapse.

In tackling the critical issue of voluntary self-destructive behavior from many perspectives, the book will be an important resource for philosophers, psychologists, psychiatrists, economists, and sociologists.

Jon Elster is Robert K. Merton Professor of Social Science at Columbia University.

Ole-Jørgen Skog is Professor of Sociology at the University of Oslo.

# Getting Hooked

## Rationality and Addiction

*Edited by*

JON ELSTER
OLE-JØRGEN SKOG

CAMBRIDGE
UNIVERSITY PRESS

CAMBRIDGE UNIVERSITY PRESS
Cambridge, New York, Melbourne, Madrid, Cape Town, Singapore, São Paulo

Cambridge University Press
The Edinburgh Building, Cambridge CB2 8RU, UK

Published in the United States of America by Cambridge University Press, New York

www.cambridge.org
Information on this title: www.cambridge.org/9780521640084

First published 1999
This digitally printed version 2007

*A catalogue record for this publication is available from the British Library*

*Library of Congress Cataloguing in Publication data*
Getting hooked : rationality and addiction / edited by Jon Elster and
Ole-Jørgen Skog.
p.    cm.
ISBN 0-521-64008-3 (hc.)
1. Addicts – Psychology.   2. Compulsive behavior – Etiology.
3. Substance abuse – Etiology.   4. Self-control.   5. Choice
(Psychology)   I. Elster, Jon. 1940–   .   II. Skog, Ole-Jørgen.
RC533.G45   1999
616.86 – dc21                                        98-17266
                                                          CIP

ISBN 978-0-521-64008-4 hardback
ISBN 978-0-521-03879-9 paperback

# Contents

# Preface and Acknowledgments

The essays collected in the present volume came out of meetings of a Working Group on Addiction that met annually from 1992 to 1997. In addition to the contributors to the volume, the group included Aanund Hylland and Jørg Mørland. Their contributions to the discussions in the group have been decisive in shaping our individual and collective views on addiction. The work of the group has been funded by the Norwegian Research Council, the Norwegian Institute for Alcohol and Drug Research, the Norwegian Directorate for the Prevention of Alcohol and Drug Problems, and the Russell Sage Foundation.

# Contributors

**George Ainslie** is Chief of Psychiatry at the Veterans Administration in Coatesville, Pennsylvania.

**James David** is Associate Professor of Psychiatry at the Albert Einstein College of Medicine.

**Jon Elster** is Professor of Political Science at Columbia University.

**Eliot Gardner** is Professor of Psychiatry and Neuroscience at the Albert Einstein College of Medicine.

**Olav Gjelsvik** is Professor of Philosophy at the University of Oslo.

**George Loewenstein** is Professor of Decision and Social Sciences at Carnegie-Mellon University.

**Karl Ove Moene** is Professor of Economics at the University of Oslo.

**Thomas Schelling** is Professor of Economics at the University of Maryland.

**Ole-Jørgen Skog** is Professor of Sociology and Human Geography at the University of Oslo.

**Helge Waal** is Professor of Psychiatry at the University of Oslo.

# Introduction

JON ELSTER AND OLE-JØRGEN SKOG

## 1. The Challenges of Addiction

Addictive behavior poses two great challenges. On a practical level, addiction ravages lives and communities. The challenge is to identify treatments and social policies that can reduce or eliminate this plague. On a theoretical level, addiction raises the paradox of *voluntary self-destructive behavior*. The challenge is to explain why people engage in behaviors that they know will harm them: Why they begin, why they persist, and why they relapse. These two tasks are clearly interrelated. To design treatments and policies that will make people quit their addictions or never become addicted in the first place, it is useful to have an understanding of the causes of addiction and relapse. Conversely, the success or failure of specific treatments and policies may confirm or falsify specific explanations of why people get addicted. Nevertheless, emphasis may fall more heavily on the practical or on the theoretical aspect.

In this book we focus mainly on the theoretical issues. At the most basic level, addiction can be seen as an instance of the classical problem of weakness of will – acting against one's own better judgment. This is the explicit theme of Olav Gjelsvik's chapter, which is organized around a confrontation between two different concepts of weakness of will and their relevance for addictive behavior. It is also the implicit theme of much of Thomas Schelling's epilogue, in which he provides an extensive analysis of the many modalities of losing control and coping with loss of control. From very different perspectives, the chapters by George Ainslie and George Loewenstein also address this issue. As we explain in more detail below, Ainslie accounts for weakness of will in terms of a general mechanism for preference reversal. Loewenstein approaches the same phenomenon in terms of a general theory of "visceral factors" that have the capacity to short-circuit rational, deliberative choice. Elster's chapter explores the problem of self-control as it arises for the compulsive gambler.

Not all writers on addiction would agree, however, that it should be understood as a form of weakness of will, that is, as a form of irrational behavior. In his influential work on "rational addiction" Gary Becker has argued that addicts choose what, for them, is their best option. In Skog's chapter he spells out some of the main assumptions and implications of Becker's theory. Moene also assumes that addicts are rational, at least before they get hooked. Rather than explaining addiction in terms of individual weakness of will, he views it as a collective action problem due to the fact that consumers impose externalities on each other.

All the addictive behaviors discussed in this book have a common and increasingly well understood neurophysiological basis, with the exception of compulsive gambling about which less is known. The chapter by Gardner and David offers a survey of the neurobiological aspects of craving, withdrawal, and other brain-related aspects of addiction. In Waal's chapter, he draws on these biological findings as well as on the work of Becker and Ainslie to discuss the successes and failures of drug policies.

In the remainder of this introduction, we provide a general framework that, we hope, will help the reader see the individual contributions in a broader perspective. We shall mainly discuss two issues: *defining addictions* and *explaining addictions*. The relation between these two tasks can be brought out by considering the homogeneity of the behaviors that are commonly classified as addictive. Alcoholism and compulsive gambling, for instance, may seem closely related in many ways, but are they really produced by similar causal mechanisms? In a discussion of the "psychomotor stimulant theory of addiction," Roy Wise and Michael Bozarth (1987) distinguish between homology and analogy as explanatory heuristics. Whereas analogies do not necessarily extend beyond the superficial similarities that were originally noted, homologies, resulting from common causal mechanisms, do allow such predictive extensions. Consider the diagram shown in Figure 1.

A key problem in the study of putative addictions is determining whether they relate to each other as bats to birds and whales to sharks or whether they are unified by a common causal mechanism. From different perspectives, this issue is addressed in the chapters by Elster and Skog. The methodological point we want to make here is that the *definition* of addiction is, in the final account, inseparable from the *explanation* of

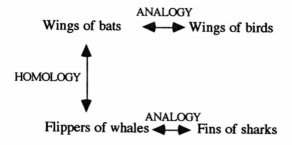

Figure 1

addiction. Although there may be some purposes for which the concepts "creatures that fly" (including flying fish!) or "creatures that live in the sea" are useful, the concepts of mammals, birds, and the various classes of fish are indispensable for scientific purposes. Similarly, theoretically grounded definitions of addiction are needed for treatment and policy purposes as well as for explanation. It is not very useful to define addiction phenomenologically as, say, "irresistible craving" if different cravings arise in different ways and are overcome or prevented by different means.

Addictions have a characteristic developmental sequence. Typically, there is an initial stage of moderate or controlled use; next, a stage characterized by loss of control, often accompanied by a desire to quit; and finally, relapse from a shorter or longer period of abstinence. To explain addictive behavior, one must offer an account for each of these stages. As Gjelsvik observes in his chapter, different explanations may be needed for different stages. Also, addictions that are causally different in earlier stages may be sustained by the same causal mechanisms in later stages. As Elster notes in his chapter, although people may start drinking and gambling for very different reasons, the reasons why drinkers and gamblers find it hard to quit may overlap.

Much of what we know about the neurophysiology of addiction is based on laboratory studies of animals. In their chapter summarizing this knowledge, Gardner and David observe the striking similarity of even identity between addictive behaviors in humans and animals. With regard to chemical addictions at least (and with the possible exception of LSD) animals can be made to self-administer all (and only) the substances to which humans are addicted. There is every reason to believe that the basic molecular machinery of addiction is the same in animals and humans. (With regard to behavioral addictions such as compulsive gambling, there are no animal studies. We do not know, therefore, whether these activities have the same neurophysiological substrate as chemical addictions.) Gardner and David also emphasize, however, that in the initial and late stages of addiction the behavior of humans often differs from that of animals. Thus, whereas the mechanism of cue-elicited craving exists both in animals and humans, only humans can prevent the triggering of the cue by crossing the street to avoid passing a bar where they used to drink. Also, what we define below as "secondary rewards" and "secondary withdrawal symptoms," which can be important factors in maintaining addiction in humans, do not exist in animals.

We now proceed as follows. In Section 2, we enumerate and classify the behaviors – substance-based or not – that have been described as addictive. At this stage we neither endorse nor deny the validity of that description but simply offer a catalogue of prima facie addictive behaviors. In Section 3, still proceeding at a preanalytical or phenomenological level, we distinguish the addictions from a number of related but apparently different patterns. In Section 4, we move closer to a theoretical analysis, by identifying and discussing a number of features that have been cited as characteristic or even defining of the addictions. In Section 5, we survey some of the main explanations that have been offered to account for addictive behavior.

## 2. Putative Addictive Behaviors

The following list of things and activities for which there is prima facie evidence for something like addiction is taken from Ainslie (1992, pp. 3–4):

- alcohol,
- drugs,
- food,
- gambling,
- prescription tranquilizers,
- nicotine,
- caffeine,
- sugar,
- chocolate,
- water (which, in large quantities, intoxicates by diluting the electrolytes of the blood),
- romantic relationships,
- emotional dependence,
- promiscuous sexual encounters,
- masturbation,
- deviant sexual practices,
- television games and video games,
- haste,
- work,
- shoplifting,
- self-inducible epileptic seizures,
- physical self-mutilation,
- aggression toward others,
- spending money,
- religiosity and fasting,
- maladaptive personality traits such as overcompetitiveness, procrastination, and obsessional jealousy, and
- compulsions to repeat.

In addition, we might cite addiction to risk taking (Bromiley and Curley 1992, p. 119, citing Keyes 1985), to pyromania (Fenichel 1945, pp. 371–2), to TV watching (Smith 1986), to reading (Fenichel 1945, p. 381; Nell 1988, p. 211 ff., and Ch. 11), to religious confessions (Lewis

1992, p. 136), to status (Scitovsky 1992, p. 130), and to emotional experiences such as hubris (Lewis 1992, p. 78). More recently, newspaper articles increasingly refer to addiction to the Internet. According to Peele (1985, p. 25), "Addiction may occur with any potent experience." In his view, if somebody derives a great deal of satisfaction from, say, collecting stamps or watching birds, that activity is potentially addictive.

We may distinguish between the addictions that are based on the intake of a substance and those that are not. Adopting the terminology of Marks (1990), we refer to these as, respectively, chemical and behavioral addictions. Within the former, there is a further subset that we shall refer to as the "core addictions": addiction to nicotine, alcohol, opiates, cocaine, caffeine, and amphetamines. Any definition or explanation of addiction is constrained by the need to attach particular importance to these cases. Within the core addictions, nicotine addiction stands out. Many generalizations about drug dependence break down because they do not cover nicotine addiction. It is not mood altering, nor does it become an all-dominant concern that drives out all other activities, a feature sometimes used to define addiction (e.g., Seeburger 1993, p. 83). Within the core addictions one may, furthermore, distinguish between stimulants (amphetamines, cocaine) and depressants (alcohol, barbiturates, opiates). Although nicotine is technically a stimulant, many people report that they smoke in order to relax ("Nesbitt's Paradox"; see McKim 1991, p. 168).

We may also distinguish between activities that are observed at nonzero levels in all individuals, as a matter of physiological survival, and those that many, perhaps most, members of the population never adopt at all. Eating is necessary for survival; overeating is arguably a form of addiction (Hoebel, 1998). Some degree of risk taking similarly is necessary for survival; the risk seeking observed in pathological gamblers is arguably a form of addiction (see Elster's chapter in this volume). By contrast, most people have never used hard drugs; a large fraction of the population has never smoked; and many have never taken a drink. This difference can matter both in explaining the onset of addiction and in designing policies or treatments.

## 3. Addictions, Habits, and Compulsions

As we further discuss in Section 4, one approach to addictions is to define them as activities that the individual wants to quit but is unable to. Whatever its other problems, this definition seems too broad. It covers a number of activities that intuitively do not belong with addictions. For one thing, people may have bad *habits* that they want to give up but cannot. For another, they may be subject to *compulsions*, which they try to resist but cannot. Scratching a sore is an example of the former; the need to double- and triple-check that the door is locked an example of the latter. At their face, at least, these activities do not seem to belong with alcoholism and heroin abuse.

Yet here, too, we cannot simply look at the surface. Remember, again, that the flippers of whales may be more closely related to the wings of bats than to the fins of sharks. Perhaps a fuller understanding of the causal processes underlying habits and compulsions would make us classify them, or some of them, as species of addiction. Or, conversely, addictions might turn out to be a subvariety of compulsions. Also, theoretical analysis might enable us to say something precise about the differences between addictions on the one hand and habits and compulsions on the other, rather than simply asserting that they are "obviously different."

Some of the theories that we survey in Section 5 do in fact have implications of this kind. For Gary Becker (1992, p. 329), "An *addiction* is defined simply as a strong habit." In this statement, "habit" is defined by the fact that "greater consumption earlier stimulates greater, not lesser consumption later." If the habit is "strong," the effects of past consumption "are sufficiently strong to be destabilizing." We refer to Skog's chapter for an explanation of this statement. Intuitively, it asserts that an addiction is a habit that has gotten out of hand. Becker does not go very far, however, in specifying the actual mechanisms that give rise to habit and addictions. As observed by Skog in his chapter, Becker's formal assumptions can be supported by a large variety of such mechanisms.

George Ainslie's theory, summarized in Section 5, has even greater potential for integrating these diverse phenomena. Ainslie asserts that bad habits and addictions are two different species of the same genus, namely behavior caused by hyperbolic time discounting. People who have decided to stop drinking may change their minds when offered a drink, because the earlier reward of drinking comes to dominate the delayed reward of good health. Similarly, somebody may indulge in an itch, "which the person wants to be rid of and which will abate if ignored, but which he usually maintains because of brief preference for the sensation of scratching" (Ainslie 1992, p. 100).

Ainslie's theory also purports to explain compulsive behaviors. He does not say that compulsions are addictions. Rather, he implies that they arise as side effects of successful attempts to control addictions. As further explained in Ainslie's chapter, and in Gjelsvik's discussion of his views, the impulses that give rise to addiction, procrastination, and a number of other undesirable phenomena may be overcome by constructing personal rules. These rules may become very rigid, if the addict or procrastinator fears that any exceptions might start him down the slippery slope to relapse. He may want to relax his rules yet is overwhelmed by panic when he tries. This rigidity is a hallmark of compulsive behavior.

Habits can be bad or good, welfare reducing or welfare enhancing. We might ask whether the same is true of addictions. Although talk of a beneficial addiction seems strange in ordinary parlance, theoretical analysis might enable us to identify behaviors that have all the features of (what we usually call) addiction except that of being harmful. In that case, we could either make the terminological decision to distinguish between good and bad addictions or coin two new words, one for the beneficial analogue to addiction and another for the general genus of which that analogue and addiction proper would be species. In the next few paragraphs we take the first option; in later sections "addiction" will refer exclusively to harmful phenomena.

Among the theoretical approaches to addiction surveyed in Section 5, only the model of Becker and Murphy (1988), based on Stigler and Becker (1977), has room for the idea of positive addictions. As more fully discussed in Skog's chapter (see his Figure 1 and accompanying explanation), negative addictions have two features. On the one hand, higher past consumption decreases the level of utility one derives from a given amount of consumption in the present (Becker's property P1). On the other hand, it increases the marginal utility of present consumption (Becker's property P2). If we observe P2 without P1, we have a case of beneficial addiction. A person may find, for instance, that the more he listens to classical music and learns to appreciate it, the more pleasure he derives from it. At the same time, his suffering when prevented from listening also goes up. As Skog notes in his chapter, the production of withdrawal symptoms could be one mechanism underlying property P2, which is common to both harmful and beneficial addictions.

Suppose now that the music lover's wife does not like classical music, and in fact becomes furious with exposure to it, both because she cannot stand it and because it takes up too much time she could have spent doing other things with her husband. Because he is affected by her anger, the welfare of her husband goes down. In that case, property P1 might well be satisfied. The addiction, once beneficial, has become harmful. To take another example, the so-called workaholic might initially be subject to a positive addiction, which then, by a similar feedback from the environment, turns into a negative one. Some overeaters (assuming that overeating can usefully be viewed as a form of addiction) might have been perfectly happy in the absence of the social stigma imposed on the obese. This is one sense in which the etiology of (negative) addictions may have a social component: The negative reactions of other people to the addictive behavior may depress the addict's welfare to the point that property P1 is satisfied. Other social aspects of addiction are discussed in the chapters by Moene and Waal.

## 4. Characterizing and Defining the Addictions

Attempts to define addiction tend to emphasize one of two clusters of criteria. On the one hand there are proposals to define addiction in terms of (more or less) objective factors, notably (i) tolerance, (ii) withdrawal, and (iii) objective harm. On the other hand, there are more subjectively oriented proposals, which define addiction in terms of (iv) craving, (v) a desire to quit, and (vi) an inability to quit. Most authors tend in fact to give some weight to all six criteria, but, as we said, emphasis tends to differ. In discussing the criteria, we shall try both to disambiguate them and to make recommendations about the most useful acceptations. In doing so, we are guided by three concerns. First, the criteria must be broad enough to fit all the core addictions. Second, they must not be so broad as to include any kind of sustained pleasure-seeking or pain-avoiding behavior. Third, they should not invite accusations of confusing bats and birds: Even at the level of phenomenological analysis, some thought should be given to the underlying causal mechanisms.

### *Tolerance*

In common parlance, tolerance is the phenomenon that, as time passes, the agent needs more of a given substance (or activity) to obtain the same "thrill" or "high." This effect is very marked for the opiates and alcohol, but much less so for cannabis and cocaine. Tolerance can also pertain to other effects of drugs, notably their lethality. The regular heroin dose of a heavy user would be lethal to the novice or to the previously heavy user who has abstained for some time. As explained by Gardner and David, tolerance with respect to the euphoric effects of drugs may be caused either by neuroadaptation in the brain reward system or by an increased rate of metabolism. Less is known about tolerance with regard to the behavioral addictions, which do not rely in well-understood ways on such mechanisms. In his chapter, Elster discusses the claim that something akin to tolerance occurs in gambling.

Tolerance with respect to the lethal effects of drugs may be caused by conditioning, as demonstrated by Siegel et al. (1982) in an experiment that deserves to be described at some length:

> Rats were given daily intravenous injections [of heroin] for 30 days. The injections, either a dextrose placebo or heroin, were given in either the animal colony room or a different room where there was constant white noise. The drug and the placebo were given on alternate days and the drug condition always corresponded with a particular environment so that for some rats the heroin was always administered in the white noise room and the placebo was always given in the colony. For other rats the heroin was always given in the

colony and the placebo was always given in the white noise room. Another group of rats served as control: These were injected in different rooms on alternate days but were injected only with dextrose and had no experience with heroin at all.

All rats were then injected with a large dose of heroin.... The rats in one group, labeled the ST group, were given the heroin in the same room where they had previously been given heroin. The other rats, the DT group, were given the heroin in the room where they had previously been given the placebo. Siegel found that 96 percent of the control group died, showing the lethal effect of the heroin in nontolerant animals. Rats in the DT group who received heroin were partly tolerant, and only 64 percent died. Only 32 percent of the ST rats died, showing that the tolerance was even greater when the overdose test was done in the same environment where the drug had previously been administered. (McKim 1991, p. 46)

Similar conditioned tolerance occurs among human opiate addicts, who are less likely to die of overdose if the drug is injected in known surroundings.

### Withdrawal

The phenomenon of withdrawal, or the production of abstinence symptoms, is often considered the most important feature of addiction. In its most general form, withdrawal simply means that upon cessation of the behavior some unpleasant consequence occurs. That concept, however, is much too broad to be useful. For one thing, we need to define the baseline with respect to which the consequence is said to be unpleasant. For another, we need to understand the nature of the unpleasant consequence and the mechanism by which it is brought about.

We shall refer to the normal state of the organism as state A, the addictive one as state B, and the immediate postaddictive one as state C. In addiction, these relate to each other as shown in Figure 2 (with time measured on the horizontal axis and welfare on the vertical axis).

We stipulate, in other words, that the baseline for assessing the withdrawal symptoms in state C is state A rather than state B. If one chose B as the baseline, one would certainly risk confusing sharks and whales. Insulin

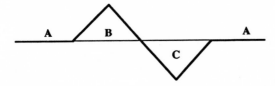

**Figure 2**

and aspirin, for instance, would then be said to produce withdrawal symptoms. When people engage in activities such as TV watching or reading to escape from the misery of everyday life, the return of the misery upon cessation of the activity does not, on this more restricted definition, count as a withdrawal symptom. Similarly, it has been argued that

> Among runners for whom the activity serves to modify dysphoric mood states of psychophysiological distress, return of distress once the effects of the run have decreased may be misunderstood as symptoms of physiological withdrawal. In this instance, withdrawal may not be the pain associated with the body adjusting to the physiological changes of nonrunning, but a reexperience of the pain felt *before* the physiological changes of running. (Peele 1985, p. 98, citing Robbins and Joseph 1982).

Whether or not this observation is factually correct (see Goldstein 1984, p. 82 for withdrawal symptoms caused by loss of sensitivity to endogenous opioids such as those produced by running), the conceptual point is well taken.

By contrast, when people drink or take heroin to escape from a drab life, the cessation causes their life to be even worse than the one they escaped from. Similarly, when people have difficulties getting off tranquilizers, it is not simply because their old problems reappear when they do so. The withdrawal symptoms are "untypical for the kind of anxiety for which the drug was probably prescribed in the first place" (Orford 1985, p. 67). This is a qualitative statement about the nature of the problems in stages A and C, not a quantitative comparison of welfare levels. An explicit comparison of the latter kind, offered by Smith and Wesson (1983) with regard to the use of benzodiazepines, is shown in Figure 3 (intensity of symptoms measured on the vertical scale).

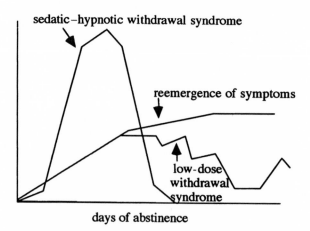

**Figure 3**

Although the reemergence of preaddictive problems should not be confused with dysphoric primary withdrawal (discussed momentarily), the two phenomena may interact. "If the user has taken the drug or alcohol to relieve particular feelings of distress, the [dysphoric] symptoms may seem magnified, markedly increasing craving for the drug as a means to relief" (Hyman 1995, p. 32).

The reduction of welfare in stage C compared to stage A that characterizes addiction must be distinguished from the general tendency for welfare to drop momentarily upon the cessation of any pleasurable activity (Solomon and Corbit 1974). A sudden interruption of sexual experience, for instance, causes welfare to drop below the preintercourse level and to remain there for a while before the subject returns to the baseline level. In George Ainslie's phrase (personal communication), this mechanism is part of "the natural history of consumption." It does not (*pace* Scitovsky 1992, p. 130) suffice to define a behavior as addictive. To distinguish between this tendency and the more specific phenomenon of withdrawal, one can note that the temporal profile of addiction is very different. Addiction takes time to build. The withdrawal symptoms are not caused by single episodes, but by a cumulative history of consumption. The symptoms persist for days, weeks, or occasionally for months, rather than minutes or hours. Also, in addiction, repeated episodes of consumption and abstention have a pattern not found in the consumption of ordinary goods (see Figure 4).

The reduction of welfare in stage C compared to stage A may be caused by the recollection of stage B. There are several ways in which memory may be involved in such welfare losses. Consider first the person who looks back at a wonderful experience with LSD. The memory, together with the knowledge that LSD is currently unavailable, makes the person more unhappy than before the experience occurred. Loss of a sexual partner can have the same effect: It may be *worse* to have loved and lost

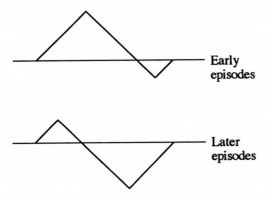

Early
episodes

Later
episodes

**Figure 4**

than never to have loved at all. (Or consider Donne's "Tis better to be foul than to have been fair.") This negative "contrast effect" usually coexists, however, with a positive "endowment effect," caused by the fact that the memory of a pleasurable experience is a pleasurable memory (Tversky and Griffin 1991). In general, the net effect of these two mechanisms is indeterminate.

Consider next the alcoholic who drinks to escape the awareness of the fact that he is an alcoholic. Here the welfare loss experienced upon cessation takes the form of an acutely unpleasant recollection of the way he has been ruining his life and that of others by drinking. This mechanism obviously cannot explain why people get hooked on addictive uses and behaviors. The alcoholism that the alcoholic is trying to forget by drinking cannot itself have been caused by such escapism. Such *secondary withdrawal symptoms*, as we shall call them, can help explain the persistence of addiction but hardly its emergence in the first place. Moreover, they do not seem equally important for all addictions. They may play a role in sustaining alcoholism, overeating, and compulsive gambling, but not in maintaining smoking behavior or cocaine abuse.

These memory-mediated withdrawal symptoms do not (we assume) play any role in animal addiction. The physiological or *primary withdrawal symptoms*, common to both animals and humans, fall into two categories (see the chapter by Gardner and David): somatic symptoms, such as tremors, sweating, and the like; and feelings of dysphoria and anhedonia. Some addictive drugs, such as cocaine, do not produce somatic withdrawal symptoms. All addictive drugs, however, produce dysphoria upon cessation. Gardner and David argue that these symptoms are produced by the brain-reward system and are indissociable, therefore, from the euphoric effects. Again, little is known about primary withdrawal symptoms in behavioral addictions (see Elster's chapter for a discussion of withdrawal in gambling).

### Harm

Addiction, as we said, can ravage lives and communities. For an outside observer, this is perhaps the most striking aspect of the phenomenon. There are good reasons, however, for considering the harm caused by addiction as a frequently occurring effect of the behavior rather than as a constitutive and invariable component. Caffeine is uncontroversially addictive, yet the damage to body, mind, or purse caused by coffee drinking is minimal or nil. Methadone users are addicted but otherwise as normal and healthy as nonaddicts. A compulsive gambler with a large fortune to draw on need not suffer any harm – unless the thrill from gambling depends on there being a real possibility of losing everything (see Elster's chapter).

|  | Positive | Negative |
|---|---|---|
| Primary effect | (1) | (2) |
| Secondary effect | (3) | (4) |

**Figure 5**

*Craving*

The varieties of craving can be classified along two dimensions, as shown in Figure 5.

1. Craving may refer to the intensely pleasant experience caused by release of dopamine in the brain-reward system. This is a common element in all chemical addictions. The specific mechanisms by which drugs increase the amount of dopamine differ from drug to drug, but the final result is the same. Nothing is known about similar mechanisms for behavioral addictions. In many cases, however, what is craved is not a positive experience of euphoria but rather an escape from a miserable existence. Alcohol and heroin are often sought for their numbness-inducing effect, not for any euphoric qualities (Peele 1985, p. 64).

2. Craving may also derive from the desire to get rid of primary withdrawal symptoms, whether these are somatic or psychological (dysphoria). Gardner and David argue, in their chapter, that earlier writers on addiction tended to overestimate the desire for relief from somatic withdrawal as a component of craving. Animals will self-administer drugs directly to the reward centers of the brain even when there are no somatic withdrawal symptoms. By contrast, the desire for relief from dysphoria is probably an important component of craving in most cases.

3. Craving may derive from what we shall call *secondary reinforcers*. One of us is a former heavy smoker, who quit twenty-five years ago, when his consumption reached forty cigarettes a day. He remembers vividly what it was like to organize one's whole life around smoking. When things went well, he reached for a cigarette. When things went badly, he did the same. He smoked before breakfast, after a meal, and when he had a drink; he smoked before doing something difficult and after doing something difficult. He always had an excuse for smoking. In addition, smoking became a ritual that served to highlight salient aspects of experience and to impose structure on what would otherwise have

been a confusing morass of events. Smoking provided the commas, semicolons, question marks, exclamation marks, and full stops of experience. It helped him to achieve a feeling of mastery, the feeling that he was in charge of events rather than submitting to them. (For a related discussion, see Klein [1993].) This craving for cigarettes amounts to a desire for order and control, not for nicotine. For such smokers, the main aspect of having a cigarette is the act of lighting up. Elster, in his chapter, also discusses the emergence of secondary reinforcers in gambling. Psychologists who have written on addiction (Orford 1985, Peele 1985) tend to emphasize this aspect of the phenomenon.

4. Finally, craving may derive from secondary withdrawal symptoms. The awareness that one is ruining one's life and perhaps that of others may be so intensely unpleasant and induce so much guilt or shame that one craves for relief.

These different forms of craving will appear at different stages. The desire to achieve euphoria or to escape dysphoria are prior to the fear of primary withdrawal symptoms, which in turn will tend to appear before the fear of secondary withdrawal and secondary rewards. Their place in the etiology of addiction will differ correspondingly. We hypothesize that the cue-elicited cravings that are responsible for many cases of relapse (Siegel et al. 1982; Siegel, Krank, and Hinson 1988) may belong to any of the four categories.

## Inability to Quit

This feature of addicts may plausibly be supposed to be fully explained by the various forms of craving. To be addicted *is* to be subject to craving of such a strength that it is or would be difficult to quit. (Note that this criterion may be satisfied even if there is no desire to quit.) The inability to quit has an important time dimension, in that it may be either a "within-episode" phenomenon or a "between-episode phenomenon." Jellinek (1960) draws a distinction between "gamma alcoholism," characterized by "loss of control," and "delta alcoholism," characterized by "inability to abstain." With the latter, he writes (p. 38), "there is no ability to 'go on the water wagon' for even a day without the manifestation of withdrawal symptoms; the ability to control the amount of intake on any given occasion, however, remains intact." Similar distinctions apply to overeating, cocaine addiction, and gambling, but not to smoking or use of opiates. (There are no out-of-control "binge smokers.")

## Desire to Quit

Many writers use the desire to quit as an important indication of addiction. For some writers, this desire must be an actual subjective fact. Thus Peele (1985, p. 24) argues that it is absurd to say that people "can depend on what they can't detect and don't care about." We disagree. Consider the pre-1950 cigarette smoker who lived (and died) in happy ignorance that he was destroying his body by smoking. We would still claim he was addicted if it were true that had he known the facts about smoking he would have wanted to quit (but would not have been able to). Although, as we have seen, the causal process of addiction may be speeded up by the addict's knowledge that he or she is addicted (by the production of secondary withdrawal symptoms), this is far from being a necessary feature.

## 5. Theories of Addiction

Writers on addiction have drawn on a large number of theories to explain the emergence and persistence of addictive behaviors, as well as later relapse. Herrnstein and Prelec (1992a) list four explanations, and there are several others that need to be considered. The following survey does not aim at anything approaching completeness. We focus on behaviorally oriented theories, whereas more traditional approaches from psychiatry or psychoanalysis are considered more briefly or not at all. Our premise is that addictive behavior is most usefully considered as the outcome of (more or less rational) *choice* that can be studied in terms of the reward structure and information of the agent.

### *Neurophysiological Approaches to Addiction*

We begin, nevertheless, by considering an approach that might appear to deny the relevance of choice altogether. The neurophysiological study of the chemical addictions, as summarized by Gardner and David in their chapter, might appear to support a view of the addict as driven by irresistible cravings that leave no room for choice. A closer reading of their chapter will, however, dispel that impression. The neurophysiological study of addiction is entirely compatible with a choice-oriented approach. It may even be compatible with a rational-choice approach, although that question is, as we shall see, more controversial.

The central topic in the neurophysiological study of the addiction is the reward system of the brain – the fine grain of the mechanisms by which consumption of drugs, and its interruption, can produce extremes both of euphoria and dysphoria. While craving, tolerance, withdrawal, conditioning, and the other phenomena described by Gardner and David change the parameters of choice, they need not undermine the possibility of choice. One might well view the addict as making optimal choices within the reward structure induced by the consumption of drugs (or interruption of consumption).

This is one view of the pharmacological action of drugs: They affect only the reward structure, while leaving the capacity for making rational choices unaffected. If drug use interferes with the time preferences of the agent, causing the user to discount the future more heavily than in a nonaddicted state, that, too, affects the reward structure rather than the capacity to make rational choices. Another view is that drugs also undermine that capacity itself. Because the action of drugs is intimately connected with emotional and volitional centers in the brain, they might give rise to one or several of the known forms of irrationality, notably weakness of will or wishful thinking (see below). This second view is defended by Loewenstein in his chapter. He argues that visceral factors such as drug craving tend to overwhelm rational considerations, much as a person in a state of acute fear takes to flight rather than pausing to think whether his ends would not be better served by staying put.

### Rational-Choice Theory

The standard version of rational-choice explanation of behavior can be set out in the diagram shown in Figure 6 (see also Elster 1983, 1986, 1989). An action is rational if it satisfies three optimality conditions, represented by the unblocked arrows. (The significance of the blocked arrow from desires to beliefs will be explained shortly. The significance of the blocked arrows from action to desires and to beliefs is explained in Elster's chapter on gambling.) First, the action has to be the best means of realizing the agent's desires, given the agent's beliefs about ends–means relationships and other factual matters. Second, these beliefs themselves have to be optimal, given the information available to the agent. The process of belief formation must not be distorted by "cold" mistakes in information processing or "hot" mistakes caused by motivational biases. The blocked arrow from desires to beliefs excludes, for instance, wishful thinking as a rational mechanism of belief formation. Third, the amount of information or, more accurately, the amount of resources spent on acquiring information, must itself be optimal, given the agent's prior beliefs about the costs and benefits of information acquisition and the importance of the decision to him.

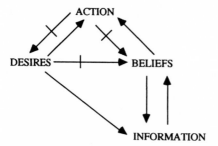

**Figure 6**

In the standard version, desires cannot be classified as rational or irrational. They act as the unmoved mover of the theory – used to assess the rationality of action, belief, and information gathering, while not themselves subject to any such assessment. This argument applies not only to substantive preferences for one good over another, but also to what one might call "formal preferences" such as degrees of risk aversion or time discounting. A time preference is just another preference. Some like chocolate ice cream, whereas others have a taste for vanilla: This is just a brute fact, and it would be absurd to say that one preference is more rational than the other. Similarly, it is just a brute fact that some like the present, whereas others have a taste for the future. If a person discounts the future very heavily, consuming an addictive substance may, for him, be a form of rational behavior.

The argument may seem counterintuitive. We believe, however, that if we want to use rational-choice theory to explain behavior on the bare assumption that *people make the most out of what they have*, the standard version is exactly right. If some individuals have the bad luck to be born with genes or be exposed to external influences that make them discount the future heavily, using drugs may, for them, be their best option. We cannot expect them to reduce their rate of time discounting, because to want to be motivated by long-term concerns ipso facto *is* to be motivated by long-term concerns (Elster 1997). If they do not have that motivation in the first place, they cannot be motivated to acquire it. This is not to say that rational-choice explanations of addiction are successful, only that they cannot be impugned simply by saying that a high discounting of the future is irrational.

Pathologies of irrational behavior can arise at each of the three stages of optimization distinguished above. An agent may fail to choose the action that, according to his own judgment, will best promote his desires. In that case, the irrationality takes the form of weakness of will (see below for a discussion of this phenomenon in the context of addiction). He may also fail to form the beliefs that are adequate in light of the available evidence. Finally, the agent may underinvest or overinvest in the acquisition of new information. The role of these forms of cognitive impairment in the explanation of addiction will be further considered below.

### Addiction as Rational Self-Medication

Several psychological theories of addiction explain alcohol or drug use as coping behavior in relation to some perceived problem. The so-called tension reduction theory is based on two hypotheses: (1) that alcohol reduces tensions and (2) that individuals drink alcohol for its tension-reducing properties (Capell and Greeley 1987). The closely related theory of stress response dampening starts off from the fact that the stressed individual reacts physiologically in several different systems, and it hypothesizes that alcohol dampens this physiological response, subjectively alleviating stress and thereby reinforcing drinking in similar stress situations (Sher 1987). Other traditions are more concerned with deprivation, inadequate socialization, poor socioeconomic conditions, etc. as predisposing factors. However, in all of these approaches, use, and ultimately abuse, are seen as attempts to handle subjectively perceived problems. This is also at the core of the rational-addiction theory proposed by Becker and Murphy (1988) and further discussed in Skog's chapter.

From the point of view of rational choice, these theories treat addiction as essentially rational self-medication. In this perspective, the addict feels that the substance he consumes (or the behavior he chooses) makes him better off, all things considered. If he has been aware of the risks being involved from the very beginning of his career, but still feels that addiction is a better option than abstaining, then he is a consonant or "happy" addict. This person is a rational addict, given his preferences, beliefs, and the circumstances. He has no desire to quit. Current prevalence estimates for different types of addictions may severely underestimate the number of consonant addicts, as their problem presumably is less visible than that of other addicts.

If the individual has misjudged his vulnerability, and acted on what has turned out to be an erroneous belief that he would not become addicted, or if he has severely underestimated the harmful consequences of his abuse, he may ultimately wish to quit. The price has become too high, compared to his original problem. Finding that he is now unable to quit, he would be conceived as a dissonant addict. Whether this addict is rational or not (i.e., whether or not he fits the description in Becker and Murphy [1988]) depends on whether or not his initial beliefs about the risks were rational, given the evidence (and whether the evidence was optimally acquired). In the special case of gambling (see Elster's chapter), one must also consider the rationality of the gambler's beliefs in the likelihood of winning.

### The Primrose Path

This account (proposed in Herrnstein and Prelec 1992a) focuses on the way into addiction through a series of incremental decisions with consequences that are not perceived by the agent until it is too late. The work arises out of Herrnstein's theory that human behavior is better explained by assuming that people *meliorate* than by assuming that they *maximize* (Herrnstein and Prelec 1992b). Assume that a person confronts two alternatives, such as drinking and not drinking. In any given period, he can choose the rate at which he will engage in one or the other activity, that is, how much of the time he will drink. Higher amounts of past drinking lower the pleasure he gets from drinking in the present, simply because of the decreasing marginal utility of consumption. One drink a day is more enjoyable than each of ten drinks taken on the same day. Yet, according to Herrnstein and Prelec, when a person decides whether to have a drink, he typically does not take into account the externality (or "internality") that arises from the fact that a drink now devalues drinks in the future. Rather, he simply compares the value of a drink now with the value of abstaining now. As long as the former is greater, he will choose to drink. If he discovers his mistake and tries to cut down on consumption in order to enhance the overall value from drinking, he will encounter withdrawal symptoms that sustain the addictive behavior.

The idea of melioration follows directly from Herrnstein's *matching law* (see the articles collected in Herrnstein 1997). It assumes that the addictive agents are completely myopic, in the cognitive sense just described. The assumption may be appropriate in the case of animal behavior, but it is far from universally valid in dealing with human choice. Human beings are uniquely capable both of identifying the future effects of their present behavior and of being motivated by them in choosing among present alternatives (Elster 1984). At the same time, they are also capable of acting against their own better judgment of what is in their long-term interest. Consider Saint Paul's statement, "I do not do the good I want, but the evil I do not want is what I do" (Romans 7:19).

## Addiction as the Result of a Divided Self

According to this account, suggested by the statement just quoted from Saint Paul, a person can have different selves or, more neutrally, different interests, which interact to cause addiction. As explained in Gjelsvik's chapter, this idea can be taken in two different ways. On the one hand, philosophers such as Donald Davidson (1969; 1980, Ch. 2) and David Pears (1984) have tried to explain addiction and related phenomena in terms of weakness of will, defined as follows: The person has to choose one of two options, both of which have something to be said in their favor. He judges that, all things considered, the reasons for choosing one option are stronger, yet he chooses the other. In this approach, the desire that wins out is the one that the person himself *at the time of choosing* judges to be more weakly supported. A person may sincerely want to stop drinking, yet accept a drink when offered one at a party, knowing *as he does so* that he should not.

A problem with this view is the difficulty of finding reliable evidence that the agent really thought that, all things considered, he should not take the drink. It is easy enough to find independent evidence that the driver, before going to the party, did not want to have more than two drinks. He may have told his wife, for instance, "Stop me if I have more than two drinks." After the party, too, he may regret his behavior as contrary to his real interest and take steps to ensure that it doesn't happen again. But how can we know that this all-things-considered judgment exists at the very moment that he is accepting the third drink? By assumption, there is no observable behavior that can support this interpretation.

George Ainslie (1975, 1992) tries to overcome this problem by explaining addiction in terms of preference reversal. Well ahead of the time of choice, the person prefers the option, say, of not smoking. Yet when an occasion for smoking comes closer in time, the attractions of smoking come to loom larger than those of good health, as when the smaller of two buildings comes to overshadow a larger one behind it when the spectator moves up closer. Less metaphorically, Ainslie's theory depends on the assumption that people typically discount the future by a function that is hyperbolic in shape rather than exponential, as assumed by most economists. Because of the central importance of Ainslie's theory in several chapters in this book, we shall devote some space to expounding it. Before we do so, however, we note that the key assumption of hyperbolic discounting is derived directly from Herrnstein's matching law. Whereas Herrnstein relied on that law to explain how myopia leads to addiction, Ainslie uses it to show that addictive behavior can arise even when people do take account of the future consequences of present behavior.

Addicts face a choice between the imminent pleasure of consuming and the delayed benefits from abstaining. Although these benefits are usually spread out over time, they will be represented here, without loss of generality, as a single delayed reward. They face this choice, moreover, on a number of successive occasions. The situation, then, can be represented as shown in Figure 7.

Initially, the agent faces the choice between an early small reward (e.g., smoking) at $t_1$ and a larger, delayed reward at $t_2$. Regardless of whether he or she chooses to take the smaller reward when it becomes available or

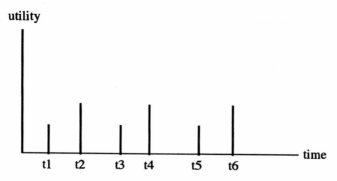

**Figure 7**

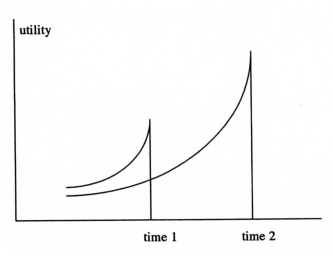

utility

time 1          time 2

**Figure 8**

to wait for the larger reward, he or she will face similar choices at $t_3$–$t_4$, at $t_5$–$t_6$, and so on. First, we focus on the single initial choice. Later, we shall see how the embeddedness of this choice in a series of similar choices can make a difference in the outcome.

Let us now consider an agent faced with a choice between a smaller, earlier reward and a larger, delayed reward (see Figure 8). At time 1, a small reward is made available to the agent. He can either take it or wait until time 2 to get a larger reward. The curves, reflecting time discounting, indicate the present values of these rewards at times before they are made available. They immediately tell us that the agent will take the smaller reward rather than wait for the larger one. At time 1, the present value of the larger reward is certainly less than the smaller reward. Moreover, at any time before time 1, the present value of the earlier, smaller reward is larger than that of the delayed, larger reward. If we ask the agent, well ahead of time 1, what he will do at time 1, he will answer that he intends to take the earlier reward. And when the time to choose arrives, he will in fact do what he said he would. This is *not* an instance of weakness of will because there is no conflict between what the agent intends to do and what he in fact does.

The shape of the time preference curve in Figure 8 reflects an assumption that people discount the future *coherently*, in the following sense. Consider three moments: Time 1, time 2, and time 3. At time 1, the agent is indifferent between getting a large reward at time 3 and a smaller reward at time 2. At time 2, a time-coherent agent will also be indifferent between getting the small reward at time 2 and the large reward at time 3. In other

words, the relative evaluation of the rewards offered at times 2 and 3 is
not affected by the time at which the evaluation is made, although the
absolute evaluation is.

By contrast, if the relative evaluation was time dependent, the agent
might not be able to stick to his decisions. At time 1, he might think that
at time 2 he will be indifferent between the two options, and yet at time
2 find himself to prefer the earlier, smaller reward. More to the point,
at time 1 he may prefer the larger reward to the smaller reward, and yet
he may find that his preferences are reversed at time 2. Such preference
reversal can be interpreted as weakness of will. It seems reasonable to
assume that the preferences that the agent forms well ahead of the time
of choice reflect his well-considered judgment. Before he goes to a party
where he knows that drinks will be offered, he fully believes that the
long-term benefits of abstaining are more important than the short-term
pleasures from drinking. However, when the time for the party comes
nearer, he changes his mind and decides to drink.

This predicament is expressed in Figure 9, which shows time preference curves that cross each other at t* before the early reward becomes
available. Prior to that time (e.g., at time 1) the agent believes that he
ought to take the greater, delayed reward. However, as the time of choice
approaches, the earlier, smaller reward becomes preferred. The agent,
we typically say, yields to temptation. In many cases, this is indeed an accurate description. If one takes a drink at the party, it may be because one
is tempted by the physical presence of alcohol. The preference reversal
might also occur, however, in the taxi on the way to the party, because *the
structure of subjective time is warped* in the way described in Figure 9. Ainslie
(1975, 1992) has marshaled empirical evidence that suggests that such
time preferences are pervasive.

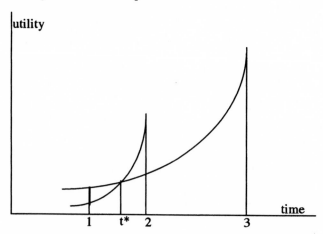

**Figure 9**

Ainslie's model has immediate implications for treatment and policy. The policy implications turn on enabling the agent to hold out in the time during which he is most at risk, between time t* and time 2 in Figure 9. These are considered in Waal's chapter. Here we offer brief comments on treatment and self-treatment.

Treatment can take the form of helping the agent to *precommit himself* to the larger delayed reward by imposing extra costs on the choice of the earlier reward that will shift the discounting curve from that reward downward. (For the general idea of precommitment, see Elster [1984] and Schelling [1986].) Antabuse, including subcutaneous implantations, is one example. Another is offered by Schelling (1992, p. 167):

> In a cocaine addiction center in Denver, patients are offered an opportunity to submit to extortion. They may write a self-incriminating letter, preferably a letter confessing their drug addiction, deposit the letter with the clinic, and submit to a randomized schedule of laboratory tests. If the laboratory finds evidence of cocaine use, the clinic sends the letter to the addressee.

In addition to treatment that requires external assistance of some kind, the agent can bootstrap himself out of addiction by a mental accounting arrangement. Ainslie (1975, 1992) shows that if the agent can "bunch" his choices to appear as a single choice between always choosing the small rewards at $t_1$, $t_3$, $t_5$... (see Figure 7) or always choosing the large rewards at $t_2$, $t_4$, $t_6$... he is more likely to go for the large rewards. At the very least, the "risk interval" between $t_0$ and $t_1$ will be compressed; they may even disappear altogether so that there is no time at which the agent prefers the smaller rewards. This bunching typically takes the form of *personal rules*, whose nature and consequences are further discussed in the chapters by Ainslie and Gjelsvik.

Among the three choice-based accounts that we have discussed, Becker's rational-choice model assumes foresight and exponential discounting; the melioration model of Herrnstein and Prelec assumes cognitive myopia and a fortiori no discounting; Ainslie's model assumes foresight and nonexponential discounting. The choice among these models turns on the realism of their assumptions and the accuracy of their predictions – and, at the meta level, on the relative importance one attaches to realism and predictive success as criteria for assessing scientific theories. We now proceed to discuss a number of other explanations that can be found in the literature on addiction.

### Social Learning Theory

Scholars with a background in mainstream psychology (rather than psychoanalysis or psychiatry) tend to explain addiction in the light of social learning theory (Orford 1985, Peele 1985). Although the theory partly

relies on classical ideas of reinforcement, it goes beyond them in arguing that some reinforcers are created by the process of addiction itself.
The order-creating effects of cigarette smoking mentioned earlier are an
example. The gambler's spurious belief in his competence is another.
Also, social learning theory allows for the fact that the expectation of
(relative) reward may be more important in sustaining addictive behavior than reward itself. For one thing, "Even if anxiety increases as a result
of prolonged drinking, this may still be reinforcing if it is less distressing
than the frustration, anxiety, or withdrawal symptoms that the person
*expected* to experience if he or she had not continued to drink." (Orford
1985, p. 137). For another, "research has consistently shown [...] that
alcoholics drink in the *expectation* of reducing tensions, even though – as
their drinking proceeds – they do not experience this effect and instead
become even more tense." (Peele 1985, p. 100)


### Cognitive Impairment

If people choose addictive behaviors despite their bad consequences,
one reason may be their inability – whether motivated or not – to perceive these effects correctly. Melioration theory takes this idea to the
extreme, by arguing that addicts have no understanding of the consequences of their choices. But there may also be more specific mechanisms that distort perception. In his chapter, Elster cites a number of
studies that indicate that gamblers are prone to various "hot" and "cool"
cognitive errors, which may sustain their behavior in various stages of
their careers. Loewenstein, in his chapter, argues that most people tend
to misjudge the subjective impact of future visceral experiences.
    More generally, the strong cravings that go together with addiction
may induce a misperception of the real dangers. Heavy smokers, for
instance, are motivated to think that "It won't happen to me." (Viscusi
[1992] argues that although both smokers and nonsmokers overestimate
the risks of smoking, the estimates made by smokers are closer to the true
risks. His data do not show, however, that the typical smoker has a realistic
perception of the risks *to him* of smoking.) Mind-altering drugs induce an
additional blunting of perception and judgment. Discussing the relation
between habits and addiction, Becker (1992, p. 329) writes that "A habit
may be raised into an addiction by exposure to the habit itself. Certain
habits, such as drug use and heavy drinking, may reduce the attention to
future consequences – there is no reason to assume discount rates on the
future are just given and fixed." Here, Becker tacitly assumes that the
knowledge about the future consequences is not impaired – it is simply
that they are given less weight in the utility function. But how can he

tell the difference? Certainly, by stipulating that the drug works on the discounting and not on the beliefs, he can still claim that the addiction is rational, given the rational-choice premise that desires and preferences cannot be assessed as more or less rational. This cannot, however, be a sufficient reason for making the stipulation. What we observe is simply that the addict is less swayed by future consequences than he was before he took up the drug.

## Social Influences

Addictive behavior does not take place in a social vacuum. Individual desires and beliefs are social products, which are shaped and reshaped through social interaction, and individual decisions are directly and indirectly influenced by other people's decisions. This is true for any type of behavior – from suicide to music consumption – and the consumption of potentially addictive substances is no exception. Most of the theories mentioned so far do not directly address the social aspect; as they are mainly focused on processes within the individual. However, if one wants to understand the large-scale variations in the prevalence rates of different types of addictions across cultures and historical epochs, one clearly needs to take into consideration the interdependencies among individual actors.

Although social learning theories (e.g., Abrams and Niaura [1987]) acknowledge the importance of social factors, their focus tends to remain on the individual actor rather than on the social system. Moene's chapter brings the aggregate-level consequences of micro-level interactions into focus. Starting from the assumption that individual consumers are to some extent conformists, he demonstrates that this may produce spillover and ratchet effects, and these may cause the prevalence of addictions to more easily go up than down. Social interaction may also produce multiple equilibria. This implies that societies that are quite similar in most relevant aspects could nevertheless be quite different in terms of rates of drug abuse, simply because of differences in consumption history. Hence, once a high-consumption culture has become established, it may not be easily removed by political measures.

The basic assumption in Moene's model is well supported by empirical evidence. For instance, both observational and experimental studies have repeatedly demonstrated that people who interact also tend to influence each other's alcohol consumption habits (e.g., Skog [1980]). This interdependence has the effect of producing a strong collective component in the drinking culture: The population tends to move in concert up and down the consumption scale, and as the consumption level among "normal" drinkers goes up, so does the consumption level among heavier drinkers, as well as the prevalence rate of heavy drinkers. Thus, the prevalence of heavy consumers tends to vary considerably across cultures and within cultures over time, in direct response to the aggregate consumption level (Skog 1985, Rose 1992).

Waal's chapter on the pros and cons for legalization draws on these and related ideas. He argues that society has a right, as well as an obligation, to control drug use for at least three different reasons. First, the vulnerable user is influenced by the consumption habits of the better-off users. Second, by a different kind of externality, drug abuse may have direct or indirect negative consequences for nonusers. And third, dependence-producing drugs may reduce the individual's capacity for making rational choices – changes that the inexperienced user has no realistic possibility of predicting in advance.

## 6. Conclusion

We conclude by stating our view that the future of addiction studies is likely to be heavily shaped by developments in brain chemistry. The most promising line of research might involve the integration of neurobiological and decision-theoretic approaches. Although this general idea is now steadily gaining in importance (Damasio, Damasio, and Christen 1996), it has not been extensively applied to the analysis of addiction. One might do so, perhaps, by thinking about how one could design a molecular-level test of the two competing views of the impact of drug-induced euphoria and dysphoria discussed above. For instance, as suggested to us by David Laibson (personal communication), if it could be shown that chemically defined states of drug craving induce rats to discount future nondrug-related rewards at a higher rate than they otherwise do, this would indicate that the effect of drugs do not simply operate by changing the reward parameters. By contrast, if this discounting remained unaffected, we would not be able to tell whether impatience for getting drugs is due to the rewards or to the rate of time discounting (or both). Although following up this particular idea may not turn out to be worthwhile, the general idea it illustrates is, we believe, of fundamental importance. The neurobiological study of addiction, like similar studies of emotion (LeDoux 1996), promises to be a key to progress in understanding of the mind–body problem.

## BIBLIOGRAPHY

Abrams, David B. and Raymond S. Niaura (1987), "Social Learning Theory," in Howard T. Blane and Kenneth E. Leonard (eds.), *Psychological Theories of Drinking and Alcoholism*, New York, The Guilford Press, pp. 131–78.

Ainslie, George (1975), "Specious reward," *Psychological Bulletin* 82, 463–96.
(1992), *Picoeconomics*, Cambridge, UK, Cambridge University Press.
Becker, Gary (1992), "Habits, addictions, and traditions," *Kyklos* 45, 327–46.
Becker, Gary and Kevin Murphy (1988), "A theory of rational addiction," *Journal of Political Economy* 96, 675–700.
Bromiley, P. and S. P. Curley (1992), "Individual differences in risk-taking," in J. F. Yates (ed.), *Risk-Taking Behavior*, New York, Wiley, pp. 87–132.
Capell, Howard and Janet Greeley (1987), "Alcohol and Tension Reduction: An Update on Research and Theory," in Howard T. Blane and Kenneth E. Leonard (eds.), *Psychological Theories of Drinking and Alcoholism*, New York, The Guilford Press, pp. 15–54.
Damasio, A. R., H. Damasio, and Y. Christen, eds. (1996), *Neurobiology of Decision-Making*, New York, Springer-Verlag.
Davidson, Donald (1969), "How is weakness of the will possible," reprinted as Ch. 2 of his *Essays on Actions and Events*, Oxford, UK, Oxford University Press, 1980.
Elster, Jon (1983), *Sour Grapes*, Cambridge, UK, Cambridge University Press.
(1984), *Ulysses and the Sirens*, rev. ed., Cambridge, UK, Cambridge University Press.
(1986), "The nature and scope of rational-choice explanation," in E. LePore and B. McLaughlin (eds.), *Actions and Events: Perspectives on the Philosophy of Donald Davidson*, Oxford, Blackwell, pp. 60–72.
(1989), *The Cement of Society*, Cambridge, UK, Cambridge University Press.
(1997), "Review of Gary Becker's *Accounting for Taste*," in *University of Chicago Law Review* 64, 749–64.
Fenichel, Otto (1945), *The Psychoanalytic Theory of Neurosis*, New York, Norton.
Goldstein, Avram (1984), *Addiction*, New York, Freeman.
Herrnstein, Richard (1997), *The Matching Law*, Cambridge, MA, Harvard University Press.
Herrnstein, Richard and Drazen Prelec (1992a), "A theory of addiction," in G. Loewenstein and J. Elster (eds.), *Choice Over Time*, New York, The Russell Sage Foundation, pp. 331–60.
(1992b), "Melioration," in G. Loewenstein and J. Elster (eds.), *Choice Over Time*, New York, The Russell Sage Foundation, pp. 235–64.
Hoebel, Barney G. (1998), "Neural systems for reinforcement and inhibition of behavior: Relevance to eating, addiction and depression," in D. Kahneman, E. Diener, and N. Schwartz (eds.), *Understanding Quality of Life: Scientific Perspectives on Enjoyment and Suffering*, in press.
Hyman, Stephen (1995), "The addicted brain," *Harvard Medical Alumni Bulletin*, Winter 29–33.
Jellinek, E. M. (1960), *The Disease Concept of Alcoholism*, New Haven, CT, Hillhouse Press.
Keyes, R. (1985), *Chancing It*, Boston, Little, Brown and Company.
Klein, R. (1993), *Cigarettes Are Sublime*, Durham, NC, Duke University Press.
Lewis, Michael (1992), *Shame*, New York, The Free Press.
LeDoux, Joseph (1996), *The Emotional Brain*, New York, Simon and Schuster.
Marks, Isaac (1990), "Behavioural (non-chemical) addictions," *British Journal of Addiction* 85, 1389–94.

McKim, William A. (1991), *Drugs and Behavior*, Englewood Cliffs, NJ, Prentice-Hall.

Mello, N. K. and J. H. Mendelson (1965), "Operant analysis of drinking patterns of chronic alcoholics," *Nature* 206, 43–6.

(1966), "Experimental analysis of drinking behavior of chronic alcoholics," *Annals of New York Academy of Sciences* 133, 828–45.

(1972), "Drinking pattern during work contingent and non-contingent alcohol acquisition," *Psychosomatic Medicine* 34, 139–64.

Nell, Victor (1988), *Lost in a Book: The Psychology of Reading for Pleasure*, New Haven, CT, Yale University Press.

Orford, J. (1985), *Excessive Appetites*, Chichester, UK, Wiley.

Pattison, M., M. Sobell, and W. Schmidt (1977), *Emerging Concepts of Alcohol Dependence*, New York, Springer-Verlag.

Pears, David (1984), *Motivated Irrationality*, Oxford, UK, Oxford University Press.

Peele, Stanton (1985), *The Meaning of Addiction*, Lexington, MA, Lexington Books.

Robbins, J. M. and P. Joseph (1982), "Behavioral components of exercise addiction," unpublished manuscript, Jewish General Hospital, Montreal.

Rose, Geoffrey (1992), *The Strategy of Preventive Medicine*, Oxford, UK, Oxford University Press.

Schelling, Thomas C. (1986), *Choice and Consequence*, Cambridge, MA, Harvard University Press.

(1992), "Self-command: A new discipline," in G. Loewenstein and J. Elster (eds.), *Choice Over Time*, New York, The Russell Sage Foundation, pp. 167–76.

Scitovsky, Tibor (1992), *The Joyless Economy*, rev. ed., Oxford, UK, Oxford University Press.

Seeburger, Francis (1993), *Addiction and Responsibility*, New York, Crossroad.

Sher, Kenneth J. (1987), "Stress response dampening," in Howard T. Blane and Kenneth E. Leonard (eds.), *Psychological Theories of Drinking and Alcoholism*, New York, The Guilford Press, pp. 227–71.

Siegel, Shepard, et al. (1982), "Heroin 'overdose' death: Contribution of drug-associated environmental cues," *Science* 216, 436–7.

Siegel, Shepard, Marvin D. Krank, and Riley E. Hinson (1988), "Anticipation of pharmacological and nonpharmacological events: Classical conditioning and addictive behavior," in Stanton Peele (ed.), *Visions of Addiction*, New York, Lexington Books, pp. 85–116.

Skog, Ole-Jørgen (1980), "Social interaction and the distribution of alcohol consumption," *Journal of Drug Issues* 10, 71–92.

(1985), "The collectivity of drinking cultures. A theory of the distribution of alcohol consumption," *British Journal of Addiction* 80, 83–99.

Smith, Robin (1986), "Television addiction," in Jennings Bryant and Dolf Zillmann (eds.), *Perspectives on Media Effects*, Hillsdale, NJ, Erlbaum, pp. 109–28.

Solomon, Richard L. and J. D. Corbit (1974), "An opponent-process theory of motivation," *Psychological Review* 81, 119–45.

Stigler, George and Gary Becker (1977), "De gustibus non est disputandum," *American Economic Review* 67, 76–90.

Tversky, Amos and Dale Griffin (1991), "Endowment and contrast in judgments of well-being," in R. J. Zeckhauser (ed.), *Strategy and Choice*, Cambridge, MA, MIT Press, pp. 297–318.

Viscusi, Kip (1992), *Smoking*, Oxford, UK, Oxford University Press.

Wise, Roy and Michael Bozarth (1987), "A psychomotor stimulant theory of addiction," *Psychological Review* 94, 469–92.

# Addiction and Social Interaction

KARL OVE MOENE

## 1. Introduction

Many forms of drug use and drug abuse are clearly social in character. Heavy consumption is allowed in some social situations and banned in others. Collective intoxication may sometimes signal friendship and virility, while outsiders may be offended by the abuse. Drug use is also affected by geographic and ethnic belongings where values and rewards of drug use seem to be inherited from previous generations. Most societies differ, for example, in drinking customs. Citizens who are members of several small societies within their community seem to drink differently within each. Use of narcotics is often initiated by friends, gang members, or neighborhood acquaintances, and habits may change once gang membership is abandoned. Some subgroups or cults develop legal and illegal drug ceremonies that resemble religious drug use in more primitive societies. (Encyclopedia Britainica)

These social characteristics of drug use do not contradict the fact that people may rationally choose their way of living. People may act rationally, but not necessarily within social circumstances chosen by themselves. In the theory of rational addiction, however, the focus is on how one person may develop addictive behaviors in situations from which interaction between potential drug users can be abstracted (Becker and Murphy [1988], Orphanides and Zervos [1992], and others). As a contrast to these rational addiction models, this paper focuses on long-range equilibria of social interaction within a group of persons and neglects addictive dynamics within each person separately. To do this, I study an abstract and very stylized model of social interaction with consumption externalities that have features in common with Schelling's tipping models (Schelling 1978, Ch. 7). (For a theoretical and empirical overview of related approaches to population dynamics in drug use, applying computer-based simulation techniques; see Skog [1980].)

At the outset, I have to warn the reader that I have not tried to kick my habit to accept strong simplifications without necessary qualifications. The paper is deliberately organized to facilitate the presentation of each aspect I want to focus on. After presenting the basic assumptions about how pleasure and pain of drug use depend on group behavior (in Section 2), I proceed with simplified expositions of various aspects of the model. In Section 5, I outline the most reasonable case, of the ones considered, where potential drug users start out as nonaddicted individuals who use the drug whenever they like and abstain when they prefer to do so. Their preferences, however, depend on how many others there are who like to use the substance and how many who have no choice because they are addicted. In that setup, each individual is aware of the risks of becoming hooked and some of them do indeed become addicts. Before exploring this case in more detail, I consider the interaction of nonaddictive individuals who are sure not to become addicted and who never interact with addicts (in Section 3). Next, addiction and abstention are considered as the only possible choices (in Section 4), in order to derive how average consumption may depend on (i) the costs of obtaining the drugs, (ii) the existence of precommitted teetotalers, and (iii) the possibility that users and nonusers are segregated.

## 2. Preferences

Even though the type of social externalities captured in the figures presented here can be justified in several ways, I have chosen to concentrate the discussion around a rather specific and simplistic microfoundation. The first simplifying assumption is that choices are binary. Each person can either take drugs ($D$) or not ($N$), which means that he either consumes a given quantity of the drug or abstains from consuming the drug at all. A person's utilities can be separated in two parts: one that reflects the pleasure from consumption ($v$) and one that reflects possible pain or side effects ($q$) of consumption. Total utility is $V = v - q$. I abstract from the facts that both pain and pleasure of drug use may be affected by past consumption and that pleasure is immediate whereas pain is delayed and possibly long lasting.

The pleasure of consumption is represented by an individual utility function, $v = v(x, y)$, where $x$ indicates the person's own choice and $y$ what the others choose. The temptation to drink or to take drugs is assumed to be social in character. Thus, when the others drink, the person prefers to drink as well and, when the others do not drink, the person also prefers to abstain. Formally, we have

$$v(D, D) > v(N, D) \tag{1}$$

and

$$v(N, N) > v(D, N), \tag{2}$$

which simply state that the individual does not like to deviate from what the others do. In addition, within a group of similar individuals a deviant behavior is assumed to impose a negative externality on the others. All else being equal, drinkers would rather interact with another drinker than with a nondrinker; and persons who prefer not to drink would rather interact with other nondrinkers than with drinkers. Stated formally, this can be expressed as

$$v(D, D) > v(D, N) \tag{3}$$

and

$$v(N, N) > v(N, D). \tag{4}$$

The preferences indicated by equations (1)–(4) are conformist in two ways. On the one hand, (1) and (2) state that people like to imitate what others do. On the other hand, (3) and (4) state that people would like others to imitate their own behaviors.

While, in the model, all individuals are assumed to have the same $v(x, y)$ function, the possible pain or side effects of consuming the drug may vary among persons. Let the expected or perceived pain for person $i$ of using the drug be indicated by $q_i$. The distribution of $q$ over the population is assumed to be bell shaped with a cumulative density function $F(\cdot)$, where, for any arbitrary value of $k$, $F(k)$ expresses the fraction of the population with a lower perceived psychic cost or pain of drug use than $k$.

The total utility of a committed drug user who interacts with drug users a fraction $\gamma$ of the time and with nonusers the rest of the time $(1-\gamma)$ is simply $V = \gamma v(D, D) + (1-\gamma)v(D, N) - q_i$. The monetary costs of acquiring the drug is implicit in $v(D, y)$. (With the price of the drug equal to $p$, we could have written $v(D, y) = v^*(D, y) - p$ for $y = D, N$.) There are no side effects of being a nonuser, and so, the nonuser's utility is $V = \gamma v(N, D) + (1 - \gamma)v(N, N)$ (where, of course, $p$ does not affect $v(N, y)$).

What else affects the utilities of both users and nonusers? The presence of more users lowers the utility of a nonuser since $V(N)$ can be rewritten as $V(N) = v(N, N) - \gamma[v(N, N) - v(N, D)]$, which is decreasing in $\gamma$ since the expression within brackets is positive according to (4). Whereas the presence of users in this way imposes negative externalities on nonusers, the presence of nonusers imposes similar negative externalities on users. The utility of a user is a decreasing function of the number of nonusers as $V(D)$ can be rewritten as $V(D) = v(D, D) - (1 - \gamma)[v(D, D) - v(D, N)] - q_i$, which is decreasing in $(1-\gamma)$ as long as (3) holds.

To simplify the presentation below, I neglect the reasonable possibility that some persons will never take the drug, namely those for whom $v(D, D) - q_i < v(N, D)$. This case could easily be incorporated, but only at the cost of more algebra. In Section 4, however, I return to a related issue while discussing the impact of precommitted nonusers.

## 3. Nonaddictive Interaction Between Casual Users

People who are not addicted to the drug or committed to a lifestyle that is characterized by $D$ can choose freely in every encounter whether to take the drug or not. We can think of drinking customs within a group of non-alcoholics who are sure not to become addicted by their consumption. Let us denote such nonaddictive and noncommitted drug users by $C$, indicating casual users. When two casual users with preferences (1)–(4) meet, each of them has, in principle, a veto over whether the two shall use the drug or not. Each of them knows that whatever he chooses the other will follow. Thus both of them either use it or do not. The expected (or average) utility of a casual user in a world of similar individuals is

$$
\begin{aligned}
V(C) &= \gamma v(D, D) + (1 - \gamma)v(N, N) - \gamma q_i \\
&= \gamma(v(D, D) - v(N, N) - q_i) + v(N, N),
\end{aligned}
\tag{5}
$$

where $\gamma$ is the fraction of meetings that result in drinking. Average consumption is proportional to $\gamma$. In the case described by (5) there is no direct feedback mechanism from average consumption to individual ranking of alternatives. In each encounter, those for whom $v(D, D) - q_i \geq v(N, N)$ would like to use the drug, whereas those with the inverse inequality would prefer not to consume it. As we shall see, average consumption may nevertheless be affected by social interaction.

Let us first calculate the fraction of the population with a sufficiently low $q_i$ to prefer use to nonuse. This fraction is denoted $\delta$ and is determined by

$$
\delta = F(v(D, D) - v(N, N)),
\tag{6}
$$

as illustrated in Figure 1. The value of $\delta$ gives a simple expression of the overall or social preferences for using the drug.

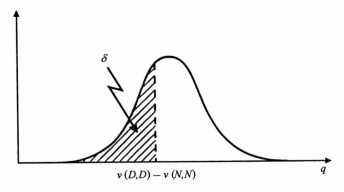

**Figure 1**

Next, think of a situation with random pairwise meetings on a bar. To derive average consumption, proportional to $\gamma$ in equation (5), we must calculate how many of the random meetings end up in drinking. A fraction of the meetings $\delta^2$ consists of pairs where both prefer to drink; a fraction of $2(1 - \delta)\delta$ consists of pairs where one person prefers to drink and another person prefers to abstain; a fraction $(1 - \delta)^2$ consists of pairs where both prefer not to drink. For drinking to occur, at least one person from the low-$q$ segment of the population has to be present. If the other person also belongs to the low-$q$ segment, both agree to drink. If the other person has a higher $q$ than $[v(D, D) - v(N, N)]$, the two, in principle, disagree on whether they both should drink or not. In that case let us assume that a proportion $\theta$ of the meetings, to be discussed below, results in drinking, whereas the rest do not. With these assumptions the fraction of all meetings that result in drinking is determined by

$$\gamma = \delta^2 + 2\theta(1 - \delta)\delta. \tag{7}$$

As equation (7) demonstrates, the outcome of mixed encounters (when one who does and one who does not prefer to drink meet) may be of great importance to average drinking. On the one hand, if the one who does not want to drink decides in all mixed encounters, $\theta = 0$ and $\gamma = \delta^2$. If, on the other hand, the one who does want to drink decides in all mixed encounters, $\theta = 1$ and $\gamma = 2\delta - \delta^2$. None of the extreme cases seems particularly reasonable. More likely, mixed encounters will sometimes result in drinking and sometimes not. If, for example, drinking or not is decided by the one who just happens to arrive first, the outcome with mixed encounters can be considered the result of coin tossing. In this case, $\theta = 1/2$ and $\gamma = \delta$ and the average level of drinking is equal to what social preferences indicate even though people who prefer to drink sometimes abstain from drinking while people who would like to abstain sometimes drink.

A more plausible possibility is that the value of $\theta$ is influenced by social customs or average drinking behavior in society. The long-run equilibrium value of $\theta$ could, for instance, adjust to $\gamma$, which means that the fraction of mixed encounters that results in drinking is equal to the fraction of overall encounters that result in drinking. In that case the equilibrium value of $\gamma$ is the solution to (7) with $\theta = \gamma$, given by

$$\gamma = \frac{\delta^2}{1 - 2\delta + 2\delta^2}. \tag{8}$$

This case is illustrated in Figure 2, where the stipulated straight line is the 45-degree line and the bold curve indicates $\gamma$ as a function of $\delta$ as described by (8).

From Figure 2, we can read how preferences in society translate into aggregate behavior when individual behavior is affected by social customs.

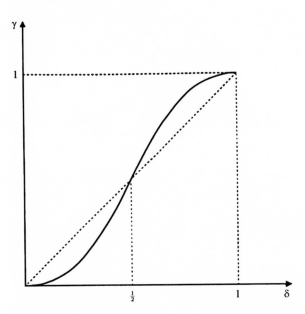

**Figure 2**

The stipulated 45-degree line represents cases where social preferences for drug use equal average consumption, that is, where $\delta = \gamma$. The bold S-shaped curve is actual use. As the figure demonstrates, only when exactly half of the population prefers use to nonuse does actual use equal the level indicated by social preferences. Actual use is lower than what is socially preferred, when $\delta < 1/2$. This means that, when less than half of the population prefer drinking, actual drinking is less than $\delta$ because less than half of the mixed encounters as a consequence end up in drinking. When more than half of the population prefer drinking, however, actual drinking overshoots social preferences because more than half of the mixed encounters end up in drinking.

## 4. To Use or Not to Use

In this section, each person is assumed to be committed to his choices once they are made either because he has become addicted to the drug or because he is committed to his lifestyle. Thus, after a person has made his choice about $D$ and $N$, he cannot easily adjust his behavior when he interacts with persons who have chosen differently. It is maintained, however, that to use or not to use the drug is decided by comparing the alternatives, including their binding consequences.

The perceived utility of a person who chooses $x = N, D$ and takes $\gamma = \gamma_{t-1}$ as an indication of the consumption of the drug for the relevant future is

$$V(D) = [\gamma_{t-1}v(D, D) + (1 - \gamma_{t-1})v(D, N)] - q_i \quad \text{and}$$
$$V(N) = [\gamma_{t-1}v(N, D) + (1 - \gamma_{t-1})v(N, N)], \tag{9}$$

where $\gamma_{t-1}$ is the fraction of committed drug users in the previous period. Whether a person will use the drug or not is now supposed to be decided by comparing the perceived utilities of the two choices. Thus a person becomes a user if he has

$$V(D) - V(N) \geq 0. \tag{10}$$

Using (9), we see that those with the lowest $q_i$ values become $D$, namely those for whom

$$V(D) - V(N) = A\gamma_{t-1} - B - q_i \geq 0, \tag{11}$$

where

$$A = [v(D, D) - v(N, D)] + [v(N, N) - v(D, N)] > 0,$$
$$B = [v(N, N) - v(D, N)] > 0. \tag{12}$$

Those who, according to (11), have lower $q_i$ than $A\gamma_{t-1} - B$ choose to be users. Hence, the long-run addictive population dynamics are described by

$$\gamma_t = F(\gamma_{t-1}A - B), \tag{13}$$

where $\gamma_t$ indicates the fraction of the present generation that chooses to become users. Since $A$ is positive, the higher is the fraction of users in the previous period $(\gamma_{t-1})$, the more people there are who become users. When use is more frequent, abstainers have to interact more with users. To abstain in a high-use society is more costly than in a low-use society simply because of the negative externalities that users impose on nonusers. Thus the more people that already consume the drug, the less attractive it is to be a nonuser relative to being a user. There is a snowball effect in total consumption of the drug in the sense that the higher is $\gamma_{t-1}$, the higher is the induced value of $\gamma_t$. As long as total consumption of the drug in period $t$ is proportional to $\gamma_t$, this has direct implications for how total consumption evolves over time.

It is interesting to study which levels of drug use can be inherited and sustained over periods in a population. Such a steady-state equilibrium in this setup is a value of average consumption that is self-enforcing and consistent with rational behavior in each period. Formally, values of $\gamma$ that solve (13) with $\gamma_t = \gamma_{t-1}$ are consistent and self-enforcing. As illustrated in Figure 3, there may be more than one such equilibrium. In the figure the bold S-shaped curve indicates a case with two locally stable equilibria:

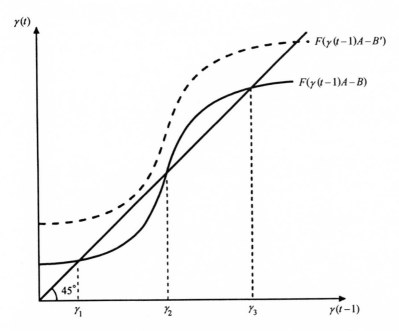

**Figure 3**

one at $\gamma^1$ with low average consumption and one at $\gamma^3$ with high average consumption. The intermediate $\gamma^2$ is an unstable tipping point.

If we start out with $\gamma$ higher than the critical mass $\gamma^2$, the process converges to $\gamma^3$, since in each period the average consumption generated by the habits inherited from the past induces an even higher consumption level. The new higher consumption level forms the environment in which new users make their choices, and average consumption increases step by step until $\gamma = \gamma^3$. Similarly, an initial point below $\gamma^2$ would converge step by step to the low-use equilibrium at $\gamma^1$. In the rest of the chapter, however, we neglect such dynamics and focus on steady-state situations such that time subscripts on $\gamma$ can be omitted.

In the low-use equilibrium $\gamma^1$, the negative externalities imposed on potential users by the fact that they have to interact with many abstainers are large enough to discourage further use. Or, expressed differently, the positive externalities that nonusers have on other potential nonusers in a low-use society are large enough to prevent further use. Thus, only the most susceptible individuals with the lowest $q_i$ values choose to consume the drug. In the high-use equilibrium $\gamma^3$, however, the balance of externalities has changed in favor of more use. A social environment with a large number of users makes it less attractive to abstain and more tempting to use. Thus, more people would find that the pleasure of consuming the drug together with all the other users more than outweighs the perceived side effects represented by their $q_i$ values.

### Drug Prices

To see how the equilibria move as we change the parameters of the model, let us consider a decline in the price of drugs. Since the monetary costs of the drug are just subtracted from utilities of consumption $v(D, y)$ for $y = N, D$, the value of $A$ is unaffected by price changes, whereas the value of $B$ decreases with the drug price according to (12). A lower value of $B$ leads to an upward shift in the $S$-shaped curve, as indicated by the stipulated (dashed) curve in Figure 3. Accordingly, for each level of drug use in the previous period, the induced use in the present period increases as the the drug price decreases.

Gradual upward shifts in the $S$-shaped curve in Figure 3 imply that both $\gamma^1$ and $\gamma^3$ increase, while the tipping point $\gamma^2$ is reduced. Moreover, for a sufficiently low price the low-use equilibrium would no longer exist. This means that a substantial price drop in a low-use equilibrium triggers a process of increasing use that converges to a high-use equilibrium (as illustrated by the stipulated (dashed) curve in Figure 3). In a similar way a price increase would shift the $S$-shaped curve downward. A sufficiently high drug price would therefore eliminate the high-use equilibrium.

Figure 4 derives the general relationship between the price of drugs and total consumption (in steady state). To explore this relationship, let us start out with such a high drug price that there is a low-use equilibrium only. Gradual price declines would then lead to an increasing demand for drugs along the left curve in the lower panel of Figure 4. This part of the demand schedule just shows how the low-use equilibrium $\gamma^1$ moves with the drug price. When the price has dropped to $p'$, which is consistent with $B = B'$ in the upper panel of Figure 4, we have reached the lowest price that can sustain a low-use equilibrium. If the drug price is reduced below $p'$, which is equivalent to $B$ being higher than $B'$, there is no low-use equilibrium and, as a consequence, demand jumps to a high-use equilibrium, depicted as the demand schedule at the right in the lower panel of the figure. This demand schedule shows how the high-use equilibrium $\gamma^3$ moves with the drug price. Further price declines below $p'$ lead to continuous increases in demand along the high-demand schedule.

Starting out with a sufficiently low drug price, followed by reductions, would not produce the identical pattern of a subsequent price decline in reverse. The reason why the situations are not the same is that a high-use equilibrium can be sustained with higher prices than $p'$. As the figure shows, the highest price that can sustain a high-use equilibrium is $p''$ (consistent with $B = B''$ in the upper panel of Figure 4). Prices between

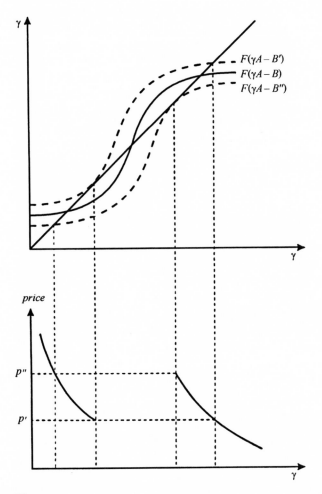

**Figure 4**

$p'$ and $p''$ may lead to demand for drugs on either schedule, depending on past consumption in society. For drug prices in this range, drug use is history or path dependent.

The existence of two locally stable equilibria implies that temporary changes may have lasting consequences. On the one hand this may act as a warning. A low-use society may easily change to a high-use society if availability of drugs increases and prices drop. Even after prices have gone up again, the population may have developed new habits and society may be captured in a high-use equilibrium that new generations inherit. On the other hand the picture may also seem optimistic. Temporary campaigns may work. One may, for instance, move from a high-consumption society to one with low consumption by reducing availability or charging a higher price for a sufficiently long period to induce a shift from the high- to the low-demand schedule. After the shift has taken place, prices may be lowered again without relapsing back to the high-demand schedule. With addicted users, however, the transition from a high-use to a low-use equilibrium is less immediate than the reverse (as we shall see more clearly in Section 5). The shifts among possible equilibria in Figure 4 should be interpreted as the final result of long-run adjustments where new generations have made their choices within the environment inherited from the past.

### Teetotalers

To study how committed nonusers may affect average consumption, let us assume that there is a fraction $\beta$ of the population that is committed never to use the drug. It is of great importance from which segments of the $q$ distribution these teetotalers are recruited. For simplicity, I assume that the committed teetotalers are a representative sample of the population as a whole when it comes to the distribution of their $q_i$ values. With $\tilde{\gamma}$ indicating the fraction of the *rest* of the population that rationally chose between being users or not, the question is how the size of the committed nonuser group $\beta$ affects $\tilde{\gamma}$.

The presence of teetotalers implies that everybody else has to interact with committed nonusers a fraction $\beta$ of the time. Thus the relevant comparison of a potential drug user is now between

$$V(D) = \beta v(D, N) + (1 - \beta)[\tilde{\gamma}v(D, D) \\ + (1 - \tilde{\gamma})v(D, N)] - q_i \quad \text{and} \tag{14}$$
$$V(N) = \beta v(N, N) + (1 - \beta)[\tilde{\gamma}v(N, D) + (1 - \tilde{\gamma})v(N, N)].$$

An increase in the number of teetotalers, captured by an increase in $\beta$, implies less pleasure from use and more pleasure from abstention. From (14) we find that $V(D) - V(N) = (1 - \beta)A\tilde{\gamma} - B - q_i$, where $A$ and $B$ are given by (12). The steady-state equilibria are determined by values of $\tilde{\gamma}$ that solve

$$\tilde{\gamma} = F[(1 - \beta)\tilde{\gamma}A - B]. \tag{15}$$

An increase in $\beta$ shifts the S-shaped curve downward, as illustrated in Figure 5. Thus the higher is $\beta$ the lower are the two stable values of $\tilde{\gamma}$. Hence committed nonusers have a preventive spillover effect on the habits in the rest of the population. Starting from a high-use equilibrium, an increase in $\beta$ may also lead to a situation where only a low-use equilibrium remains, as illustrated in Figure 5. For the committed nonusers

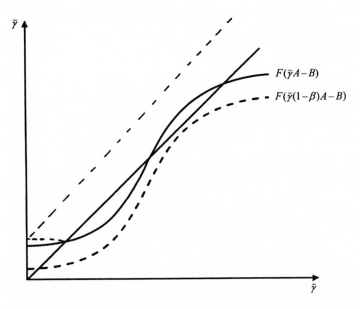

**Figure 5**

to affect the average use, it is essential, however, that they interact with potential users. Thus committed nonusers of alcohol have the greatest impact on alcohol consumption if they spend their time in bars.

## Segregation

For some types of drugs, heavy users may interact more frequently with each other than with the rest of society. In extreme cases, this kind of voluntary segregation becomes complete. Identification of users is then totally with the addict group, which may develop its own culture and live apart from ordinary community life. To see how average consumption is affected when those who choose to use the drug also freely choose to live separately from those who choose not to use the drug, we return to the case without committed nonusers.

Clearly, in our setup, nonusers benefit from segregation because they do not have to interact with users. Yet the answer to our question is not obvious: Some of the potential nonusers may be more tempted to use the drug than otherwise since they do not have to bear the costs of being deviants among nonusers. In a society where all users automatically become segregated from nonusers, the option is to use the drug within a community of similar individuals and obtain $v(D, D)$ or not use the drug and live together with other nonusers to obtain $v(N, N)$. People with sufficiently low $q$ values choose $D$, that is, those for whom $v(D, D) - q_i \geq v(N, N)$. Thus the fraction of users in this case becomes equal to $\delta$ defined in (6), $\delta = F(v(D, D) - v(N, N))$. The equilibrium values of $\gamma$ in the unsegregated society are implicitly defined by (13) for $\gamma_{t-1} = \gamma_t$.

It turns out that (i) when the externalities that users impose on non-users are negligible, or formally $v(N, N) = v(N, D)$, voluntary segregation leads to higher drug use, whereas (ii) when the externalities that nonusers impose on users are negligible, or formally $v(D, D) = v(D, N)$, voluntary segregation leads to lower drug use.

To see (i) that voluntary segregation may *increase* drug use, we insert $\gamma_{t-1} = 1$ in (13) to find that the highest equilibrium value of $\gamma$ must be lower than $F(A - B)$. By inserting for $A$ and $B$ from (12), we can derive the following upper bound on possible equilibrium values of $\gamma$ in the unsegregated case (with $v(N, N) = v(N, D)$):

$$\gamma < F(v(D, D) - v(N, N)) = \delta. \tag{16}$$

Hence, if the presence of a user does not affect a nonuser's utility much, voluntary segregation leads to a higher use than in the high-use equilibrium within an unsegregated society. Intuitively, this result is easy to understand. When $v(N, D) = v(N, N)$, utility levels of nonusers are independent of the number of users. Thus, when users leave, nonusers obtain the same well-being as before. Users, however, obtain a higher well-being since they do not have to interact with nonusers anymore. Thus people who were on the margin of using the drug before segregation (but did not) would choose $D$ after segregation since well-being of users has improved.

To see (ii) that voluntary segregation may *decrease* drug use, we insert $V(D, D) = v(D, N)$ in the expression of $B$ to obtain

$$\gamma = F(A\gamma + v(D, D) - v(N, N)) > F(v(D, D) - v(N, N)) = \delta. \tag{17}$$

Hence, if the presence of nonusers does not affect the utilities of users much, voluntary segregation leads to lower use of the substance. When users leave in this case, their utility levels do not change. The utility levels of nonusers go up, however, when users are not present anymore. Thus, on the margin, some potential users would rather choose to abstain within segregated societies.

Case (i) may be realistic for socially accepted drugs such as alcohol, whereas (ii) may capture some illegal drug use, where users do not care about what others do, but the rest of society does. When neither (i) nor (ii) holds, drug use can go either way as a consequence of users being voluntarily segregated from nonusers. Segregation may also be used by the authorities in an attempt to prevent the spread of what they consider harmful drugs: One possibility is to try to isolate the persons most susceptible to drug use (that is, those with the lowest $q_i$ values) from the rest. These persons may use the drug in any case, but if isolated they would not tempt others to start.

Isolating the most susceptible individuals may be problematic, not only because of possible human rights violations but also because authorities may be unable to identify who they are as long as the $q_i$ values are not observable. The latter problem may be circumvented, however, if we start out with a low-use equilibrium, since the users in this case must be the ones with the lowest $q_i$ values. The most susceptible can then be identified as the fraction of the population that are already users, $\gamma^1$. If the authorities are afraid that an increasing supply of drugs may shift the situation into one of high use, they may consider isolating those who are already users.

If the users in the low-use equilibrium can be prevented from interacting with the rest of the population, the high-use equilibrium may cease to exist. A high-use equilibrium requires that individuals with rather high psychic costs be tempted to use the drug. Individuals with high $q_i$ values would only use the drug, however, if others with whom they can interact go first. When the most susceptible individuals are isolated from interaction with the rest, there may be no situation where enough of the others use the drug to tempt anybody beyond the $\gamma^1$ fraction to start. The case is illustrated in Figure 5, where the 45-degree line is shifted upward (to the dotted parallel line) as the fraction $\gamma^1$ is isolated from the rest. After the shift, there may be no other equilibrium than zero use in the rest of the population. This is an example of a more general policy discussion related to segregation and integration, explored by Schelling (1978, Ch. 5).

## 5. Users as Potential Addicts

So far, addiction has been considered a deliberate choice. More realistically, users of the drug run a certain chance of becoming addicted. Rational individuals take this risk into account when they decide whether to use the drug or not. To capture this, let $\phi$ be the probability of becoming hooked and let $\alpha$ represent the fraction of users who are addicted. We have then three groups: the committed nonusers, the nonaddicted users, and the addicted users. Addicted users have no choice. They use the drug in all encounters. Nonaddicted users act as hybrids. They use the drug when they interact with addicts and nonaddicted users. A fraction $\phi$ of them eventually become addicts and all addicts have started out as hybrids. Committed nonusers never use the drug. Note that no consumption takes place when a hybrid and a nonuser meet. Alternatively, such meetings could have been modeled similarily to mixed encounters among casual drinkers, as we did in Section 3, but only with additional complications. Instead, it is simply assumed that hybrids respect nonusers' commitment to abstain.

A committed nonuser interacts a fraction of his time $(1-\gamma)$ with other nonusers. The rest of his time $(\gamma)$ he interacts with users. A fraction $(1-\alpha)$ of the users are hybrids who abstain from using the drug when they meet a committed nonuser, and a fraction $\alpha$ are addicts who use the drug also when they interact with nonusers. Thus the utility of a committed nonuser is equal to

$$V(N) = (1-\gamma)v(N,N) + \gamma[(1-\alpha)v(N,N) + \alpha v(N,D)]. \qquad (18)$$

Correspondingly, the utility of an addict is

$$V(A) = \gamma v(D,D) + (1-\gamma)v(D,N) - q_i, \qquad (19)$$

since he consumes the drug in all encounters. He consumes together with his mates when he meets other users (hybrids and addicts), but he has to consume alone when he meets committed nonusers. Finally, the utility of a nonaddicted user is the weighted sum of the utility of acting as a nonaddicted hybrid and of becoming an addict with the relevant probabilities as weights or, formally,

$$V(H) = (1-\phi)[\gamma v(D,D) + (1-\gamma)v(N,N) - \gamma q_i] + \phi V(A). \qquad (20)$$

Nonaddicted persons have the choice between being a hybrid user and abstaining. Accordingly, persons for whom

$$V(H) - V(N) \geq 0 \qquad (21)$$

choose to become users with the chance of becoming addicts in the end. Straightforward calculations reveal that (21) is equivalent to

$$\frac{[A-(1-\alpha)C]\gamma}{(1-p)\gamma + p} - B \geq q_i,$$

where $A$ and $B$ are positive as defined in (12), and

$$C = v(N,N) - v(N,D) > 0 \qquad (22)$$

such that $[A-(1-\alpha)C] > 0$. The steady-state equilibrium values of $\gamma$ are solutions to

$$\gamma = F\left(\frac{[A-(1-\alpha)C]\gamma}{(1-\phi)\gamma + \phi} - B\right). \qquad (23)$$

For given values of $\alpha$ and $\phi$, the argument of the function $F$ in (23) is increasing in $\gamma$. Thus this case may also give rise to two locally stable equilibria, one with low drug use and one with high drug use. The description of the equilibria is not yet complete since in any steady-state equilibrium the number of addicts must depend on the probability of being hooked $\phi$ and the incidence of use $\gamma$. For a constant fraction of users $\gamma$, we must, in the long run, have that the probability of becoming an addict equals the proportion of addicts among users or, formally, $\phi = \alpha$.

In steady state the fraction of addicts in the population is then given by

$$\eta = \alpha\gamma.$$

The value of $\eta$, however, is more responsive to increases than to decreases in average consumption $\gamma$. If $\gamma$ goes up the number of addicts rises proportionally. If $\gamma$ goes down again, however, the number of addicts does not decline in tandem simply because they are hooked. The number of addicts is therefore path or history dependent.

The dependence of $\eta$ on previous high-consumption episodes produces yet another ratchet effect of increases in drug use. In addition come spillover effects since a higher number of addicts also stimulates others to use the drug both in the high-use and the low-use equilibrium cases. This can be seen from (23) in the following way: After a high-use episode, the fraction of addicts among users is higher than the probability of becoming addicted if one starts out as a user; that is, we have $\alpha > \phi$. From (23), we see that an increase in $\alpha$ for a given value of $\phi$ increases the argument of the function $F$. This means that every initial consumption level induces a higher consumption level than before $\alpha$ went up (for every initial value of $\gamma$, the induced values of $\gamma$ are higher). Moreover, just as the presence of committed nonusers may eliminate the high-use equilibrium (as discussed in Section 4), the presence of a large number of addicts may eliminate the low-use equilibrium. In fact, addiction may cause the low-use equilibrium to vanish as a consequence of the habits induced by a temporary high-use episode in society.

## 6. Conclusions

The main message of this paper is that history matters for total drug use in a society. The simple model that we have explored identifies spillovers and ratchets in drug use that cannot so easily be captured in the theory of rational addiction by Becker and others. Social interaction in drug use easily produces multiple equilibria, which in itself implies that temporary changes may have lasting consequences. Each equilibrium is self-enforcing once society has reached it. In addition, drug use more easily goes up than down. Thus, if society first has been in a high-use situation, the likelihood that there still exists a low-use equilibrium falls, and if the low-use equilibrium still exists, it has a higher level of drug consumption. Those who are addicted today are the victims of the drug use in previous periods and have an stimulating impact on drug use today.

## Acknowledgments

This paper is based on my presentation at the Addiction seminar in Collioure, France, September 27–30, 1994, where I received very helpful comments from the participants. A draft of the paper was as later read by Jon Elster, Aanund Hylland, Tone Ognedal, Tom Schelling, and Ole-Jørgen Skog. I am grateful for all suggestions, comments, and criticism. Remaining errors and shortcomings are my own responsibility.

## BIBLIOGRAPHY

Becker, Gary S. and Kevin Murphy (1988), "A theory of rational addiction," *Journal of Political Economy* 96, 675–700.
Orphanides, Athanasios and David Zervos (1992), "Rational addiction with learning and regret," unpublished manuscript.
Schelling, Thomas C. (1978), *Micromotives and Macrobehavior*, New York, Norton.
Skog, Ole Jørgen (1980), "Social interaction and the distribution of alcohol consumption," *Journal of Drug Issues* 10, 71–92.

# Addiction, Weakness of the Will, and Relapse

OLAV GJELSVIK

## 1. Introduction

Addiction is a puzzle. In some cases, at least, it seems to be a form of voluntary, self-destructive behavior. It may then plausibly be taken as an instance of weakness of will, in the sense (roughly) of acting against one's better judgment. Many addicts want to quit but don't. Many smokers, for instance, believe it would be better, all things considered, if they stopped smoking, but they still continue. In this chapter, I discuss how addiction can be illuminated by two very different conceptions of weakness of will, presented by Donald Davidson and George Ainslie, respectively. Davidson offers a philosophical theory to show that weakness of will is *possible*, without offering any specific causal mechanism by which it might be brought about. Ainslie, by contrast, offers a highly specific causal mechanism that determines the circumstances in which a person will knowingly act against his interest. Each theory, I shall argue, has strengths and weaknesses. Each may account for some aspect of weakness of will in general, and of addiction more specifically.

For my purposes, addiction will be characterized in terms of (i) a desire to quit and (ii) the production of withdrawal symptoms when the person tries to quit.[1] (The desire may be actual or counterfactual, the latter case being that of an addict who is unaware of the harmful consequences of addiction but would have wanted to quit had he known about them.) Although the addict wants to quit, he may not be able to, as vividly described by Harry Frankfurt(1982, p. 87):

> He hates his addiction and always struggles desperately, although to no avail, against its trust. He tries everything that he thinks might enable him to overcome his desires for the drug. But these desires are too strong for him to withstand, and invariably, in the end, they conquer him. He is the unwilling addict, helplessly violated by his own desires.[2]

Note that this description is neutral between a craving for the drug experience and a fear of the withdrawal experience.

In the normal case, the desire to quit is caused by a correct assessment of information about the harm of the addiction, and especially by the insight that, in the long run, you stand to gain in overall utility or welfare by quitting. Interesting models of addiction allow for this insight in some way or other, including models that display the addicted state as a product of consecutive rational choices. An insight into what is best in the long run, which in its turn causes a strong desire to quit, can only be found in thinking agents, such as people. It is something that other animals are unlikely to achieve.

What does the inability to quit consist of, in the case of an unwilling addict? In many cases the commonsense, or "folk," answer is that the inability consists of weakness of the will. Were the agent to have a sufficiently strong will, he would have the ability in question. Cases of actual quitting might be attributed to a strong will. We can easily imagine cases of relapse, where common sense ascribes a relapse to a weak will, and we can imagine cases where we explain the fact that a person was not able to quit in time (and thereby developed the full addiction) by pointing to his weak will. These commonsense answers may have little value, but since we have sophisticated concepts of weakness of the will in the literature, it may be worthwhile to explore the answers given in the light of these concepts. If such an exploration were to bring positive results, a concept of weakness of the will might have a quite direct role in an account of these puzzling, but also central and profoundly human, cases of addiction we shall concentrate upon.

As the editors explain in their introduction to the present volume, putative addictions might relate animals such as whales and sharks, that is, their similarities might make them look like subvarieties of a common general kind although they in fact belong to quite distinct general kinds. The same might hold for weakness of the will: The different employments of the concept of weakness of the will in the commonsense use in the previous paragraph might denote quite distinct mechanisms. Intuitively, weakness of the will is considered a failure of the agent to act in accordance with what he recognizes to be the best choice. In a standard case, weak will is exhibited when we have to choose between A (quitting) and B (for example smoking), and we have reasons for doing B (we enjoy smoking) but better reasons for doing A (we enjoy being a healthy nonsmoker more than being a smoker). In a weak-willed case, we still do B (smoking) freely and intentionally, knowing or believing that doing A (quitting) is better. A weak-willed person is stereotypically someone who often gives in to temptations while knowing or believing he is better off not giving in.

A main aim of this paper is to explore the role of weakness of the will in the account of addiction. In Section 2, I discuss the relationship between two accounts (Davidson's and Ainslie's) of weakness of the will. In Sections 3 and 4, I relate these accounts of weakness of the will to the preliminary account of addiction by focusing on the explanation of relapse. Theorists of addiction typically aim to show how a person can become addicted, and they see addiction as an entrapment exhibited as the result of certain rational, quasi-rational, or irrational processes and choices. I agree completely with the view that one major adequacy condition on a theory of addiction is that it can explain how people become addicted. But a theory of addiction also needs to be compatible with typical aspects of quitting and relapse. In particular, it has to be able to account for the fact that ex-addicts resume their habit at a time when withdrawal symptoms are assumed to have disappeared. As I see it, a theory of addiction that is not compatible with the fact that we are prone to relapse cannot amount to an adequate theory of addiction. Gary Becker's theory, for instance, seems to fail on this account.

## 2. Ainslie and Davidson on Weakness of the Will

In their introduction, the editors outline George Ainslie's and Donald Davidson's theories of weakness of the will. I shall limit myself to some additional remarks about Davidson's theory and suggest that we need something like it to supplement Ainslie's account.

In what sense does one hold A better in cases when one freely but weak-willedly does B? Different answers to this question lead to different accounts of weakness of the will. Donald Davidson requires that in weakness of the will a judgment that, "all things considered, A is best" be held *simultaneously* with an all-out judgment that "B is best" (the latter judgment is the intention acted upon). This is clearly irrational. By contrast, George Ainslie's model does not ascribe such conflicting simultaneous judgments to the weak-willed.[3]

As we try to refine the essential concepts needed to understand action, it becomes increasingly questionable whether it is at all possible to act contrary to our judgment about what course of action is best. The pressure against allowing for such a possibility stems from the need to account for what it is to do something intentionally, and especially from the role we must give to reason in the account of intention. The present-day standard account of intention, expounded by Davidson, accounts for an intention by representing it as an unconditional judgment about what is best to do. Acting intentionally is then thought of as something we do, that is correctly described as intentional in some way or other. When something we do is correctly described as intentional some way or other, there is a corresponding intention. Davidson used to think that he could give an account of intention by using only the concepts of belief, desire, and primary reason, but he later abandoned this reductive strategy.[4] As I understand it, Ainslie's theory works without an independent role for intention, and thus it stays within Davidson's original and more parsimonious framework.

For Davidson the reason for which an action was done (i.e., the reason we give if we explain the action) is a rational cause. To put it in a slightly dangerous way: A reason has in a way two sets of causal properties: the content-related properties, which give the action its point, and other causal properties. All the causal properties – rational, content-related, and other – normally march in step, and a reason will causally influence acts and other mental states by virtue of its content. If this were not so, we would not be speaking of reasons. We have no independent access to the causal properties of reasons apart from their content-related manifestations in thought and other intentional activities. All access to reasons is for Davidson the access of a radical interpreter who tries to make sense of the agent's talk and deeds. To explain an action we need to find a reason whose content gives the action a purpose and which also caused it.

Here is the problem Davidson tries to solve in his account of weakness of the will. Let us assume that doing A intentionally is being caused to do A (and caused, moreover, in the right sort of way) by one's judgment that doing A is best. Assume, also, that there is

1. a conceptual tie between judging that A is best among exclusive options and wanting A most among these options,
2. a new and separate conceptual tie between wanting A most and doing A when freely doing either A or another option.

We are here only considering cases in which one truly believes oneself free to realize more than one option and where A is among the options one believes oneself free to realize. If we accept these two conceptual ties, which connect judging A to be best, wanting A most (preferring A), and intentionally doing A, it seems very hard to maintain that we can intentionally and freely act contrary to what we think best. If weakness of the will is to knowingly do A contrary to what we think best, that is, believing that some other available action B is better than A, then weakness of the will does not seem possible if (1) and (2) both are true. But (1) and (2) seem to be true.

Davidson's account of weakness of the will is meant as a solution to this conceptual problem about whether weak-willed action is at all possible. His goal is to show the possibility of weak-willed action without renouncing the conceptual ties expressed in (1) and (2). What Davidson does is to loosen another conceptual tie instead, the tie that seems to exist between beliefs and desires on the one hand and judging something best (preferring something) on the other. Davidson keeps the rational tie between beliefs and desires and the all-things-considered judgment (errors of calculation excepted), but he sees as possible an irrational causal transition from this all-things-considered judgment to actual preferences, or to actual all-out ranking of the options. What then happens is that reasons in support of B turn out to be stronger in causal terms in the production of preferences and of action, despite the fact that reasons supporting B have rational properties that the subject recognizes to be weaker than the rational properties of contrary reasons in support of A.

There is at this stage no need to enter the more detailed Davidsonian story, which encounters difficulties at many points.[5] We need not, however, think of the story with the all-things-considered judgment as describing psychological reality from the subject's point of view. We should rather think of it as a way of characterizing the state of an agent whose preferences conflict with his beliefs and desires and who is aware of this fact. Note that this conflict may persist after all time discounting is taken into account. Consider an "Ainslie diagram" such as Figure 9 in the Introduction to this book, which charts belief-and-desire–based estimation of reward value. For Davidson it is possible to form a preference for a smaller and earlier good (smoking) before this preference can be accounted for by time discounting (before the curves cross at $t^*$ in Figure 9). Conversely, one can form a preference for a larger and more distant good (quitting) even if one's present reasons favor smoking (after the curves cross at $t^*$ and before time 2 in Figure 9).

Should we believe that Davidson describes real cases? We may try to settle this by looking at cases where time considerations are not present or where they are irrelevant for the comparison of options. Here is a case based upon an example brought forward by Jon Elster: A self-neglecting housewife receives a lump sum of money, which she can use either on herself or on her family. She knows or believes that, all things considered, she should spend this money on herself, get some new clothes, see some new places, etc. She knows or believes that this is best not only for her, but for all concerned parties, both in the long and in the short run, morally and otherwise. Still she chooses not to spend the money on herself. In this case there is no difference in temporal perspective and thus time discounting cannot account for the weakness. If cases of this sort exist, there may be more to weakness of the will than Ainslie can account for and a need for something akin to the Davidsonian concept.[6] The argument does not show, of course, that we can make do solely with the Davidsonian concept.

Ainslie might be able to give a plausible interpretation of this housewife case within his own theory, for instance, as a case of too much will for the person's own good: The housewife has been forced to adopt what Ainslie calls rules in the "sell-out range" (see his chapter in the present volume) about spending next to nothing on herself in order to make her family happy and is thus unable to act rationally in the face of the new opportunities she is faced with in the example. She is seen as unable to make the proper exceptions to the personal rules that have been necessary for her to adopt.

Against this explanation I would argue that Ainslie has given no compelling reason for thinking that a housewife capable of recognizing that some exceptions are rational will always make them in practice. She might

normally make exceptions when she is able to recognize the need for
them, but she might also fail to make exceptions she believes she ought
to make even when she is able to make them. I believe having the ability to
make exceptions is compatible with failing to exercise this ability every
time she believes she ought to.[7]

I see the housewife example, and others like it, as supporting the view
that we need Davidson's concept of weakness of the will as well as Ainslie's.
I do not see them as competitors. I shall assume that Ainslie's view has both
theoretical and empirical support. I shall also maintain that there are obvious conceptual arguments in support of the view that we cannot make do
just with Davidson's concept to account for the intuitive concept of weakness of the will. Consider someone who experiences preference reversals
in Ainslie's sense constantly and always gives in to temptation. Common
sense deems such a person as weak willed. But he need not be weak willed
according to Davidson's conception of weak will, if he never holds conflicting judgments at the same time. There will therefore be cases of weak will
that Davidson cannot account for. Neither concept by itself, Davidson's
or Ainslie's, captures all there is to the intuitive idea of weakness of the
will, the concept we used in the beginning of the essay (a concept that
really seems to denote things related, as whales and sharks).

## 3. Relapses

Consider a smoker who has quit after many years of smoking, perhaps
an unwilling addict who has turned willing abstainer. Nevertheless, the
ex-smoker is prone to relapse. Avram Goldstein (1994, p. 220) says about
relapse:

> Relapse is, of course, always preceded by a decision to use, however vague and
> inchoate that decision may be. It is an impulsive decision, not a rational one,
> and it is provoked by craving – the intense and overwhelming desire to use the
> drug.[8]

In this insightful phenomenological description of a case of relapse,
Goldstein relies on commonsense ideas, as I did at the beginning. Let
us explore some of the theoretical ways of explaining why this decision,
which is "impulsive and not rational," is made. I shall discuss two kinds of
relapse: relapse into a bad habit and relapse into an addiction. I shall use
smoking as an example of both a bad habit and an addiction, assuming
that there is a significant difference in one's ability to quit between the
two cases. The fundamental aim still is to throw light on what addiction is.

### Relapse into a Bad Habit

Let us look at a person who has managed to quit the bad habit of smoking
and relapses. In Ainslie's picoeconomic perspective, prior to the relapse

this person lives by a personal rule not to smoke. I shall first assume that the person has simply overcome a bad habit, similar to a person who has adopted a personal rule about going to bed at eleven, or brushing his teeth before going to bed, or not having wine before playing the piano publicly at night. As explained in the Introduction to this volume, such rules are supported by considerations of *bunching*. Independently of the question of whether the adoption of personal rules can be justified as a rational decision (see below), we assume that this strategy is in fact adopted. The will is strengthened in the sense that the agent no longer has preference reversals in this particular area and is not losing out in the long run by constantly giving in to temptation. The agent continuously prefers nonsmoking, and so does not smoke. In case of a relapse, the agent defects from the rule, returns to giving in to temptations, and is soon smoking as heavily as before.[9]

How does the Ainslie-type framework account for relapse in this case? The obvious way to account for a relapse is to bring in some external cause that changes beliefs and/or desires. Since the adoption of the rule determines preferences, and there is no slack between adopting the rule and having a preference for A, it is not possible that the agent's preferences undergo a change from favoring A to favoring B while the personal rule is still operative. There is no room in Ainslie's theory for the possibility of defecting from the rule, giving in to temptation, and acting contrary to what the rule says, while the rule is still in place.

The external cause might change beliefs or desires or both. I shall ignore cases where it changes both beliefs and desires and look at cases where it exclusively changes either beliefs or desires. In the latter case something might bring on craving or a very strong urge for a cigarette, and the internalized rule might not be strong enough to prevent a preference reversal in favor of smoking. In this case we maximize utility when we smoke: We do what we prefer at that point in time. In the case of changing beliefs, the perception of the current smoking as a precedent for future choices might be undermined in one way or another: We might, for instance, deceive ourselves into being confident that a few cigarettes will not lead to erosion of the rule. In this case we act upon false or irrational beliefs, but we maximize utility relative to the (false or irrational) beliefs we have. The actions are therefore minimally rational, whereas the preference reversal is due to newly acquired false or irrational beliefs. These actions are not weak willed in Davidson's sense of the word, but we deem them irrational if the preferences are determined by irrational beliefs, especially if these beliefs are themselves motivated by the craving for cigarettes.

These cognitive cases are plausible, but I shall concentrate on the cases where some external cause changes the desire and brings on craving. In the real world, relapse will normally be a mixed case; the desire to smoke might easily cause various irrational beliefs, by wishful thinking or by self-deception, and thereby preference reversal. (See Schelling's epilogue, this volume, for a typology of such cases.) One might come to believe that a few cigarettes cause no harm, that they do not influence one's general ability to control smoking, and so forth. Perhaps motivated irrational belief formation is necessary in many actual cases of relapse. But to compare the Davidsonian concept of weakness of the will to Ainslie's, it is better to concentrate on clean rather than on mixed cases, and clean cases are surely possible even if not frequent.

Michael Bratman has recently criticized Ainslie's account of the rationality of bunching choices and adopting personal rules. I shall simply assume that someone who succeeds in quitting is acting rationally when he lives by a personal rule since he believes in precedence.[10] We then have a case where a belief in precedence forces a bunching of choices, which again supports the rule, and the subject has a stable preference for not smoking through time. Ainslie says about such rules: "They are self-enforcing insofar as the expected value of co-operation exceeds that of defection at the times when the choices are made." Let us concentrate on the case where a change in desire accounts for the occurrence of preference reversal and defection where there used to be stability. This is indeed a very natural situation for a smoker's relapse: It is likely to be caused by a significant change in craving brought about by some situation, perhaps a situational cue. The person still has the fundamental insight that choices make precedents, that the rule not to smoke can easily be eroded, and that he therefore might lose out quite drastically in the long run by smoking today.

Davidson's theory is capable of explaining this behavior, or more accurately, of accounting for its possibility. The agent judges that, all things considered, it is best not to smoke, but he still gives in to the craving and starts smoking. His actual preferences are in conflict with what his beliefs and desires dictate and his action is irrational. By contrast, Ainslie's theory does not seem to have the conceptual requisites for explaining relapse into the bad habit. By assumption, beliefs are not changed in the cases we are now considering. The perception of choices as precedents is firmly in place and not altered. The person we are considering once quit on the basis of the insight about what is best in the long run, and this insight remains in place. Moreover, Ainslie's aims are more ambitious than Davidson's: He does not merely want to account for the possibility of certain kinds of behavior but actually seeks to identify the conditions under which they will occur. He cannot simply say, therefore, that relapse will occur whenever the craving becomes strong enough to undo the bunching considerations, unless he also can say something about the conditions under which that will happen. And as far as I can see, his theory offers him no way of doing that.[11] Furthermore, even if Ainslie were to supply an extended theory that fills this gap, there would remain a question of whether that theory could be empirically adequate. Intuitively, it seems very unlikely that all cases of relapse within this setting could be accounted for by a craving larger than the craving felt when quitting the bad habit.

Thus we need Davidson's concept of weakness of the will, or something of that structure, to model what goes on in some cases of relapse into a bad habit for which we do not have irrational belief formation. I already argued, from the case of the housewife, that we need a concept with this structure anyway. It should come as no surprise that I suggest we employ this concept in the cases where Ainslie's theory does not provide an account. Davidson's concept can provide the gap between adoption of a rule and actual preferences, which I claimed that Ainslie could not allow for. Imagine that we have acquired the rule in the process of quitting. That very fact makes it rational for us not to smoke. Since we have the rule, we judge that, all things considered, we should not smoke. But we defect from the rule and smoke nevertheless, preferring to smoke while holding that, all things considered, it is best not to. This behavior might soon lead to the erosion of the rule, by a rationally based belief in the low likelihood of abstaining tomorrow if we smoke today. Ainslie can account for the progressive erosion of the rule once defection behavior has started. The start of the defection is, however, hard to account for in picoeconomic theory.[12] When the rule is eroded, we are back to where we started before we were able to quit.

Even if this reasoning is correct, there is a catch. Davidson's concept allows for causal/irrational deviations from what is considered best, all things considered. In theory, there is no reason to expect any particular pattern in these causal/irrational deviations. They might favor a long-term perspective or a short-term one. Davidson's theory gives no support to specific predictions and, in a sense, it therefore simply represents noise for a theory that attempts to predict people's behavior on the basis of their beliefs and desires. Davidson's focus is instead on the explanation of an individual piece of (irrational but) free and intentional behavior. Even if Davidson can account for a particular start of a defection from a rule, he will equally well be able to account for cases where defection does not occur, even if the desire for a cigarette is so strong that in the normal case it should have led to smoking because that is rationally considered best, all things considered, when the choice was made.

We might hold that noise of this sort is a natural human phenomenon and believe that our concepts should allow for it and not make it impossible. Nevertheless, actual deviations from rationality seem to have a pattern that Davidson cannot account for. It is surely more common for people to smoke against their own better judgment than for them to abstain from smoking against their own better judgment. Davidson's general account needs to be supplemented by a detailed explanatory story about causal mechanisms that generate weakness of the will, and this story, when given, might favor the "temptations," and thereby reduce the impression that the theory is useless for general prediction.[13]

### Relapse into an Addiction

Smoking is an addiction and relapses are frequent after someone quits smoking. When the person in our example quit smoking, he experienced withdrawal symptoms and the craving for cigarettes must have been very strong. Still he was able to quit. If we think of quitting as solely based upon starting to live by personal rules, and consider the fact that withdrawal symptoms were very strong, then the long-term gains must be very substantial when the time-discounting agent prefers quitting and quits. When such is the case, it seems very unlikely that the agent should experience a relapse, since it is very unlikely that the strength of craving at some future point should match the craving when trying to quit. It seems as if only a Davidsonian mechanism can account for relapse.[14]

I have maintained that if an account of addiction makes it very unlikely that a person who has been able to quit should relapse, then the account of addiction in question is inadequate. Relapse is a much too prominent phenomenon to be ignored, and the account of addiction must connect quitting with an account of relapse. An account of addiction that makes relapse after quitting very unlikely is a priori unacceptable as an account of addiction. We must therefore look for a richer account of quitting than what I called quitting a bad habit.

When the person quits, additional precommitment techniques might be applied to overcome the preference reversal, not merely personal rules. The three other Ainslean types of such techniques, as for instance the Ulysses-type technique or attention control, will represent an additional cost at the moment to serve the long-term interest. At the time of employing such techniques, additional temporary costs must be justified by a long-term gain. Let us consider a specific agent who has been addicted and who has quitted smoking. The agent we are considering has used such additional precommitment techniques. It has been rational for him to use them when quitting. We might think that in times of crisis (relapse threatening) it might be rational for this agent to use them again if needed to overcome a craving, since it was rational to use such techniques to overcome withdrawal symptoms. The long-term gain must be very considerable for it to be rational to quit, and this long-term gain is just as large when one is in danger of relapsing as when one is quitting. There is therefore no reason we should not apply these techniques again when there is danger of relapse; thus it seems as if explaining relapse proves to be no easier even if additional strategies have been employed when quitting.

This reasoning overlooks important facts about the interaction of pre-commitment strategies. To adopt an extra-psychic, Ulysses-type strategy to quit might be rational if it is done early enough, so that the cost is incurred when the long-term interest is strong. Such a strategy makes certain options unavailable, which, if they had been available, one would have gone for them. Thomas Schelling (1992) has described strategies to quit an addiction, and a main feature is to make it very difficult and temporarily impossible for an agent to act upon a craving when he has it.[15] This is done by arranging for externally enforced delays, for instance, very slow and cumbersome procedures for how to be released from a clinic. Such strategies are then employed to overcome the period when withdrawal symptoms and craving are at their strongest.

Just to be far away from cigarettes and smoke might steer attention away. A simple form of self-control of one's mind in connection with quitting might be to concentrate on all the good things that accompany nonsmoking. These good things might offer permanent, conflict-free satisfactions. Such concentration might involve a cost, but the cost must be incurred at a time before the preference reversal was to take place. The result of the concentration might be a change in the present assessment of the value of nonsmoking compared with smoking. Let us suppose that we have before us a case in which the desire to smoke is very strong, and where bunching by itself is insufficient to do the job of preventing preference reversal. In such a case a small readjustment of the absolute value of smoking compared with nonsmoking might add up to a lot through the bunching and thereby make a large impact. Concentration of one's mind might be just as effective in keeping something good in sight as keeping something bad out of sight. Emotion control might work by inducing feelings of disgust in connection with cigarettes after routine exposures to cigarette ashes and remains, which then create disgust reactions, which undermine the pleasure in smoking.[16]

In his discussion of the interaction of precommitment methods, Ainslie does not calculate how smaller changes in the absolute value of the alternatives, brought about by emotion control or concentration, will magnify in bunching when choices are seen as making precedents. He discusses how attention control can be symbiotic with personal rules and be crucial to get through periods of great vulnerability. But concentration on permanent goods and emotion control will have an effect that gets multiplied in the bunching. The effect of emotion control cannot be limited to one period, but will, once one is aware of it, constitute a permanent devaluation of smoking.

When discussing relapse into a bad habit, I looked at a case where effective bunching of choices was sufficient to quit. The interim conclusion at this point is that if the interactive, symbiotic use of many precommitment strategies is needed for quitting, then relapse might become more easily explainable than in the case where bunching is sufficient by itself. It therefore looks as if it should be part of a picoeconomic theory of addiction that bunching in itself won't suffice for quitting once one has become addicted. This follows if being able to account for our tendency toward relapse is an adequacy condition for a theory of addiction. To illustrate: The active smoker knows his craving and thus takes all these additional measures to serve his long-term interest. To do this requires time and preparation, training, and conditioning. Nonetheless, the smoker might succeed in quitting. Facing an unexpected craving, brought on by some situation later on, he might not have time to assemble these resources, and he might have lost much of the ability if this ability required training or conditioning that would fade after a while. (If conditioned emotion control fades, then the fading gets multiplied in the bunching.) It will therefore be possible to relapse even if the craving is far from being as strong as at the time of quitting.[17]

As discussed in the editorial introduction, craving might be caused by the desire to get rid of withdrawal symptoms, including secondary withdrawal symptoms. We might speculate: The stronger the craving derived from such sources, the stronger the need for additional precommitment strategies to succeed in quitting. The reasoning above, the interim conclusion, might in that case be further strengthened, since the need for a very sizable craving to cause relapse is reduced further. This is because quitting is likely to require a very sophisticated use of symbiotic precommitment strategies, a use that takes much to re-create. This might make one vulnerable to relapse even if the craving at that point in time were substantially less intense than when quitting, since it is very hard, and takes considerable time, to re-create the abilities to withstand the craving one once had.

What matters is the relative value of smoking compared with nonsmoking at various point in time. The relative value of smoking compared with nonsmoking is naturally thought of as increasing as one is in the process of becoming addicted.[18] One passes from a state where bunching might be sufficient to quit into a new state where bunching is no longer sufficient to quit and, as one becomes more and more addicted, one needs more and more complex symbiotic uses of precommitment methods to be able to quit. When bunching is no longer sufficient, then we have passed from a bad habit into an addiction. After quitting, we get the opposite development, a reduction of the relative value of smoking compared with nonsmoking. This will account for a number of facts, among them that it takes less to stick to the long-run interest A after a certain period of abstaining and, at the same time, that the strength of the desire needed to account for relapse need not match the strength of the desire to smoke when quitting. On such a view of addiction, relapse into an addiction will be much more plausible with an Ainslie type of view.

## 4. Conclusions and Speculations

Are there any conclusions? There is a suggestion that addiction is the development of an habitual activity, which in its turn causes changes in one's evaluation of the utility of this activity, making it more or less impossible to act upon a strong desire to quit just by bunching consideration and a cooperative strategy in dealing with tomorrow's self. The suggestion is, however, based upon the example of an unwilling addict and therefore might not be thought to be generally valid. We must, however, remember the counterfactual element in our definition: The addict would be unable to quit were he to develop a strong desire to quit. The reasoning should therefore be generally valid, and it seems to give weakness of the will a prominent role in the account of addiction.

There is one important caveat, and that concerns time considerations. I have made a claim about the significance of the change from the case of bad habit, where personal rules and bunching considerations can be sufficient for quitting, to the case of addiction, where bunching considerations are insufficient for quitting. In my example, this change takes place in the perspective of a person who cares about a finite number of choices between smoking and nonsmoking.[19] Agents who care about a larger number of choices will have a smaller chance of becoming addicted, in a similar way to how people who discount the value of events a year ahead are less likely to become addicted. But the perspective that people have on value in time need not remain fixed. In theory, one strategy to quit might be to try to influence a change in one's perspective on value in time.[20] I shall not go into such possibilities but just note that an expected change when acquiring some addictions is a tendency to care less about events in the fairly distant future. Such a change will make it harder to quit, and it might in itself be sufficient to turn a habit into an addiction under given circumstances.

In what light can we now view our initial commonsense explanations and answers at the outset, where we employed the concept of weakness of the will? The explanation of relapse due to weakness of the will does not specify any explanatory mechanism and is compatible with both a Davidsonian mechanism and an Ainslie-type mechanism. The more detailed causal story in the Davidson case is still missing, but this gap might be filled some day. With this qualification I turn to the Ainslie-type mechanisms I have discussed.

There is a relationship between the ability to quit employed at a prior stage and the danger of relapse. The latter depends upon the type of precommitment strategies employed when quitting: If one is able to quit by bunching considerations and the adoption of personal rules alone, then the danger of relapse is very small.[21] Depending on the type and nature of other precommitment strategies one has used in combination with the adoption of personal rules, the danger will increase. To rely heavily on the use of extra-psychic mechanisms might make one prone to relapse, since these mechanisms might not be available. Furthermore, one needs time (which one does not have) to make a number of preparations. The effect of emotion control might fade and directly influence the bunching considerations. An explanation of relapse by reference to weakness of the will can therefore be substantiated in various ways by an Ainslie-type account of why we suddenly have preference reversal in cases where we had no such reversal in the preceding period.

If we imagine a gambler who depends heavily on the extra-psychic strategy of staying far from any gambling table, the explanation of relapse can be expanded into a plausible explanation within the Ainslie-type framework. In their Introduction to the present volume, the editors also suggests the need for order as a possible cause of relapse in connection with smoking. The quitter might have such a need, and if alternative ways of satisfying it, already employed among the precommitment strategies, are suddenly missing, then this might cause preference reversal and relapse. A general point is that what offsets a recurrence of preference reversal, and relapse, after a long period of stable abstaining, will depend closely on the properties of the type of addiction at hand and on the types of precommitment strategy used when quitting.

In the picoeconomic framework, we can also fill in an explanation of a failure to quit, which refers to weakness of the will. An ability to quit is seen as an ability to control oneself in the sense of preventing preference reversal. The case of the unwilling addict is someone who does not have this ability or does not have access to the help he needs to get the ability. It is an ability that can be reduced or lost, and then relapse is likely to occur, which again can be explained by reference to weakness of the will. This inability to quit consists in a failure to achieve the mastery of self-control techniques with sufficient causal power to serve the long-term interest and prevent preference reversal. Such failure might be due to many things: One has no access to the extra-psychic strategies needed to overcome a certain period of withdrawal symptoms; one lives in an environment that regularly induces cravings after one has quit, which would require extremely powerful self-control techniques; one is not very receptive to emotion control conditioning or its effect fades very fast; etc.

We also see that it is much harder for Davidson than for Ainslie to account for an inability to quit in the face of a recognition that one ought to quit. An account of the inability requires a causal account of why certain reasons (desires) are much more prone to undermine an all-things-considered judgment than others.[22] In the absence of such an account, an explanation of a failure to quit, where the reference to weakness of the will is to an inability to quit in spite of what one thinks best in the long run, can only work if one is referring to weakness of the will of the Ainslie type. In general, it is hard to connect up Davidson's account of weakness of the will with accounts of abilities or inabilities, and this is, in my judgment, due to the fact that his theory is geared toward explanation of individual (exceptional) actions, not toward explanations of tendencies to do one thing or the other. Such tendencies are linked to abilities in the cases that concern us.

The description of the unwilling addict given by Harry Frankfurt is therefore a case that is much harder to make sense of in Davidson's framework than in Ainslie's. Frankfurt's case has been used to shortcut the standard link between valuing something and desiring it, which has shaped the problem of weakness of the will, because of the connection between judging something best and wanting it. Davidson's aim is to keep that connection. However, it seems that we need Ainslie's framework to make sense of Frankfurt's case. It therefore looks as if we need hyperbolic discounting to keep the connection between valuing something and wanting it.

## Acknowledgments

George Ainslie, Jon Elster, Eliot L. Gardner, Aanund Hylland, George Loewenstein, Karl Ove Moene, Ole-Jørgen Skog, and Helge Waal listened to me giving this paper. I am very grateful to all of them for help and comments. I am also grateful to Nancy Cartwright and Gabriel Segal and to an audience at the London School of Economics. Al Mele and Ole-Jørgen Skog gave clear, constructive, and helpful comments in writing, and discussions and exchanges with Michael Bratman on closely related issues have been of considerable help. I am pleased to acknowledge a longstanding debt to Donald Davidson as well as help from a recent conversation. I thank the Norwegian Research Council for generous support and SIFA, the Norwegian National Institute for Alcohol and Drug Research, for access to a stimulating research environment. I am especially grateful to Jon Elster in more ways than one.

### NOTES

1. See the introductory chapter for definitions of these concepts. The withdrawal symptoms in their turn produce craving, and craving can also be produced by secondary withdrawal symptoms. Perhaps we can simply speak of craving and ignore its causes.
2. Harry Frankfurt, "Freedom of the Will and the Concept of a Person," in Watson, *Free Will*, Oxford University Press, Oxford 1982, p. 87.
3. We can say that Ainslie's agent is always minimally rational.
4. The strongly reductive view is Davidson's classical position in "Action, Reasons and Causes" in 1963. Although it is explicitly given up in the article "Intending" from 1978, it actually was given up in the earlier article on "How

Is Weakness of the Will Possible." Davidson accounts for the changes in the preface to his 1980 collection, *Essays on Actions and Events*, which contains the articles I have mentioned. (See Davidson [1980].) Davidson's new position remains a "reductive" approach to intention, since he uses beliefs, desires, and belief-desire–based evaluations to account for intention. Michael Bratman (1985) criticizes Davidson's view and argues that the concept of intending must be explained by using the closely related concept of planning. I defend a Davidsonian "reductive" view on intention in Gjelsvik (1996).

5. The difficulties might be very severe indeed – in this paper, I ignore them.

6. The first part of this conclusion is obviously on more secure ground than the second. One can imagine that other things besides time should be taken into account and that an adequate general account could agree with Ainslie's view that all choices are minimally rational. The need to go all the way to Davidson's view is not documented by this example.

7. In response to this paper, George Ainslie argued along these lines: The case might be analogous to a teeth-brushing case that Davidson discusses at length in "How Is Weakness of the Will Possible" (Davidson 1980), which Ainslie also is likely to see as a case of too much will. See Ainslie's paper in this volume for an illuminating discussion of similar cases of too much will. In my example, I am imagining a case that cannot be fitted into such a background story. I am grateful to Jon Elster for questioning me about this point.

8. Goldstein 1994, p. 220.

9. The assumption that there might be people who smoke who are not addicted to nicotine might be wrong. If it is, and we are obliged to use only realistic examples, substitute "drinking" for "smoking" throughout the chapter.

10. Bratman, in "Planning and Temptation" (1996) argues that the belief in precedence has no rational foundation. This might be true. Nevertheless, a person who has this (irrational) belief is (minimally) rational when he maximizes utility relative to the beliefs he has.

11. I am grateful to Jon Elster for this theoretical point.

12. This does not mean that picoeconomic theory does not have resources that can be used to account for the beginning of relapse in many cases. Having rules without bright lines is one good candidate, but I cannot see how these resources can do all the work. I thank Ole-Jørgen Skog for bringing this up. He also raised the issue that this seems to imply that a rational person should maintain the abilities to withstand craving. I reply that this might be very costly, and much too costly if one's estimate of the chance of increased craving is very low.

13. But there is always a danger: The supplementation of Davidson might turn out to be a replacement instead, if one eventually provides mechanisms that work in such a way that we make do with minimally rational choices and avoid the extreme irrationality of all-out judgments, contrary to all-things-considered judgments.

14. Gabriel Segal has suggested that we see the Davidsonian concept as accounting for all cases with this structure. Relapse is, after all, a rare event in a person's life, he argues.

15. See Schelling 1992.

16. See Ainslie (1992a, p. 139).

17. In thinking about self-control, I have been helped considerably by Alfred Mele's writings, especially Mele (1987), but also Mele (1992).

18. One can here imagine a causal mechanism somewhat analogous to the Becker/Murphy-type causal mechanism. In their case the consumption of the addictive good causes an increase in the marginal utility of the addictive good, while the overall welfare/utility level is reduced. See the Introduction to the volume and also the discussion in Ole-Jørgen Skog's contribution.

19. It is fairly simple to give a general mathematical formula for how large the finite number of choices one cares about must be in order for bunching to be a sufficient means to prevent preference reversal.

20. Jon Elster has convinced me that character planning to change one's rate in time discounting makes no sense on the assumptions of standard decision theory with dynamic consistency and a given rate for time discounting. My theoretical remark is made in the context of dynamic inconsistencies due to hyperbolic discounting. A person who discounts hyperbolically and who is generally good at getting around temptations by bunching might consider ways of changing his discount factor and comparing that strategy with other strategies when bunching fails to be sufficient in the particular case of addiction at hand. Empirically, there might not be any methods for changing the discount factor, and in that case this strategy is not an option.

21. As long as the rules have "bright lines." This assumption applies throughout this discussion.

22. Someone might hold that the inability to quit involves a compulsion. If that is right, I should skip this paragraph and the next. Philosophers normally treat compulsions as cases where one is no longer acting freely, most likely as cases where one is no longer acting, and weak-willed cases as cases where one is acting (freely). Of course there is a different use of compulsion: one compatible with agency. If that use is reflected in the first sentence of this footnote, it might fail to express something I disagree with.

## BIBLIOGRAPHY

Ainslie, George (1985), "Beyond microeconomics," in Jon Elster (ed.), *The Multiple Self*, Cambridge University Press, Cambridge, UK.

(1992a), *Picoeconomics. The Strategic Interaction of Successive Motivational States Within the Person*, Cambridge University Press, Cambridge, UK.

(1992b), "Hyberbolic discounting," with Nick Haslam, in George Loewenstein and Jon Elster (eds.), *Choice over Time*, Russell Sage Foundation, New York.

(1992c), "Self-control," with Nick Haslam, in George Loewenstein and Jon Elster (eds.), *Choice over Time*, Russell Sage Foundation, New York.

(1993), "Where there's a will there's a won't," Presentation for the Symposium *Contemporary Perspectives on Self-Control and Drug-Dependence*, Chicago.

Becker, Gray and Kevin Murphy (1988), "A theory of rational addiction," *Journal of Political Economy* 96, 675–700.

Bratman, Michael (1985), "Davidson's theory of intention," in Ernest LePore and Brian McLaughlin (eds.), *Actions and Events, Perspectives on the Philosophy of Donald Davidson*, Blackwell, Oxford, UK, pp. 14–28.

(1987), *Intentions, Plans and Practical Reason*, Harvard University Press, Cambridge, MA.

(1996), "Planning and temptation," in L. May, M. Friedman, and A. Clark (eds.), *Mind and Morals*, Cambridge University Press, Cambridge, UK.

Davidson, Donald (1980), *Essays on Actions and Events*, Oxford University Press, Oxford, UK.

(1982), "Paradoxes of irrationality," in Richard Wollheim and James Hopkins (eds.), *Philosophical Essays on Freud*, Cambridge University Press, Cambridge, UK.

(1985), "Deception and division," in Jon Elster (ed.), *The Multiple Self*, Cambridge University Press, Cambridge, UK.

Frankfurt, Harry (1982), "Freedom of the will and the concept of a person," in Gary Watson (ed.), *Free Will*, Oxford University Press, Oxford, UK.

Gjelsvik, Olav (1996), "Intention and alternatives," *Philosophical Studies*, 82, 159–77.

Goldstein, Avram (1994), *Addiction*, Freeman, New York.

Mele, Alfred (1987), *Irrationality*, Oxford University Press, Oxford, UK.

(1992), *Springs of Action*, Oxford University Press, Oxford, UK.

Schelling, Thomas, "Self-command, a new discipline," in George Loewenstein and Jon Elster (eds.), *Choice over Time*, Russell Sage Foundation, New York. pp. 167–76.

# The Dangers of Willpower

GEORGE AINSLIE

Addiction and dissociation are puzzling phenomena that are not usually thought of as related, although they are often prominent in the same individuals. Both violate our conventions of rationality. Addiction entails the voluntary choice of options that the person himself reports he does not want. Dissociation is a temporary reversal of preference so extensive as to change what the person acknowledges as his "self"; such reversal, for which the person is amnesic, is seen to an extreme degree in multiple personalities and to a lesser extent in fugue episodes, "blackouts," and the experience of spirit possession. Economic Man, the conventional utilitarian model of how people evaluate choices (Stigler 1980), explains neither, much less suggests any reason why they tend to appear together.

Empirical research on the relationship of dissociation with volitional lapses such as addictions has been sparse. There is a high correlation between dissociation and other self-control disorders: Of 100 substance-abuse patients, 39 percent have been reported to also have a dissociative disorder (Ross et al. 1992), as have 41 percent of 265 male veterans in a substance abuse program (Dunn et al. 1993). Patients with eating disorders also have high rates of dissociative disorder (McCallum et al. 1992, Zerbe 1993). Furthermore, a large proportion of drug addicts have post-traumatic stress disorder (e.g., 59 percent of a female drug rehabilitation population [Fullilove et al. 1993]), which entails many dissociative symptoms. However, these findings only suggest an important relationship between addiction and dissociation; they do not shed light on what it is.

The boundaries of the concept of addiction are in dispute, but the core meaning of the term is evident from its etymology: The term originally meant judicial enslavement, as when a person was sentenced (addicted) to serve another (*Oxford English Dictionary*), so that as a metaphor it clearly means enslavement by an appetite. Ample experience with addicts has shown that this enslavement comes not from a fear of withdrawal symptoms but from the continuing wish for a high, which often causes relapse after years of sobriety. Modern science has had increasing success in isolating the reward mechanism that makes the substance-based addictions extraordinarily attractive (Gardner 1992 and this volume), but this attractiveness does not explain the sense of slavery. Missing is an explanation for the addict's ambivalence, that is, why he regularly pursues a goal that he says he wants to get away from.

Scientific theories have avoided confronting the conundrum of ambivalence: They hold either that the addict does not realize the contingencies he faces or that the pain is worth it to him; Economic Man has so little trouble maximizing his prospects that he cannot knowingly be enslaved. True, he can suffer from erroneous expectations and thus stumble innocently into a downward spiral of conspicuous pleasure followed by insensibly diminishing options, the "primrose path" described by Herrnstein and Prelec (1992b); and he can have a very steep temporal discount function, which makes him simply take no interest in the future, like the "rational addict" described by Becker and Murphy (1988). However, continual maximizer that Economic Man is, he cannot have the familiar human experience of looking forward with apprehension to a behavior that he knows he will regret; nor does he ever have a reason for buying disulfiram or naloxone, the means for limiting his own future choices to forestall such a behavior. In short, he cannot have motivational conflict beyond an uncertainty about magnitudes.

Thus, conventional utility theory could explain without further assumptions both a naive subject's entry into addiction and an experienced user's unambivalent preference for his substance use over sobriety; but it does not explain an addict's internal conflict, as evidenced in the extreme case by his attempts to restrict his own future freedom of choice.

Despite these difficulties, addiction could theoretically be explained by a variability in the addict's estimate of his future prospects, however unaccountable, in someone with consistent values. Dissociation is more mysterious by far; it represents a regular reversal of those values, a change that may block access to all memory of times when the person's values were different. Such changes of character might seem to be out of the person's control, a neurological calamity such as epilepsy, but actually they are well known to be motivated (Putnam 1989). If utility theory has had difficulty explaining addiction, it has not even attempted to analyze something as irrational as the harboring of whole contradictory selves.

I will show that it is possible to reconcile both addiction and dissociation with strict maximization of utility, in light of recent evidence that a basic assumption of conventional utility theory has been wrong. I will also deduce a relationship of these two seeming paradoxes with a reliance on willpower for self-control and suggest a relationship between them.

## 1. Picoeconomics Predicts Self-Defeating Behaviors

I have argued elsewhere (Ainslie 1975, 1992) that the exponential discount curve by which people evaluate delayed goods in conventional utility models cannot predict irrational choice. However, controlled experiments have found a substantially different curve describing how the effect of a reward declines with delay, a curve that can be elicited in all higher organisms; this curve is not exponential but hyperbolic (Ainslie 1974, Ainslie and Herrnstein 1981, Ainslie and Haendel 1983). It is an aspect of Herrnstein's (1961) matching law, which has been confirmed by a number of researchers (Green, Fry, and Myerson 1994; Kirby and Herrnstein 1995; Stevenson 1986).

Hyperbolic curves predict that people will regularly form temporary preferences for the smaller but earlier of many possible pairs of alternative rewards, a preference pattern that in turn can account for a number of phenomena that had previously seemed paradoxical (an analysis I have called *picoeconomics*; Ainslie [1992]).[1] Many people balk at accepting a hyperbolic discount curve as fundamental, since at first glance it seems incompatible with the exponential discount curves that accurately describe a great deal of human economic behavior. However, the aggregate effect of hyperbolic curves on whole classes of choice can produce the appearance of exponential curves under some circumstances (Ainslie 1991). The identification of exponential discount curves as special cases within a framework of hyperbolic discounting liberates motivational theory from these curves' relentless prediction of rationality.

I cannot present a comprehensive exposition of picoeconomics here; but since several of its predictions combine to offer a rationale for addiction and dissociation, I will summarize them and refer the reader to specific parts of a fuller discussion (Ainslie 1992).

The effect of regular temporary preference is to make all motivated processes compete for survival against incompatible processes and to give them an incentive to strategically forestall these competitors. The "mind" or "self" is a population of reward-seeking operations that survive insofar as they actually obtain reward. The mental operations selected for by a particular reward or class of rewards constitutes the person's *interest* in that reward; interests within the person are very like interests within a community – those factions that are rewarded by ("have an interest in") the goal that names them (e.g., "the petroleum interest," "the arts interest"). Since a common marketplace of reward[2] keeps a person's purposes coherent except when conflicting rewards dominate at successive times, it makes sense to name an interest only where that conflict exists, that is, where the success of one process depends on its forestalling another process that would otherwise become dominant and undo the work of the first process. I would not be said to have separate chocolate and vanilla ice cream interests, even though these are often alternatives, because at the time when I prefer chocolate I do not increase my prospective reward by forestalling a possible switch to vanilla. However, I may have an ice cream interest and a diet interest, such that my expectable reward from the diet is intermittently threatened by an immediate prospect of ice cream. I do not increase my prospective reward in either the long or the short range by defending my choice of chocolate against the possibility that I may change to vanilla; but I increase my prospective long-range reward by defending my diet against ice cream, and I increase my prospective short-range reward by finding evasions of my diet for the sake of ice cream. Whichever faction promises the greatest reward, discounted from its expected time of occurrence to the present moment, gets to decide my move at this moment; the sequence of moves over time determines which faction ultimately gets its way.

Where alternative rewards are available at different times, each will build its own interest, and one interest will forestall the other only if it can leave some enduring commitment that will prevent the other reward from occurring: If my diet interest can arrange for me not to get too close to ice cream, the discounted prospect of ice cream may never rise above the discounted prospect of the rewards for dieting, and the diet will have effectively won. However, whenever the value of ice cream spikes above that of dieting, the ice cream interest may suddenly undo the effect of many days of dieting. The ultimate determinant of a person's choice is not his simple preference, any more than the determinant of a legislature's action is simple voting strength; in both processes, strategy plays a major part.

This model of hyperbolic discounting might seem to make self-defeating behaviors such as addiction a straightforward problem. Once a person has identified a recurring preference as temporary, he should be able to commit himself not to give in. However, the solution is not that simple, as we will see.

Self-commitment is certainly a familiar behavior. Even pigeons have some ability to do this: After varying amounts of experience with their own strong tendencies to choose the poorer but earlier of two alternative food rewards, they can learn to forestall these tendencies somewhat. If a particular route to the largest available reward goes through some point A, where they can choose a poorer, earlier alternative reward, many subjects learn to take the longer or more effortful route through a different point B that avoids this peril (Ainslie 1974). To some extent, pigeons can even achieve this internally, that is, without the experimenter offering them a route through point B that physically keeps them away from point A (Mazur and Logue 1978).

This last finding raises the question of what other committing tactics are possible, for pigeons or for people. Perhaps these subjects have learned to keep their attention away from cues that, once seen, offer the choice of a temporarily more valued smaller reward; perhaps they are learning to think "cool thoughts" instead of building their appetites for the reward, as the Mischels' five-year-old children report doing (Mischel and Mischel [1983]; more discussion in Ainslie [1992, pp. 130–42]). The most interesting possibility is that they are forming elements of willpower – resolutions or intentions as the philosophers of mind picture them (Bratman 1987). That is, they may be evaluating choices as members of larger categories.[3] For exponential discounters, this would have no effect on choice, but for hyperbolic discounters it would let the disproportionate effectiveness of an immediate temptation be averaged in with the more objective, albeit discounted, evaluations of many similar prospective choices in the future. Categorical choice might allow subjects to evaluate and reject temptations with "both alternatives steadily held in view," as William James (1890, p. 534) characterized the effort of will.

The stabilizing effect of deciding "on principle" has been recognized since Aristotle (Barnes 1984, 1,147a24–b17) and was well known to the Victorian psychologists (see Sully's quote in note 3, as well as James [1890, p. 534]). It has recently been verified by the same kind of experiments that demonstrated the matching law: Even pigeons will choose a larger, later reward over a smaller, earlier one more often if this choice is part of a series of choices than if it stands alone, an effect that Rachlin (1995) has attributed to his subjects' adoption of a "molar" (i.e., global) framework of the choice in place of a "molecular" (i.e., one-by-one) framework. Similarly, Heyman (1996) has demonstrated how a consistent signal associated with the better long-range choice leads pigeons to increase that choice, a change he explains in terms of the signal's having supplied his subjects with an "overall" versus a "local" perspective on the outcomes.

However, the increase in both pigeons' and children's capacity to wait for the larger reward is small in these experiments (usually less than double). There is reason to believe that even grouping choices together in series, while necessary for genuine willpower, will not be sufficient. That is, there is nothing in the process of molar or overall categorization per se that prevents a short-range interest from distinguishing each current choice from the molar category. Choices in potential series will all have unique as well as common features, which can be a basis for excepting them; addictive motives are notorious for subverting general plans of conduct by establishing the example at hand as a special case (as in James's famous list of drunkard's excuses [James 1890, p. 565]). Somewhere, perhaps in the long exploration of social rules that takes place in the grade-school years (Piaget 1965), humans discover the power of the test case, of focusing on their own choice between molar and molecular interpretations of a current example as a predictor of what they can expect of themselves in similar cases in the future.[4] People soon learn that the outcome of such tests weighs on subsequent choices that look similar and that the threat of losing one's expectation of future self-control can marshal a great deal more motivation than depends on the single case at hand. Intention policed by such a strategy is experienced as something transcendent: will, or resolve, or moral determination. Perhaps this is even the "knowledge of good and evil" that gave Man self-will and mythically ended his career in the Garden of Eden (Genesis 3).

The perception of test cases, in individuals or in interacting groups, gathers motivation remarkably. Relevance to a diet greatly changes the incentives for eating versus not eating a single piece of candy, just as fluctuations in the price of a "bellwether" stock have a disproportionate effect on the whole stock market.[5] Furthermore, it can be shown that perception of a series of choices as test cases for a common rule should shape the relationship of successive choosing selves into a familiar relationship, limited warfare (Schelling 1960, pp. 21–80), the properties of which are described by a well-known bargaining game, the repeated prisoner's dilemma (Ainslie 1992, pp. 142–79). This is to hypothesize that willpower achieves deterrence against each individual impulse through the fear of setting precedents for whole strings of future impulses. The *personal rules* that define what is to be seen as cooperation in this bargaining process seem identical to the principles specified in Kant's categorical imperative (Kant 1960, pp. 15–49) and Kohlberg's highest stage (VI) of morality (Kohlberg 1963), and thus they appear at first glance to represent rationality itself. Certainly they give molar or overall views of reward great leverage over molecular or local ones. It might indeed seem that they should solve the problem of addiction.

## 2. Willpower Is an Awkward Expedient, Not the Ultimate Rationality

Unfortunately, a person's perception of the relationship of the prisoner's dilemma and the willpower that results from this perception do not really solve the problem of temporary preference. Willpower may be the best expedient we have[6]; but it turns out to have serious side effects that become major factors in people's lives. I argue that these side effects are what shape the problem of addiction as the clinician encounters it in a developed society; that they link addiction to other phenomena, particularly dissociation, that seem anomalous in any rigorous theory of behavior; and that they are little recognized, leading even the best-intended advice to produce perverse results both in individuals and in social policies.

Although personal rules can sometimes lead an individual to approximate an exponential discount curve for future events, they do not give him the prelapsarian trait of maximizing his expected utility whenever he makes a choice, nor do they preserve the experience of spontaneity in choice making. Rule-governed choice has four properties that cause it to fall short of these utilitarian ideals:

1. Categories of choice come to overshadow their individual members, resulting in a legalistic manner of choice making.

2. Rules make lapses disproportionally damaging and tend to turn them into permanent symptoms.
3. Rules create a motive to distort the perception of reality.
4. Rules need not be in the person's longest range interest.

### Categories of Choice Overshadow Their Individual Members

The perception of choices as precedents often makes a choice much more important for its expected effect on future choices in the intertemporal prisoner's dilemma than for the rewards that literally depend upon it. Insofar as this is true, choice becomes detached from the properties of its objects and takes on an aloof, legalistic quality. In the parlance of existential therapists the person becomes "inauthentic" (Kobasa and Maddi 1983).

A person is often hard put to predict how his own future selves will perceive the precedent his current choice is setting. This makes cooperation in intertemporal prisoners' dilemmas both rigid and tenuous. Unless chance provides clear lines that can be used as boundaries it may be difficult to tell whether, facing a choice in the future, one will look back at the current choice and judge it to have been a lapse.

The difficulty of this task depends on topography of the range of options. A person trying to give up a heroin habit at least benefits from the *bright line*[7] between some heroin and no heroin; but a person trying not to overeat has to make judgment·calls continually about what food to allow himself, even if he has committed himself to one single diet. In consequence a short-term interest within the individual can usually offer a colorable exception to a diet, and it may escalate such proposals by degrees until the diet has been rendered useless without ever having been clearly violated.

Under the pressure of temptation, a person may claim an exception to a rule but later see the claim as unsupportable, that is, see himself as having had a lapse. Conversely, he may be cautious beyond what his long-range interest requires, for fear that he will later see his choice as a lapse – a rationale that exacerbates compulsiveness. Errors in either direction impose costs that would never result from the exponential curves of Economic Man, since these curves would create no reason for discerning precedents in the first place.

### Rules Magnify Lapses

When a person violates a personal rule, the cost is a fall in his prospect of getting the long-range rewards on which it was based. This prospect is what he uses to stake against the relevant impulses; a lapse suggests that his will is weak, a diagnosis that may actually weaken his will in the recursive pattern described long ago by James, Lange, and Darwin (James

1890, vol. 2, p. 458; Ainslie 1992, pp. 200–5). To save his expectation of controlling himself generally, he will be strongly motivated to attribute the lapse to a particular aspect of his present situation; the consequence may be that he abandons his attempts at willpower whenever that aspect is present. That is, he may create a class of exceptions rather than suffer a general loss in the credibility of his will – to decide that he *can't* resist the urge to panic when speaking in public, or to lose his temper at incompetent clerks, or to smoke after meals. Thereafter the occasions for these urges will seem to bring on the behaviors automatically, without an intervening moment of choice.

In other words, exceptions to personal rules need not arise through deliberate rationalization; an exception can impose itself on the person's intentions in the most awkward of places, wherever a lapse has threatened a broad loss of impulse control. When she has been using her willpower to control panic, or rage, or smoking in a particular setting, and her will has been overwhelmed, she will be under pressure to distinguish that setting from all others so that she will not see her lapse as a precedent for her choices, in general. Her discrimination of this special circumstance has a perverse effect, since whenever she faces it she sees only failure predicting further failure. I have called this area, where the person dares not attempt efforts of will, a lapse district, by analogy to the vice districts in which Victorian cities tolerated the vice that they lacked the political will to suppress (Ainslie 1992, pp. 193–7). Where the encapsulated impulses are clinically significant, clinicians call a lapse district a symptom. In this way the perception of repeated prisoner's dilemmas stabilizes not only long-range plans but lapses as well.

The availability of boundaries to circumscribe a potential lapse district may determine whether it will form in the first place. Lapses are goal-directed behaviors, and thus they are not beyond the influence of long-range rewards; lapses endanger these rewards less when there is a boundary that can limit their implications. Short-range interests prosper most when they parasitize, as it were, rather than kill, long-range interests. Thus the uniqueness of a vacation trip may make a spendthrift more apt to go off a budget; likewise, an alcoholic may find lapse districts forming in time-limited circumstances (e.g., only when she has just completed a project or a school year or an election campaign).

The boundary may be intrinsic to the kind of reward involved. Many "out of control" consumption patterns commit the addict to withdrawal sickness followed by a period of abstinence before the substance becomes rewarding again. The crude periodicity of such a cycle may permit the addict to stably apportion his ambivalence into two successive, contradictory activities. Then the trigger for a binge may be nothing more than a perceived lapse itself: His willpower governs until it stumbles but, as soon as he has a drink or fix, he experiences a "loss of control" and winds up on a bender (Evenson et al. 1973; for a similar loss of control in dieting, see Polivy and Herman 1985); his will when sober will be preserved by his perception of the drunken state as a lapse district. In the period of exhaustion that ends the bender, his "normal" will can reassert itself, but only until a regenerated appetite for the addictive activity again asserts itself in a lapse. He will have two distinct selves, an intoxicated one and a sober one.[8] By contrast, a rapidly satiating activity such as smoking will never reach the proportions of a binge; here, any regular alternation between control and loss of control must be cued by something other than intrinsic exhaustion and recovery.

### Rules Motivate Misperception

Personal rules depend heavily on perception – on noticing and remembering one's choices, the circumstances in which they were made, and their similarity to the circumstances of other choices. Because personal rules organize great amounts of motivation, they naturally create an incentive to suborn the perception process. When a lapse is occurring or has occurred, it will often be in both the person's long- and short-range interests not to recognize that fact: His short-range interest is to keep the lapse from being detected so as not to invite attempts to stop the forbidden behavior. His long-range interest is also at least partially to keep the lapse from being detected, because acknowledging that a lapse has occurred would lower the expectation of self-control that he needs to stake against future impulses.

After a lapse, the long-range interest is in the awkward position of a country that has threatened to go to war in a particular circumstance that has then occurred. The country wants to avoid war without destroying the credibility of its threat and may therefore look for ways to be seen as not having detected the circumstance. The person's long-range interest will suffer if he catches himself ignoring a lapse, but perhaps not if he can arrange to ignore it without catching himself. This arrangement, too, must go undetected, which means that a successful process of ignoring must be among the many mental expedients that arise by trial and error; these are retained simply because they make the person feel better without his realizing why.[9] Money disappears despite a strict budget, and people who "eat like a bird" mysteriously gain weight. Clouding of consciousness in the face of temptation has been reported by observers from Aristotle (Bogen and Moravcsik 1982) to Sjoberg and Johnson (1978). Here is a motivational pattern that could easily create a black market, indeed an underworld, of those behaviors that include blockage of notice and recall.

### Rules Need Not Serve the Person's Longest Range Interest

There is a puzzling class of behaviors that are more stable than the addictions but that a person still perceives not to be in his "best" interest.

Whereas bouts of addictive behavior are preferred for periods of minutes to days, these more stable behaviors are preferred for years, or indefinitely, but are still accompanied by a sense that they will be regretted. Compulsions, dieting in anorexia nervosa, and making oneself impervious to emotion in alexithymia (Nemiah 1977) are clinical examples, but many highly systematic "character flaws," such as miserliness, fastidiousness, and overcontrol, never come to a clinician's attention. These maladaptively narrow behaviors lack a generally accepted name; I have called them *sellouts.*[10] Like addictions, sellouts create a sense of enslavement, but they are apt to be more systematic and may even seem rational, because they are often based on personal rules. That is, sellouts can combine against both longer and shorter range interests.

Although the combinatory mechanism of personal rules obviously requires them to serve longer range interests against shorter range ones, they need not serve the person's longest range interests. Some rules may even group such mid-range payoffs together so as to steal dominance from longer range payoffs, without violating the strict logic of hyperbolic discounting (Ainslie 1992, pp. 216–24). The relationship of a person's longest range interest with sellout- and addiction-range interests is illustrated by Jon Elster's example:

> I wish that I didn't wish that I didn't wish to eat cream cake. I wish to eat cream cake because I like it. I wish that I didn't like it, because, as a moderately vain person, I think it is more important to remain slim. But I wish I was less vain. (1989, p. 37 note)

Assuming that his wish to be less vain does not merely serve his wish for cream cake, it reveals a perception that vanity is not in his longest range interest – that he will regret it even though it dominates his current choice. That is, he sees vanity as an overly narrow trait, a sellout. His vanity is in turn threatened by a tendency to eat cream cake; assuming that episodes of seeking cream cake dominate his choice for a matter of minutes to hours, they represent temporary preferences of roughly the same duration as those in addictions.[11] Under these circumstances the vanity will be able to foster a personal rule against eating the cake (i.e., a diet), even though it may contradict the still longer range interest in not being vain. This will be true as long as this longest range interest cannot find effective criteria that would make a rule against the vanity practical. It is on the availability of such criteria (bright lines) that contests among relatively long-range interests seem to depend.

In seeming inversions of the interests' power relationships – where a sellout-range interest that is protected by a rule dominates the person's longest range interest – the decisive factor may not be how well a rule would pay if enforced, but how well it can be enforced. Enforceability depends in turn on how clearly each choice is either a member or not a member of the relevant series.[12] That is, personal rules operate most effectively with countable criteria. Thus rules against acts of vanity are apt to be much less enforceable than rules against overeating.

The impact of having rewards marked by discrete stimuli is illustrated by recent experiments on "melioration": Human subjects had to choose between amounts of money such that choice A produced a conspicuously larger reward than choice B, but choice A led to poorer subsequent payoffs for both choices A and B (Herrnstein and Prelec 1992a). Where choice of a larger amount reduced the *amounts* to choose from on subsequent turns, most subjects soon discovered the strategy of picking the smaller amount in the current choice. However, where choosing the larger amount led not to smaller amounts but to greater *delay* before subsequent choices, thus reducing total income in a game of fixed duration, subjects tended to keep picking the larger amounts and getting smaller returns (Herrnstein et al. 1993). Amounts are eminently countable; delays are vague unless someone specifically thinks to count the seconds. As we might expect, when Herrnstein pointed out to his subjects the greater delay that came from choosing the larger reward, they also generally started choosing the smaller.[13]

Thus when sellout-range interests are based on well-marked rewards, and their richer, longer range alternatives are harder to define, the sellouts may win the protection of personal rules. Rules that serve sellouts are particularly apt to become dominant when the person has had a conspicuous addiction-range interest that has motivated strict controls, as in the case of the anorectic patient who finds his draconian diet worthwhile to end a history of overeating. It is easier to enforce specific rules about diet than more subtle rules such as "eat what you need" or "eat what you will be glad of in retrospect," though if the latter were enforceable rules they would permit the most reward in the long run. When a person seeks the comparative safety of the most clearcut criteria for his personal rules, he may be forestalling not only short-range impulses but also the richest long-range rewards.

Extreme commitments to personal rules are widely recognized as compulsions. But even short of frank compulsiveness, the systemization that lets personal rules recruit the greatest motivation may undermine the very purposes that inspired them. The attempt to optimize our prospects with rules confronts us with the paradox of definition: That to define a concept is to alter it, in this case toward something more mechanistic. A person who concludes that he should maximize money becomes a miser; one who rules that he should minimize his openness to emotional influence becomes alexithymic (Nemiah 1977); if he concludes that he should minimize risk, he becomes obsessively careful; and so forth. The logic of rules may so come to overshadow a person's responsiveness to experience that his behavior becomes formal and inefficient. A miser is too rigid to optimize his chances in a competitive market, and even a daring financier undermines the productiveness of his capital if he rules that he must maximize each year's profit (Malekzadeh and Nahavandi 1987). Similarly, strict autonomy means shielding oneself against others' ability to invoke his passions, but the alexithymics who have accomplished this cannot effectively use the richest strategy available for maximizing reward, the cultivation of human relationships (Ainslie, 1995 and in preparation). And avoidance of danger at any cost is poor risk management.

Furthermore, beyond the inefficiency of hidebound rules in obtaining their ostensible goals, picoeconomic analysis predicts a reduction in their emotional payoff that occurs insofar as they *do* succeed: Optimal exploitation of the available reward for any gamelike activity requires the maintenance of suspense, but hyperbolic discount curves create a shortsighted impatience for resolution that can be effectively resisted only by committing oneself to be surprised (Ainslie 1992, Ch. 7). That is, imagination attenuates through an innate impatience to entertain its high points at the cost of prematurely resolving emotional tension, thus increasingly wasting the relevant appetite as the person gains experience with a given situation. The more efficient a person learns to be at overcoming a challenge, or the more familiar he becomes with a story, the more he will anticipate its resolution and undermine the longing needed for relatively intense satisfaction. Thus the various mental diets that let the person maximize wealth, or autonomy, or safety reduce by their very efficacy the amount of surprise he is subject to. Since surprise is the key factor in appetite for emotional experience, the maximization process is apt to become stale, even if it is working well. This seems to be how nature keeps organisms exploring novel areas instead of resting on their laurels. A consequence is that clarity per se predisposes rules for pacing emotional rewards to serve sellout-range interests.[14]

Of course, in many cases a person never regrets maximization schemes such as anorexia and miserliness, so that these are held to be inferior choices only in an observer's estimation (raising, as with alleged addictions, that the person himself does not recognize, the question of tastes); but often the person regrets them intermittently, or blames them for spoiling his happiness without being able to devise a rule structure sufficient to motivate their abandonment. Perhaps the person initially tried less concrete rules, such as to do what he would be glad of in retrospect, and found they could not hold their own against more specific prescriptions; his "consistent preference" for the more concrete rules is then just acquiescence in their seeming inevitability.

Personal rules convert changes of preference that depend on proximity to temptation into the simultaneous conflicts that seem more numerous (Ainslie 1992, p. 193). Getting drunk no longer depends on how close one gets to a bottle but on whether an ongoing search for excuses finds a believable one. With characterologic choices such as anorexia or miserliness, the temporal basis of the conflict is harder still to see, but the payoffs even for these abstemious behaviors are clearly a current sense of some kind of well-being, at the expense of any realistic expectation of feeling glad of one's choices later.

In these four ways, elementary motivational conflict is sharpened and its stakes raised when it is structured by personal rules. After the need for clarity has taken its toll on subtlety, and overcaution on flexibility, and undercaution with its consequent failures on resolve and self-observation – in short, after the makeshift nature of our attempt at global perception has caught up with us – the conflict between global and local approaches to choice making is no longer simply one of long- versus short-range interests. Given the distorting effects of both hyperbolic discounting and the personal rules that compensate for it, "rationality" becomes an elusive concept. Insofar as it depends on personal rules demanding consistent valuation, rationality means being systematic, but systemization readily goes too far and winds up advancing a person's mid-range interests against her longest range ones. Sometimes a particular global approach is less productive in the long run than local, myopic alternatives, as anorectics and misers discover to their bewilderment.

### 3. Side Effects of Willpower Foster an Interaction of Dissociation and Addiction

Experiential underworlds (classes of goal-directed behavior that the person cannot report) have often been described, but theorists have been hard put to make sense of them in motivational terms.[15] Modern parlance characterizes the formation of underworlds as "dissociation," a person's blockage of information about one experience while he is having another. Hypnosis experiments (Hilgard 1977) and observations of unusual natural phenomena such as multiple personalities (Putnam 1989) and psychic amnesia (Schacter and Kihlstrom 1989) have characterized the experiencing entities (the various "selves") as parallel and potentially autonomous, with radically divergent value systems. One of these value systems is almost always conspicuously impulsive, whereas another is conventionally prudent.

Current belief about dissociation attributes it to a combination of innate cognitive predisposition and a strong acquired motive to avoid intrusive traumatic memories (Spiegel 1991). The relation between these two factors is in dispute, but there is usually agreement that dissociation is motivated by the dysphoria of intrusive thoughts. I will refer to this as *hypothesis A.*

This hypothesis suggests only a minor relationship between dissociation and addiction: Concomitant abuse of some substances may physiologically augment the repression, but nonsubstance addictions should neither cause repression nor be caused by it. I will briefly comment about recent research on this mechanism and then suggest two additional motives for dissociation that arise from personal rules and have a more intimate relation to addiction-range motives: Dissociation can protect useful personal rules (*hypothesis B*) and may offer relief from oppressive ones (*hypothesis C*); in both cases it would do this by strengthening the encapsulation of lapse districts, which would in turn provide occasions for the dissociations. Any of these three mechanisms might operate side by side with any of the others.

### Dissociation Avoids Intrusive Thoughts

Some individuals seem to have more of a bent for dissociating than others. Perhaps 10 percent of a general population have spontaneously entered experiences that they could not report afterward or that they discovered only by external evidence – "waking up" in a different place or being told of it; 2 percent do so repeatedly (Ross, Joshi, and Currie 1990). The latter are said to have a dissociative disorder. Observers have long noticed that dissociation seems to go along with an unusual aptitude for directing one's attention. High dissociators do not readily compare one part of their experience with other parts but become totally "absorbed" in one to the exclusion of others (Crawford, Brown, and Moon 1993, Roche and McConkey 1990). Hypnotizability is another associated trait. Whether from heredity (Crawford and Gruzelier 1992) or learning, about a fifth of the population can follow a suggestion to experience events that they cannot remember at other times (Hilgard 1965). These highly hypnotizable people also report a great degree of absorption (Smyser and Baron 1993).

The relationship of dissociation with these attentional factors is not surprising. In motivational terms, hypothesis A states that dissociation represents an extreme use of attention control – the restriction of information gathering – as a tactic for controlling very short range urges[16]: Those trauma victims who have predispositions to dissociate use their powers of absorption to divert their attention from the triggers of intrusive memories, until the strength of the unsatiated intrusive urge is enough to attract it back; and during their subsequent surrender to these memories they protect their long-range interests from association with them by repressing those interests in turn.

The source of the intrusive memories has seemed obvious: A large percentage of dissociators report a history of trauma (Putnam 1989), and a large percentage of people with post-traumatic stress disorder (PTSD) dissociate (Branscomb 1991). PTSD is increasingly recognized. It is now said to affect 12 percent of the population, or at least of its females, at some time, and 5 percent at any given time (Resnick, Kilpatrick, and Dansky 1993). However, the role of trauma in dissociation is complicated by the relationship of PTSD with another trait, fantasy proneness. There is a group of people who readily generate vivid fantasies of both rapture and dread; 1 to 2 percent of the population are said to be capable of fantasy experiences comparably vivid to those occasioned by actual physical stimuli, even food and sex (Wilson and Barber 1983, Rhue and Lynn 1987). Like PTSD patients, the fantasy-prone have intrusive thoughts, which are easily triggered and which may undermine long-range activities that require sustained attention.[17] However, the fantasy-prone are not merely *like* PTSD patients: They often *are* PTSD patients, reporting histories of trauma at an extremely high frequency (Lynn and Rhue 1988).

It has been impossible to say to what extent fantasy-proneness is a way people learn to cope with urges to entertain real traumatic memories and to what extent an innate fantasy proneness lures the person into elaborating or fabricating trauma fantasies, which then have the vividness of memories. Certainly some people form convincing memories of demonstrably impossible experiences such as prior lives, and they can do so either spontaneously or under hypnotic direction (Spanos et al. 1991, Labelle et al. 1990); however, a large proportion of people who report childhood traumata can find independent corroboration of them (Herman and Schatzow 1987), although this has not been studied specifically in people who are fantasy-prone. Whatever the interaction of trauma and fantasy, we know that fantasy proneness is closely associated with attentional absorption (Rhue and Lynn 1989), raising the additional question of whether an aptitude for directing attention creates exceptional fantasy abilities or whether a proneness to exceptionally vivid fantasies motivates attention-controlling strategies such as high absorption. Hypothesis A is obviously complex and in need of systematic study. In any case, it should probably be broadened to include intrusive thoughts that do not come from trauma.

### Dissociation Protects Personal Rules in the Person's Longest Range Interest

We would expect the processes of partitioning volitional lapses (side effect 2 of willpower, above) and repressing them (side effect 3) to reinforce each other, in that each limits the scope of personal rules. Either of these responses (the lapse-district or the information avoidance) may occur by itself, but there is no reason that one need exclude the other. The cue that warns the person not to attempt willpower may tell him to block access to memory as well: Defining a lapse district will not completely protect the person's other prospects for impulse control, since even after distinguishing the circumstances of a lapse the person cannot be sure of how important his future selves will think the distinction is; it is hard to be sure that future selves will not see predictive implications in that lapse. However, forgetting a lapse will end its particular danger, albeit at the expense of strengthening the person's tendency to forget lapses in the future. Thus there is the potential for a synergy of repression and lapse-district formation.

Once a lapse district has become established, its circumscribed extent will invite the person's other short-range interests to exploit it as an opportunity for expression. For instance, the alcoholic's binges offer not only a limited period of drinking but also an occasion for a vacation from other rules. Other temptations that have heretofore been under tenuous control can thrive using the period of the binge as an exception to the rules that forbid them, a holiday like Saturnalia. Modified rules such as, "I will be faithful, respectful, and prudent, but not when the alcohol is talking," are supported by a reduction in the pressure of urges between binges, which may make up for the aftereffects of the periodic adultery, rage, and/or dissipation, particularly if other people accept the attribution to the alcohol. The drunken and sober selves will take on a whole panoply of different characteristics, often under the general rubric of hero and villain.

The greater the scope of the rules threatened by the person's impulsive behaviors, the more necessary the blockage of memory to maintain his confidence in his will when sober, that is, the more he will be motivated to use dissociation to further separate his lapse district from the rest of his life. Although a person may learn to accept a circumscribed weakness of will against a "normal" temptation such as drinking, he might find that a disgusting paraphilia or outbursts of vicious rage at someone he loves require ignorance. A person who is vegetarian because of a concern for world food supplies might not be threatened by episodes of eating meat and might even recognize periodic occasions for it; but for one who is vegetarian out of a tenet that killing animals is murder, eating meat would threaten a larger belief structure, and he would be motivated to "not be himself" during any such episode. Dr. Jekyll could not accept Mr. Hyde, even as a lapse. A person with enough blockage will have a "split ego."

Thus some dissociations may be extreme forms of that spontaneous pressure valve, the lapse district. Just as a lapse district itself offers other impulses the occasion of a natural exception to rules, the concealment from these rules afforded by dissociation will further attract the other major addiction-range interests that the person has tried to outlaw. Once an exception is thus doubly protected from the review of personal rules, it becomes a formidable focus for organizing other impulses. Thus dissociated selves are apt to become very bad citizens, but primary selves will be proportionately virtuous.

### Dissociation May Evade Rules That Serve Sellout-Range Interests

There is a more speculative possibility that sometimes appears in the lore of addictionology: That a person's will may have become so confining that a pattern of regular lapses actually makes him better off in the long run. This lore attributes binging to a patient's inhibitedness in the rest of his life; his general overcontrol is said to set up periodic episodes of breaking loose.

The model of intertemporal bargaining predicted by hyperbolic discount curves provides a specific rationale for this pattern: Ruling out any large source of emotional reward will create a proportional motive for the person to bypass or break his rules. If these rules have, in William James's phrase, "grown too narrow for the actual case" (James [1890, p. 209]; side effect 2, above), even his long-range interest will lie in partially escaping from them. Thus personal rules that serve sellout-range interests potentially create alliances between long- and short-range interests. The person's occasional binge comes to serve as a correction to the comparative sterility of such rules, a means of providing richer experiences while still limiting the scope of behaviors that pay off in the addiction range. The longest range interest of an alcoholic who is too rigid when sober may be to tacitly foster the cycle of drunkenness and sobriety, rather than be continuously imprisoned by his rules.

An alcoholic is sometimes described who becomes nicer, or more genuinely creative, or more fully human when drunk. Furthermore, some addicts plan binges in advance. Such people may believe that their binges are undesirable (indeed, "rationality" will almost certainly dictate such a belief), but the therapists they hire find them mysteriously unresponsive to treatment. The patient who arranges for drinking several days in advance – goes off his disulfiram, for instance, or brings bottles with him to his rehabilitation program for later use – cannot simply be yielding to a short-range impulse. This is behavioral evidence that he experiences his rational plans as sellouts, which, even at a distance, appear to need hedging, although he may be unable to report any such thing.

Evasion of sellout-based rules is thus a third incentive for dissociation, beyond the avoidance of intrusive thoughts and the protection of useful personal rules.[18] Insofar as this mechanism is important, a simplistic policy of "the more willpower, the better" will contradict the experience of many addicts. They are able to "listen to reason" only when they have somehow learned to ease the strictures that starve their own long-range interests.

Pervasive personal rules may arise in response not only to extraordinary temptation or ineptness in dealing with temptation but also to an environment's extraordinary demands for systematic decision making. As a society develops a complex, interdependent economy, it generates both better means for individuals to maximize their efficiency and more pressure to do so. This is not to say that one has to obey particular people or otherwise narrow one's choices; on the contrary, the range of substitutable behaviors grows enormously. But a person who chooses these substitutions on a basis that ignores economic advantage loses conspicuous benefits.

Even as parents and rulers have less control, the logic of an increasingly comprehensive marketplace has more. The implications of a person's choices comes to extend beyond a set of related behaviors in a circumscribed context (how to satisfy this customer, make love to this partner, fix this machine) to most of one's behaviors in a common universe, and the behaviors of many other people whom he may never meet. I list three of the many manifestations of this progression: First, cash prices and wages, which make disparate decisions comparable, have penetrated choice making ever more minutely, so that goods and services that used to be bartered as part of relationships are increasingly paid for. It is indicative that the smallest unit of money in use was half a day's wages in medieval times but is now barely worth picking up from the floor (ironically, the penny in both cases; Burnett 1969). Second, and similarly, the long-term records that result from one's behavior, which once consisted (beyond a few major documentations such as births, marriages, and deeds) of the emotional memories of neighbors, are now automated, quantified, and increasingly collated. The consequence is greater comparability of past and current choices; job reports, credit ratings, and traffic tickets issued a decade ago are increasingly available and used to predict a person's behavior. Third, formal acculturation by schooling is increasingly lengthy and gets increasingly audited according to standards. A person's performance in one subject or at one time can be compared to her performance elsewhere, or to another person's, with increasing precision, comparisons that are apt to determine her career choice, her advancement, or at least her morale. In these and many other ways, each of a person's choices is made comparable to, and thus predictive of, a range of other choices. Attention to this aspect of choice is rewarded by greater efficiency in any systemizable endeavor; but, as we have just discussed, it may lead to less productive occasioning of reward in the long run.

These changes do not feel forced upon us by alien interests. On the contrary, they are means to the ends we ourselves have defined, means that are increasingly selected for efficiency by the competition of the marketplace. We freely adapt our personal rules to be compatible with them; but these rules may come to serve sellout-range interests.

Attuned as we are to modern efficiency in the developed world, we do not recognize the oppressiveness of an environment so rationalized that much of our natural idiosyncrasy has been anticipated and harnessed or selected out. Yet newcomers accustomed to more backward economies find our relationships superficial; and our own fictional heroes are increasingly those who rage against systems. The costs of basing decisions only on countable outcomes never appear in cost-benefit analyses; indeed they are recognized only obliquely, as anomie or other imponderable moral problems, part of the "X-inefficiency" of workers that somehow limits their responsiveness to monetary incentives (Leibenstein 1976). Only within the past two decades has there been retrenchment where systemization is most advanced – in large corporations – in the form of decentralization, quality circles, self-directed work teams, and other retreats from the conventional approach of time/motion efficiency (Macdonald and Piggott 1993).

The systemization of modern society may be making the evasion of personal rules an increasingly important motive for dissociation. Certainly the apparent increase in multiple-personality disorder in modern times has been perplexing. The condition was known in Victorian times and as demonic possession even earlier (Ellenberger 1970, pp. 13–22). Granted that it has recently received a great deal of publicity, if there were a substantial incidence of it in earlier days, one would expect there to have been more discussion of it. The supposed causative agent, trauma in childhood, must have been more widespread in earlier generations, an increase in reportage notwithstanding: Historical cultures encouraged physical discipline, neglected children's experiences (Aries 1965), and had scant means or will to interfere with abusive families. The violence of the life children saw in earlier times is attested to by the cruelty of their games.[19] If trauma were the main cause of dissociative disorder, we would expect the incidence to be decreasing, and this, at least, does not seem to be happening. The evasion of an increasingly systematic world is a speculative cause at best, but it makes some sense. Dissociation in such a cause would represent another alliance of convenience between addiction-range and long-range interests.

### 4. Summary

The strategy of controlling temporary preferences by perceiving one's choices as sets of precedents is far different from the rationality of exponential discounting envisioned by conventional utilitarians. Instead of being an elementary process, that rationality seems to be a legal fiction, a convention that has been shaped by practical experience to be the most useful goal of the intertemporal bargaining process. We undertake to make choices as if this goal represented our spontaneous preferences, and perhaps even to suppress our awareness of this very undertaking. We do so to give our long-range interests an advantage over shorter range interests and to give ourselves an advantage over economic and social competitors, where self-control is a factor in the competition. However, this rationality is a somewhat clumsy artifice, seemingly cobbled together in the form of personal rules without having evolved in lower species, as soon as the human race realized that our spontaneous preferences did not maximize our long-range prospects.

I have described four side effects of personal rules that interact to produce two behavior patterns that we find pathological, patterns that in turn interact to stabilize each other. The four properties are

1. rigidity leading to legalism;
2. magnification of lapses, leading to encapsulated symptoms;
3. perceptual distortion, leading to limited self-knowledge;
4. inordinate dependence on concrete criteria, which suborns personal rules away from the person's longest range interests.

The two pathological processes are addiction and dissociation. My analysis of their interaction uses the picoeconomic concept of durations of temporary preferences, in particular, addictions (hours to days) and sell-outs (months to years).

The artificiality of personal rules (side effect 1) may make them seem like prisons. Formation of lapse districts (side effect 2) leads to stable behavioral "symptoms" with an addiction range of preference. Distortion of perception (side effect 3) may both conceal and strengthen lapse districts. The selective advantage that rules with concrete criteria have over those without (side effect 4) often leads to the dominance of rules that serve sellout-range interests, an effect that enhances the sense of imprisonment. When a personal rule no longer serves a person's longest range interest, lapse districts that have broken away from this rule ironically may start to serve this interest, forming an alliance that can explain why some addictions are highly resistant to therapy.

For these reasons, two incentives for dissociation may well be added to the conventional one of avoiding intrusive thoughts: The protection of desirable personal rules and the evasion of the personal rules that serve sellout-range interests. Incidentally, fantasy proneness may be added to traumatic memories as a source of such thoughts.

Neither addiction nor dissociation represent the straightforward functioning of an elementary principle; rather, hyperbolic discount curves can be expected to create them semistably in the course of intertemporal bargaining. Significant clinical addictions will usually occupy lapse districts (areas that the will has stabilized by its failures) and these addictions may ally with other addiction-range interests and even long-range interests. Likewise, dissociation has other motives besides the management of traumatic memories.

As theories of this complex subject proliferate, a unifying discipline will be indispensable: that of specifying how each tenet explains robust contradictory behaviors within the constraint of maximizing expected utility. This discipline seems attainable if and only if we understand the discount curves from expected rewards to be hyperbolic.

## Acknowledgments

A preliminary version of this paper was presented to The Norwegian Research Council Working Group on Addiction, Collioure, France, September 28, 1994.

Coatesville Department of Veterans Affairs Medical Center and Temple University Medical School. I thank Barbara Gault, David Renfrow, and Elizabeth Ainslie for extensive help in discussing drafts of this article.

## NOTES

1. People's preference for an addictive substance is sometimes not temporary, especially early in their consuming careers. An observer with superior foresight might say that it would be temporary, *if only they knew* . . .

   > If a person does *not* wish to quit under the prevailing circumstances, he would still be considered addicted if he found it very difficult to quit under circumstances that generated a wish to quit. This person is called a consonant addict [Skog, this volume].

   However, addiction in this sense is an ordinary taste; such a taste would not puzzle us if it did not typically lead to a stage in which the person recognized his error but could not escape – in other words, to enslavement.

2. The broad substitutability of behaviors in a limited channel of expression must constrain diverse possible reward centers to be comparable along a single dimension for purposes of selection. That dimension is best called reward (Ainslie 1992, pp. 28–32; Shizgal and Conover 1996).

3. When "particular actions are united under a common rule, they are viewed as members of a class of actions subserving one comprehensive end. In this way the will attains a measure of unity" (Sully 1884, p. 631).

4. It turns out that pigeons do *not* discover the power of the test case; that is, even when they have learned some resistance to temptation, they do not come to perceive their own choices as precedents (Ainslie 1989).

5. The movements of a bellwether stock affect the market proportionately as investors are sensitive to test cases, that is, as they behave like "portfolio insurers" rather than "value-based investors" (Ferguson 1989).

   Similarly, the sensitivity of an individual's self-control to the outcome of test cases may vary. A person who is not greatly worried about overeating or smoking, but is "just trying to cut down," may have frequent fluctuations into greater consumption without noticeably damaging his willpower. At the other end of the continuum, someone who is strongly motivated to cut out these behaviors and is threatened by any sign that they are returning may subject himself to such scrutiny that every relevant choice becomes a crucial test. He will stake such importance on a single lapse that, if it ever occurs, it will lead him to helpless surrender. The "first-drink" phenomenon has been such a conspicuous cause of alcoholics' loss of sobriety that it was once thought to be a physical reflex (Evenson et al. 1973). This will be discussed in the section on how personal rules magnify lapses.

6. The empathic disengagement that characterizes a cosmopolitan society makes the most obvious alternative form of impulse control – tolerating one's vulnerability to social pressure from the community – unreliable and sometimes treacherous. The bigger the community in functional terms, the more often one encounters disengaged predators who can exploit her openness to engagement, a situation that encourages her to cultivate disengagement in turn. This disengagement is concealed by the friendly informality that is actually one of its symptoms, a sign of a "growing aversion to emotional intensity, [an aversion] that such informality requires" (Stearns 1994, p. 11). The change is well expressed by the twentieth-century cultivation of emotional "cool." Beginnings may be visible in Beau Brummel's introduction of the "stiff upper lip" to fashionable Regency society, which was at least a conspicuous milestone of our escalating competition in imperviousness to influence (Cole 1977). However, there may be important gender differences in the progress of this trend (Gilligan 1982).

7. Lawyers and other negotiators developed this useful term, meaning a boundary that stands out in some unique way from other boundaries that might be proposed. Bright lines have the effect of stabilizing negotiated settlements against shifts in boundaries from small changes in the balance of bargaining power. See Ainslie (1992, pp. 163–73).

8. This description of symptom formation as a product of intertemporal bargaining is not meant to negate the importance of biological preparedness for temptations in motivating lapses. The tastes for alcohol or thrills that make some risk-taking styles highly heritable are increasingly being traced to innate differences in the physiology of emotion (Cadoret et al. 1986, Grove et al. 1990), as are shorter range urges such as fearfulness and pain sensitivity (Kendler, Neale, and Kessler 1992, Skre et al. 1993, Panocka et al. 1986). Great urges may overcome even well-drawn rules. However, even a middling urge may overcome badly functioning rules. Rules that are overly strict or just poorly drawn may permit too little reward to sustain then against ordinary challenges. Thus bulimic patients may just be poorer lawyers than the anorectics who succeed in never bingeing, in that they cannot formulate sustainable rules for this purpose; and anorectics in turn feel a need to resist longings that people with more adaptive rules can gratify without fear of losing control.

9. As Erdelyi (1990) has pointed out, the unconscious but goal-directed effort to forget that the psychoanalysts call repression does not differ in nature from the conscious kind (suppression). I would suggest that its unconsciousness is shaped by the incentive to avoid losing the stakes of personal rules.

10. The person might be said to have "sold out" his subtler or richer interests for the reliability of a system.

Two ranges of temporary preference shorter than addictions – itches and pains – can also be discerned in common experience (Ainslie 1992, pp. 98–114), but they are not important for this discussion.

11. I use overeating and dieting as illustrations frequently, not because they seem to be pivotal, but because they are probably the best-known concerns about temporary preference in common experience.

12. Another factor – how sharply this series stands out against alternative series that could be substituted – was discussed above with bright lines.

13. Admittedly, melioration procedures with humans study subjects' awareness of rewards rather than their self-control; there should be little urge to favor small, early cash rewards when the cash can't be spent until the end of the experiment anyway. However, the advantage that countable rewards have over subtler ones in this purely informational problem should also be present when self-control is involved.

14. However frustrating this phenomenon is to the hedonist, it is liberating for motivational theory because it suggests how "process rewards," those that do not depend on a hardwired releasing stimulus, can compete on equal terms with biological need-satisfiers. A person is physically able to summon the most powerful of emotions – joy, terror, love, hate, etc. – without external stimuli, but insofar as he does so without occasions that are both adequately rare and adequately unpredictable, the absence of suspense will turn them into mere daydreams; such direct approaches will generally extinguish.

    This phenomenon selects for strategies that use optimally unpredictable events to cue their process rewards (e.g., joy) and demands continual growth or replacement of these strategies as their finding of occasions becomes so efficient that these occasions become common or predictable (Ainslie 1992, Ch. 8). This model frees the observer from a search for "curiosity drives" and "conditioned emotional reactions" and brings all motives into a single marketplace.

15. Freud's "unconscious" organized centuries of puzzled observations (Ellenberger 1970, Whyte 1962), but the "repression" that he said created it confounds the impulsive diversion of attention from unpleasant truths with the impulse-controlling diversion of attention from temptations; it can be reconciled with strict utilitarian accounting, but only by the additional assumption of hyperbolic discounting (Ainslie 1992, pp. 35–9, 133–5).

16. Certainly processes with very short latency periods from suggestion to adoption – obsessions, hypochondriacal worries, vivid fantasies, traumatic memories, and other mental processes – are poorly controlled by personal rules, probably because there is not time enough between the urge and the process itself to test the urge as to whether it is permissible (Ainslie 1986). Diversion of attention from the pathway that brings up the urge should indeed work better than personal rules against very-short-latency processes.

17. Both groups also develop related self-destructive activities with a range of preference duration like that of addictions: Many traumatized patients voluntarily repeat their traumata (van der Kolk 1989), and many high fantasiers become addicted to their fantasies at the expense of richer human relationships (Firestone 1993).

18. Of course, such evasion could also be said to be preserving these rules, in that it prevents their outright confrontation. The interest that supports the rules may also support their evasion.

19. Torture of animals, for instance, is uncommon today compared with even recent times. If we go far enough back, we encounter village games where children nailed a cat to a wall and took turns trying to butt it to death with their heads (Origo 1959, pp. 40–3).

## BIBLIOGRAPHY

Ainslie, G. (1974), "Impulse control in pigeons," *Journal of the Experimental Analysis of Behavior* 21, 485–9.
  (1975), "Specious reward: A behavioral theory of impulsiveness and impulse control," *Psychological Bulletin* 82, 463–96.
  (1986), "Manipulation: History and theory," in M. P. Nichols and T. J. Paolino, Jr. (eds.), *Basic Techniques of Psychodynamic Psychotherapy*, New York, Gardner Press.
  (1989), "Internal self-control in pigeons," unpublished manuscript.
  (1991), "Derivation of rational economic behavior from hyperbolic discount curves," *American Economic Review* 81, 334–40.
  (1992), *Picoeconomics: The Strategic Interaction of Successive Motivational States Within the Person*, Cambridge, UK, Cambridge University Press.
  (1995), "A utility-maximizing mechanism for vicarious reward: Comments on Julian Simon's 'Interpersonal allocation continuous with intertemporal allocation,'" *Rationality and Society* 7, 393–403.
  (in preparation), *Empathy: A Picoeconomic Understanding of the Basic Good.*
  (in press), "A utility-maximizing mechanism for vicarious reward," *Rationality and Society.*
Ainslie, G. and V. Haendel (1983), "The motives of the will," in E. Gottheil, K. Druley, T. Skodola, and H. Waxman (eds.), *Etiology Aspects of Alcohol and Drug Abuse*, Springfield, IL, Charles C Thomas.
Ainslie, G. and R. Herrnstein (1981), "Preference reversal and delayed reinforcement," *Animal Learning and Behavior* 9, 476–82.
Aries, Philippe (1965), *Centuries of Childhood: A Social History of Family Life*, New York, Random House.
Barnes, Jonathan (ed.) (1984), *The Complete Works of Aristotle*, Princeton, NJ, Princeton University Press.
Becker, G. and K. Murphy (1988), "A theory of rational addiction," *Journal of Political Economy* 96, 675–700.
Bogen, J. and J. Moravcsik (1982), "Aristotle's forbidden sweets," *History and Philosophy* 20, 111–27.
Branscomb, Louisa P. (1991), "Dissociation in combat-related post-traumatic stress disorders," *Dissociation* 4, 13–20.
Bratman, Michael E. (1987), *Intention, Plans, and Practical Reason*, Cambridge, MA, Harvard University Press.
Burnett, J. (1969), *A History of the Cost of Living*, Baltimore, MD, Penguin Books.
Cadoret, R. J., E. Troughton, T. W. O'Gorman, et al. (1986), "An adoption study of genetic and environmental factors in drug abuse," *Archives of General Psychiatry* 43, 1131–6.
Cole, Hubert (1977), *Beau Brummel*, Woodstock, NY, Beekman.

Crawford, Helen J. and J. H. Gruzelier (1992), "A midstream view of the neuropsychology of hypnosis: Recent research and future directions," in E. Fromm and M. Nash (eds.), *Contemporary Perspectives in Hypnosis Research*, New York, Guilford, pp. 227–66.

Crawford, Helen J., Audrey M. Brown, and Charles E. Moon (1993), "Sustained attentional and disattentional abilities: Differences between low and highly hypnotizable persons," *Journal of Abnormal Psychology* 102, 34–43.

Dunn, Gary E., Anthony M. Paolo, Joseph J. Ryan, and Jay Van Fleet (1993), "Dissociative symptoms in a substance abuse population," *American Journal of Psychiatry* 150, 1043–7.

Ellenberger, Henri F. (1970), *The Discovery of the Unconscious*, New York, Basic Books.

Elster, J. (1989), *Nuts and Bolts for the Social Sciences*, Cambridge, UK, Cambridge University Press.

Erdelyi, Matthew Hugh (1990), "Repression, reconstruction and defense: History and integration of the psychoanalytic and experimental frameworks," in Jerome L. Singer (ed.), *Repression and Dissociation: Implications for Personality Theory, Psychopathology, and Health*, Chicago, University of Chicago Press.

Evenson, R., H. Altman, J. Sletton, and R. Knowles (1973), "Factors in the description and grouping of alcoholics," *American Journal of Psychiatry* 130, 49–54.

Ferguson, Robert (1989), "On crashes," *Financial Analysts Journal*, March–April.

Firestone, Robert W. (1993), "The psychodynamics of fantasy, addiction, and addictive attachments," *American Journal of Psychoanalysis* 53, 335–52.

Fullilove, Mindy T., Robert E. Fullilove, Michael Smith, Karen Winkler, et al. (1993), "Violence, trauma, and post-traumatic stress disorder among women drug users," *Journal of Traumatic Stress* 6, 533–43.

Gardner, Eliot L. (1992), "Brain reward mechanisms," in J. H. Lowinson, P. Ruiz, R. B. Millman, and J. G. Langrod (eds.), *Substance Abuse: A Comprehensive Textbook*, 2d ed., Baltimore, Williams & Wilkins, pp. 70–99.

Gilligan, Carol (1982), *In a Different Voice: Psychological Theory and Women's Development*, Cambridge, MA, Harvard University Press.

Green, Leonard, Astrid Fry, and Joel Myerson (1994), "Discounting of delayed rewards: A life-span comparison," *Psychonomic Science* 5, 33–6.

Grove, W. M., E. D. Eckert, L. Heston, et al. (1990), "Heritability of substance abuse and antisocial behavior: A study of monozygotic twins reared apart," *Biological Psychiatry* 27, 1193–304.

Herman, Judith L. and Emily Schatzow (1987), "Recovery and verification of memories of childhood sexual trauma," *Psychoanalytic Psychology* 4, 1–14.

Herrnstein, R. (1961), "Relative and absolute strengths of response as a function of frequency of reinforcement," *Journal of Experimental Analysis of Behavior* 4, 267–72.

Herrnstein, Richard J. and Drazen Prelec (1992a), "Melioration," in G. Loewenstein and J. Elster (eds.), *Choice Over Time*, New York, Russell Sage Foundation, pp. 235–64.

(1992b), "A theory of addiction," in George Loewenstein and Jon Elster (eds.), *Choice Over Time*, New York, Russell Sage Foundation, pp. 331–60.

Herrnstein, R. J., G. Loewenstein, D. Prelec, and W. Vaughan, Jr. (1993), "Utility maximization and melioration: Internalities in individual choice," *Journal of Behavioral Decision Making* 6, 149–85.

Heyman, Gene M. (1996), "Resolving the contradictions of addiction," *Behavioral and Brain Sciences* 19, 561–610.

Hilgard, Ernest R. (1965), *Hypnotic Susceptibility*, San Diego, CA, Harcourt Brace Jovanovich.

(1977), *Divided Consciousness, Multiple Controls, and Human Thought and Action*, New York, Wiley.

James, W. (1890), *Principles of Psychology*, New York, Holt.

Kant, I. (1960), *Religion Within the Limits of Reason Alone* (T. Green and H. Hucken, transl.), New York, Harper and Row, pp. 15–49.

Kendler, Kenneth S., Michael Neale, and Ronald C. Kessler (1992), "The genetic epidemiology of phobias in women: The interrelationship of agoraphobia, social phobia, situational phobia, and simple phobia," *Archives of General Psychiatry* 49, 273–81.

Kirby, Kris N. and Richard J. Herrnstein (1995), "Preference reversals due to myopic discounting of delayed reward," *Psychological Science* 6, 83–9.

Kobasa, S.C. and S.R. Maddi (1983), "Existential personality theory," in R. J. Corsini, and A. J. Marsella (eds.), *Personality Theories, Research and Assessment*, Itasca, IL, Peacock.

Kohlberg, L. (1963), "The development of children's orientations toward a moral order: I. Sequence in the development of moral thought," *Vita Humana* 6, 11–33.

Labelle, Louise, Jean-Roch Laurence, Robert Nadon, and Campbell Perry (1990), "Hypnotizability, preference for an imagic cognitive style, and memory creation in hypnosis," *Journal of Abnormal Psychology* 99, 222–8.

Leibenstein, H. (1976), *Beyond Economic Man: A New Foundation for Microeconomics*, Cambridge, MA, Harvard University Press.

Lynn, S. J. and J. W. Rhue (1988), "Fantasy proneness: Hypnosis, developmental antecedents, and psychopathology," *American Psychologist* 43, 35–44.

Macdonald, John and John Piggott (1993), *Global Quality: The New Management Culture*, San Diego, CA, Pfeiffer.

Malekzadeh, Ali, R. and Afsaneh Nahavandi (1987), "Merger mania: Who wins? Who loses?," *Journal of Business Strategy* 8, 76–9.

Mazur, J. E. and A. W. Logue (1978), "Choice in a self-control paradigm: Effects of a fading procedure," *Journal of Experimental Analysis of Behavior* 30, 11–17.

McCallum, Kim E., James Lock, Mary Kulla, Marcia Rorty, and Richard D. Wetzel (1992), "Dissociative symptoms and disorders in patients with eating disorders," *Dissociation* 5, 227–35.

Mischel, H. N. and W. Mischel (1983), "The development of children's knowledge of self-control strategies," *Child Development* 54, 603–19.

Nemiah, J. C. (1977), "Alexithymia: Theoretical considerations," *Psychotherapy and Psychosomatics* 28, 199–206.

Origo, Iris (1959), *The Merchant of Prato: Francesco di Marco Datini*, New York, Octagon.

Panocka, Izabella, Przemyslaw Marek, and Bogdan Sadowski (1986), "Differentiation of neurochemical basis of stress-induced analgesia in mice by selective breeding," *Brain Research* 397, 156–60.

Piaget, J. (1965), *The Moral Judgment of the Child*, New York, Free Press.

Polivy, J. and C. P. Herman (1985), "Dieting and binging: A causal analysis," *American Psychologist* 40, 193–201.

Putnam, F. W. (1989), *Diagnosis and Treatment of Multiple Personality Disorder*, New York, Guilford.

Rachlin, Howard (1995), "Self-control: Beyond commitment," *Behavioral and Brain Sciences* 18, 109–59.

Resnick, Heidi S., Dean G. Kilpatrick, and Bonnie S. Dansky (1993), "Prevalence of civilian trauma and posttraumatic stress disorder in a representative national sample of women," *Journal of Consulting and Clinical Psychology* 61, 984–91.

Rhue, Judith W. and Steven Jay Lynn (1987), "Fantasy proneness: The ability to hallucinate as real as real," *British Journal of Experimental and Clinical Hypnosis* 4, 173–80.

—— (1989), "Fantasy proneness, hypnotizability, and absorption – A re-examination," *International Journal of Clinical and Experimental Hypnosis* 37, 100–6.

Roche, Suzanne M. and Kevin M. McConkey (1990), "Absorption: Nature, assessment, and correlates," *Journal of Personality and Social Psychology* 59, 91–101.

Ross, Colin A., S. Joshi, and R. Currie (1990), "Dissociative experiences in the general population," *American Journal of Psychiatry* 147, 1547–52.

Ross, Colin A., Jeff Kronson, Stuart Koensgen, Ken Barkman, et al. (1992), "Dissociative comorbidity in 100 chemically dependent patients," *Hospital and Community Psychiatry* 43, 840–2.

Schacter, D. L. and J. F. Kihlstrom (1989), "Functional amnesia," in F. Boller and J. Grafman (eds.), *Handbook of Neuropsychology*, vol. 3, pp. 209–31. Amsterdam, Elsevier.

Schelling, T. C. (1960), *The Strategy of Conflict*, Cambridge, MA, Harvard University Press.

Shizgal, Peter and Conover, Kent (1996), "On the neural computation of utility," *Current Directions in Psychological Science* 5, 37–43.

Sjoberg, L. and T. Johnson (1978), "Trying to give up smoking: A study of volitional breakdowns," *Addictive Behaviors* 3, 149–67.

Skre, Ingunn, S. Onstad, S. Torgersen, S. Lygren, et al. (1993), "A twin study of DSM-IIIR anxiety disorders," *Acta Psychiatrica Scandinavica* 88, 85–92.

Smyser, Cameron H. and David A. Baron (1993), "Hypnotizability, absorption, and subscales of the dissociative experiences scale in a nonclinical population," *Dissociation* 6, 42–6.

Spanos, P. Nicholas, Evelyn, Gabora, Menary, J. Natalie, C. DuBeuil, Susan, et al. (1991), "Secondary identity, enactments during hypnotic past-life regression: A sociocognitive perspective," *Journal of Personality and Social Psychology* 61, 308–20.

Spiegel, David (1991), "Dissociation and trauma," in A. Tasman and S. Goldfinger (eds.), *American Psychiatric Press Review of Psychiatry*, vol. 10, pp. 261–75, Washington, DC, American Psychiatric Press.

Stearns, Peter N. (1994), *American Cool: Constructing a Twentieth-Century Emotional Style.* New York, New York University.

Stevenson, M. K. (1986), "A discounting model for decisions with delayed positive or negative outcomes," *Journal of Experimental Psychology: General* 115, 131–54.

Stigler, George (1980), "The economist as preacher," Tanner Lectures delivered at Harvard Univ., April 1980.

Sully, J. (1884), *Outlines of Psychology*, New York, Appleton.

van der Kolk, Bessel A. (1989), "The compulsion to repeat the trauma: Re-enactment, revictimization, and masochism," *Psychiatric Clinics of North America* 12, 389–411.

Whyte, Lancelot Law (1962), *The Unconscious Before Freud*, Garden City, NY, Doubleday.

Wilson S.C. and T. X. Barber (1983), "The fantasy-prone personality: Implications for understanding imagery, hypnosis, and parapsychological phenomena," in A. A. Sheikh (ed.), *Imagery: Current Theory, Research, and Application*, New York, Wiley.

Zerbe, Kathryn J. (1993), "Selves that starve and suffocate: The continuum of eating disorders and dissociative phenomena," *Bulletin of the Menninger Clinic* 57, 319–27.

# The Neurobiology of
# Chemical Addiction

ELIOT L. GARDNER AND JAMES DAVID

Jeanette, a single unmarried mother of two, lives in subsidized housing in an economically depressed inner-city region of a major American city. She works as a countergirl in a fast-food hamburger restaurant, earning close to the minimum legal wage. She ekes out an existence on her wages, government-supplied food stamps, subsidies for her two children, and assistance with both food and child care from her mother, who lives nearby and works as a domestic housecleaner. One Friday evening, after getting her week's wages, she receives a telephone call from one of her occasional boyfriends, who informs her that he has just acquired some "crack" (free-base) cocaine and some beer and is planning a party for that night with some friends. Jeanette is invited to "come on over, do a few rocks with us, and have some fun." After some moments of indecision, Jeanette accepts the invitation. She is told to "bring some money, to pay for the crack you use." Jeanette then carefully counts her week's wages, estimates the amount she will need over the coming week for food, rent, and other necessities, and then "precommits" herself to use for the crack party only those dollars she will not need for "necessary money" over the coming week. She gives her children to a girlfriend in the same building to watch for the night and also gives the girlfriend all her "necessary money" for the coming week, telling the girlfriend to "not give it back to me before Monday, no matter how hard I beg." Jeanette goes to the party and begins to smoke the crack. At first she attempts to pace her drug use, using more beer than crack. But the intense pleasure of each crack "hit" (inhalation of crack smoke) overwhelms her. Within a short time her cocaine use increases dramatically and takes on an insistent and frantic quality; she grabs for the crack pipe out of turn and pleads for extra "hits" of the crack cocaine smoke. Her "party money" used up, she is soon back in her own building, begging her girlfriend for the "necessary money" – screaming and threatening when it is refused. She runs back to her own apartment, grabbing items to sell for crack money. Back at the party, her behavior becomes even more frantic, driven, and debased. She is totally focused on obtaining the desired drug. Her money and trade goods exhausted, she begins to perform sex acts for crack money. By the time the crack is exhausted and the party over, she has performed multiple sex acts on total strangers, in full view of other party participants, for as little as a single "hit" of crack.

A laboratory rat has been surgically implanted with a very small (1 mm diameter) electrode device in the middle of the pleasure/reward circuitry in its brain. After appropriate recovery from the surgery, the rat is placed daily for one hour in a test chamber containing a wall-mounted lever, which is connected to an electrical brain stimulator, the output of which is fed – via ultra-thin wires and an ultra-small electrical connector mounted on the top of the rat's head – to the electrode in the pleasure/reward circuitry. The rat rapidly learns that pushing the wall-mounted lever delivers a brief (250 ms) train of mild electrical stimulation (just strong enough to activate the brain cells immediately surrounding the electrode tip deep in its brain). Because of the electrode tip's location in the pleasure/reward circuitry, the rat experiences a brief "hit" of intense pleasure each time it depresses the lever. The rat rapidly acquires the lever-pressing "habit" – giving itself approximately 5,000–10,000 pleasure/reward "hits" during each one-hour daily test session. During these test sessions, the animal is totally focused on obtaining the desired electrical stimulation – lever-pressing at maximum speed and completely ignoring other attractions within the test chamber (food, water, playthings, sexually receptive rats of the opposite sex). After several weeks, the rat suddenly faces a new and unexpected behavioral contingency. An electrified metal floor grid has been placed in the test chamber, between the entrance and the wall-mounted lever. This floor grid delivers intensely painful footshock. The rat enters the chamber, receives a footshock, and jumps back off the floor grid. It stands in the entrance, looking alternately at the aversive floor grid and the appealing wall-mounted lever. After some minutes of indecision, it crosses the floor grid, receiving intensely painful footshock with every step (and flinching and squealing in pain), to reach the lever and once again self-administer the pleasurable brain stimulation.

The existence of reward or pleasure circuits in the mammalian brain had been postulated either explicitly or implicitly as part of every behavior theory from Darwin's time onward (ranging from the older Darwinian, Freudian, neo-Freudian, Pavlovian, and Skinnerian theories to the integrated brain-behavior theories that dominate modern psychology). However, no one knew for certain that such hypothetical reward sites existed or where they were until the seminal discovery by Olds and Milner (1954) that such reward circuits do exist and can be directly activated by electrical stimulation delivered through electrodes deep in the brain. The reward elicited by such stimulation (termed "intracranial self-stimulation" or "brain-stimulation reward"), and the brain substrates that support it, have been much studied and well characterized over the past thirty-five years (Rolls 1975, Routtenberg 1978, Olds and Fobes 1981, Gardner 1997).

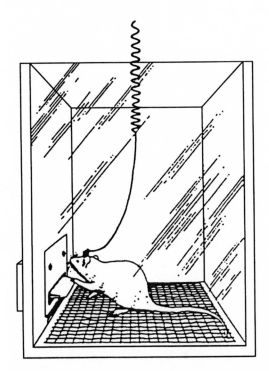

**Figure 1. Laboratory rat connected to apparatus that provides intracranial self-stimulation. (From Grzimek's *Encyclopedia of Ethology*, Coron Verlag Press, 1977, with permission.)**

As studied with behavioral paradigms in which animals volitionally self-administer the rewarding electrical stimulation themselves (see Figure 1), such direct brain-stimulation reward is intensely powerful. Hungry animals ignore food to get it; thirsty animals ignore water to get it. Male animals ignore sexually receptive females to get it. Animals even endure pain to get it. Response rates of animals self-stimulating for electrical brain reward are extremely high, often in excess of 100 lever-presses per minute. In short, electrical brain-stimulation reward is one of the most powerful rewards known to biology, rivaled only by the reward of the most intensely addicting drugs (e.g., cocaine). The few human studies of electrical stimulation of brain reward areas confirm this; the human experience is one of intense subjective pleasure or euphoria (Heath 1964).

## 1. Neuroanatomy of Brain Pleasure/Reward Mechanisms

Anatomical mapping studies of brain-stimulation reward carried out in the 1950s and 1960s showed that electrical brain reward could be elicited

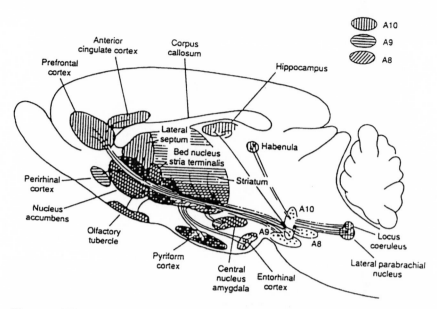

**Figure 2.** The mesotelencephalic dopamine (DA) circuitry of the mamalian (laboratory rat) brain. The primary brain-reward–relevant portion appears to be a subset of the mesolimbic projections originating in the ventral tegmental area (DA nucleus A10) and terminating in the nucleus accumbens. (From Cooper J. R., Bloom F. E., and Roth R. H., *The Biochemical Basis of Neuropsychopharmacology*, 5th ed., New York: Oxford University Press, 1986, with permission.)

in laboratory animals from a variety of brain-stem, midbrain, and fore-brain loci, including most importantly the ventral tegmental area, sub-stantia nigra, hypothalamus, medial forebrain bundle, septum, amygdala, neostriatum, nucleus accumbens, olfactory tubercle, and portions of the cingulate and frontal cortices (see Figure 2). This seeming hodge-podge of sensory, motor, limbic, midbrain, diencephalic, and cortical loci initially made little sense in terms of classical understandings of brain-behavior relationships. It was soon realized, however, that all these areas are interconnected by the ascending and descending tracts of the me-dial forebrain bundle – the nuclei, tracts, and the projections of which connect all major brain sites positive for electrical brain-stimulation re-ward. The hypothesis soon arose that a subset of the medial forebrain bundle is dedicated to carrying reward-related or pleasure-related neural signals.

## 2. Neurochemistry of Brain Pleasure/Reward Mechanisms

When movable electrodes were used to three-dimensionally map brain-reward substrates, brain-stimulation reward thresholds were found to vary as a function of the density of dopamine-containing brain cells

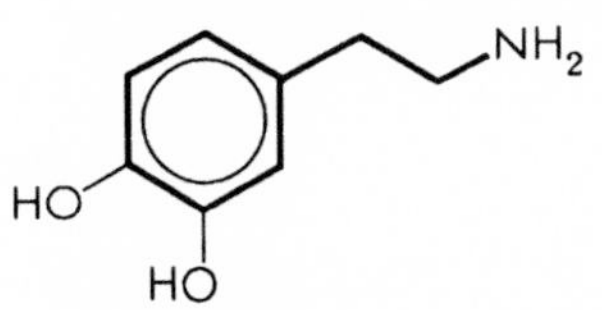

**Figure 3. Dopamine, the brain's "pleasure" molecule.**

surrounding the electrode tip (Corbett and Wise 1980). It was apparent that the neurotransmitter dopamine (see Figure 3) and dopamine-rich neural circuitry played a fundamental role in brain reward. Guided by this anatomical–neurochemical correspondence, workers in many laboratories began to study the effects of dopaminergic pharmacological manipulations on brain-stimulation reward, soon discovering that brain reward is critically dependent upon the functional integrity of the mesotelencephalic dopamine system (Wise and Rompre 1989), the projections of which are carried through the medial forebrain bundle. More specifically, it is a subportion of dopamine neurons originating in the ventral tegmental area and projecting through the medial forebrain bundle to the nucleus accumbens that appears most crucially specialized for carrying reward-related or pleasure-related signals (Wise and Bozarth 1984).

Speculation that addicting drugs might derive their rewarding properties by activating existing brain-reward circuits had been presented as early as the 1940s (more than a decade prior to the actual discovery of brain-reward sites) by Donald Hebb, the brilliant pioneer of modern biological psychology. The first experimental evidence for this was presented by Killam, Olds, and Sinclair (1957) and has been amply confirmed by three decades of subsequent work (Gardner 1992, 1997; Kornetsky 1985; Wise 1980a).

The effects on electrical brain-stimulation reward of a wide range of addicting drugs, including cocaine, amphetamines, opiates, barbiturates, benzodiazepines, nicotine, dissociative anesthetics, ethyl alcohol, and marijuana, have been well studied in many laboratories over the past thirty years. With the exception of the LSD-like hallucinogens, all addicting drugs produce robust enhancement of brain-stimulation reward. In other words, addicting drugs act on the brain's pleasure/reward circuitry to produce higher levels of pleasure/reward than occur in the drug-free state. Operationally stated, animals with stimulation electrodes in their pleasure/reward circuits will lever-press for markedly lower intensities of electrical brain-stimulation reward when under the influence of addicting drugs than when not under the influence.

Intracerebral self-administration of drugs in laboratory animals (as opposed to the self-administration of electrical stimuli) has also been used to map out the brain areas mediating the reinforcement (i.e., pleasure) produced by the addicting drugs (see Figure 4). These brain loci

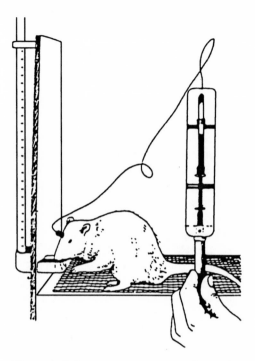

**Figure 4. Laboratory rat connected to apparatus that provides intracerebral self-administration of drugs. (From Grzimek's *Encyclopedia of Ethology*, Coron Verlag Press, 1977, with permission.)**

correspond to specific portions of the circuitry mapped in the electrical self-stimulation paradigm, as noted earlier. Thus, cocaine and amphetamines are voluntarily self-administered into the nucleus accumbens and medial prefrontal cortex, but not into other brain sites. Opiates are voluntarily administered into the ventral tegmental area, the lateral hypothalamus, and the nucleus accumbens, but not into other brain sites. These findings are an important contribution to the current view that addicting drugs produce their euphorigenic effects by acting on dopaminergic reward neurons that constitute a subcomponent of the mesotelencephalic dopaminergic circuitry of the forebrain.

In addition to such drug self-administration into brain-reward sites, laboratory animals will also voluntarily (indeed, avidly) self-administer drugs systemically (e.g., intravenously). The total number of compounds voluntarily self-administered by laboratory animals is no more than a few score. These include opiates, ethyl alcohol, nicotine, cocaine, amphetamines, methylxanthine stimulants (e.g., caffeine), benzodiazepines, barbiturates and barbiturate-like sedative-hypnotics, anesthetics, and some volatile solvents and hydrocarbons. Strikingly, these are the same compounds that humans use recreationally and to which vulnerable humans become addicted (see Table 1). Furthermore, these drugs constitute

Table 1. *Addictive chemicals by pharmologic class*

| | |
|---|---|
| **CLASS:**<br>Alcohol | **EXAMPLES:**<br>Beer, Wine, Whiskey, Vodka, etc. |
| **STRUCTURE:** | $CH_3CH_2OH$<br>Alcohol |
| **CLASS:**<br>Sedatives, Hypnotics, Anxiolytics | **EXAMPLES:**<br>Barbiturates (Seconal®, Nembutal®, etc.)<br>Benzodiazepines (Valium®, Xanax®, etc.)<br>Methaqualone (Quaalude®) |
| **STRUCTURE:** | |

Pentobarbital

Diazepam

| | |
|---|---|
| **CLASS:**<br>Amphetamines | **EXAMPLES:**<br>Dextroamphetamine, Methamphetamine ("speed"),<br>3,4-Methylenedioxymethamphetamine ("MDMA," "ecstacy")<br>Methylphenidate (Ritalin®) "Diet pills" |
| **STRUCTURE:** | |

Methamphetamine

MDMA

Methylphenidate

| | |
|---|---|
| **CLASS:**<br>Cocaine | **EXAMPLES:**<br>Cocaine hydrochloride (cocaine powder), Cocaine alkaloid/base ("crack"), Coca leaves, Coca paste |
| **STRUCTURE:** | |

Cocaine

(*cont.*)

but a very small subset of the more than fourteen million different chemicals catalogued to date. What distinguishes these compounds from the fourteen million other compounds? Why is this subset appealing to humans and laboratory animal alike, whereas humans and animals eschew other drugs? The answer is not to be found in chemical or structural similarities, because addicting drugs have no overall stereochemical or structural commonalities. Nor is the answer to be found in pharmacological

Table 1. *(Continued)*

| CLASS:<br>Caffeine and related methylxanthine stimulants | EXAMPLES:<br>Caffeine (coffee, tea, cola, chocolate, over-the-counter headache pills, alertness pills, diet pills), Theophylline (tea), Theobromide (chocolate) |
|---|---|
| STRUCTURE: | |

Caffeine

| CLASS:<br>Cannabis | EXAMPLES:<br>Marijuana, Hashish, Hash oil |
|---|---|
| STRUCTURE: | |

$\Delta^9$-Tetrahydrocannabinol

| CLASS:<br>Hallucinogens | EXAMPLES:<br>Lysergic acid diethylamide (LSD)<br>Mescaline<br>Psilocybin ("magic mushrooms") |
|---|---|
| STRUCTURE: | |

Lysergic acid
diethylamide

Mescaline

Psilocybin

| CLASS:<br>Nicotine | EXAMPLES:<br>Cigarettes, Cigars, Pipe tobacco, Snuff, Chewing tobacco |
|---|---|
| STRUCTURE: | |

Nicotine

*(cont.)*

similarities, because addicting drugs have no pharmacological commonalities (by traditional pharmacological categorization); some drugs, for example, are stimulants whereas others are sedatives. Nor is the answer to be found in the interrelated phenomena of tolerance, physical dependence, and withdrawal (see fuller discussion of these phenomena later), because animals will voluntarily self-administer addicting drugs in the

Table 1. *(Continued)*

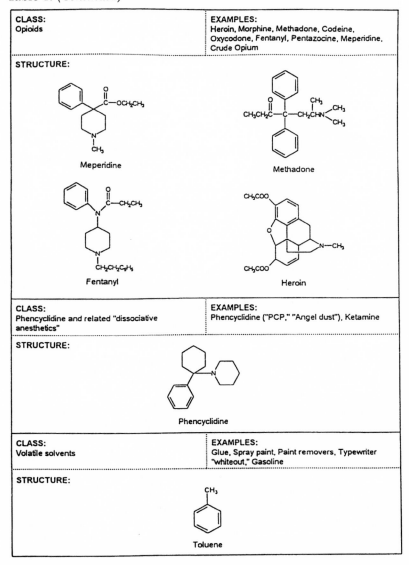

| CLASS:<br>Opioids | EXAMPLES:<br>Heroin, Morphine, Methadone, Codeine, Oxycodone, Fentanyl, Pentazocine, Meperidine, Crude Opium |
|---|---|
| STRUCTURE: | |

Meperidine

Methadone

Fentanyl

Heroin

| CLASS:<br>Phencyclidine and related "dissociative anesthetics" | EXAMPLES:<br>Phencyclidine ("PCP," "Angel dust"), Ketamine |
|---|---|
| STRUCTURE: | |

Phencyclidine

| CLASS:<br>Volatile solvents | EXAMPLES:<br>Glue, Spray paint, Paint removers, Typewriter "whiteout," Gasoline |
|---|---|
| STRUCTURE: | |

Toluene

absence of tolerance, physical dependence, or withdrawal (indeed, they will self-administer in the absence of any prior history of drug taking). The importance of this can hardly be overstated, because it clearly shows that drug-taking behavior cannot be explained simply in terms of the ability of addicting drugs to ameliorate the withdrawal discomfort associated with abstinence from prior administration of such drugs. Withdrawal symptoms cannot, in and of themselves, account for the phenomenon of addiction.

In fact, *the single essential commonality of the addicting drugs is the neurobiological one – their ability to acutely enhance the pleasure/reward circuitry of the brain.* The hypothesis that addicting drugs act on these brain mechanisms to produce the intense subjective pleasure/reward that constitutes the "hit" or "rush" or "high" sought by drug users is, at present, the most compelling hypothesis available on the neurobiology of drug abuse.

## 3. Characteristics of Systemic Drug Self-Administration by Laboratory Animals

As already noted, laboratory animals will voluntarily self-administer, by systemic (e.g., intravenous) routes, the same drugs that human beings self-administer (with the exception of the LSD-like hallucinogens). The characteristic patterns of drug intake seen in self-administration by laboratory animals vary by drug class and are provocatively similar to intake patterns seen in humans. Opiate self-administration by laboratory animals is constant, moderate, measured, and lacking in voluntary abstinence periods. Heroin addiction in humans is commonly a seven-day-a-week, steady-dosing, low-key affair. Stimulant self-administration in laboratory animals is characterized by alternating binge and abstinence periods. During binge periods, stimulant self-administration reaches frenzied levels, accompanied by markedly reduced food and water intake and insomnia. During abstinence periods, a semblance of normal eating, drinking, and sleep returns. The alternating binge and abstinence pattern can continue for months, reminiscent of the natural history of stimulant abuse (cocaine or amphetamines) in humans – a "run" followed by a "crash," which is followed by a relatively short period of voluntary abstinence. Alcohol self-administration in laboratory animals is also characterized by alternating binge and abstinence periods, much like the syndrome of severe alcoholism in humans. Barbiturate and dissociative anesthetic (e.g., phencyclidine or "angel dust") self-administration is characterized by maximum self-administration, without abstinence periods. Benzodiazepine (e.g., Valium®) self-administration is characterized by more moderate intake patterns.

The self-administration paradigm in animals can be modified to assess the *relative appetitive value* of different addicting drugs. One such modification is the "progressive ratios" self-administration paradigm, in which the amount of work an animal has to expend to receive a single intravenous injection is progressively increased in ratio fashion (e.g., one lever-press for the first injection, two lever-presses for the second injection, four lever-presses for the third injection, eight lever-presses for the fourth injection, etc.) In any such progressive-ratio run, there comes a point where the animal simply gives up and abruptly stops lever-pressing (the "Oh hell, this ain't worth it anymore" point). This is the so-called break point. By comparing break points between different classes of addicting drugs, one can establish hierarchies of appetitiveness. Such hierarchies closely resemble those observed in humans (e.g., cocaine, extremely appetitive; morphine, moderately appetitive; benzodiazepines, marginally appetitive). Of course, there are individual differences among animals just as there are among humans. However, cocaine is so appetitive to most laboratory animals that, if given continuous access, they will spend most of their waking hours self-administering the drug and will self-administer it to the point of starvation and death, even if hundreds or thousands of lever-presses are needed to obtain one dose of the drug (Pickens and Harris 1968; Johanson, Balster, and Bonese 1976; Bozarth and Wise 1985). This has remarkable parallels to the extreme appetitiveness of crack cocaine in vulnerable humans.

## 4. Volitional Intent and the Activation of Brain Pleasure/Reward Mechanisms by Addicting Drugs

A long-standing clinical observation of addicting drug action is that a more intense "high" is produced when self-administered than when exogenously administered. This appears true for many addicting drugs, but especially so for those that are only moderately euphorigenic. A laboratory animal homolog of this human observation appears to have been recently demonstrated. When administered exogenously in genetically inbred ethanol-nonpreferring rats (see the next section for further discussion of genetic variation in brain-reward substrate activation by addicting drugs), ethanol has little or no facilitating effect on electrical brain-stimulation reward. However, when the very same animals are allowed to *voluntarily* self-administer the same dose of ethanol, brain reward is robustly and reliably enhanced (Gardner 1992, Moolten and Kornetsky 1990). This suggests that there must be neural circuitry encoding volitional intent that feeds into the reward system and summates with the acute pharmacological sensitization produced by the drug.

## 5. Genetic Influences on Addiction

At the human level, genetic variation in vulnerability to addicting drugs has been long suspected and is especially well documented for alcoholism (Pickens et al. 1991, Cadoret et al. 1986, Cloninger 1987, Cloninger and Begleiter 1990). Concordance rates for alcohol and drug addiction are significantly higher in monozygotic twins than in dizygotic twins (the former sharing 100 percent of their genes, the latter sharing approximately 50 percent of their genes; Pickens et al. [1991]). Children of drug addicts, when adopted and raised by nonaddict parents, show an increased rate of drug addiction as compared to adopted-out children of nonaddict parents (Cadoret et al. 1986). From twin studies, it is estimated that genetic influences account for approximately 38 percent of the vulnerability to alcohol abuse, 60 percent of the vulnerability to alcohol dependence, and 31 percent of the vulnerability to drug abuse or dependence (Pickens et al. 1991). The most reliable evidence to date suggests that genetic influences on drug addiction are most pronounced in the most severe forms of addiction (Pickens et al. 1991, Cadoret et al. 1986, Cloninger 1987). Because family studies have failed to show strong evidence for single-gene Mendelian inheritance, genetic influences on addiction are believed to be polygenic, with low penetrance (i.e., low expression of the genotype) and a relatively high degree of environmental determinism in expression (Cloninger and Begleiter 1990).

At the laboratory-animal level, genetic factors are well known to influence both drug preference and propensity for self-administration of many addicting drugs (e.g., ethanol, morphine). In laboratory rats, a number of inbred strains have been shown to exhibit high ethanol preference and high ethanol self-administration. One such strain, the Lewis rat, generalizes this vulnerability to cocaine, heroin, and marijuana, relative to otherwise comparable rat strains. Thus, Lewis rats are more sensitive to the stimulant effects of cocaine; show consistently higher self-administration of cocaine, opiates, and alcohol; show greater degrees of persistent preference for environments in which they have previously received morphine or cocaine; and show unique vulnerability to $\Delta^9$-tetrahydrocannabinol (the psychoactive constituent of marijuana and hashish) in the electrical brain-stimulation reward paradigm, compared to other genetically well-characterized inbred rat strains (George and Goldberg 1989; Suzuki, George, and Meisch 1989; Miserendino et al. 1992; Guitart, Beitner-Johnson, and Nestler 1992; Gardner and Lowinson 1991).

Recently, it has become clear that the dopaminergic reward neurons projecting to the nucleus accumbens of Lewis rats are uniquely different from those of other rat strains (Guitart et al. 1992, 1993; Beitner-Johnson, Guitart, and Nestler 1991; Chen et al. 1991). Specifically, these reward neurons in Lewis rats show markedly enhanced extracellular dopamine overflow when exposed to addicting drugs, compared to the same reward neurons in the brains of other rat strains exposed to the same drugs. Thus, Lewis rats may well get more of a euphorigenic effect than other rats from the *same* dose of a given addicting drug. In addition, Lewis rats are genetically endowed with a highly specific alteration in a neuronal molecular transport system for dopamine in their reward-relevant dopamine neurons (Guitart et al. 1992, Nestler 1993). Provocatively, chronic exposure to heroin or cocaine in non-Lewis strain rats produces the *same* specific alteration in the *same* neuronal molecular transport system for dopamine as the Lewis rats are born with (Nestler 1993). Thus, Lewis rats have, by genetic endowment, the same kind of neurobiological vulnerability to drug abuse normally imparted by chronic exposure to addictive drugs in other, nongenetically vulnerable, rats. This convergent outcome of genetic endowment and environmental drug exposure at the subcellular neuronal level (specifically involving neurotransmitter mechanisms in the dopamine pleasure/reward neurons of the forebrain) is striking.

## 6. Tolerance

Tolerance is defined as a need to use increasingly larger and larger amounts of drug to achieve the intended effect (in the case of addicting drugs, the euphoric "high"). Concomitantly, the same dose of a drug, over time, has less and less of the desired effect on the user. The degree of tolerance that develops varies widely from drug to drug, and from user to user. Tolerance to opiates, alcohol, and sedative-hypnotics is marked, whereas tolerance to cannabinoids and hallucinogens is limited. Also, tolerance develops differentially to the various effects of a drug. For example, tolerance to the pupillary-constricting effect of heroin and to the acute nausea and vomiting produced by heroin in beginning users may be pronounced, but tolerance to opiate-produced constipation may be insignificant or even absent.

Tolerance operates in both the short and long term and is mediated by mechanisms both in the periphery of the body and in the central nervous system. Peripherally mediated tolerance occurs largely in the liver and involves acceleration of the enzymatic detoxification of addictive drugs that normally takes place in the liver.

> When the elimination of the drug is largely by metabolism, an increase in the rate of metabolism reduces its availability to sites of action. The metabolism of most drugs occurs largely in the liver, because of its mass, high blood flow, and concentration of enzymes that metabolize drugs. The initial step in metabolism of many drugs is executed by a group of mixed-function oxidase isoenzymes in the endoplasmic reticulum. These enzyme systems containing cytochrome $P_{450}$ oxidize the molecule by a variety of actions including aromatic hydroxylations, $N$-demethylations, $O$-demethylations, and sulfoxidations. The products of these reactions are usually more polar (and more readily excreted by the kidney).
>
> The biosynthesis of some of the mixed-function oxidase isoenzymes is under regulatory control at the transcriptional level, and their content in the liver can be induced by a number of drugs. Phenobarbital is the prototype of these inducers, and all barbiturates in clinical use increase mixed-function oxidase isoenzymes. Induction with phenobarbital can occur with doses of as little as 60 mg daily. Mixed function oxidases also are induced by rifampin, carbamazepine, phenytoin, and glutethimide, by occupational exposure to chlorinated insecticides such as DDT, and by chronic alcohol ingestion [Wilson et al. 1991].

Tolerance within the central nervous system is less well elucidated than hepatically mediated tolerance and – significantly – can develop quite rapidly. When one ingests alcohol, measurable levels of alcohol appear in the bloodstream within minutes, and blood alcohol level (BAL) is considered useful in monitoring one's state of intoxication or impairment

Table 2. *Signs of intoxication correlated with blood alcohol levels*

| Blood alcohol level (mg/dl) | Signs of intoxication |
| --- | --- |
| 25–99 | Muscular incoordination<br>Impaired sensory function<br>Changes in mood, personality, and behavior |
| 100–199 | Marked mental impairment<br>Incoordination<br>Prolonged reaction time<br>Atexia |
| 200–299 | Nausea and vomiting<br>Diplopia<br>Marked Atexia |
| 300–399 | Hypothermia<br>Severe dysarthria<br>Amnesia<br>Stage 1 anesthesia |
| 400–700 | Coma<br>Respiratory failure<br>Death |

*Source:* From *Review of General Psychiatry*, 2nd ed., Appleton and Lange, 1988, with permission.

(see Table 2). Laws restricting drunk driving uniformly use BAL to set a threshold value, above which one is legally considered to be "driving while intoxicated."

If a person begins drinking at 8:00 P.M. and has one or two drinks per hour until midnight, the BAL curve will rise during the period of continued intake, will peak at approximately 1:00 A.M., and will then start downward – returning to a level of near zero at approximately 5:00 A.M. If this person is approached during his or her fourth drink, with a BAL of approximately 100 mg/dl, he or she might well be expected to report feelings of expansive mood, gregariousness, positive self-esteem, and moderate euphoria. Moving to the downward limb of the BAL curve, at around 4:00 A.M., when BAL is again approximately 100 mg/dl, one observes a very different clinical picture – one of irritability, headache, somnolence, and general dysphoria – in contrast to the same BAL on the upward side of the curve. This hypothetical person has rapidly developed tolerance to a BAL of 100 mg/dl, that is, the same amount of drug now has a considerably less euphorigenic effect.

Tolerance develops not only to the euphorigenic or brain-reward–related effects of drugs, but to other, undesirable, drug effects. In methadone maintenance treatment to block heroin craving, a single daily dose of methadone is commonly 80 mg, taken by mouth as a liquid. If this same dose is given to someone who is a pharmacologic "virgin" to opiates, they will likely develop respiratory depression and asphyxiate in the absence of emergency medical attention. The methadone maintenance patient, however, is tolerant to the respiratory depressant effects of opiates. Methadone dosages well above 100 mg are easily tolerated by tolerant individuals, who have built up their tolerance by gradually increasing their intake of opiate drugs.

Clinical tolerance to opiates has been suggested to occur primarily in the central nervous system and to be mediated at several neuronal sites. Opiate drug use may alter the number of opioid receptors on nerve-cell membranes (Zukin, Tempel, and Gardner 1984; Davis, Akera, and Brody 1979). Such a shift in the "population dynamics" of the ratio of drug molecules to drug receptors could account for some of the tolerance that occurs. In the brain, most receptors activated by addicting drugs activate, in turn, other proteins and/or enzymes (2nd messengers) that, in their turn, activate yet other proteins and/or enzymes (3rd messengers, 4th messengers, ... *n*th messengers) in a lengthy biochemical cascade (see Figure 5) that mediates between receptor activation and the ultimate cellular end point or "effector mechanism." Some authorities feel that alterations within this postreceptor biochemical cascade of 2nd, 3rd, 4th, and *n*th messengers may also underlie some aspects of tolerance within the central nervous system. For example, cell-wall and intracellular concentrations of 2nd-messenger G-proteins and/or cyclic nucleotides may be altered by chronic opiate exposure. Such cellular changes, for opiates and other addicting drugs, may partly underlie the mechanism(s) of neuroadaptation that mediate the phenomena of tolerance to and withdrawal from addicting drugs.

## 7. Physical Dependence and Withdrawal

Withdrawal can fundamentally be conceptualized as a physiological "rebound" phenomenon. If chronic drug administration causes one bodily effect, withdrawal from chronic drug will cause an opposite rebound effect. For example, if a chronic drug (heroin) causes intestinal *hypo*motility (constipation), withdrawal from that drug will cause intestinal *hyper*motility (diarrhea).

> The hospitalized patient is in his late forties, and his attending physicians are at their wits' end in attempting to manage their patient's agitation. The patient has all four limbs tied to the bed and a cloth restraint holding his chest to the bed. He continues to shout at the staff (and into thin air), switching languages, becoming angry, threatening, disoriented, alternately still and then suddenly violent, intermittently working a restrained limb loose and striking out wildly. One staff member is struck forcefully atop the head, at which point consultants are called from the divisions of Critical Care and Psychiatry. The treating physicians have

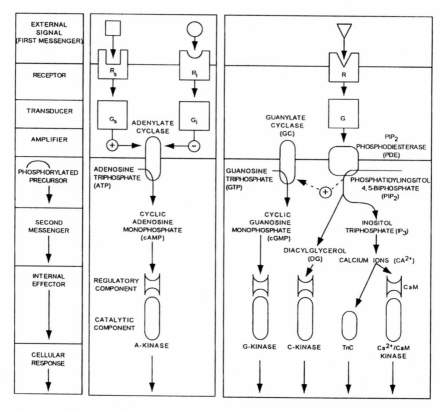

**Figure 5.** Diagram of neurotransmitter binding to receptor, receptor activation of G-protein, G-protein activation of 2nd messenger, kinase, etc.

already administered extremely large doses of sedating medications, first by intramuscular injection and finally via intravenous infusion – with little effect. The patient is febrile, hypertensive, soaked in sweat and urine, tearing at the intravenous catheter in his forearm, and actively hallucinating.

The consultants concur that the treating team have correctly made the diagnosis of delirium tremens, have appropriately used the recommended medications in the recommended dosages, and have appropriately resorted to physical restraints to prevent injury to the patient and others. They suggest that the patient be transferred to an Intensive Care Unit, where otherwise dangerous doses of sedatives can be given in a highly monitored setting in the hope of overcoming this patient's feverish and frenzied agitation. As a last resort, the patient can be anesthetized (becoming paralyzed and unconscious), placed on a respirator, and medicated appropriately.

Delirium tremens ("rum fits") is perhaps the best-known withdrawal syndrome, and it is certainly the most dangerous, with approximately one in six patients not surviving the full-blown syndrome just described. In this vignette, the patient's last drink of alcohol was four days before, and he had already suffered at least one generalized tonic-clonic seizure. Abrupt cessation of chronic alcohol intake (or abrupt cessation of the chronic use or abuse of virtually any sedative-hypnotic medication) puts one at risk of developing this frightening syndrome.

*Withdrawal syndromes tend to be substance-specific and are fairly consistent within a given class of addictive substances.* The severity of the symptoms and signs vary among individuals and vary roughly in proportion to the dosage of the addictive substance from which one is withdrawing. In the above case, the patient reported a daily intake of approximately two to three 750-ml bottles of hard liquor, a severe habit. Had his intake been two to three cans of beer daily, abrupt cessation might well have made him uncomfortable, anxious, and restless; and he might well have had difficulty sleeping for several days (rebound insomnia); but he almost certainly would not have suffered the full-scale withdrawal delirium syndrome.

As already noted *withdrawal symptoms tend to be opposite to the symptoms associated with intoxication and chronic use.* If one is withdrawing from sleep medications (sedative-hypnotics), one can expect to have insomnia. If one is withdrawing from amphetamines, which give one increased energy and self-esteem and a decreased need for food or sleep, one can expect to be exhausted, hypersomnic, famished, and deeply depressed. Opiate use has the side effect of constipation; the opiate withdrawal syndrome includes diarrhea. Opiate use produces "pinpoint" pupils; opiate withdrawal produces dilated pupils. Opiates are potent analgesics; opiate withdrawal is associated with joint pain, back pain, and, ironically, extreme sensitivity to transcutaneous needle insertion (as used in medical treatment to obtain blood samples or give intravenous medications). Obviously, many withdrawal symptoms are subjectively highly unpleasant and dysphorigenic – even, in many cases, overtly painful.

Physical dependence, then, is the state produced by the combined actions of tolerance and withdrawal. The drug addict (or self-administering animal) becomes tolerant to many of the effects of the drug being chronically administered. Upon cessation of drug taking, exceedingly unpleasant and even painful physical withdrawal symptoms emerge, which can be easily and quickly abolished by more drug taking. The addict (or laboratory animal) is now said to be physically dependent, because he or she needs to continue drug taking to ward off the emergence of the unpleasant and painful physical withdrawal symptoms. It is easy, however, to overstate the importance of physical dependence in drug addiction, since it is almost always possible to avoid cessation-induced withdrawal symptoms by simply slowly decreasing the amount of drug taken each day until the drug-free state is reached. Although such "weaning" regimens may sometimes need to be quite prolonged, it is almost always possible to keep the addict comfortable until the drug-free state is reached. Such weaning regimens can be accelerated by the adjunctive use of medications (e.g., clonidine) to block some of the unpleasant withdrawal symptoms. Such schemes are typically referred to as "detoxification," or simply "detox," and are a standard medical procedure for safe rapid weaning of drug addicts from their drug habits. However, in the absence of further aggressive and comprehensive treatment to control drug-craving and drug-taking triggers (environmental cues associated with prior drug taking, stress, cross-priming from other drugs), return to habitual, compulsive drug taking after successful detoxification is a virtual certainty. Thus, explanations of continued drug taking that are predicated solely on tolerance, physical dependence, and avoidance of withdrawal symptoms are not satisfactory.

Equally important to understand is the fact that, although withdrawal usually has unpleasant and dysphoric physical manifestations, it is not simply the reversal of the acute brain reward produced by addicting drugs. Intracerebral microinjection techniques have been used to dissociate the different brain sites mediating the various properties of addicting drugs. Such studies are very important, because they clear up a number of surprisingly common misconceptions about addicting drugs, such as the misconception that the brain loci and systems subserving physical dependence/withdrawal and those subserving drug self-administration are identical. Thus, intracerebral microinjection studies have shown that the analgesic effect of opiates is mediated by local action on endogenous opioid peptidergic (enkephalinergic or endorphinergic) circuits within the pontine periaqueductal gray matter, whereas the pleasure/reward effects are mediated by action on reward-dedicated portions of the meso-accumbens dopamine system. Very importantly, physical dependence upon opiates has been shown by intracerebral microinjection studies to be mediated by action on brain-stem loci anatomically distinct and far removed from the meso-accumbens dopaminergic loci mediating opiate-induced reward, and repeated opiate microinjections into the meso-accumbens dopaminergic loci critical for drug reward utterly fail to produce physical dependence (Bozarth and Wise 1984).

At the same time, dysphoric mood, a part of virtually all withdrawal syndromes, may well be a "reversal" of brain reward. A number of experiments over the past fifteen years have demonstrated that, just as administration of addicting drugs enhances brain-reward processes, withdrawal from chronic administration of addicting drugs depresses these same brain-reward processes (Kokkinidis, Zacharko, and Predy 1980; Wise 1995; Simpson and Annau 1977). In contrast to the physical symptoms of withdrawal, which are referable to neurobiological changes in brain circuits and brain loci distinct from the meso-accumbens pleasure/reward circuitry, this withdrawal-induced depression of brain-reward mechanisms clearly involves the meso-accumbens pleasure/reward system. The resulting dysphoria, or anhedonia (Wise 1982), is relieved by additional drug taking, which thus constitutes an important additional motivational ("negatively reinforcing") factor in chronic substance abuse. Koob and his colleagues (1989) have recently cast these aversive, negatively reinforcing aspects of chronic drug abuse into the previously existing framework of "opponent process" motivational theory (Solomon 1980). This theory holds that most reinforcers arouse both positive (appetitive, pleasurable) and negative (aversive, dysphoric) hedonic processes in the brain and that these processes oppose one another in a simple dynamic system. Moreover, the time dynamics and tolerance patterns of the two processes are hypothesized to differ. The positive hedonic processes are hypothesized to be simple, stable, of short latency and duration, to follow the reinforcer closely, and to develop tolerance rapidly. The negative hedonic processes are hypothesized to be of longer latency and duration; thus, they build up strength more slowly and decay more slowly. They are also hypothesized to be resistant to the development of tolerance. Therefore, if self-administration of an abusable substance is frequently repeated, two correlated changes in hedonic tone are postulated to occur. First, tolerance to the euphorigenic effects of the substance develops while the withdrawal or abstinence syndrome becomes more intense and of longer duration (Koob et al. 1989, 1993; Koob and Bloom 1988). Thus, the positively reinforcing properties of the drug diminish while the negatively reinforcing properties (relief of withdrawal-induced anhedonia) strengthen. Koob and his colleagues (1993) propose that not only are the positively reinforcing properties of abusable drugs mediated by drug effects in the nucleus accumbens, but that opponent processes within these same brain-reward circuits become sensitized during the development of dependence and thus become responsible for the aversive stimulus properties of drug withdrawal. They are therefore ultimately responsible for the negative reinforcement processes that come, in this view, to dominate the motivation for chronic drug abuse. Thus, brain pleasure/reward mechanisms, and the regulatory neural mechanisms controlling them, are conceptualized in this theory to dominate not only the positively reinforcing acute "hit," "rush," or "high" resulting from early administration but also the negatively reinforcing properties that develop with chronic administration and that are important in the maintenance of drug habits.

## 8. Drug Craving and Brain Pleasure/Reward Systems

A seemingly closely related concept to this opponent-process anhedonia is that of craving. Craving is experienced by chronic substance abusers when they have been deprived of their drug for a period of time. By definition, then, craving must differ from the acute pleasure/reward engendered by electrical brain-stimulation reward or by acute drug self-administration. Two important questions arise: (1) How does drug craving affect function within the dopaminergic reward circuitry of the meso-accumbens forebrain? (2) Is drug craving per se neurally coded within this reward circuitry (perhaps as an opponent-process neural substrate)?

Since craving is known to be engendered at the human level by abstinence following chronic use of addicting drugs, most workers have modeled craving in laboratory animals (and looked for craving-induced effects on brain reward) by using a simple abstinence model in which animals are given a chronic regimen of an addicting drug, the drug administration is stopped, and some direct or indirect aspect of brain reward function is measured. Using this paradigm, several groups have found acute drug abstinence to produce alterations in brain-stimulation reward or in the neurotransmitter substrates believed to underlie brain reward. As already noted, acute abstinence from repeated injections of addicting drugs produces marked inhibition of electrical brain-stimulation reward (Kokkinidis et al. 1980, Wise 1995, Simpson and Annau 1977). Furthermore, it is surmised that this reflects a functional diminution in hedonic tone, since it can be overcome by increasing the electrical-current level of the rewarding brain stimulation. At the level of neurotransmitter function within the meso-accumbens pleasure/reward circuits, abstinence from repeated cocaine administration has been shown to produce decreased presynaptic dopamine synthesis (Trulson and Ulissey 1987, Kalivas et al. 1988), decreased somatodendritic (Kalivas and Duffy 1988) and axonal (Parsons, Smith, and Justice 1991) dopamine release, and supersensitive release-modulating dopamine autoreceptors (Dwoskin et al. 1988). Such findings have led some (Dackis and Gold 1985b) to posit that drug craving is engendered by, and neurally mediated by, dopamine depletion within the meso-accumbens dopaminergic reward-related circuitry of the ventromedial forebrain. This "hypo-dopaminergic" hypothesis of drug craving has, in fact, spawned clinical trials (Dackis and Gold 1985a). Unfortunately, although this hypo-dopaminergic hypothesis of drug craving has the initial appeal of simplicity and parsimony, there are many grounds for believing that it is either incomplete or wrong (Gardner and Lowinson 1993).

## 9. Positive and Negative Brain Pleasure/Reward Mechanisms Simultaneously Activated by Addicting Drugs

One conceivable way out of the conceptual dilemma posed by the fact that some evidence supports the hypo-dopaminergic hypothesis of craving while other evidence contradicts it (Gardner and Lowinson 1993) is the possibility that there may well be functional heterogeneity within the dopaminergic pleasure/reward substrates of the forebrain, with dopaminergic activation within some subcomponent encoding positive hedonic tone and dopaminergic activation within another subcomponent encoding negative hedonic tone.

Supporting this possibility is the finding that there are anatomically and functionally different subdomains of the forebrain dopaminergic pleasure/reward systems with respect to opiate action on electrical brain-stimulation reward (Gardner and Lowinson 1993; Nazzaro, Seeger, and

Gardner 1981). Although robust electrical brain-stimulation reward can be elicited from electrode placements throughout the entire medial-lateral extent of the medial forebrain bundle and the corresponding medial-lateral domains of the mesencephalic dopamine cell fields from which these pleasure/reward circuits arise (Seeger and Gardner 1979; Gardner, Walker, and Paredes 1993), and although electrical brainstimulation reward throughout these medial-lateral domains can be robustly modulated by direct pharmacological manipulation of underlying dopaminergic substrates (i.e., by chronic administration of dopamine antagonists to pharmacologically upregulate the sensitivity of postsynaptic dopamine receptors) (Seeger and Gardner 1979; Gardner et al. 1993; Eichler, Antelman, and Fisher 1976; Ettenberg and Wise 1976), addicting drugs do not appear to uniformly enhance brain-reward substrates throughout these medial-lateral domains. To the contrary, we have consistently found that the medially lying brain-reward–relevant dopaminergic circuitry, originating in the ventral tegmental area and projecting through the medial portions of the medial forebrain bundle to terminate in (among other areas) the nucleus accumbens, appears uniquely sensitive to the brain-stimulation reward-enhancing properties of addicting drugs (Gardner 1992, Nazzaro et al. 1981). The differential response of these medial and lateral brain pleasure/reward domains to opiate administration is illustrated in Figure 6. With electrodes in the medial (mesolimbic) portions of the pleasure/reward circuitry, morphine produces a clear enhancement of brain reward; this enhancement dissipates as time passes following each daily injection, and pronounced tolerance to this brain-reward enhancement develops with repeated daily morphine injections (see Figure 6; Nazzaro et al. 1981). However, with electrodes in the lateral (mesostriatal) portions of the reward circuitry, morphine *inhibits* brain-stimulation reward (i.e., is *dysphorigenic*); this inhibition dissipates as time passes following each daily injection, and a progressive augmentation of this brain-reward inhibition develops with repeated daily morphine injections (Nazzaro et al. 1981). That the brain-stimulation reward elicited from both the medial (mesolimbic) and lateral (mesostriatal) loci has a dopaminergic substrate is strongly suggested by the robust and comparable enhancements (supersensitivity) in brain reward produced in both loci by chronic administration of dopamine antagonists (Seeger and Gardner 1979, Gardner et al. 1993, Eichler et al. 1976, Ettenberg and Wise 1976). Thus, opiates appear to simultaneously activate both excitatory and inhibitory brain pleasure/reward mechanisms, and the complex interplay between these two functionally distinct neurobiological pleasure/reward substrates may well determine not only the acute "high" achieved, but may also contribute importantly to the phenomenon of craving. There is also suggestive evidence that other addicting drugs operate similarly.

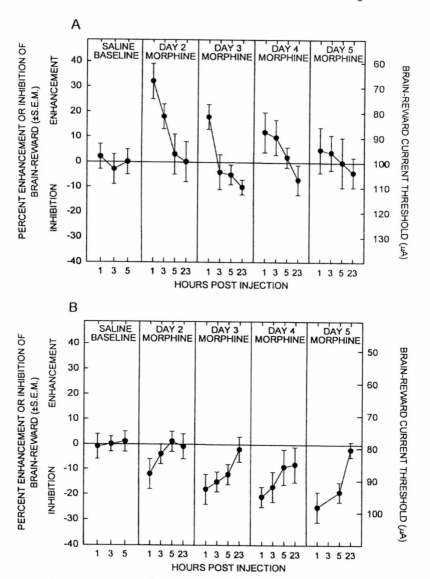

Figure 6. Differential effects of morphine on brain-stimulation reward in mesolimbic versus mesostriatal dopaminergic reward-relevant loci. Enhancement of brain reward is operationally defined as a decrease, and inhibition of brain reward as an increase, in electrical brain-stimulation reward threshold levels (Gardner 1992). (A) Effect of repeated once-daily acute systemic administration of morphine (5.0 mg kg⁻¹ day⁻¹, subcutaneous administration ) on brain reward in the ventral tegmental area (mesolimbic dopamine nucleus A10). (B) Effect of repeated once-daily acute systemic administrations of morphine (5.0 mg kg⁻¹ day⁻¹, subcutaneous administration) on brain reward in the substantia nigra (mesostriatal dopamine nucleus A9). (From Gardner and Lowinson [1993], with permission.)

## 10. Cue-Elicited Craving

Craving at the human level is very often elicited by sensory stimuli previously associated with drug-taking.

> American saloon-keepers of the 1800s were well familiar with the phenomenon of sensory cue-elicited craving. Each day, they kept a "slops bucket" behind the bar, into which the unfinished portions of each patron's glass were dumped. By the end of each business day, the slops bucket was full of whiskey. The next morning, as they opened for business, they would sprinkle the contents of the slops bucket on the sidewalk in front of their establishment, so that the pronounced aroma of liquor would attract customers.

Since cue-elicited craving is so strong at the human level, various conditioning paradigms have been used to model craving in laboratory animals. One of the most widely used is conditioned place preference (van der Kooy 1987, Bozarth 1987, Phillips and Fibiger 1987). In this paradigm, animals are tested (when free of drug) to determine whether they prefer an environment in which they previously received drug as compared to an environment in which they previously received saline or vehicle. If the animal, in the drug-free state, consistently chooses the environment previously associated with drug delivery, the inferences are drawn that not only was the drug appetitive but also that the appetitive hedonic value was encoded in the brain and is accessible during the drug-free state.

Such cognitive association of brain-encoded positive hedonic valence with brain-encoded sensory or perceptual representations of environmental stimuli would appear to be closely related to craving. The question obviously arises: Do pharmacological manipulations and/or lesions of the dopaminergic pleasure/reward circuitry alter conditioned place preferences induced by addicting drugs? On the basis of much work (Phillips and Fibiger 1987), it is now clear that pharmacological manipulations or lesions of the forebrain dopaminergic pleasure/reward system profoundly alter place conditioning of addictive substances and that the dopamine pleasure/reward system almost certainly serves as an important substrate for the central encoding in the brain of the hedonic value imparted by abusable substances. Furthermore, and very provocatively, White and Hiroi have recently demonstrated (Hiroi and White 1990; Hiroi, McDonald, and White 1990; Hiroi 1990; White and Hiroi 1993) that different aspects of conditioned hedonic value appear to depend upon different neurochemically specific dopaminergic substrates. Specifically, in amphetamine place conditioning, the newly synthesized intraneuronal dopamine pool appears to subserve the neural encoding of hedonic value, whereas the vesicular intraneuronal dopamine pool appears crucial for the behavioral expression/readout of that previously encoded hedonic value (Hiroi 1990, Hiroi and White 1990, Hiroi et al. 1990, White and Hiroi 1993). Furthermore, although systemically administered dopamine $D_1$ and dopamine $D_2$ receptor antagonists block both acquisition and expression of conditioned place preference for amphetamine, selective $D_1$ antagonism is significantly more effective at blocking behavioral expression/readout of the previously encoded hedonic value than $D_2$ antagonists. Also, preconditioning and postconditioning lesions of the lateral amygdaloid nucleus impair the conditioned place preference for amphetamine.

On the basis of these experiments we can conclude that the behavioral expression/readout of conditioned incentive stimuli for amphetamine (i.e., the animal homolog of amphetamine craving) is mediated by a dopaminergic neural system that involves the intraneuronal vesicular dopamine pool and the $D_1$ dopamine receptor in the nucleus accumbens and the lateral amygdaloid nucleus (Hiroi 1990, Hiroi and White 1990, Hiroi et al. 1990, White and Hiroi 1993). Thus, we may well be close with our animal models to understanding the neurochemical substrates for the craving that drug addicts feel when confronted visually with syringes, needles, crack vials, smoking pipes, or even the street corner where they buy their illicit drugs. We could, therefore, ultimately be able to pharmacologically manipulate these substrates of craving in the brains of vulnerable humans, and to develop therefrom rational therapeutic approaches for treating uncontrollable drug cravings.

## 11. Abstinence and Relapse

For most drug addicts, reduction of their drug use patterns to nonharmful, occasional, recreational use is not a realistic goal. Indeed, on their way to becoming addicted, all drug users go through a period of occasional recreational use, but they are unable to maintain their use pattern at such a level. Abstinence, then, is the goal of most drug addiction treatment programs. As indicated in the section on physical dependence and withdrawal, it is relatively easy to bring many drug addicts to the abstinent state by either a weaning or detoxification process. Even for drug addicts who present themselves in hospital emergency rooms in the throes of acute withdrawal, appropriate detox use of adjunctive medications and physiological supports can usually alleviate or mitigate the worst withdrawal symptoms. Following successful detoxification, the addict is virtually free of withdrawal discomfort and is drug-abstinent. However, as already noted, it is extremely rare for this abstinence to continue, without significant social, psychological, and physiological interventions. Why? One possibility is that there may actually be two withdrawal syndromes, one acute and one protracted, both of which produce unpleasant and uncomfortable withdrawal symptoms (Satel et al. 1993, Ashton 1991, Schuckit and Hasselbrock 1994). Under this hypothesis, it is only the acute withdrawal that is terminated by detoxification regimens, while the protracted withdrawal (also termed "late withdrawal") persists for an extended period (even for months). It is hypothesized that the persistent discomfort and unpleasant symptoms of protracted withdrawal can be alleviated by drug use just as those of acute withdrawal can be. These symptoms are thus hypothesized to be a major cause of relapse to drug use. However, the very existence of such "protracted withdrawal" states has been sharply questioned (Schuckit and Hasselbrock 1994). Another possibility is that strong and persistent drug craving may outlast drug detoxification and withdrawal by months or years. From clinical interviews with former drug users, it seems quite clear that craving persists for extended time periods, and this can defeat even lengthy recoveries from drug addiction.

The Psychiatry Emergency Room was dependably packed when the Saturday day shift began at 8:00 A.M. A large number of patients had arrived over the previous twelve hours – some by themselves, some brought by friends or families, and some carted in either peaceably or by force by the New York City police. We're always double staffed on Saturdays, and our task was to sort through our patients, one by one, ascertain what drugs they had taken, how much, what had then occurred, confirm the stories with whomever was available, and to then either admit the patients to locked psychiatric wards or to discharge them with referrals to drug and alcohol treatment clinics. There are rarely any residential drug treatment center beds available for these patients on such short notice.

The patients and their drugs come in all varieties. One learns to distinguish the drug classes by the patients' Saturday behaviors:

There are the skinny ones who are dead asleep all morning but who climb off their stretchers when the meal cart arrives – and who wolf down two or three trays of hospital food before falling off into a deep sleep again. Crack cocaine.

There are the ones who sleep intermittently and fitfully, awakening with shouts and sometimes violent outbursts, as though their nightmares can't be contained. These patients are often given heavy sedation but sometimes still need physical restraints, depending on their level of assaultiveness. We start the wilder ones on "four-point" restraints (both arms and legs physically tied down), and as time wears on and they improve, the restraints are removed limb by limb over a period of hours. "Angel Dust" (phencyclidine).

There are the ones who start asking for headache medication after breakfast. They complain about their back pains, their stomach cramps, and their joint pains. They explain (and then plead) that they need Valium or some other sedative-hypnotic medication. And they finally add that they have to leave the hospital soon. Heroin, usually mixed with other drugs.

Then there are the ones who look the worst: miserable, hung over, and nauseous; some of them are vomiting. They might try a bite of breakfast, but they rapidly become nauseated and go back to their stretchers. They suffer from headaches and bellyaches, feelings of guilt and hopelessness, and are exhausted since they are unable to sleep either restfully or for long. They have tremors and shaky hands, are anxious, and are requesting medications. Alcohol.

After a few months of working this shift, and after the initial cynicism wears off, one comes to appreciate the power of drugs on people – lots of people – lots of different kinds of people. But the more seasoned staff members know what is most needed by these patients. They know that, other than shelter and food and sometimes medications, what these patients really need is to talk about relapse, about "slips." *Every single patient, whether their drug is cocaine or heroin or alcohol or whatever, is in the hospital that day because they had relapsed.*

Some patients had been clean for two days; some for two years. Some had been attending self-help groups such as Alcoholics Anonymous daily for months or years. Some had been clean since their last paycheck – and Friday had been payday and the cash was too much of a "trigger." Some had been clean since their New Year's day resolutions. Some had just finished doing prison time for drug-related offenses, and the sights and sounds of their old neighborhood triggered their drug hunger and unleashed vivid and euphoric and seductive memories of getting high – even though they hadn't had a drug hit in years. But whatever the details, every stretcher held someone who had relapsed.

When you get to know these patients and their stories, you find periods in their lives when they were clean for extended periods – often years of sobriety. Jobs were held, families begun, money was in the bank, rent had been paid, interrupted educations had begun again, and life's prospects had been looking good. And then the hunger for one's drug returns, often with a vengeance. And if one is not prepared for this intense craving (i.e., had not yet learned that one's recovery depends first and foremost on not succumbing to these episodes of craving) then we will find you waiting for us in hospital some Saturday morning.

Drug craving is not only noted for its extraordinary persistence, but also for its irrationality – even in otherwise mentally healthy and perfectly rational people.

A physician (an ex-smoker) receives a thorough medical examination as part of his routine yearly medical checkup. He has no current acute medical complaints. As part of the checkup, he undergoes a routine chest x ray, and he leaves the examining office prior to a reading of the chest film. This physician then finds himself fantasizing about the radiologist discovering a lesion on the film and of then being given a terminal diagnosis of untreatable lung cancer – and he feels a flicker of hopeful excitement – because this otherwise terrible news would free him to immediately resume smoking, no longer hindered by his prior choice to avoid the long-term consequences of smoking.

As already noted, environmental cues previously associated with drug taking are well known to trigger craving and promote relapse to drug use. In addition, other stimuli are also known to trigger craving, including environmental stressors and small "priming" drug doses. This last phenomenon – the ability of a "priming" drug dose to reinstate previously extinguished drug taking – is extremely instructive. It has been studied at the laboratory animal level by Stewart and her colleagues, in what is called the "drug reinstatement" paradigm (Gerber and Stretch 1975, de Wit and Stewart 1983, Stewart 1983). In this paradigm, the ability of drugs (or other stimuli, including stressors and drug-associated sensory stimuli) to reestablish extinguished drug-taking habits in laboratory animals can be measured and quantified. As noted by Stewart and Wise (1992),

> the most potent stimulus for renewed responding that has been demonstrated in this model is a free "priming" injection of the training drug; a priming injection of the training drug can re-establish extinguished habits much as a single drink, cigarette, or injection are thought to re-establish such habits in de-toxified ex-addicts.

Provocatively, such priming injections can be successfully given intravenously or directly into component parts of the brain-reward circuitry, such as the ventral tegmental area or nucleus accumbens. Equally provocative, successful cross-priming has been demonstrated in the reinstatement paradigm. For example, priming doses of morphine reinstate cocaine self-administration (Stewart 1984) and priming doses of amphetamine or of the dopamine agonist bromocriptine reinstate heroin-trained responding (Stewart and Vezina 1988; Wise, Murray, and Bozarth 1990). Such cross-priming between addicting drugs of different classes speaks eloquently to the existence of common neurobiological substrates within the reward circuitry of the brain (Gardner 1997).

Cigarettes are the hardest habit to give up. This is widely acknowledged by folks who have quit cigarette use and who have also quit heroin use, cocaine use, or alcohol use. The first week off nicotine is usually a subjective horror. Programs set up to help people quit smoking almost invariably forbid alcohol intake, for the first month at least, and some forbid it for six months or longer. Why? Because of the well-known and oft-experienced classic relapse to smoking: The person hasn't had a cigarette in days, weeks, or months. On her way home from work, she enters a tavern for an after-work drink with some friends. In the midst of her second drink, she suddenly turns to a friend, hastily begs a cigarette and is puffing away, enjoying the amplified rush of a first cigarette after a period of abstinence. A single drink is sufficient to elicit a major relapse/alcoholic binge in an alcohol addict. So, too, can a single alcoholic drink elicit major relapses to drug taking in people abstinent from other drugs, cocaine in particular. So, too, can a single marijuana cigarette. These all-too-frequent experiences are all examples of "cross-priming" and "reinstatement" at the human level.

Importantly, the drugs and doses known to reinitiate drug self-administration at both the human and laboratory-animal levels are drugs and doses known to *increase* dopaminergic function within the brain's reward circuitry (Gardner 1997). Thus, a series of virtually insurmountable neurobiological hurdles are erected in the path of drug addicts wishing to stay abstinent: (1) By virtue of their prior chronic drug use, the pleasure/reward circuits of their brains have been forever changed so that they now possess heightened vulnerability to addicting drugs (Miserendino et al. 1992; Guitart et al. 1992, 1993; Beitner-Johnson et al. 1991). (2) This heightened vulnerability includes a heightened cross vulnerability to other drugs that activate the pleasure/reward circuits of the brain, even drugs to which the addict may never have been exposed. (3) This heightened vulnerability can be triggered not only by drugs, but by stressors and environmental cues previously associated with drug taking.

## 12. Altering Drug Self-Administration by Pharmacological or Neurobiological Manipulations

At the laboratory animal level, pharmacological challenges that specifically disrupt individual neurotransmitter systems can obviously yield important information on the neurobiological substrates of drug-induced reward, as well as yielding suggestions for rational pharmacotherapeutic approaches for the treatment of human drug addiction. In the many experiments in which neurotransmitter-specific pharmacological manipulations have been paired with drug self-administration in laboratory animals, a striking common thread stands out: Pharmacological challenges that disrupt brain dopaminergic function interfere with the reward value of self-administered drugs. Thus, $\alpha$-methyl-para-tyrosine ($\alpha$MPT), a dopamine synthesis inhibitor, initially produces a partial-extinction-like increase in cocaine or amphetamine self-administration, followed by full extinction of the self-administration behavior as the $\alpha$MPT dose increases. Similarly, the dopamine antagonist pimozide produces an initial dose-dependent increase in self-administered amphetamine intake, followed at higher doses by cessation of drug taking. The stereoisomers (+)-butaclamol (possessing potent dopamine antagonism) and (−)-butaclamol (devoid of dopamine antagonism) have also been used to assess the dopaminergic substrates of drug-induced reward. In these studies, (+)-butaclamol produced partial and then complete extinction of amphetamine self-administration whereas (−)-butaclamol had no effect on amphetamine self-administration. Similar patterns of increased drug self-administration after low-dose dopamine blockers followed by decreased drug self-administration after higher doses have also been seen in animals self-administering a wide range of addicting drugs, including cocaine, amphetamine, and morphine. In contrast, noradrenergic blockers have no effect on drug self-administration in laboratory animals. In humans, dopamine antagonists and dopamine synthesis inhibitors blunt the euphorigenic effects of at least some addicting drugs.

Another approach to pharmacological manipulation of drug self-administration in laboratory animals involves the administration of neuro-transmitter-specific agonists. The rationale for this approach is that of substitution: Just as noncontingent administration of amphetamine temporarily decreases amphetamine self-administration, so too a neuro-transmitter-specific agonist that activates the same brain-reward substrates should temporarily decrease drug self-administration. Such, in fact, is the case. Noncontingent administrations of the dopamine agonists apomorphine or piribedil dose-dependently decrease amphetamine self-administration.

A further approach to elucidating the neurochemical substrates of drug reward is to study the effect on drug self-administration of selective lesions, induced either surgically or pharmacologically, of specific neurotransmitter systems in the brain. Obviously, such studies also help elucidate the neuroanatomical substrates of drug reward. Such studies typically are of two types. One type has assessed the effects of brain lesions on stable, previously acquired drug self-administration; the second type has assessed the effects of brain lesions on acquisition of drug self-administration. When the catecholamine-specific neurotoxin 6-hydroxydopamine (6-OHDA) is used to selectively lesion the dopamine projections to the nucleus accumbens, cocaine self-administration is disrupted but self-administration of the direct dopamine receptor agonist apomorphine in the same animals is unaffected. Similarly, when 6-OHDA is used to lesion the ventral tegmental area (site of the cell bodies of the dopaminergic reward neurons), cocaine self-administration is disrupted but apomorphine self-administration is unaffected. Such findings are congruent with the known actions of these drugs on the reward circuitry: cocaine acting on the *pre*synaptic dopamine neurons that would be killed by 6-OHDA; apomorphine acting on the *post*synaptic neurons in nucleus accumbens pleasure/reward synapses (containing the dopamine receptors) that are unaffected by 6-OHDA. Lesions induced by 6-OHDA of other brain sites do not affect cocaine self-administration. In animals with 6-OHDA lesions of either the ventral tegmental area or the nucleus accumbens, the extent of 6-OHDA-induced dopamine depletion in the nucleus accumbens is highly predictive of duration of curtailment of cocaine self-administration. The greater the dopamine depletion the longer the animal takes to recover drug self-administration behavior, and animals with the greatest dopamine loss (more than 90 percent) often fail to recover at all. The 6-OHDA lesions of the nucleus accumbens also block acquisition of amphetamine self-administration. Heroin and morphine self-administrations in laboratory animals have been similarly demonstrated to be critically dependent upon the functional integrity of the mesolimbic dopamine system.

## 13. Pharmacotherapy for Addiction

Although functional blockade, either pharmacologically induced or lesion-induced, of brain-reward substrates clearly alters drug-taking behavior in laboratory animals, the extension to the human clinical situation is not straightforward. Attempts to treat human drug addiction with dopamine antagonists (i.e., neuroleptics) have proven to be failures, although one should keep in mind that this class of dopamine antagonists is not highly specific for dopamine receptors and introduces significant unintended effects on brain neurotransmitters other than dopamine (e.g., epinephrine, norepinephrine, serotonin, acetylcholine, histamine). Interestingly, one of the main reasons for failure of dopamine antagonist therapy for drug addiction is that drug addicts are very much more vulnerable to the dysphorigenic properties of these drugs than other humans. This raises a provocative question: Are the reward mechanisms of the brains of addiction-prone individuals more vulnerable to any pharmacologically induced perturbation, either euphorigenic or dysphorigenic?

A more promising pharmacotherapy approach has been to use dopamine agonists (e.g., bromocriptine, amantadine) in a type of pharmacological substitution strategy somewhat (although not fully) analogous to methadone substitution therapy for heroin addiction. This strategy does seem to work for a limited number of patients.

Methadone substitution therapy for heroin addiction has served as a successful treatment modality for many hundreds of thousands of patients worldwide, who continue in their physiological dependence to opiates, but who no longer demonstrate the overall clinical syndrome of addiction (i.e., compulsive drug seeking and drug taking, profound interference with personal and occupational function, psychological distress, medical sequelae, legal sequelae, and social harm). Methadone, of course, is simply a long-acting opiate; and methadone maintenance is simple substitution therapy. Its pharmacological and conceptual simplicity, however, does not negate its very real success as a treatment that has given hundreds of thousands of opiate addicts their lives back. However, it is also true that a significant number of methadone maintenance patients relapse back to opiate (e.g., heroin) use or fall prey to other addicting drugs (e.g., cocaine, alcohol) while receiving methadone, partially defeating the intent of this opiate-agonist model of pharmacotherapy. There is good evidence that inadequate doses of methadone may be responsible for many of these treatment failures, and other opiate-agonist pharmacotherapies (e.g., buprenorphine, L-acetylmethadol) may hold promise for patients in whom methadone treatment fails.

Another agonist-substitution pharmacotherapy model is the treatment of nicotine dependence with nicotine "patches," which provide nicotine transdermally, in a slow-release preparation. The intent of this treatment modality is to blunt the relapse-inducing acute psychophysiologic withdrawal syndrome that accompanies cessation of cigarette smoking. Unfortunately, many smokers are unable to quit for long using this method, and some smokers smoke while wearing the patch, or in spite of chewing nicotine-impregnated chewing gum. These nicotine substitutions are best thought of as adjuncts for individuals attempting to quit smoking.

Pharmacotherapies for addiction based on attempts to directly manipulate – either by dopamine agonists or antagonists – the drug-sensitive dopaminergic pleasure/reward circuitry of the forebrain have not proven widely successful. However, strategies that attempt to transsynaptically or indirectly "buffer" these same forebrain pleasure/reward mechanisms may prove more successful. Provocatively, the brain-reward enhancement produced by numerous addicting drugs (of different pharmacological classes) is significantly attenuated by the opiate antagonists naloxone or naltrexone in most animal-model systems (e.g., electrical brain-stimulation reward). We know that there is significant endogenous opioid peptidergic innervation of the nucleus accumbens and its dopaminergic pleasure/reward synaptic neural matrix (Mansour et al. 1988; Khachaturian et al. 1985; Sharif and Hughes 1989; Pollard et al. 1977; Unterwald et al. 1989; Van Bockstaele, Sesack, and Pickel 1994), and that there is also significant opioid peptidergic synaptic innervation of the ventral tegmental area (Mansour et al. 1988; Khachaturian et al. 1985; Delay-Goyet, Zajac, and Roques 1990; German et al. 1993; Speciale et al. 1993) (the nucleus of origin of the dopaminergic pleasure/reward neurons). Further, the drug-induced pleasure/reward neural signals appear to be carried out of the nucleus accumbens, to the ventral pallidum, over yet another subset of endogenous opioid peptidergic neural circuits (Mansour et al. 1988, Khachaturian et al. 1985, Pickel and Chan 1989, Kubota et al. 1986, Nauta et al. 1978, Walaas and Fonnum 1979, Zahm et al. 1985, Graybiel 1986). It is further known that local application of opiate agonistsor antagonists into either the ventral tegmental area or nucleus accumbens can significantly alter dopaminergic tone in the dopaminergic pleasure/reward circuitry that is preferentially activated by addictive drugs (Matthews and German 1984; Ostrowski, Hatfield, and Caggiula 1982; Latimer, Duffy, and Kalivas 1987; Pentney and Gratton 1991; Spanagel, Herz, and Shippenburg 1992; Leone, Pocock, and Wise 1991; Devine et al. 1993a,b; Devine, Leone, and Wise 1993). Thus, the neural circuitry apparently exists by which the dopamine pleasure/reward circuitry can be modulated or "buffered" by its endogenous opioid peptidergic synaptic inputs, or by exogenous opiate drugs acting on these synaptic inputs (the synaptic equivalent of a "volume knob" or "gain-control knob" on the dopaminergic pleasure/reward circuitry mediated through opioid-sensitive receptors and neurotransmitters). Acting through these neural mechanisms, opioid or anti-opioid molecules could upregulate or downregulate the overall amplitude of drug-induced alterations in hedonic tone within the underlying dopaminergic reward system. Opioid-antagonist pharmacotherapy (e.g., naloxone), by this model, could logically have clinical efficacy for other nonopioid addictions, such as alcohol, nicotine, or cocaine. In fact, naltrexone, a long-lasting congener of naloxone (both of which are potent and highly specific opioid receptor blockers), appears to be successful in curbing craving and drug use in some alcoholics (Volpicelli et al. 1992, 1995). Also, naltrexone appears to be quite successful for a limited number of highly motivated opiate (e.g., heroin) addicts, although in this case the clinical effect is presumably mediated by a direct antagonism of heroin's actions on opioid receptors in the brain, thus interfering directly with the reward circuitry's responsiveness to opiate intake. Noteworthily, such opiate antagonist therapy for opiate addiction is much less successful than opiate agonist therapy (e.g., methadone) for opiate addiction, perhaps speaking to the hypothesis that opiate addicts may have some basal hypofunction within crucial endogenous opioid circuits in the brain (Dole, Nyswander, and Kreek 1966; Dole 1989).

Another transsynaptic "buffering" approach rests upon the extensive and complex anatomical and functional interrelationships between the dopaminergic pleasure/reward system and the serotonergic projections of the anterior triad of raphé nuclei (the dorsal, median, and lateral raphé nuclei) and upon extensive evidence that alterations of serotonergic activity within these projections can profoundly alter synaptic tone in the drug-sensitive dopaminergic pleasure/reward circuitry of the forebrain (de Belleroche and Bradford 1980; Chesselet 1984; Hetey and Drescher 1986; Tricklebank 1989; Westfall and Titternary 1982; Chen, van Praag, and Gardner 1991; Chen et al. 1992). Based upon this approach, much attention has focused recently on attempts to buffer or protect, by serotonergic pharmacological manipulations, the dopaminergic reward circuits against the large perturbations in functionality that they undergo when exposed to addictive drugs. This strategy works extremely well in laboratory animals (Amit et al. 1984; Gill, Amit, and Ögren 1985; Le Bourhis et al. 1981; Leccesse and Lyness 1984; Murphy et al. 1985; Naranjo, Sellers, and Lawrin 1986; Rockman et al. 1979). For example, the highly selective serotonin reuptake blocker fluoxetine (Prozac®) significantly reduces ethanol, amphetamine, and cocaine self-administration in laboratory animals (Leccesse and Lyness 1984, Yu et al. 1986, Zabik et al. 1982, Peltier and Schenk 1993, Kleven and Woolverton 1993). Clinical trials with fluoxetine for the treatment of cocaine-dependent human patients are under way at several major drug abuse treatment centers, with preliminary encouraging results reported from one center (Batki et al. 1993).

## 14. Conclusions

The preceding provides an overview of the compelling evidence for a neurobiological substrate that drives chemical addictions in both laboratory animals and human beings. More than forty years of research with electrical and chemical probes of the central nervous system has shown that animal self-administration of addictive drugs (and their congeners) can be precisely and unequivocally attributed to neuroanatomical, neurophysiological, and neurochemical substrates within the mesotelencephalic dopamine system (most importantly involving a subset of neuronal projections contained within the medial forebrain bundle, and linking the ventral tegmental area and the nucleus accumbens). This brain pleasure/reward system is composed of quite ordinary neurophysiological elements: nerve cells, synapses between nerve cells, several neurotransmitters (primarily dopamine) used at those synapses, and a complex arrangement of neurons communicating with other neurons. This pleasure/reward neural system, in addition to its self-connectedness, has complex and diffuse interconnections throughout the brain. One might imagine a political party's headquarters during a major campaign, with a dense net of telephone lines interconnecting the headquarters' staff, and many other telephone lines spreading outward into surrounding cities and towns and most especially to other relevant organizations. The campaign is managed from headquarters, but headquarters receives continuous and copious telephone input from without. Additionally, it directs and influences many elements via outgoing communications.

Animal patterns of self-administration of addicting drugs are strikingly parallel to human patterns of self-administration. This is neither analogy nor homology, but rather identity: The human central nervous system contains within it the same neuroanatomical structures encoding the same emotional, motivational, cognitive, and behavioral functions seen in laboratory animals. Rats, dogs, monkeys, and humans differ only slightly with regard to the deep-brain pleasure/reward circuits involved in encoding hedonic tone. Mammalian neuroanatomy, neurophysiology, neurochemistry, and neuropsychology at this level of the brain stem and diencephalon vary little from species to species, and the animal data are constrained to a handful of species only because of the relative ease of laboratory work with some species and their ready availability. Indeed, given the presumptive evolutionary function of the brain's pleasure/reward circuitry – to reinforce food seeking, eating, mating, and parenting behaviors (i.e., survival behaviors; Wise 1980b, Hebb 1949) – it is not at all unexpected to find a common neurobiological pleasure/reward system present throughout the mammalian line.

Of direct relevance to these considerations of evolutionary function is the fact that electrical stimulation in brain pleasure/reward areas can also evoke natural consummatory behaviors such as feeding and other species-typical biologically essential behaviors (Miller 1960; Margules and Olds 1962; Hoebel and Teitelbaum 1962; Coons, Levak, and Miller 1965). Furthermore, the directly activated neural substrates of stimulation-induced feeding and brain-stimulation reward in the lateral hypothalamus and ventral tegmental area appear identical in terms of refractory periods, conduction velocities, and medial-lateral and dorsal-ventral alignment of the nerve fibers subserving the two stimulation-induced effects (feeding and reward), suggesting strongly that the same neurons mediate both effects (Gratton and Wise 1988a,b). Intriguingly, the same mesotelencephalic dopamine circuits that appear to subserve the reward induced by addictive drugs are also biochemically activated by natural rewards, in a manner seemingly identical to the dopaminergic activation produced by addicting drugs (Hernandez and Hoebel 1988).

Thus, one may view human vulnerability to chemical addictions as simply an accident of nature. The poppy and coca plants quite unintentionally produce alkaloid chemicals (morphine and cocaine) that are capable of "pirating" or "hijacking" the pleasure/reward circuits of the brain, by virtue of the especially intense effect they have on these circuits and by virtue of individual neurobiological vulnerabilities in pleasure/reward neurons and their interconnections. Alcohol, a by-product of natural fermentation, also "pirates" the brain's pleasure/reward systems, as does every other addictive drug (with the possible exception of the LSD-like hallucinogens). Pharmaceutical manipulations have, in recent times, produced semisynthetic (e.g., heroin from morphine) and synthetic (e.g., methadone) congeners of naturally occurring reward chemicals. Humans, with their capacity to collect, cultivate, refine, synthesize, and then self-administer these remarkable chemicals were the final step in the evolution of addiction.

As in any complex neural circuit, the pleasure/reward systems of the brain have multiple interconnections and intermodulating subcircuits, which have variable influences upon the overall function of the larger circuit. Different addicting chemicals enter the brain's pleasure/reward circuitry at different sites and affect it by different neuropharmacological mechanisms. For example, heroin increases neural impulse flow within the dopaminergic afferents to the nucleus accumbens, amphetamine releases presynaptic dopamine in nucleus accumbens reward synapses, and cocaine blocks the reuptake of synaptic dopamine in the nucleus accumbens. These are three very different neuroanatomical sites of action and three very different neuropharmacological mechanisms of action, but each results in the same final common neurochemical event (augmented dopamine in nucleus accumbens dopaminergic pleasure/reward synapses). Different doses and routes of administration (e.g., oral versus intravenous) of even the same drug interact differentially with the reward system. The syndromal variability between drug classes and within drug classes reflect (1) the different loci in the system being pirated, (2) the varied degree to which a given drug or dose can impact the normal functioning of the network, and (3) the different other brain circuits (mediating other functions such as sedation, arousal, anxiety, perception) pirated at the same time that the pleasure/reward system is pirated.

Having established the neurobiological identity of addictive drug action on the pleasure/reward systems of humans and animals, we turn now briefly to the task of contrasting addicted humans with addicted laboratory animals.

A human who has never ingested cocaine (but who has knowledge of cocaine's effects from reading, television, or personal acquaintance with a cocaine user) might decline an offer to use the drug, with the conscious and volitional intent of wanting to avoid the future risks of addiction and the associated negative consequences. Rats or dogs, to the best of our knowledge, cannot do this. At the other temporal end of the addiction syndrome, a human who has successfully abstained from cocaine for years (after kicking a severe habit) might also decline an offer to use the drug, out of conscious fear of having to suffer again the many painful aspects of his prior period of active addiction (e.g., unemployment, divorce, depressive episodes, arrests, imprisonment, medical complications). To cite another example, ex-smokers, early on, commonly abstain by focusing on their desire to avoid having to reexperience acute nicotine withdrawal. Thus, at the very outset and at late stages of recovery from drug addiction, humans are perhaps less similar to laboratory animals. But during the active addictive phase, and during both the acute and short-term withdrawal and abstinence phases, we are perhaps most similar to laboratory animals (see Figure 7). This construct, distinguishing the relative contributions of ventral tegmental area/medial forebrain bundle/nucleus accumbens input from neocortical input, is obviously only descriptive in nature. However, it may prove useful in the integration of the hedonic/motivational with the cognitive/motivational phenomena seen in the human addictions. We venture to suggest that a phase-specific perspective may facilitate the micromotivational analysis of addiction at the human level. Blurring the distinctions between the markedly different stages of addiction may obscure hypotheses that have utility if applied to one or another specific phase or transition. For example, in Figure 7, the motivational economics of stage C1 are a far cry from those of stage C3.

The behavioral addictions, as well, are strongly suggestive of the neurobiological underpinnings seen so clearly in the chemical addictions (for such addictions, animal models are more difficult to design, although probably not impossibly so). Again, a phase-specific view is applied.

> A gambler, standing before a "one-armed bandit" slot machine, hypnotized and spending his rent money, dollar by dollar, lever-pulling as fast as he can insert his coins, can hardly fail to remind us of our experimental animals lever-pressing avidly and relentlessly for intracranial electrical stimulation or for intravenous drug self-administration. But this same gambler, the following year, choosing to attend a Gamblers Anonymous meeting rather than buy an airplane ticket to Las Vegas, looks a good deal less like our laboratory animals.

It is this addict's most crucial decision – responding to a craving to relapse with a constructive alternative – that we must come to understand and augment. The role of episodic craving in relapse is increasingly

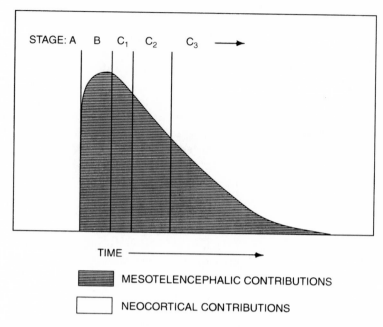

Figure 7. Stages of addiction from left to right over a *t* axis; shaded area indicates the postulated mesotelencephalic (vs. neocortical) contribution operant during each particular phase. Stage A, preaddictive phase. Stage B, addictive phase. Stage C1, acute withdrawal: 24–48 hours, maximum of 1 week. Stage C2, short-term withdrawal-abstinence: days to weeks, maximum of 1 month. Stage C3, long-term abstinence: weeks to months to years.

familiar to both clinicians and researchers, yet the neurobiological correlates of this craving remain obscure and unexplored. The Stage C dynamics warrant further elucidation (particularly C2 and C3) as to the neurobiological mechanisms in play, as well as with regard to the psychological economics of relapse "decisions." To partly redirect the editors' question in the Introduction to this volume, asking "why people engage in behaviors that they know will harm them," we must focus as well on the related question, "Why do people reengage in behaviors that have already harmed them?"

## Acknowledgments

Preparation of this article was supported, in part, by grants from the Aaron Diamond Foundation (New York) and the U.S. Public Health Service (National Institute on Drug Abuse research grant DA03622 and National Institute on Alcohol Abuse and Alcoholism research grant AA09547) to E.L.G., and by funds from the New York State Office of Alcohol and Substance Abuse Services. The authors are indebted to William Paredes for his tireless assistance and to T. Byram Karasu,

Chairman, Department of Psychiatry, Albert Einstein College of Medicine, for his support.

## REFERENCES

Amit, Z., E. A. Sutherland, K. Gill, and S. O. Ögren (1984), "Zimeldine: A review of its effects on ethanol consumption," *Neurosci. Biobehav. Rev.* 8, 35–54.

Ashton, H. (1991), "Protracted withdrawal syndromes from benzodiazepines," *Journal of Substance Abuse Treatment* 8, 19–28.

Batki, S., L. B. Manfredi, P. Jacob III, and R. Jones (1993), "Fluoxetine for cocaine dependence in methadone maintenance: Quantitative plasma and urine cocaine/benzoylecgonine concentrations," *Journal of Clinical Psychopharmacology* 13, 243–50.

Beitner-Johnson, D., X. Guitart, and E. J. Nestler (1991), "Dopaminergic brain reward regions of Lewis and Fischer rats display different levels of tyrosine hydroxylase and other morphine- and cocaine-regulated phosphoproteins," *Brain Research* 561, 146–9.

Bozarth, M. A. (1987), "Conditioned place preference: A parametric analysis using systemic heroin injections," in M. A. Bozarth (ed.), *Methods of Assessing the Reinforcing Properties of Abused Drugs,* New York, Springer-Verlag, pp. 241–73.

Bozarth, M. A. and R. A. Wise (1984), "Anatomically distinct opiate receptor fields mediate reward and physical dependence," *Science* 244, 516–17.

 (1985), "Toxicity associated with long-term intravenous heroin and cocaine self-administration in the rat," *Journal of the American Medical Association* 254, 81–83.

Cadoret, R. J., T. O'Gorman, E. Troughton, and E. Heywood (1986), "An adoption study of genetic and environmental factors in drug abuse," *Archives of General Psychiatry* 43, 1131–6.

Chen, J., W. Paredes, J. H. Lowinson, and E. L. Gardner (1991), "Strain-specific facilitation of dopamine efflux by $\Delta^9$-tetrahydrocannabinol in the nucleus accumbens of rat: An in vivo microdialysis study," *Neuroscience Letters* 129, 136–40.

Chen, J., W. Paredes, H. M. van Praag, J. H. Lowinson, and E. L. Gardner (1992), "Presynaptic dopamine release is enhanced by $5\text{-}HT_3$ receptor activation in medial prefrontal cortex of freely moving rats," *Synapse* 10, 264–6.

Chen, J., H. M. van Praag, and E. L. Gardner (1991), "Activation of $5\text{-}HT_3$ receptor by 1-phenylbiguanide increases dopamine release in the rat nucleus accumbens," *Brain Research* 543, 354–7.

Chesselet, M. F. (1984), "Presynaptic regulation of neurotransmitter release in the brain: Facts and hypothesis," *Neuroscience* 12, 347–75.

Cloninger, C. R. (1987), "Neurogenetic adaptive mechanisms in alcoholism," *Science* 236, 410–16.

Cloninger, C. R. and H. Begleiter, eds. (1990), *Genetics and Biology of Alcoholism,* New York, Cold Spring Harbor Press.

Coons, E. E., M. Levak, and N. E. Miller (1965), "Lateral hypothalamus: Learning of food-seeking response motivated by electrical stimulation," *Science* 150, 1320–1.

Cooper, J. R., F. E. Bloom, and R. H. Roth (1986), *The Biochemical Basis of Neuropsychopharmacology*, 5th ed., New York: Oxford University Press.

Corbett, D. and R. A. Wise (1980), "Intracranial self-stimulation in relation to the ascending dopaminergic systems of the midbrain: A moveable electrode mapping study," *Brain Research* 185, 1–15.

Dackis, C. A. and M. S. Gold (1985a), "Bromocriptine as a treatment for cocaine abuse," *Lancet* I, 1151–2.

(1985b), "New concepts in cocaine addiction: The dopamine depletion hypothesis," *Neurosci. Biobehav. Rev.* 9, 469–77.

Davis, N. E., T. Akera, and T. M. Brody (1979), "Reduction of opiate binding to brainstem slices associated with the development of tolerance to morphine in rats," *Journal of Pharmacology and Experimental Therapeutics* 211, 112–19.

de Belleroche, J. S. and H. F. Bradford (1980), "Presynaptic control of the synthesis and release of dopamine from striatal synaptosomes: A comparison between the effects of 5-hydroxytryptamine, acetylcholine, and glutamate," *Journal of Neurochemistry* 35, 1227–34.

de Wit, H. and V. Stewart (1983), "Drug reinstatement of heroin-reinforced responding in the rat," *Psychopharmacology* 79, 29–31.

Delay-Goyet, P., J.-M. Zajac, and B. P. Roques (1990), "Improved quantitative autoradiography of rat brain Š-opioid binding sites using [³H] DSTBULET, a new highly potent and selective linear enkephalin analogue," *Neurochemistry International* 16, 341–68.

Devine, D. P., P. Leone, W. A. Carlezon, Jr., and R. A. Wise (1993a), "Ventral mesencephalic delta opioid receptors are involved in modulation of basal mesolimbic dopamine neurotransmission: An anatomical localization study," *Brain Research* 622, 348–52.

Devine, D. P., P. Leone, D. Pocock, and R. A. Wise (1993b), "Differential involvement of ventral tegmental mu, delta and kappa opioid receptors in modulation of basal mesolimbic dopamine release: In vivo microdialysis studies," *Journal of Pharmacology and Experimental Therapeutics* 266, 1236–46.

Devine, D. P., P. Leone, and R. A. Wise (1993), "Mesolimbic dopamine neurotransmission is increased by administration of mu-opioid receptor antagonists," *European Journal of Pharmacology* 243, 55–64.

Dole, V. P. (1989), "Implications of methadone maintenance for theories of narcotic addiction," *Journal of the American Medical Association* 261, 1879–80.

Dole, V. P., M. E. Nyswander, and M. J. Kreek (1966), "Narcotic blockade," *Archives of Internal Medicine* 118, 304–9.

Dwoskin, L. P., J. Peris, R. P. Yasuda, K. Philpott, and N. R. Zahniser (1988), "Repeated cocaine administration results in supersensitivity of striatal D-2 dopamine autoreceptors to pergolide," *Life Sciences* 42, 255–62.

Eichler, A. J., S. M. Antelman, and A. E. Fisher (1976), "Self-stimulation: Site-specific tolerance to chronic dopamine receptor blockade," *Soc. Neurosci. Abstr.* 2, 440.

Ettenberg, A. and R. A. Wise (1976), "Non-selective enhancement of locus coeruleus and substantia nigra self-stimulation after termination of chronic dopaminergic receptor blockade with pimozide in rats," *Psychopharmacol. Commun.* 2, 117–24.

Gardner, E. L. (1992), "Cannabinoid interaction with brain reward systems – the neurobiological basis of cannabinoid abuse," in L. L. Murphy and A. Bartke (eds.), *Marijuana/Cannabinoids: Neurobiology and Neurophysiology*, Boca Raton, FL, CRC Press, pp. 275–335.

(1997), "Brain reward mechanisms," in J. H. Lowinson, P. Ruiz, R. B. Millman, and J. G. Langrod (eds.), *Substance Abuse: A Comprehensive Textbook*, 3rd ed., Baltimore, Williams and Wilkins, pp. 51–85.

Gardner, E. L. and J. H. Lowinson (1991), "Marijuana's interactions with brain reward systems: Update 1991," *Pharmacology, Biochemistry and Behavior* 40, 571–80.

(1993), "Drug craving and positive/negative hedonic brain substrates activated by addicting drugs," *Sems Neurosci.* 5, 359–68.

Gardner, E. L., L. S. Walker, and W. Paredes (1993), "Clozapine's functional mesolimbic selectivity is not duplicated by the addition of anticholinergic action to haloperidol: A brain stimulation study in the rat," *Psychopharmacology* 110, 119–24.

George, F. R. and S. R. Goldberg (1989), "Genetic approaches to the analysis of addiction processes," *Trends in Pharmacological Science* 10, 78–83.

Gerber, G. J. and R. Stretch (1975), "Drug-induced reinstatement of extinguished self-administration behavior in monkeys," *Pharmacology, Biochemistry and Behavior* 3, 1055–61.

German, D. C., S. G. Speciale, K. F. Manaye, and M. Sadeq (1993), "Opioid receptors in midbrain dopaminergic regions of the rat," I. Mu receptor autoradiography. *Journal of Neural Transmission – Gen. Sec.* 91, 39–52.

Gill, K., Z. Amit, and S. O. Ögren (1985), "The effects of zimelidine on voluntary ethanol consumption: Studies on the mechanism of action," *Alcohol* 2, 343–7.

Gratton, A. and R. A. Wise (1988a), "Comparisons of connectivity and conduction velocities for medial forebrain bundle fibers subserving stimulation-induced feeding and brain stimulation reward," *Brain Research* 438, 264–70.

(1988b), "Comparisons of refractory periods for medial forebrain bundle fibers subserving stimulation-induced feeding and brain stimulation reward: A psychophysical study," *Brain Research* 438, 256–63.

Graybiel, A. M. (1986), "Neuropeptides in the basal ganglia," in J. B. Martin and J. D. Barchas (eds.), *Neuropeptides in Neurologic and Psychiatric Disease*, New York, Raven, pp. 135–61.

Grzimek's *Encyclopedia of Ethology*, Coron Verlag Press, 1977.

Guitart, X., D. Beitner-Johnson, and E. J. Nestler (1992), "Fischer and Lewis rat strains differ in basal levels of neurofilament proteins and in their regulation by chronic morphine," *Synapse* 12, 242–53.

Guitart, X., J. H. Kogan, M. Berhow, R. Z. Terwilliger, G. K. Aghajanian, and E. J. Nestler (1993), "Lewis and Fischer rat strains display differences in biochemical, electrophysiological and behavioral parameters: Studies in the nucleus accumbens and locus coeruleus of drug naive and morphine-treated animals," *Brain Research* 611, 7–17.

Heath, R. G. (1964), "Pleasure response of human beings to direct stimulation of the brain: Physiologic and psychodynamic considerations," in R. G. Heath (ed.), *The Role of Pleasure in Behavior*, New York, Hoeber, pp. 219–43.

Hebb, D. O. (1949), *The Organization of Behavior: A Neuropsychological Theory*, New York, Wiley.

Hernandez, L. and B. G. Hoebel (1988), "Food reward and cocaine increase extra-cellular dopamine in the nucleus accumbens as measured by microdialysis," *Life Sciences* 42, 1705–12.

Hetey, L. and K. Drescher (1986), "Influence of antipsychotics on presynaptic receptors modulating the release of dopamine in synaptosomes of the nucleus accumbens of rats," *Neuropharmacology* 25, 1103–9.

Hiroi, N. (1990), "A pharmacological and neuroanatomical investigation of the conditioned place preference produced by amphetamine," dissertation, Montreal, Quebec, McGill University, p. 158.

Hiroi, N. and N. M. White (1990), "The reserpine-sensitive dopamine pool mediates (+)-amphetamine-conditioned reward in the place preference paradigm," *Brain Research* 510, 33–42.

Hiroi, N., R. J. McDonald, and N. M. White (1990), "Involvement of the lateral nucleus of the amygdala in amphetamine and food conditioned place preferences (CPP)," *Soc. Neurosci. Abstr.* 16, 605.

Hoebel, B. G. and P. Teitelbaum (1962), "Hypothalamic control of feeding and self-stimulation," *Science* 135, 375–7.

Johanson, C. E., R. L. Balster, and K. Bonese (1976), "Self-administration of psychomotor stimulant drugs: The effects of unlimited access," *Pharmacology, Biochemistry and Behavior* 4, 45–51.

Kalivas, P. W. and P. Duffy (1988), "Effects of daily cocaine and morphine treatment on somatodendritic and terminal field dopamine release," *Journal of Neurochemistry* 50, 1498–504.

Kalivas, P. W., P. Duffy, L. A. DuMars, and C. Skinner (1988), "Behavioral and neurochemical effects of acute and daily cocaine administration in rats," *Journal of Pharmacology and Experimental Therapeutics* 245, 485–92.

Khachaturian, H., M. E. Lewis, M. K.-H. Schaffer, and S. J. Watson (1985), "Anatomy of the CNS opioid systems," *Trends in Neuroscience* 8, 111–19.

Killam, K. F., J. Olds, and J. Sinclair (1957), "Further studies on the effects of centrally acting drugs on self-stimulation," *Journal of Pharmacology and Experimental Therapeutics* 119, 157.

Kleven, M. S. and W. L. Woolverton (1993), "Effects of three monoamine uptake inhibitors on behavior maintained by cocaine or food presentation in rhesus monkeys," *Drug and Alcohol Dependence* 31, 49–58.

Kokkinidis, L., R. M. Zacharko, and P. A. Predy (1980), "Post-amphetamine depression of self-stimulation responding from the substantia nigra: Reversal by tricyclic antidepressants," *Pharmacology, Biochemistry and Behavior* 13, 379–83.

Koob, G. F. and F. E. Bloom (1988), "Cellular and molecular mechanisms of drug dependence," *Science* 242, 715–23.

Koob, G. F., A. Markou, F. Weiss, and G. Schulteis (1993), "Opponent process and drug dependence: Neurobiological mechanisms," *Sems Neurosci.* 5, 351–8.

Koob, G. F., L. Stinus, M. Le Moal, and F. E. Bloom (1989), "Opponent process theory of motivation: Neurobiological evidence from studies of opiate dependence," *Neurosci. Biobehav. Rev.* 13, 135–40.

Kornetsky, C. (1985), "Brain-stimulation reward: A model for the neuronal bases for drug-induced euphoria," *National Institute of Drug Abuse Research Monograph Series* 62, 30–50.

Kubota, Y., S. Inagaki, S. Kito, H. Takagi, and A. D. Smith (1986), "Ultrastructural evidence of dopaminergic input to enkephalinergic neurons in rat neostriatum," *Brain Research* 367, 374–8.

Latimer, L. G., P. Duffy, and P. W. Kalivas (1987), "Mu opioid receptor involvement in enkephalin activation of dopamine neurons in the ventral tegmental area," *Journal of Pharmacology and Experimental Therapeutics* 241, 328–37.

Le Bourhis, B., A. Uzan, G. Aufrere, and G. Lefur (1981), "Effets de l'indalpine, inhibiteur spécifique de la récapture de la sérotonine sur la dépendance comportementale à l'éthanol et sur la prise volontaire d'alcool chez le rat. [Effects of indalpine, a specific serotonin reuptake inhibitor, on ethanol behavioral dependence and voluntary alcohol consumption in the rat]," *Annales Pharmaceutiques Francaises* 39, 11–20.

Leccesse A. P. and W. H. Lyness (1984), "The effects of putative 5-hydroxytryptamine receptor active agents on D-amphetamine self-administration in controls and rats with 5,7-dihydroxytryptamine median forebrain bundle lesions," *Brain Research* 303, 153–62.

Leone, P., D. Pocock, and R. A. Wise (1991), "Morphine-dopamine interaction: Ventral tegmental morphine increases nucleus accumbens dopamine release," *Pharmacology, Biochemistry and Behavior* 39, 469–72.

Mansour, A., H. Khachaturian, M. E. Lewie, H. Akil, and S. J. Watson (1988), "Anatomy of CNS opioid receptors," *Trends in Neuroscience* 11, 308–14.

Margules, D. L. and J. Olds (1962), "Identical 'feeding' and 'rewarding' systems in the lateral hypothalamus of rats," *Science* 135, 374–5.

Matthews, R. T. and D. C. German (1984), "Electrophysiological evidence for excitation of rat ventral tegmental dopamine neurons by morphine," *Neuroscience* 11, 617–25.

Miller, N. E. (1960), "Motivational effects of brain stimulation and drugs," *Federation Proceedings, Federation of American Societies for Experimental Biology* 19, 846–53.

Miserendino, M. J. D., T. A. Kosten, X. Guitart, S. Chi, and E. J. Nestler (1992), "Individual differences in vulnerability to drug addiction: Behavioral and biochemical correlates," *Soc. Neurosci. Abstr.* 18, 1078.

Moolten, M. and C. Kornetsky (1990), "Oral self-administration of ethanol and not experimenter-administered ethanol facilitates rewarding electrical brain stimulation," *Alcohol* 7, 221–5.

Murphy J. M, M. B. Waller, G. J. Gatto, W. J. McBride, L. Lumeng, and T.-K. Li (1985), "Monoamine uptake inhibitors attenuate ethanol intake in alcohol-preferring (P) rats," *Alcohol* 2, 349–52.

Naranjo, C. A, E. M. Sellers, and M. O. Lawrin (1986), Modulation of ethanol intake by serotonin uptake inhibitors," *Journal of Clinical Psychiatry* 47(4) [suppl], 16–22.

Nauta, V. J. H., G. P. Smith, R. L. M. Faull, and V. B. Domesick (1978), "Efferent connections and nigral afferents of the nucleus accumbens septi in the rat," *Neuroscience* 3, 385–401.

Nazzaro, J. M., Seeger, T. F., and Gardner, E. L. (1981), "Morphine differentially affects ventral tegmental and substantia nigra brain reward thresholds," *Pharmacology, Biochemistry and Behavior* 14, 325–31.

Nestler, E. J. (1993), "Molecular mechanisms of drug addiction in the mesolimbic dopamine pathway." *Sems Neurosci.* 5, 369–76.

Olds, M. E. and J. L. Fobes (1981), "The central basis of motivation: Intracranial self-stimulation studies," *Annual Review of Psychology* 32, 523–74.

Olds, J. and P. Milner (1954), "Positive reinforcement produced by electrical stimulation of septal area and other regions of rat brain," *Journal of Comparative and Physiological Psychology* 47, 419–27.

Ostrowski, N. L., C. B. Hatfield, and A. R. Caggiula (1982), "The effects of low doses of morphine on the activity of dopamine-containing cells and on behavior," *Life Sciences* 31, 2347–50.

Parsons, L. H., A. D. Smith, and J. B. Justice, Jr. (1991), "Basal extracellular dopamine is decreased in the rat nucleus accumbens during abstinence from chronic cocaine," *Synapse* 9, 60–5.

Peltier, R. and S. Schenk (1993), "Effects of serotonergic manipulations on cocaine self-administration in rats," *Psychopharmacology* 110, 390–4.

Pentney, R. J. W. and A. Gratton (1991), "Effects of local delta and mu opioid receptor activation on basal and stimulated dopamine release in striatum and nucleus accumbens of rat: An in vivo electrochemical study," *Neuroscience* 45, 95–102.

Phillips, A. G. and H. C. Fibiger (1987), "Anatomical and neurochemical substrates of drug reward determined by the conditioned place preference technique," in M. A. Bozarth (ed.), *Methods of Assessing the Reinforcing Properties of Abused Drugs*, New York, Springer-Verlag, pp. 275–90.

Pickel, V. M. and J. Chan (1989), "Ultrastructural basis for interactions between opioid peptides and dopamine in rat striatum," *Soc. Neurosci. Abstr.* 15, 810.

Pickens, R. and W. C. Harris (1968), "Self-administration of *d*-amphetamine by rats," *Psychopharmacologia* 12, 158–63.

Pickens, R. W., D. S. Svikis, M. McGue, D. T. Lykken, L. L. Heston, and P. J. Clayton (1991), "Hereogeneity in the inheritance of alcoholism: A study of male and female twins," *Archives of General Psychiatry* 48, 19–28.

Pollard, H., C. Llorens, J. J. Bonnet, J. Costentin, and J. C. Schwartz (1977), "Opiate receptors on mesolimbic dopaminergic neurons," *Neuroscience Letters* 7, 295–9.

Rockman, G. E, Z. Amit, G. Carr, Z. W. Brown, and S. O. Ögren (1979), "Attenuation of ethanol intake by 5-hydroxytryptamine uptake blockade in laboratory rats: I. Involvement of brain 5-hydroxytryptamine in the mediation of the positive reinforcing properties of ethanol," *Archives Internationales de Pharmacodynamie et de Therapie* 241, 245–59.

Rolls, E. T. (1975), *The Brain and Reward*, Oxford, Pergamon Press.

Routtenberg, A. (1978), "The reward system of the brain," *Scientific American* 239(5), 154–64.

Satel, S. L., T. R. Kosten, M. A. Schuckit, and M. W. Fischman (1993), "Should protracted withdrawal from drugs be included in DSM-IV?" *American Journal of Psychiatry* 150, 695–704.

Schuckit, M. A. and V. Hasselbrock (1994), "Alcohol dependence and anxiety disorders: What is the relationship?" *American Journal of Psychiatry* 151, 1723–34.

Seeger, T. F. and E. L. Gardner (1979), "Enhancement of self-stimulation behavior in rats and monkeys after chronic neuroleptic treatment: Evidence for mesolimbic supersensitivity," *Brain Research* 175, 49–57.

Sharif, N. A. and J. Hughes (1989), "Discrete mapping of brain mu and delta opioid receptors using selective peptides: Quantitative autoradiography, species differences and comparison with kappa receptors," *Peptides* 10, 499–522.

Simpson, D. M. and Z. Annau (1977), "Behavioral withdrawal following several psychoactive drugs," *Pharmacology, Biochemistry and Behavior* 7, 59–64.

Solomon, R. L. (1980), "The opponent process theory of acquired motivation," *American Psychologist* 35, 691–712.

Spanagel, R., A. Herz, and T. S. Shippenburg (1992), "Opposing tonically active endogenous opioid systems modulate the mesolimbic dopaminergic pathway," *Proceedings of the National Academy of Sciences of the United States of America* 89, 2046–50.

Speciale, S. G., K. F. Manaye, M. Sadeq, and D. C. German (1993), "Opioid receptors in midbrain dopaminergic regions of the rat," II. Kappa and delta receptor autoradiography. *Journal of Neural Transmission – Gen. Sec.* 91, 53–66.

Stewart, J. (1983), "Conditioned and unconditioned drug effects in relapse to opiate and stimulant drug self-administration," *Progress in Neuropsychopharmacol. Biol. Psychiat.* 7, 591–7.

(1984), "Reinstatement of heroin and cocaine self-administration behavior in the rat by intracerebral application of morphine in the ventral tegmental area," *Pharmacology, Biochemistry and Behavior* 20, 917–23.

Stewart, J. and P. Vezina (1988), "A comparison of the effects of intra-accumbens injections of amphetamine and morphine on reinstatement of heroin intravenous self-administration behavior," *Brain Research* 457, 287–94.

Stewart, J. and R. A. Wise (1992), "Reinstatement of heroin self-administration habits: Morphine prompts and naltrexone discourages renewed responding after extinction," *Psychopharmacology* 108, 79–84.

Suzuki, T., F. R. George, and R. A. Meisch (1989), "Differential establishment and maintenance of oral ethanol reinforced behavior in Lewis and Fischer 344 inbred rat strains," *Journal of Pharmacology and Experimental Therapeutics* 245, 164–70.

Tricklebank M. D. (1989), "Interactions between dopamine and 5-HT$_3$ receptors suggest new treatment for psychosis and drug addiction," *Trends in Pharmacological Science* 10, 127–9.

Trulson, D. L. and M. J. Ulissey (1987), "Chronic cocaine administration decreases dopamine synthesis rate and increases [$^3$H]spiroperidol binding in rat brain," *Brain Research Bulletin* 19, 35–8.

Unterwald, E. M., A. Tempel, G. F. Koob, and R. S. Zukin (1989), "Characterization of opioid receptors in rat nucleus accumbens following mesolimbic dopaminergic lesions," *Brain Research* 505, 111–18.

Van Bockstaele, E. J., S. R. Sesack, and V. M. Pickel (1994), "Dynorphin-immunoreactive terminals in the rat nucleus accumbens: Cellular sites for modulation of target neurons and interactions with catecholamine afferents," *Journal of Comparative Neurology* 341, 1–15.

van der Kooy, D. (1987), "Place conditioning: A simple and effective method for assessing the motivational properties of drugs," in M. A. Bozarth (ed.), *Methods of Assessing the Reinforcing Properties of Abused Drugs*, New York, Springer-Verlag, pp. 229–40.

Volpicelli, J. R., A. I. Alterman, M. Hayashida, and C. P. O'Brien (1992), "Naltrexone in the treatment of alcohol dependence," *Archives of General Psychiatry* 49, 876–80.

Volpicelli, J. R., N. T. Watson, A. C. King, C. E. Sherman, and C. P. O'Brien (1995), "Effect of naltrexone on alcohol 'high' in alcoholics," *American Journal of Psychiatry* 152, 613–15.

Walaas, I. and F. Fonnum (1979), "The distribution and origin of glutamate decarboxylase and choline acetyltransferase in ventral pallidum and other basal forebrain regions," *Brain Research* 177, 325–6.

Westfall T. C. and V. Titternary (1982), "Inhibition of the electrically induced release of [$^3$H]dopamine by serotonin from superfused rat striatal slices," *Neuroscience Letters* 28, 205–9.

White, N. M. and N. Hiroi (1993), "Amphetamine conditioned cue preference and the neurobiology of drug-seeking," *Sems Neurosci.* 5, 329–36.

Wilson, J. D., E. Braunwald, K. J. Isselbacher, R. G. Petersdorf, J. B. Martin, A. S. Fauci, and R. K. Root, eds. (1991), *Harrison's Principles of Internal Medicine*, 12th ed. New York, McGraw-Hill, 369–70.

Wise, R. A. (1980a), "Action of drugs of abuse on brain reward systems," *Pharmacology, Biochemistry and Behavior* 13 (suppl. 1), 213–23.

(1980b), "The dopamine synapse and the notion of pleasure centers in the brain," *Trends in Neuroscience* 3, 91–5.

(1982), "Neuroleptics and operant behavior: The anhedonia hypothesis," *Behav. Brain. Sci.* 5, 39–87.

(1995), "Munn E. Withdrawal from chronic amphetamine elevates baseline intracranial self-stimulation thresholds," *Psychopharmacology* 117, 130–6.

Wise, R. A. and M. A. Bozarth (1984), "Brain reward circuitry: Four circuit elements 'wired' in apparent series," *Brain Research Bulletin* 12, 203–8.

Wise, R. A. and P.-P. Rompre (1989), "Brain dopamine and reward," *Annual Review of Psychology* 40, 191–225.

Wise, R. A., A. Murray, and M. A. Bozarth (1990), "Bromocriptine self-administration and bromocriptine-reinstatement of cocaine-trained and heroin-trained lever pressing in rats," *Psychopharmacology* 100, 355–60.

Yu, D. S. L, F. L. Smith, D. J. Smith, and W. H. Lyness (1986), "Fluoxetine-induced attenuation of amphetamine self-administration in rats," *Life Sciences* 39, 1383–8.

Zabik, J. E, J. D. Roache, R. Sidor, and J. F. Nash, Jr. (1982), "The effects of fluoxetine on ethanol preference in the rat," *Pharmacologist* 24, 204.

Zahm, D. S., L. Zaborsky, V. E. Alones, and L. Heimer (1985), "Evidence for the coexistence of glutamate decarboxylase and met-enkephalin immunore-activity in axon terminals of rat ventral pallidum," *Brain Research* 325, 317–21.

Zukin, R. S., A. Tempel, and E. L. Gardner (1984), "Opiate receptor upregulation and functional supersensitivity," *National Institute of Drug Abuse Research Monograph Series* 54, 146–60.

# To Legalize or Not to Legalize: Is That the Question?

HELGE WAAL

## 1. Introduction

More than ten years after President Reagan promised victory in the war on drugs, drugs remain available in most parts of the United States. Moreover, the costs of the war have been high. Many leading intellectuals and some politicians are, therefore, demanding a new policy. "The war is lost." In Europe, the war has always been controversial. The English drug policy has traditionally been dominated by a medical model with doctors rather than the drug squad in central position and addicts more seen as patients in need of treatment than criminals to be prosecuted. The Netherlands has a long-standing liberal policy in criminal matters and a disinclination to use restrictive measures. In countries such as Italy and Spain, there is a strong tendency to view a ban on drugs as moralizing.

Whereas skepticism toward the war on drugs has obvious merits, surrender is no acceptable alternative. It is obviously an immense exaggeration to see drugs as the root cause of most that is wrong with our societies. But today a new and equally faulty paradigm is gaining influence: The culprit is the war on drugs rather than the drugs themselves. As in Reagan's case, the solution is just as simple as the diagnosis: The war is to be replaced by legalization. The advocates of legalization have a rapidly growing influence in the European Parliament.

### The Drug Policy Debate

There may appear to be three main positions in the debate: prohibition, partial or full decriminalization, and legalization. Partial decriminalization implies reduced use of prison and shorter sentences, whereas the goal of full decriminalization is to replace the penal code with other types of restrictions. Full legalization is the policy to treat drugs as consumer goods regulated by the classical mechanisms of supply and demand. The reality is more complex, however. Few if any advocate prohibition across the board, and few if any propose legalization across the board. The proponents of legalization usually presuppose that some restrictions and regulations will remain in place. Although the debate is heavily shaped by ideology and arguments from first principles, a closer analysis usually reveals attitudes that are located on a continuum between legalization and prohibition.

In spite of the heat of discussions, most observers strongly agree on the urgent need for a better drug policy. For this purpose, we need to consider three core themes. The first is whether the regulation of voluntary drug use in a free society is at all legitimate. If the rights of the individual supersede the need for a drug policy, there is no need for further discussion. Second, and assuming that drug policies can in fact be justified, the instruments need to be chosen in the light of what we know about the dynamics of drug abuse and dependence. There is also a need to understand the interaction between individual drug use and public drug policies. Only at this stage can we ask the third question: How do we find an optimal balance between the war on drugs and legalization?

In discussing these issues, I shall draw on three bodies of literature. The first is a set of neurobiological findings about abuse and dependence. The second is the theory of human behavior as choices characterized by limited rationality. The third is our knowledge, derived from epidemiology and social psychology, about drug use as a collective phenomenon. The conclusion is that a restrictive drug policy is not only legitimate but also in accordance with most of the logic of drug use. However, the examination of means does not support the warfare approach as victory is unrealistic and enemies difficult to delineate from allies and one's own forces. The rhetoric of war should be replaced by the everyday language of civil society. Our strategies must be found among those suited to limit societal evils in general, very much in the line with efforts to reduce pollution. The aim should not be to win victories but to reduce problems and improve conditions in long-term efforts.

## 2. Some Neurobiological Aspects of Drug Use

From the biological point of view, behavior is regulated by its consequences. Positive reinforcement (reward) increases the frequency of behavior, whereas negative reinforcement (punishment or loss of reward) decreases the frequency. This mechanism is observed in all organisms that have a central nervous system. In the lower organisms, the value associated with a given sensory input is largely hardwired. In higher organisms, the value is also shaped by learning. In humans, it is also shaped by culture and conscious thought. Yet in all cases we are dealing with the same basic mechanism: If an action is experienced as rewarding, we will tend to repeat it. The biological basis for the mechanism has been localized to specific areas in the brain. If such areas are artificially stimulated in an animal, the animal will show by its behavior whether it likes or dislikes the stimulation. If the area is destroyed, the animal will cease to have an interest in reacting. When such areas are stimulated under brain surgery, we can also learn something about human reactions. Subjects can report intensely euphoric reactions.

A central part of this system consists of neurons that connect the *ventral tegmentum* to reward areas of which nucleus accumbens has a central position. From the nucleus accumbens, there are further connections to the frontal brain area and to the limbic structures. The frontal area is important for complex mental functions such as normative evaluations and ethical considerations, and the limbic structures for memory, emotions, and complex reactions. Centers for basic drives such as thirst, hunger, sexuality, and child nurturing are also closely connected to the reward areas. Using advanced technology we can identify the parts of the brain that are active in different motivational states. When an animal begins to feel hunger or sexual excitement, we observe increased impulse transmissions in the motivational circuits and particularly in the nucleus accumbens. Actual intake of food or sexual behavior is then accompanied by a sharp increase of activity in these neurological structures.

This is only a rough sketch of the motivational system of the brain. (For details, see the previous chapter by Gardner and David.) The system has evolved by natural selection to ensure that the organism, among the innumerable potential behaviors at its disposal, sufficiently often chooses the ones that allow for necessary energy intake and reproduction. Intense neurobiological research on drug use and dependence has shown that these phenomena are based on universally observed biological mechanisms in this system. Laboratory animals will selectively prefer dependence-inducing substances over other stimuli, and they will brave various negative conditions to get access to them.[1]

As with many other substances that affect the central nervous system, drugs of abuse act on transmissions between neurons. They bind to specialized cell areas or *receptor sites*, where they give rise to reactions that influence the level (amount) of neurotransmitters in the intercellular cleft. What characterizes drugs of abuse is that these reactions directly or indirectly cause an increase of activity in the nucleus accumbens, as can be shown by increased energy consumption and increased release of dopamine. The activation of these motivational circuits in the brain causes pleasurable feelings (Abood and Martin 1992, Bloom 1993, Crabbe and Belknap 1992, Friedman 1993, Goldstein 1994, Koob 1992, Samson and Harris 1992, Wolverton and Johnson 1992).

Needless to say, such feelings can also arise from sensory stimuli such as smell, taste, and touch or through more complex phenomena such as thoughts and emotions. In these cases, too, pleasure or euphoria arises by activation of the reward areas. Not only do these experiences ensure that the individual desires and derives satisfaction from biologically necessary

behaviors, such as food intake and reproduction, they are also fundamental in learning and the development of preferences, which in turn
shape cultural patterns.

There is an obvious difference, however, between the two sources of
activation. In drug abuse, what activates the nucleus accumbens is not
a biologically important or culturally conditioned experience but drug
molecules that reach the brain through the blood. In principle, the pleasure or euphoria can be obtained independently of any other action
besides that of introducing the drug into the body, although in practice some form of learning is usually also involved. Drug abuse, to use a
metaphor, is a kind of biological cheating or short-circuiting. Artificial
and destructive behaviors are experienced as attractive and desirable. It
is not surprising, therefore, that all drugs of abuse, legal as well as illegal,
can induce behavior that violates the norms regulating ordinary human
interaction.

## Why Some Drugs Are More Dangerous Than Others

It is well known that not all drugs of abuse have the same potential influence – some are "stronger" than others. The explanation is essentially
biological. Some substances, such as cocaine and amphetamine, act directly on the synapses and their effect is almost independent of context
or learning. Others, such as alcohol, benzodiazepin, and cannabis, work
indirectly, by blocking the inhibiting effect of certain neurons. Their effect may depend on the degree of activation present. In some mental
states, their effect is more pleasurable than in others. For these drugs the
process leading to release of dopamine into the synapses of the nucleus
accumbens seems to be more dependent on learning. In the case of some
substances, such as caffeine, their effect on the central nervous system is
so weak that their use rarely affects behavior to a significant extent.

Another important factor is the speed and efficacy with which the drug
molecules reach the motivational circuits. The reward effect is strong if
the access is immediate, as with injection and inhalation. If the substance
has to be digested and absorbed through the intestine, the effect is delayed and slow. Injection and inhalation, therefore, often cause destructive habits of abuse.

The concentration of the substance also matters greatly. Whereas chewing of coca leaves has been a way of life in many South American countries
for centuries, the concentrated forms of the substance such as cocaine,
crack, and cocaine paste are vastly more effective. When crack is smoked,
the serum level of cocaine rises very rapidly and the molecules reach the
brain immediately, with correspondingly strong effects. The same dynamics explain the increased social and human problems that followed when
distilling techniques made it possible to produce hard liquor, when the

invention of cigarettes enabled effective and simple use of nicotine, and when heroin injection allowed a faster and more effective stimulation of the opioid receptors.

Any rational drug policy has to take these factors into account. Technical change has created much more potent substances and more effective consumption modes, compared to those that, in earlier centuries, could be integrated into society and regulated by cultural patterns.

## The Biological Basis of Dependence

We have also learned a great deal about the biological aspects of drug dependence, defined informally as consumption beyond what can be justified by rational, long-term considerations. (See the editorial introduction to this volume for further discussion of dependence and addiction.) Two neuronal systems seem to be involved. One is linked directly to the motivational circuits and in particular to the nucleus accumbens. The other is linked to other structures, in which the *locus coeruleus* is a central component. The locus coeruleus is centrally placed in the regulation of muscular tonus, in the activation of the sympathetic nervous system, and in anxiety states. It has been called a "moderator button" for alarm states in the brain. In both systems there appears to occur a process of adaptive change caused by long-term excessive stimulation. The cell adapts by modifying the sensitivity of the receptor sites or by corresponding intracellular changes, so that the same amount of the drug no longer produces the same effect. If the intake of the substance ceases altogether or is markedly reduced, there occurs a shorter or longer period of reduced function. (See Nestler [1992]; Nestler, Hope, and Widnell [1993]; Gardner and David, this volume.)

The consequences depend on the function of these neuronal systems. In the motivational circuits are, the consequence of suboptimal functioning is anhedonia and feelings of hopelessness. Nothing seems attractive. Abusers who quit describe long and miserable days. Animals whose nucleus accumbens is destroyed lose the motivation for many forms of behavior, including drug consumption. Suboptimal functioning of the second system implies tremors, muscle pains, anxiety feelings, and other unpleasant symptoms. If the locus coeruleus is destroyed, as has been done in rats, many of these withdrawal symptoms disappear.

In the nucleus accumbens, suboptimal functioning leads to the loss of positive reinforcement, whereas in the locus coeruleus it leads to aversion in the form of painful symptoms. Not all substances act on both systems. Although withdrawal symptoms are often understood in terms of the pain and unpleasantness caused by cessation, anhedonia and motivational problems are at least equally important. Development of tolerance involves not only the need for larger amounts to achieve the same pleasurable effect but also the need for continued consumption to avoid discomfort and dysphoria; in fact, up to a certain point, ever-larger amounts are needed to keep the withdrawal symptoms at bay. The basic mechanism is that of neuronal hypofunctioning following hyperfunctioning. During hyperfunctioning, the drug experience is sought because it creates a pleasurable and elated state. Later, the sober condition is increasingly characterized by dysphoria and other forms of withdrawal symptoms caused by hypofunctioning. The increased use of the drug almost invariably has negative effects on the user's health and finances, thus trapping him or her into a low level of welfare.

## 3. Drug Use as Rational Behavior

In the legalization debate, many writers have noted the fact that withdrawal symptoms are rarely strong enough to enslave us. It is sometimes said, for instance, that withdrawal from heroin is no worse than a bad flu. From this it is inferred that the use must be left to the choice of the individual.

Many of us know from experience that this view is an inadequate simplification. Anyone who has tried to stop smoking or drinking knows that the main problem is not to make the decision to quit. Nor is the greatest obstacle that we find ourselves overwhelmed by withdrawal symptoms. Rather, it is a matter of maintaining morale and motivation in the period of anhedonia that follows upon discontinuation of use. The earlier consumption has created a situation in which we experience not only withdrawal symptoms but also periods of dysphoria in which life does not seem to provide any pleasures. At the same time, we are constantly exposed to events that activate the longing for use. "Just one time can't be so bad." While life is experienced as boring and devoid of meaning, a solution is always available in the form of relapse.

These facts are relevant for our understanding of the user's choice and choice situation. Simply stated, rational choice means to choose among the available alternatives so that the sum total of positive and negative effects is as large as possible. Rationality in this sense requires not simply myopic adaptation to the current situation but the ability to take account of longer-term consequences. As Elster (1979, 1983) has shown in his analyses of rationality, human reason is far from perfect. Temptations and lack of judgment induce all sorts of myopic and stupid behavior. We weigh utility in a myopic manner, so that long-term benefits are overshadowed by short-term gains. As with the fox and the sour grapes, we often adjust our preferences to what seems feasible. "Our minds play all sorts of tricks on us, and we on them" (Elster 1983, p. 111).

It therefore may be rational to limit our options. Our ability to assess and compare the total effects of the available alternatives is so unreliable that restrictions on freedom may be needed. Sometimes, it makes sense to limit our freedom of choice and precommit ourselves to one alternative, as did Ulysses when he bound himself to the mast as he was approaching the island of the Sirens (Elster 1979).

Drug abuse seems to provide good examples of this predicament. Most people do not have sufficient knowledge of the long-term consequences of intake of drug molecules. Their behavior is characterized by a limited form of rationality, which is then made even more vulnerable by hypofunction in the motivational circuits with a concomitant impact on the ability to make choices. The effect is a loss of ability to deal with the future in a constructive and strategic manner. Although in a limited sense the individual is behaving rationally (i.e., choosing among alternatives in terms of their perceived consequences), this perception itself is truncated and distorted. Because of the problems this myopic perspective creates for society and for the individual, society is justified in preventing the individual from responding to the Siren-like appeal of the drugs. Admittedly, this is not a form of individual self-binding, as with Ulysses. Rather, the restriction is a form of collective self-binding, which should be subject to the normal rules of the democratic process, including respect for individual rights. I return to the latter issue in the section on alternatives to warfare.

### Drugs as Commodities

Gary Becker has pioneered the economic approach to addiction, assuming that the potential addict is acting rationally for the purpose of maximizing total (discounted) utility (Becker and Murphy 1988; Becker 1992; Skog, this volume). In his theory, addictive substances are a special type of commodity whose use can be explained by two specific features. On the one hand, earlier consumption has an impact on the utility of present consumption: The more you have consumed in the past, the lower the utility of consumption in the present (tolerance). On the other hand, the marginal utility of present consumption is very high because it tends to relieve withdrawal symptoms (which include the low utility derived from other goods in a dysphoric state). Even a small amount of the substance can relieve or reduce these symptoms. Becker shows that if these conditions are satisfied, consumption will tend to escalate. From the point of view of the addict, the addictive behavior is rational, even if the goal increasingly becomes that of avoiding discomfort. The quality of life is measured in the absence of negative consequences rather than in the presence of positive ones. From the point of view of the outside observer, the total (not discounted) sum of utility is reduced, but this is not a relevant consideration for a myopic user.

The Beckerian consumer has problems reaching a stable low level of drug consumption. With other commodities, this is achieved because of the decreasing marginal utility of consumption. After the purchase of new clothes, additional clothes will provide less utility than other commodities with regard to which the consumer is less satiated. Drug commodities differ, in that they offer both decreasing overall utility and increasing marginal utility. As a consequence, we observe an uncontrolled escalation of use. In an early stage, many consumers feel that they can limit their use but, with increasing neuroadaptation, a strong craving combined with discomfort causes them to lose control. It is only the appearance of strong negative effects that enables them to establish a new (high-level) equilibrium in which no further escalation takes place. Whereas the consumption of ordinary commodities is limited by satiation and lack of desire, drug consumption is limited by increasing problems and costs of use.

The implication of Becker's theory is that one cannot expect the addict to limit his or her consumption before the high-level equilibrium is reached. To reduce the consumption of addictive substances, society must take measures both to reduce the number of individuals who start using drugs and to counteract and reduce established use. To achieve these ends, one can increase the costs of addiction, by acting on prices and more generally making drugs more costly to obtain, and by imposing sanctions that increase the negative consequences of consumption.

### Ambivalence and Hyperbolic Discounting

Anyone who has worked with drug abusers will feel that Becker's perspective is useful but insufficient. One of the most striking features of dependence is a strong and painful feeling of ambivalence. One cannot characterize the abuser simply by saying that he or she chooses short-term gratification. An addict who at one moment is totally convinced that the drug use is destructive and reduces his or her total welfare may at the next moment plan very skilfully for the next consumption episode. Not infrequently, the explanation may be found in intervening external events or in a form of self-deception, but the phenomenon cannot be fully understood without appealing to a systematic tendency toward preference reversal.

Becker assumes, with most economists, that future utility is discounted in an exponential manner. As explained in the Introduction to the present volume (see notably Figure 6 and accompanying text), this view cannot account for preference reversals. An alternative view is offered by George Ainslie (1992) (see again the Introduction, notably Figure 7 and accompanying text). He argues that future utility is discounted in a hyperbolic fashion, allowing for preference reversal as the time of choice approaches. The theory, in other words, is able to explain ambivalence, not only with regard to addiction but also with regard to procrastination and other phenomena that exhibit a combination of small, early rewards and larger delayed rewards. There is a period of hours or days in which the addictive substance is preferred. This mechanism generates the characteristic cycles of addiction, in which the addict yields to a temptation and goes on a binge, until remorse and regret set in.

The biological features of addictive substances, surveyed at the beginning of this section, can be integrated with Ainslie's perspective. Ahead of time, the potential user who is aware of all the negative consequences of addiction will judge the discounted utility of abstinence to be greater than the discounted value of consumption. As the occasion for use approaches, however, the thoughts on possible benefits of use will activate the appetite, as shown by increased activity in the nucleus accumbens. Ainslie's perspective admittedly focuses on the discounting process on future utilities. But changes in discounting must have their cerebral correlates. It is more than feasible to hypothesize that, if an occasion of drug use approaches, memories of drug pleasures and the associations connected to them lead to activity in the reward centers (as can in fact be demonstrated by brain imaging). This would color both judgment (which depends on complex functions in the prefrontal areas) and emotions (which are affected by the limbic system). The result would be a change in appreciation of the drugs, which will come to appear as more attractive and important, and a relative increase in discounting of alternative utilities. The net result would be a more myopic drug consumer.

Like Becker's model, Ainslie's has clear implications for drug policy. If the goal is to reduce consumption and to increase the individual's capacity to take account of long-term consequences, the time interval between the appearance of an urge to consume and the occasion to get hold of the drug becomes very important. The longer the interval, the better the chances of abstention. This interval can be extended by a number of different measures. By shortening the opening hours of liquor stores, for instance, one may enable the individual to exercise self-control. A problem drinker who usually drinks in the evening, may no longer want to drink when the store opens up again in the morning. By reducing the number of retail outlets, one may increase the time needed for the average user to get access to the drug. To make a drug illegal is to determine that it is not to be bought in the shop nearby. Hence it will for most of the population also be more time-consuming to procure.

## 4. Drug Abuse as a Social Phenomenon

Because individual choices are strongly shaped by social factors, we need to understand the social interactions in which drug abuse is embedded. For this purpose, it is useful to distinguish among experimental use, habitual use, and uncontrolled use. Who become users? Who are at risk?

From prospective, longitudinal studies (e.g., Pedersen [1991]), we know quite a lot about those who experiment with drugs and the factors that affect their behavior. The findings are simple and compelling: Availability and social norms are the most important factors. The main determinants of an adolescent's use of cannabis (or alcohol or nicotine) are the number of peers who are users and the opinions of peers toward use. Parental attitudes are also very important: The more liberal their attitudes toward alcohol consumption or cigarette smoking, the more likely that their children will use these drugs – and to a significant extent also that they will use illegal drugs.

If we examine who become habitual users, and notably who become problem users, other factors also have to be considered. In the simple and self-confident perspective of the 1960s, the dominant opinion was that abuse was a symptom of social deprivation and individual problems. There is some evidence to support this view. Animal experiments show that rats deprived of maternal care consume more drugs or brave more obstacles to get them than rats that are reared normally. Rats that live in poorly equipped cages with few opportunities for play and movement develop especially destructive habits (McKim 1991, p. 77). Many studies show that, in populations of drug abusers in treatment, many had problems as children and when growing up. We also find more signs of poor mental health and higher frequency of social problems. Epidemiological studies invariably show that drug abuse is more frequent and has more destructive consequences in inner-city slums and in groups that are victims of social discrimination.

Yet asserting that abuse is a symptom is a simplification. A preference for drugs arises in animals independently of environment and earlier experiences and, even if many patients have a difficult background, this is far from true of all. Health personnel have the highest prevalence of addiction to prescription drugs. High alcohol consumption is correlated with the upper middle class (in the United States also with the Caucasian race), a high income, liberal attitudes, and professions such as bartender (see, e.g., Brun-Gulbrandsen [1988], Goodwin [1992]). There is even evidence that high income and liberal attitudes on alcohol in the parental generation are correlated with early initiation of drinking and with higher levels of alcohol use in the offspring (Pedersen 1991). Such findings point to the importance of the availability.

### Drug Availability

Much work has been done on the effects of availability. (Because most of it deals with alcohol consumption, this will also be the focus of the following discussion.) One has shown how sales volumes change following the outbreak of war, strikes by personnel in retail outlets, boycotts, or changes in the number of retail outlets. One has also examined the effect on consumption of price changes, taxation, and prohibition.

Well-substantiated conclusions were drawn as early as two decades ago (Bruun et al. 1975). Under the auspices of the World Health Organization, Griffith Edwards recently gathered a group of experts to summarize what is now known about alcohol policy (Edwards et al. 1994). The conclusion is clear: Changes in availability are followed by changes in consumption. As predicted by Becker's model, increases in price and other costs to the consumer reduce consumption. As predicted by Ainslie's model (but not by Becker's), measures that increase the time needed to get hold of the drug also have an impact.

The dependent variable in these studies is not simply, as often assumed, only alcohol consumption as measured by sales statistics or questionnaires. Studies have also been done on the impact on cirrhosis of the liver, alcohol-induced psychosis, and alcohol-related violence, and these have been found to be even more sensitive to changes in availability. In periods of prohibition and other significant reductions in availability, it is precisely these indicators that fall significantly, more than the bare consumption figures. Even small reductions in availability that do not significantly affect the ordinary consumer can reduce problem drinking as measured by the amount of public drunkenness or violence (Edwards et al. 1994, p. 137). There is therefore more than enough evidence to conclude that availability – both the physical presence of drugs and the social norms that make their use acceptable – has an independent and important significance. At the same time, availability has a disproportionate negative impact on those who already are in trouble. What may appear to be unproblematic and a natural right for the better-off can easily become a fate and a burden for others.

### Total Consumption and the Paradox of Prevention

Total consumption is the sum of all consumption by a population. Because changes in availability have a greater impact on problem consumption than on normal consumption, one might expect problem consumption to vary with normal consumption in a systematic manner. In a study of the effect of wine harvests and prices, Ledermann (cited by Edwards et al. 1994, pp. 83–84) found not only that total consumption increased with good harvests, but that the incidence of cirrhosis of the liver increased even more. Specifically, he found that, when total consumption doubled, the incidence of cirrhosis increased by a factor of three to four. To fight cirrhosis of the liver, the most effective policy is to reduce total consumption.

Conversely, of course, changes in an independent variable that has a relatively small effect on normal consumption can have a big impact on problem consumption. This is related to what has been called *the paradox of prevention*, a mechanism that is also known from prevention of tuberculosis and vascular disease: Apparently, small measures that target many individuals can have a larger impact than strong measures targeted on the individuals at especially high risk. Many drug-related incidents, involving accidents and violence, are caused by episodic and moderate use by normal consumers. A policy aiming to reduce alcohol-related problems should therefore target the use by the majority, those not considering themselves to have drinking difficulties (Kreitman 1986).

## Drinking Patterns as a Social Phenomenon

"Ledermann's law" has been criticized for being too mechanical. Also, later studies do not give exactly the same result. Use of more sophisticated time-series methodology nevertheless confirms the general proposition that alcohol-related problems increase faster than total consumption (Edwards et al. 1994, Ch. 4). One factor that has a modifying influence on this connection is the presence of different use patterns in "wet" and "dry" cultures. Where alcohol is a normal and accepted part of everyday life, as in the Mediterranean countries, people drink not only more, but in different patterns.

Skog (1985) has analyzed Ledermann's law using two testable hypotheses. First, drinking patterns are the result of a number of factors that interact in a multiplicative fashion. Second, the individual alcohol consumer is affected by the drinking habits in his or her social network. These hypotheses were incorporated in a stochastic mathematical model and tested against data for total consumption and individual variations in a large number of countries. In this way he showed that Ledermann's law can be generated as the result of stochastic interaction among individuals in a multiplicity of drinking situations. Alcohol consumption is a social and collective phenomenon.

These findings have two important implications. First, they underline the reciprocal influence of alcohol consumers on each other. The individual not only influences his or her own family but also the drinking patterns of neighbors, colleagues, and friends. These influences create ripples throughout society that add up to aggregate patterns of consumption. At the same time, the individual is influenced by the surroundings. When people drink to celebrate, to relax, to console themselves, or simply to pass the time, drinking becomes embedded in innumerable social contexts. To drink becomes an important part of being with others. Not to drink becomes a deviation, which requires strength and courage. This is a significant fact for the problem drinker who is trying to abstain. The problem consumer falls victim to the habits of the ordinary consumer.

The second implication is that although consumption might increase rapidly in periods of general social unrest or cultural change, such as the

1960s, established patterns of use will tend to change slowly. The chain reactions described above take time to work themselves out before a new equilibrium is established. One cannot, therefore, evaluate the effect of policy changes on the basis of observations over a short period. By waiting until the new equilibrium has been established, however, one incurs the risk that the consequences, if undesirable, might be irreversible. If a reform turns out to cause greater acceptance for and higher use of a drug, it may be difficult to reverse the situation by restrictions and prohibitions. The irreversibility might be due to the addictive nature of the drug or to the social dynamics described by Moene (this volume).

### *"Wet" Cultures of Other Drugs?*

Many of these conclusions from alcohol research can be generalized to other addictive substances. One can talk about "wet" cultures with regard to other substances as well as alcohol. In particular, much is known about the use patterns of American veterans when they returned from Vietnam. In Vietnam, cannabis and heroin were extremely accessible, the attitudes of the soldiers were extremely tolerant, and there was need for self-medication and escape from a depressive reality. As a result, many veterans came back from the war as addicted users. The majority nevertheless stopped using hard drugs such as heroin, in spite of the fact that the drug is easily available in most parts of the United States (Robins, Davis, and Goodwin 1974, Robins 1993). The explanation is that in the United States heroin is not a part of everyday life and its use is largely incompatible with ordinary social existence. Schelling (1992) emphasizes similar factors behind the reduction in nicotine consumption in the United States. As the result of complex social processes smoking has become stigmatized in an increasing number of settings.

There are strong reasons to believe that drug use in general is a collective phenomenon and that the lessons from alcohol policy research are relevant for policy with regard to other drugs. It is important to keep total consumption down. Even moderate liberalizing measures can cause serious damage and be difficult to reverse.

### 5. Drug Use and Individual Rights

The attitude toward drugs is not only a function of beliefs about the consequences of drug use. Islamic countries ban alcohol on religious grounds that are quite independent of the harmful effects of consumption. Some religious groups such as the Amish or the Seventh-Day Adventists believe that the body is a temple of God and that it is a sin against creation to use any kind of psychoactive drug. In contrast, some cultures prescribe the use of drugs, notably hallucinogens, in their rites. (The amount of wine involved in Christian rituals is too small to have any intoxicating effect.) In the 1960s and 1970s, the somewhat pathetic figure of Timothy Leary was central among the believers in "consciousness-expanding" drugs as the path to wisdom and happiness.

These attitudes are mainly relevant for those who adhere to these religions and beliefs. Because they mainly interact among themselves, the chain reactions described in the preceding sections do not occur. It is generally relevant, however, to observe the importance of values and attitudes. The Amish and Seventh-Day Adventists show a remarkable ability to avoid social traps and to maintain their mental health even when the environment is highly permeated by drug use.

## Drugs, Morality, and Individual Rights

In the modern liberal state the individual's right to self-determination is a core value. There must exist compelling reasons before society can interfere with the free choice of the individual. Some advocates of legalization do in fact base their argument on the basis of the right of the individual to use any drug he or she might want to use. An instance is the Italian Radical Party (Partito Radicale, now Partito Federalista Europeo), which has seen the fight against the moralizing and oppression of the Catholic Church as its particular mission and which deserves a major part of the credit for the legality of divorce and use of contraceptives in Italy. This party is now a strong and vocal advocate of legalization, arguing that prohibition is an outmoded and repressive form of moralizing.

The Radical Party has a strong support in the European Union Parliament and from various more or less influential groups.[2] An often-cited decision by a German state court found it unconstitutional to permit alcohol while punishing the use and possession of cannabis.[3] Academics from different disciplines have also argued for legalization. In the following, I shall discuss the views of the American philosopher Douglas N. Husak (1992), who has offered a sustained analysis of this issue, with clear and strong conclusions. According to Husak, prohibition is indefensible not only because its negative consequences are greater than the positive ones, but even more importantly, because the individual has a moral right to choose to consume psychoactive substances that can be used recreationally. This right can be set aside only by appeal to even stronger moral arguments. Although Husak does not recommend drug use, he defends the right to use drugs on the same basis as he would argue that "Adults have the moral right to preach communism or practice Buddhism" (Husak 1992, p. 252). The first argument is consequentialist and utilitarian. Its validity is ultimately an empirical issue. The second argument, on which I shall focus here, is nonconsequentialist.

## Drug Use as a Moral Category

According to Husak (1992, p. 210), utilitarianism is "an adequate theory to govern that sphere of behavior unprotected by moral rights." Recreational drug use, by contrast, is protected by a moral right. His definition of this concept is as follows: "By 'recreational use' I mean consumption that is intended to promote pleasure, happiness, or euphoria of the user" (p. 44). Furthermore, "only a near catastrophe or a conflict with other rights [...] override the moral right to use drugs recreationally" (p. 212).

Husak draws a distinction between preferences and rights. The former are less important and can be regulated if necessary. Although I may like ice cream, as Husak writes, I have no moral right to it. The state is free to impose restrictions on the sale of ice cream for health-related and other reasons. Nobody has a moral right to violate speed limitations when driving, although some may derive pleasure and even euphoria from doing so. These are activities that can be regulated by society.

The question is obviously why drugs would have a different status. Husak argues that they often produce happiness and pleasure and that their negative sides tend to be exaggerated. Whereas the use in itself is morally neutral, the intention behind the use – to increase pleasure or happiness – turns it into a right. Paradigmatic examples are use for the purpose of heightening pleasure (e.g., party drugs) and use to make trivial and monotonous chores more endurable (e.g., housewives using Dexedrine). As long as nobody is hurt by the use, it is unambiguously positive.

It is hard to see why these features of drugs should give them a special status compared to goods and activities that many of us would see as far more important. Strangely enough, Husak is not alone in thinking that the right to use drugs ought to be written into the law (see, e.g., Hamaide [1993]). The most natural explanation of such views must be that they are based on empathy with the user's situation. When a person has become habituated to the drug, abstention will be difficult and painful. In that case, the special status of drugs is linked to their negative properties, related to the biological mechanisms we surveyed, and not to their positive properties.

From a moral point of view, however, there is more at stake than just the dependency-inducing effect. As I have argued, drugs play directly into the motivational circuits and can produce strong and positively valued experiences that are entirely dissociated from effort, skills, and behavior. This short-circuiting of the biological system may very well be considered morally dubious and socially undesirable. Not infrequently, the use of drugs leads to an increase in the drug-searching behavior, at the expense of other activities. Because the drugs for a short while also tend to dampen both justified and unjustified dissatisfaction, they will often reduce the motivation to "change the things that can be changed." The claim that drug use is morally dubious rests not only on consequentialist considerations, but it can also be supported by arguments similar to those invoked by Kant to argue that suicide is wrong, that is, if everybody behaved in this way the world would be a very bad place.

## The Imperialistic Action of Drugs

The defense of the right of access to drugs of abuse rests on three assumptions, all of them unrealistic. The first is that the individual user can be considered in isolation from the effect on others. However, as we have seen, drug use is very much a collective phenomenon.

The second assumption is that it is possible to distinguish between those drugs with negative consequences and those without. Husak emphasizes that it is possible to use drugs in a fully controlled way, without any negative effects. Research is increasingly showing, however, that the distinction between harmful and harmless use is untenable. The consensus today is that the less use, the better.[4] With regard to the choice of drugs, the consensus is that the weaker the drug, the smaller the problems. Control is affected by the user's environment and social network; in addition, it can change with life circumstances and crises. Very few have a constant use pattern over time. The so-called recreational user is not a different kind of person from the abuser. They have the same motivation for use – to achieve intoxication or to reduce discomfort.

The third assumption is that each individual consumption episode can be considered in isolation from others. One of the differences between addictive substances and other goods, however, is that each episode increases the frequency of later episodes. Over time, the drug comes to take an increased importance in the life of the user. As a young doctor influenced by the language of the 1960s, I used to refer to "the imperialistic action of drugs." Drugs of abuse represent a problem precisely because they become too important for many users. Addicts show, in action if not always in words, that the drugs have become a priority compared to other goods and needs. When choosing among alternative rewards, they often behave in a destructive fashion. Faced with boredom or problems, they choose to drug themselves rather than trying to change the situation. Husak's Dexedrine-using housewife would be better off developing pride in her work or talking to her husband about sharing the burdens. Instead, she may have to resort to increasing doses of Dexedrine. After a while, the use may even impede her housework.

In conclusion, harmless use is an illusion created by artificial isolation of a single consumption episode in an individual that is neither influenced by nor exerts an influence on others. In reality, each episode has an indefinite influence on future situations. Each user contributes to the overall use pattern in society. In particular, the vulnerable user is influenced by the consumption habits of the better-off.

### Autonomy and Social Regulation

Discussions of the autonomy of the individual in a liberal society are often traced back to John Stuart Mill (Husak 1992, Trebilcock 1993). In *On Liberty*, Mill argued that only harm to the life and property of others could justify interventions that reduced the right of the free and well-informed individual to make his or her own autonomous choice. Responsibility for any negative consequences of the choice belongs to the individual, not to society. The only exceptions, Mill thought, were choices that undermine the autonomy itself. For instance, one does not have the right to sell oneself into slavery.

The choice to use addictive drugs is arguably analogous to selling oneself into slavery – an act that may be kept outside the scope of autonomous choice precisely because it undermines autonomy. Husak (1992, pp. 117–30) argues that the loss of autonomy caused by drug use is not total and that not everybody will become dependent on the drug. However, the same might also be said about slavery: Some masters are kind, and some people may be able to maintain their inner fortitude even as slaves. If we nevertheless ban slave contracts, it is because of the great potential for loss of autonomy that is created. An analogous argument applies to drugs.

Two other arguments are more important, however (Trebilcock 1993). In complex modern societies, the notion of free individual choice is an artificial one. An individual has no right to choose without taking account of the externalities involved. Society has the right to impose the use of motorcycle helmets, because head injuries cause grief and suffering among relatives and because they involve costly treatment and care. Similarly, use of addictive drugs has many externalities. Smoking may harm others both through passive smoking and by making it more difficult for others to stop. In the words of Trebilcock (1993, p. 75), "at least in the context of externalities, rights-based theories of individual autonomy and utilitarian or welfare-based theories of the public good are not nearly as sharply divergent as many of their respective proponents claim."

The (often tacit) assumption of full information is also problematic in this context. For the choice to be autonomous, the choosing person must possess the necessary information and be competent to assess it. The choice must not be the result of coercion, weakness, manipulation, or of a temporarily confused state of mind (Trebilcock 1993, p. 148). As I showed in the section on the neurobiological effects of drug use, the individual who experiments with drugs rarely has such information. It is very hard to predict the extent of future dependence. Moreover, many start using drugs in a period of life when they are in fact under the confusing influence of temporary factors (adolescence, restlessness, illness, social problems, etc.). At the same time, the choices themselves can lead to lasting changes in the perception of one's welfare, as pointed out also by Becker (1992, p. 329): "A habit may be raised into an addiction by exposure to the habit itself. Certain habits, like drug use and heavy drinking, may reduce the attention to future consequences."

## 6. Drug Policy and Its Instruments

Given this background of neurobiology, rational choice, and individual rights, what can be said about a rational drug policy? The policy must obviously take account of the collective nature of drug use. It should aim at low levels of total consumption and promote restrictive norms and attitudes in the population. According to Becker (1992), one should aim at increasing the costs of use, thereby decreasing the marginal utility of consumption. According to Ainslie (1992), the obvious aim is to focus on another aspect of availability, by increasing the time interval between purchase and consumption. Even small time margins can make a difference. By contrast, a drug policy that makes drugs more available and their use more acceptable is highly undesirable.

As can be seen, the body of evidence supports a restrictive drug policy of reduced availability and norms against use. But any policy needs instruments and, as I shall demonstrate, an examination of effectiveness and costs casts serious doubts on the present warlike policy (even though legalization does not seem to provide an acceptable alternative).

### Variations in What Is Regulated by the Law

There are large differences among countries with regard to the practices that are regulated by the law and the sanctions that are seen as acceptable. Behavior that in one society is seen as a crucial right for the individual may in another be subject, quite uncontroversially, to control and regulation.[5] There are also large variations in the attitude of the citizens to the state apparatus itself. Laws are more frequently violated when the state is seen as remote and oppressive. For this reason, members of groups that are subject to discrimination or are vulnerable in other ways, tend to violate the law more frequently. In addition, much depends on social attitudes toward the behavior that is to be regulated. If one tries to regulate behavior that is widely seen as acceptable, and especially if it is part of everyday life of friends and relatives, violations will be frequent.

These factors are clearly relevant for drug policy. In the United States, the drug legislation stipulates severe penalties and is implemented by considerable use of police resources. At the same time, illegal drug use is widespread in inner-city populations, notably among Blacks and Hispanics.

The outcome is massive imprisonment, which does not, however, seem to have much impact on the drug problem.[6] When whole societies are demoralized such that the state apparatus loses its legitimacy, there will be an impact on law enforcement, including the implementation of drug policy.[7] If social conditions are sufficiently bad, it is pointless and inhumane to counteract abuse with prohibition and draconian sentencing. Once many have become habituated to a substance, prohibition will create a disproportionate amount of criminality, as observed during the prohibition of alcohol in the period after the First World War. A ban on tobacco, therefore, is unrealistic. These lessons cannot be transferred, however, to substances that are not widely used. They do not, for instance, justify demands for the abolition of the ban on alcohol in Islamic countries. Nor can we generalize the experiences from societies in which there is widespread alienation from the state apparatus and from law enforcement agencies.

### Criminal Law as a Regulator of Behavior

For many, punishment is mainly a moral issue. The wrongdoer deserves to be punished. If public opinion singles out drug use as one of the worst social evils, there will be a demand for heavy punishment of drug-related crimes, quite independently of what the public believes about the effect of punishment. Drug policies must be built on better foundations.

What do we know about the behavioral effects of the criminal law? It is usual to distinguish between general and specific deterrence. The first operates through the effect of the law on attitudes, social norms, and on the propensity of the individual to obey the law. The effect can be indirect, through social control and internalization of norms, or direct, through fear of stigma and punishment. The second involves the effect of punishment on the person who has been punished. The question is whether punishment reduces the likelihood of new infractions.

Although research on general deterrence has not yielded many clear findings, some conclusions do emerge (Andenæs 1975, 1994; Gibbs 1986; MacCoun 1993). Even a writer such as MacCoun (1993), who criticizes deterrence theory for employing an economistic model of rationality that is needlessly cynical in its view of human nature, believes that the criminal law has a regulating effect on behavior. Although behavior may be more strongly influenced by informal interactions and social norms than by cost-benefit calculations, the law can also shape the former in several ways. In the first place, legislation has a general impact on the development of society. In the second place, there is empirical support for the view that active use of legislation can strengthen attitudes and norms in a given society. Bonnie (1986) reaches a similar conclusion. Andenæs (1994, p. 51) summarizes the situation by saying that "The question is not whether the criminal law system has a general deterrent effect, but in which areas and under what circumstances this effect obtains."

There seems to be widespread agreement that the deterrent effect does not work universally. Gibbs (1986) observes, for instance, that use of the death penalty has little or no impact on homicide frequencies. More generally, it is hard to find any correlation between length and severity of punishment on the one hand and the level of criminal behavior on the other. This conclusion holds whether we use perceived or actual levels of punishment as the independent variable. Andenæs (1994) and MacCoun (1993) are somewhat less categorical, but the general view seems to be that what matters is the risk of discovery and especially the perceived risk. Gibbs (1986) emphasizes that our doubts concerning the effect of punishment mainly concern the impact of the severity of the penalty. Criminalization in itself, the fact that an action is prohibited, does matter, especially if the action is highly visible. Along these lines Bonnie (1986) claims that the law may be used paternalistically to reduce the frequency of health-damaging or troublesome behaviors. Generally speaking, research seems to support the general deterrence effect of legislation, although some of the effects arise indirectly rather than directly.

With regard to recidivism, the most plausible conclusion is a different one. Those who abstain from new criminal acts are mainly those who would have done so in any case. Those who violate the law frequently are hardly affected or not at all. If there is an effect, it may be offset by stigmatization and difficulties in social adjustment after sentencing. Most of the research shows therefore that punishment fails to reduce the likelihood of future lawbreaking. This is especially true if the punishment is seen as unfair or oppressive, in which case it can actually increase the likelihood of recidivism. It is true, of course, that crimes are prevented from taking place during the period of imprisonment.[8] But as a solution to the overall crime problem, imprisonment is not only inhumane and costly but also ineffective.

As mentioned, there is a connection between risk of detection and future lawbreaking. If the risk is large enough, especially the perceived risk, the frequency of lawbreaking goes down. The problem, however, is that for many types of crime the risk of detection is very small. Also, psychological research shows that the impact of aversive stimuli are stronger the sooner they follow upon behavior. We may conclude that punishment may work, but only if there is a high risk of detection and a swiftness of reaction and these are usually hard to realize in practice.

### Deterrence and Drug Abuse

MacCoun (1993) offers an extensive survey of what is known about the effect of legislation on drug use. The findings are largely in agreement with what is known about the impact on other forms of criminal behavior. The frequency of illegal drug use is affected by the risk of discovery, but not by the severity of punishment. Again, actual risk is less important than perceived risk. The risk is most accurately perceived by those who have some experience with the system (i.e., by those who have broken the law in the past). Habitual users and members of their circles know that the risk is small. Although they exercise some caution, they are not much affected, even when sentencing is severe. Whereas the nonusing part of the population has an exaggerated perception of the risk and is therefore less likely to become users, this effect obtains even when sentencing is mild.

This is an important message. One of the most characteristic features of drug legislation is the high level of sentencing. This is notably true of the United States and many countries in Northern Europe. In Norway, for instance, the law – and the courts – place drug dealing on a par with treason, homicide, and serious sexual offenses. Research tells us that this solution is ineffective. There will always be a steady stream of new dealers to replace those who are incarcerated.

MacCoun (1993) is less convincing when discussing whether it is at all possible to affect drug use by legislation. He argues, as noted, that deterrence assumes that the potential lawbreaker behaves rationally. For the drug user, MacCoun states, this assumption is satisfied only in the initial stages. When dependence sets in, the user's behavior is increasingly shaped by unconscious, automatic, and conditioned reactions. Whereas the user may be reached by legislation in the early, experimental stages, the full-blown addict is affected only by the social and health-related consequences of use.

I believe this is a simplification, for two reasons. First, as we saw, drug use is usually a collective phenomenon, in the sense that total consumption affects problem consumption. Second, I believe that MacCoun's concept of addiction is too simple. As shown by Becker (1992) and Ainslie (1992) from two different perspectives and as amply demonstrated by alcohol research, increased costs (including the costs arising from the abuse) and reduced availability can have a significant impact on the addicted user. Even addicts can behave rationally within their myopic perspective.

## 7. The Alternatives to Warfare

In Norway, as in many other countries, the use of criminalization to fight drugs was exposed to criticism early on (see, e.g., Christie and Bruun [1968]). The main argument was that there are many forms of dependence for the different types of drugs. When cannabis is criminalized, many otherwise law-abiding young individuals will be stigmatized and brought into contact with criminal groups and hard drugs. Half-truths about the dangers of drug use will undermine the credibility of all information about drugs. Once prohibition has been introduced, decriminalization will be difficult and costly.

Later, heavier ammunition was brought out. According to Christie and Bruun (1991), addictive drugs have become "the good enemy" that all can fight with a good conscience and at low risk. The victims in the war on drugs are the poor and disadvantaged. The real problems in society and in the world are swept under the carpet, while the costs of control continue to escalate. Ever more resources are diverted to build more prisons and hire more police officers, while personal security and privacy are being undermined by new investigative techniques. Yet, the whole effort seems to be in vain. The war will have only losers, no winner. (For discussions of these views, see also Albrecht [1993], Cotts [1994], Derks and Kalmthout [1993], Goldstein [1994], Husak [1992], Inciardi and McBride [1991], Jarvik [1990], Kleiman [1992], Nadelman [1991], Nadelman and Wenner [1994], Reuter [1993], Schmoke [1994], Taradash [1993], Vasseur [1993], Wisotsky [1991].) In the following subsections, I will examine the most important arguments.

### The War on Drugs – Is It Lost?

In one sense, the war effort – the buildup of narcotics squads, frontier controls, heavy sentencing – seems to be in vain. The proof is that drugs remain available (Husak 1992, Nadelman 1991, Nadelman and Wenner 1994, Schmoke 1994). But if we forget the rhetoric of war and look at some everyday facts, the picture has many more nuances. In the affluent warring countries, consumption has stagnated, especially in the middle and upper classes. The increase takes place in the producer countries and in the countries along the transportation routes. The total number of illegal drug users is much lower than that of users of legal drugs. In no country with reliable statistics is the number of regular users of any illegal drug as high as one third as the number of regular users of alcohol (Reuter 1993). The war is certainly not won, but it is not lost either.

### Prohibition – Does It Work?

The United States, Norway, and Finland introduced prohibition of alcohol in the 1920s. It is often assumed that the reason why prohibition was lifted was that it had no impact on alcohol consumption and alcohol-related problems. In fact, both assumptions are false. Public health data for the United States show a marked decline of both alcohol consumption and alcohol-related damages during Prohibition (Goldstein 1994, pp. 257–61; Kleiman 1992, pp. 245–6). Kleiman (1992, p. 102) concluded that "the ban on selling alcohol actually reduced the volume of alcohol consumption is not open to serious debate."

The reasons why prohibition was abolished lie elsewhere. Public opinion turned against prohibition because of smuggling and the related criminal activities. At the same time, the population underwent a change from puritanical to more hedonistic attitudes. There were also some opportunistic reasons at work, as shown by the debates in the Norwegian parliament. Many deputies abandoned prohibition because of pressure from Spain, which threatened to boycott Norwegian fish unless Norway resumed its wine purchases from Spain. For many puritanical deputies from the Norwegian periphery, the fear of economic loss ultimately weighed heavier than the ideology of prohibition.

### Are Legal Drugs More Dangerous Than Illegal Drugs?

We often read that a restrictive drug policy is misguided because the wrong drugs are targeted. The reason given is that legal substances create far greater health problems. Whereas the annual victims of illegal drugs are counted in hundreds, the victims of cigarette smoking are counted in thousands or tens of thousands. Although heroin does create problems, alcohol is far more important in its destructive impact on families, child abuse, violence, traffic accidents, reduced work effort, and so forth. Let us remember, however, that alcohol and nicotine research shows that these effects of problem consumption are closely related to total consumption. Moreover, a high total consumption of a substance presupposes that it is legally available. Hence the serious problems created by alcohol and nicotine are in fact an argument against legalizing more drugs.

### Does Prohibition Make Drugs Less Available?

The weighted sum of alcohol research is that bans and restrictions reduce availability and consumption (Bruun et al. 1975, Edwards et al. 1994, Kleiman 1992). Another and not unexpected finding is that small and insignificant restrictions lead to, at most, insignificant changes in consumption.

Research on illegal drugs are, for natural reasons, far more scarce and the evidence is often ambiguous. When the use of marijuana was decriminalized in ten American states in the early 1970s, only one state (Alaska) saw an increased prevalence. In the other nine states, the trend was about the same as in the rest of the United States. It is worth noting that the decriminalization did not extend to sale. What happened in most of the nine states was only that possession of small amounts was downgraded from a crime to a misdemeanor and punished with fines. Only Alaska introduced a full decriminalization of possession and storage for personal use. Here, the increase in consumption continued until these provisions were abolished.

The Alaska findings can be interpreted in two ways. In the period in question there was a general reaction against all drugs, and not least against marijuana, all over the United States, except in Alaska where such trends reportedly arrive with some delay. It is possible, therefore, that any tendency for decriminalization to increase drug use was simply swamped by cultural factors working in the opposite direction. One could also argue, however, that the Alaskan experience shows that the *extent* of liberalization makes a difference. One could also argue that the downgrading of use to a misdemeanor is an acceptable reform from a drug-use prevention perspective.

The Netherlands provides another well-known example. Although cannabis has not been legalized in that country, nobody is prosecuted for use. There is also a sort of official double standard with acceptance and regulation of sale in so-called coffee shops. The policy states that a sharp distinction should be drawn between soft and hard drugs. Sale of heroin and cocaine will be prosecuted, albeit with lower sentences than in many other countries.

The Dutch case has been used to both show that a liberal drug policy reduces consumption and to show the opposite: that this policy would lead to a sharp increase in problems. Many believe, for example, that there is a difference between The Netherlands and Germany that can be explained by the different drug policies. In his comparison of the two countries, however, Reuband (1993) found a striking similarity between consumption in the liberal Netherlands and in its more restrictive neighbor. The conclusion seems to be that consumption patterns are similar because both countries are subject to the same cultural trends.

Reuband (1995) concludes in an analysis of European prevalence findings that this seems to be a general finding. He points out that the European pattern is one of high prevalence of addiction to heroin in the southern and Mediterranean countries while the northern and middle parts exihibit low prevalence. The prevalence of cannabis use varies following other lines, but neither follows the pattern of restrictive or liberal drug policies. Reuband concludes that "Within all probability, informal social control and sociocultural attitudes are more important than formal controls and drug availability (as determined by drug policy)." If that is so, the importance of drug policy is foremost in its influence on attitudes in the population and on the informal sides of the control.

One tendency should be noted. There are several examples showing that, when a pattern has taken hold in an area or a segment of the population, this may be difficult to change. For a long time, there were significant differences in consumption habits between residents of the American East and West Coasts, with heroin in a more dominant position in the East and a more mixed pattern in the West, where heavy use of central stimulants and hallucinogens was seen. In Sweden, abuse of amphetamines emerged in the 1950s because of large supplies left over from the war. This pattern still dominates in the Gothenburg area. In Malmö the preferred drug is heroin because of the proximity to Copenhagen, where heroin use is prevalent. These cases underline what I said earlier about irreversibility. If possible, it is more important to prevent the development of abuse because, once established, use is hard to influence.

Even if the research results are scanty, a tentative conclusion might be drawn. It is highly probable that the use of illegal drugs would follow the same patterns as those of legal drugs. This would mean that relatively minor reforms would have minor impacts. A gradual and partial decriminalization of cannabis will probably not have a major impact on consumption. Methadone programs and even heroin dispensing through controlled and medically oriented treatment systems would not increase the number of addicts. The effect of full legalization, allowing commercial marketing and sale, might be much more dramatic. Also, periods characterized by cultural unrest have a great potential for development of increased use, and the countries in the formerly heavily controlled Eastern Europe might experience a problematic rise of consumption. But I repeat: Whatever the cause of the increase, it may be hard to reverse.

## What Does the Most Damage – Drugs or Drug Control?

Ten years ago, Christie and Bruun (1991) introduced the idea of "control-related damages" into the Norwegian debate. It remains central in current discussions (Husak 1992, Karel 1991, Nadelman 1991, Reuter 1993). The claim is that more harm is caused by control and prohibition of drugs than by their use. If the prohibited drugs are legalized, the user may enjoy safe sterilized equipment and drugs of controlled strength and purity. The criminality that is linked to the illegal market for drugs would disappear. The number of prisoners would go down and civil rights would be better protected. With the disappearance of the enormous sums of money circulating in the illegal economy, we would no longer risk corruption of police officers, customs officials, and judges in consuming and producing countries.

These arguments have varying strength. It is clear enough that the crime rate would go down if no one could be arrested for use of drugs. It is also probable that legalization of sale would reduce illegal sales and smuggling, but not necessarily if other restrictions limit distribution. The experience from Norway and Sweden, where wine and liquor are sold by state monopolies and heavily taxed, shows that illegal sale and crime may remain at relatively high levels. High prices and a small number of retail outlets will re-create the illegal market. Age limits induce illegal sales to minors. In Norway the illegal markets made possible by high taxation and retail monopoly also go together with a significant amount of violence, as can be seen from the police statistics. (These conclusions also apply, albeit if to a lower extent, to cigarette sales and cigarette smuggling.)

The conclusion is that, to reduce the incentives for illegal sale and other criminal behaviors, legalization is insufficient. One must also ensure lower prices and easy access. Drugs will have to be sold over the counter in ordinary stores at prices that reflect costs of production. Although this would undermine the illegal distribution, the consequences of an increase in availability of this magnitude, although hard to predict, are likely to be dramatic.

Advocates of legalization sometimes hold out the prospect of significant revenue from taxing legal sale of drugs. Taxation would limit consumption, and the revenue could be used for drug prevention. This reasoning is dubious. If taxes are high, significant illegal sales will still take place. If taxes are low and prices are correspondingly low, substantial tax revenues would require a very large volume of sales and, of course, a large total consumption.

Schmoke (1994) of Baltimore and other mayors in large American cities have argued that legalization is necessary to reduce the problem in inner-city slums. So far, however, no study has been able to isolate the violence caused by drug crimes from the violence caused by the environment itself. Poor inner-city areas with alienated and destructive inhabitants exist all over the world. In demoralized societies and societies with high degrees of racial discrimination, destructive subcultures emerge even if there is no ban on drugs. For young men in the inner-city slum with few opportunities for legal employment, legalization will not eliminate the search for illegal incomes. Nor will it do away with their need for excitement and an outlet for aggression. In sum, crime will continue even though a reduction would be likely since the crime rate of addicts is higher when they are using.

Some also object to the traditional view of the drug user as colored by stigmatization and criminalization. There are in fact well-known examples of users who have been able to consume heroin on a controlled basis and remain socially well adjusted (Zinberg and Jacobsen 1976). William S. Halstead, the father of modern surgery, combined lifelong use of morphine with an impressive professional career (McKim 1991). The overall picture is nevertheless one of social problems and individual misery, as we can see in the difficult life of alcoholics everywhere or in the opium abuses that made nineteenth-century Chinese emperors fight the British opium trade. Any discussion of greater availability of opiates and central stimulants has to account for the fact that controlled use of freely available and strongly addictive substances requires considerable personal strength and a benign environment. The reason why there are not more heavy users must be found in external pressures such as limited availability, social norms, and risk of prosecution. It is often reported that among cocaine users, only 10 to 20 percent go on to become addicts. It is overwhelmingly likely that, had it not been for the illegality of use and distribution and the negative social reactions, this proportion would have been much higher.

### The Problems of the Producer Countries

An important aspect of legalization concerns the possible ripple effects in the drug-producing countries. As is well known, these are mainly poor countries, where prohibition has led to large-scale corruption, illegal economic activities, and drug-related crimes. Many of them have been subject to strong pressures from the United States and other consuming countries. It has been asserted that legalization of drugs in the latter countries would transform the illegal economy into a legal and orderly one, thereby eliminating many of the social problems created by the drug economy.

A detailed analysis of these issues is beyond the scope of the present article, but a few remarks are in order. It is probably true that the prohibition policy has caused considerable damage in many of the producer countries, but it is far from clear how much of the violence, oppression, crime, and poverty can be ascribed to the drug policies or how much would be solved by legalization. We know for certain that production costs in these low-cost countries are so small that confiscation and criminalization do not cut much into profits. The income potential in the high-cost consuming countries is too great. It is virtually inconceivable that policing and customs efforts can have significant effects (Kleiman 1992). However, assuming that legalization has positive effects is also not well founded.

Two matters are important here. The first is that any legalization that could have an effect on the problems of the producer countries would have to establish legal channels for drug trade that are able to compete with the illegal ones. This means organized sales and marketing, with increased consumption as a result. International capital would be sure to enter, perhaps also demands for free trade.[9] The other is that the problems of these countries are to a large extent linked to international trade. Most of them are losers in the international competition and are subject to severe economic restrictions, during a time when the prices of their traditional products such as coffee or rice have fallen. A former president of Peru is reported to have said that "In South America, the drug trade is the only profitable line of business." The solution to these problems must be sought elsewhere than in drug legalization.

### Harm Reduction

As an alternative to the "war on drugs," many have proposed "harm reduction." This goal need not of course imply legalization because most of the measures of harm reduction are fully acceptable in generally restrictive countries. In the city of Oslo, for instance, with a population of

Table 1. *The drug problem in some European countries: Prevalence of addiction and incidence of drug deaths*[a]

| Country | Addicts per thousand inhabitants[b] | Drug deaths per million ihabitants[c] |
|---|---|---|
| Portugal[d] | 4.5 | 28.0 |
| Spain | 3.0 | 20.3 |
| United Kingdom[d] | 3.0 | 5.8 |
| Italy[d] | 2.6 | 22.2 |
| France | 2.5 | 6.9 |
| Luxembourg | 2.0 | 44.0 |
| Denmark | 2.0 | 37.6 |
| Sweden[e] | 1.7 | 12.5 |
| Belgium | 1.7 | 9.1 |
| Greece | 1.5 | ? |
| Germany | 1.3 | 26.6 |
| Netherlands | 1.5 | 5.8 |
| Norway | 1.1 | 22.0 |
| Ireland | 0.6 | 4.2 |

[a]The European Monitoring Centre for Drugs and Drug Addictions (EMCDDA), located in Lisbon, is presently working to improve epidemiological data on drug use and drug use problems in Europe.
[b]In most countries the number of addicts covers primarily or only heroin addicts. The figures are often rough estimates.
[c]The term "drug deaths" is used differently in different statistics. The methods of data gathering, also, vary in reliability.
[d]Prevalence is based on a mean between a high and a low estimate of number of addicts.
[e]The Swedish figures on addicts cover all types of serious abuse, where illegal substances dominate.
*Source:* EU data are mainly from Knaack (1993). Norwegian and Swedish data are from a report on the drug situation to the Nordic Council of Ministries (Olsson 1993).

500,000 and approximately 3,000 drug addicts, about 1,000,000 disposable needles are handed out each year; yet Norway is generally regarded as a restrictive country. It might also very well be argued that legalization would result in an increase in consumption that might increase and not reduce harmful consequences.

Many have tried to compare the extent of abuse and the incidence of harm in various countries with different drug policies (Reuter, Falco, and Maccoun 1993). A survey is offered in Table 1. The picture is confusing. Liberal Great Britain has a high prevalence, whereas the even more liberal Netherlands has low prevalence. Very restrictive Norway has an especially low prevalence but not very much lower than The Netherlands and Germany, which have very different drug policies. Restrictive Sweden has a lower prevalence than neighboring liberal Denmark but the difference is not very marked (even though it should be remembered that the Swedish figures include abusers not considered addicts in most statistics). Relatively restrictive France seems to have a low prevalence compared to Italy and Spain with their liberal policies. But it might be said that a factor of public sentiment opposing governmental regulations in the two latter countries is more important than the differences in policies. Figures for the United States complicate the picture even more. Jonas (1991) gives a figure of one million U.S. heroin addicts, a prevalence of 3.9/1,000 population. The number of cocaine addicts is about double the number of those addicted to heroin and this skyrockets the U.S. problem. However, the United States has had a drug problem for a more extensive period than many European countries.

These data should be interpreted with considerable caution because only a few of the countries have reliable bases for their estimates. It might nevertheless be noted that we find a low prevalence in the more restrictive countries in Northern Europe, whereas the drug-liberal Mediterranean countries with their alcohol-accepting culture seem to have especially high prevalence. But even they cannot compete with the home country of the "war on drugs." It is difficult to see that differing policies in neighboring countries result in different drug use patterns in any systematic direction. Comparing the situation in several European countries, Reuband (1995) reaches a similar conclusion. The cultural factors determining attitudes and the societal factors influencing behavior seem to be more important than drug policy.

The mortality data should be interpreted even more cautiously as there are widely differing practices and principles in counting drug deaths. From Table 1, it might be seen that restrictive Norway has a relatively high mortality in spite of its low prevalence of drug addiction while the incidence in liberal Great Britain and Netherlands is very low. It might appear as if those who become users in a restrictive environment are especially at risk but, then again, Denmark, Spain, and Portugal (and Switzerland, which is not included in the table) are liberal countries with as high or higher mortality figures. The variations therefore may be due to cultural and geographical factors rather than to drug policy to the extent that statistical artifacts are not the root cause. Reuter (1993), who has headed a large comparative project financed by the Rand Corporation, finds it difficult to draw any firm conclusions.

It is often argued that legalization is necessary to fight the AIDS epidemic. This argument is not supported by the figures. Extensive anonymous testing in prohibitive Oslo and Stockholm has secured a user population with unusually high levels of HIV testing. The findings are an unusually low incidence of seroconversion. The proportion of seropositives in the user population is markedly higher in liberal countries such as Denmark and Spain. But again, some liberal countries such as The Netherlands and Great Britain also have low rates of seroconversion. The reason for the confusion is simple: The important harm-reducing strategies are anonymous testing, information, and access to clean needles and to treatment. These measures can be used independently of the choice of a restrictive or a liberal policy.

### Some Evidence in Favor of Restrictions

Evidence of benefits of restrictions stem mostly from the field of alcohol research. Prohibition decreases total consumption and health costs, whereas less comprehensive restrictions have smaller effects. Marginal restrictions have insignificant or no effect. However, the restrictions also have their costs, and the choice of policy should seek to balance the costs and benefits. There is some evidence that restrictions on harmful use of alcohol might have similar benefits. Up until the mid-1970s, the Norwegian vagrancy law had the effect that many alcoholics regularly stopped drinking because repeated public drunkenness could cause incarceration for significant periods. After the law was abolished, the mortality in this group went up (Amundsen and Hauge 1978).

Some studies indicate similar effects of restrictive drug policies (see, e.g., Winick [1964] and Vaillant [1970]). The costs of abuse, such as prison experiences and compulsory detoxification, influence the behavior of the addicts. The tendency for one to mature out of abuse seems to be affected by the costs of illegal drugs, as Becker's model would lead us to expect. Until the late 1960s, Californian legislation required compulsory treatment of addicts if they had committed crimes or had other dependency-related problems. If they relapsed within a seven-year period, the compulsory treatment could be extended, whereas successful treatment and abstention allowed a reduction of this period. Time-series studies based on these experiences show that this system increased the proportion of addicts that stayed in treatment and continued to abstain. Compulsory treatment reaches a larger number of users and is at least as effective as voluntary treatment (Anglin, Brecht, and Bonett 1986, Anglin and Hser 1991, Powers et al. 1991). Finally, Norwegian and Swedish experiences with the so-called Hassela collectives favor restrictions. Follow-up studies of compulsory treatment of adolescent drug addicts according to the child care law seem to demonstrate high retention rates and impressive treatment results (see, e.g., Berglund et al. [1991]).

### 8. Neither Peace nor War

There are no simple answers in the debate on drug policy. The central question is not to decide whether we should opt for legalization but to identify the policy and measures that will reduce total harm as much as possible. This is a harm-reduction perspective, but without a one-sided focus on the harms caused by restrictive policies.

The costs of the war on drugs are unacceptably high, and many of the policies have very little effect. Meanwhile, many exaggerate the advantages of liberalization and ignore how liberal attitudes and increased availability lead to higher consumption. Although some of the negative side effects of prohibition can be reduced by liberalization, this gain may be offset by concomitant increases in consumption. A policy of full legalization that also includes unrestricted sales, is hard to defend.

It seems useful to shift from the language of war to a more nuanced policy that weighs the costs of various restrictions against their benefits. Different policies may be appropriate for different drugs. One cannot proceed as if all drugs are as bad as the worst drugs. The goal must be to find the optimal balance between the negative and positive effects of policy, measured perhaps by using what Kleiman (1992) calls a "grudging tolerance." This involves a continuous fight to reduce distribution and consumption with a variety of means.

Giving up the war metaphor and weighing the goal of reduced drug consumption against other values is actually not principally different from existing U.S. practice. Fighting drugs has never been at the top of the hierarchy of goals. During the Vietnam War the United States supported opium cultivation by minority groups whom they wanted to enlist on their side. "Air America" shipped opium as well as military equipment. Many of the South Vietnamese generals were deeply involved in heroin production and smuggling. The American authorities kept a closed eye.

The problem is not so much that these priorities and trade-offs were morally unacceptable (although I believe they were), as that they were hidden from the public. A rational drug policy must be based on an open acknowledgment that not all good things go together. This would enable us to focus attention on the increased number of prison inmates brought there by draconian legislation and on the alienation of many citizens from the society they live in. In many countries, notably the United States, these questions do not, however, seem to capture the attention of the majority. On the contrary, the demand is for more severe sentencing and for sending more people to prison. Often it might appear that reactions against restrictive policies appear mainly when the customs control interferes with the ordinary traveler or when the ordinary citizen feels his or her civil rights invaded by police procedures.[10]

Perhaps what is mostly needed is *a new metaphor for drug policy,* a metaphor that can generate commitment and motivation and allow both for consideration of the side effects of policy measures and for alternative values. The increased use of psychoactive, dependence-inducing substances is a kind of pollution of the psychosocial environment that must be fought in the same way as pollution of the physical environment. This analogy also helps us to see the goal in a more realistic perspective. The ideal of a totally unpolluted physical environment is chimerical. Achieving it would involve unacceptably high costs. Similarly, we have to accept the idea that a drug-free environment is chimerical within the time horizon that current drug policies can address. In both cases, the only adequate approach is to adopt a variety of long-term strategies to reduce and contain the severest problems.

## NOTES

1. Some substances (heroin and cocaine) create dependence in all animal species. Others (cannabis) will only become attractive to some species. Some substances (alcohol, nicotine) are initially unattractive, and the animals have to be tricked into using them for some time before they begin to prefer them.

2. Thus in 1993, the Association of European Democratic Lawyers, with members from many countries, adopted a resolution demanding the legal right to drug use and the ending of repression. The resolution

> conclut à la necessité de réglementer le droit à la consommation des substances actuellement illicies, plutôt que de poursuivre et d'accentuer sans cesse la répression et l'exclusion d'une population de plus en plus marginalisée, ce qui constitue un facteur d'insécurité publique. (L'Association d'Avocats Européens Démocrates, Brussels Feb. 10, 1993, cited after Hamaide 1993).

3. The appellate court of Lübeck found that an accused could not be punished for possession of cannabis as long as alcohol is legal (Dok no. 713 Js 16817–90. St ad Lübeck-2 Ns (Kl.1067–90).) After the prosecutor appealed, the Constitutional Court decided that use of cannabis is against the law but not punishable (*Achtenzeichen* 2 BVL no. 43, 1992). The decision leaves room for local decisions with regard to the quantities that can be ignored as uninteresting because destined for personal use. The acceptable quantities vary considerably across the German states (Pappendorf 1992).

4. Alcohol is to some extent an exception, in that it has been shown that moderate intake is correlated with lower risk of heart disease (Edwards et al. 1994). The beneficial effect is linked to a very low regular consumption and pertains mainly in conjunction with a healthy lifestyle. The marginal effect compared to other factors is small and applies in any case almost solely to individuals who are at high risk for heart disease. A general recommendation in favor of moderate consumption would, therefore, do more harm than good (Edwards et al. 1994, pp. 51–3).

5. In the United States, many see the possession of handguns as an inalienable right, despite the extreme costs in terms of murders and accidents. In Germany, a similar attitude exists with regard to the absence of speed limitations on the motorways. In many other countries, however, both spheres are regulated as a matter of course.

6. The United States today, with a prison population of one and a half million, has a greater percentage of its population in prison than any other modern society. A strikingly high proportion consists of Black and Hispanic youths. One of three American Blacks between 15 and 30 years is in prison or on probation. The tendency is toward harsher sentencing and heavier use of prison. A considerable proportion of the sentences concern drug-related crimes.

7. An example is the massive increase in criminality in almost all of the former Soviet Union. There are many hardships, poverty is on the increase, and respect for the state is on the decline. Under the these circumstances, criminal behavior, including drug dealing, may appear to be the best option. If, in addition, conditions of civil war create a need to finance weapons purchases, organized crime will flourish. This development has had a major impact on the market for illegal drugs in Western Europe.

8. This is the reason why, in the United States, imprisonment is being favored as the solution. The Criminal Reform Act of 1994 includes provisions both about minimal-level punishment and about life sentences without reduction in the case of repeated law violations: "Three strikes and you're out" rule. For many crimes, minimal punishment is very high. Life sentences are not infrequently meted out for minor crimes. On top of this, the death penalty is being reintroduced in more and more states. The American legal system seemingly is becoming a draconian one.

9. In Norway, Sweden, and Finland, the state monopolies for sales of wines and spirits have been judged to violate the EU and EEA regulations of free trade. So far, the countries have had to give up the import and wholesale monopolies, and it is not clear whether the retail monopolies will survive. The argument that the state monopolies are instruments in public health policies is not found to be legally sustainable.

10. The plenary session of the 1993 "European Seminar on Strategies and Policies to Combat Drugs," in Florence, was chaired by Mathilde van den Brink, a well-known member of the European Parliament. In her introductory speech, she complained about restrictive policies, notably that the control of ingredients for "designer drugs" might include the acetone she uses to remove her nail varnish and thus render her suspect of running an illegal laboratory.

## REFERENCES

Abood, M. E. and B. R. Martin (1992), "Neurobiology of marijuana abuse," *Trends in Psychopharmacological Science* 13, 201–204.

Ainslie, G. (1992), *Picoeconomics, The Strategic Interaction of Successive Motivational States Within the Person*, New York, Cambridge University Press.

Albrecht, H.-J. (1993), "Drug policies and national plans to combat drug trafficking and drug abuse," European University Institute Doc. IUE 415/93, Florence.

Amundsen, A. and R. Hauge (1978), "Dödeligheten blant löslatte fra Opstad (Mortality among those released from Opstad)," *Tidsskrift om Edruskapss- prrsmD1* 2(18), 6–7.

Andenæs, J. (1975), "General prevention revisited," *Journal of Criminal Law and Criminology* 66, 338–65.

(1994), *Straff som Problem*, Oslo, Exil forlag.

Anglin, M. D., M. L. Brecht, and D. G. Bonett (1986), "An empirical study of maturing out: Conditioning factors," *International Journal of Addictions* 21(2), 233–46.

Anglin, M. D. and Y.-I. Hser (1991), "Criminal justice and the drug-abusing offender: Policy issues of coerced treatment," *Behavioral Science and the Law*, 9, 243–67.

Becker, G. (1992), "Habits, Addictions and Traditions," *Kyklos* 45, 327–46.

Becker, G. S. and K. M. Murphy (1988), "Theory of rational addiction," *Journal of Political Economy* 96, 675–700.

Berglund, G. W., A. Bergmar, B. Björling, L. Grönblad, S. Lindberg, L. Oscarsson, B. Olsson, V. Segraeus, and C. Stensmo (1991), "The Swedate project: Interaction between treatment, client background and outcome in a one-year follow-up," *Journal of Substance Abuse Treatment* 8, 161–9.

Bloom, F. E. (1993), "Brain research for today and tomorrow: Recent advances and research frontiers," in C. R. Hartel (ed.), *Biomedical Approaches to Illicit Drug Demand Reduction*, Washington DC, National Institute for Drug Abuse, pp. 9–26.

Bonnie, R. J. (1986), "The efficacy of law as a paternalistic instrument," in Gary B. Melton (ed.), *The Law as a Behavioural Instrument*, Lincoln and London, University of Nebraska Press, pp. 131–212.

Brun-Gulbrandsen, S. (1988), "Drinking habits in Norway," in O.-J. Skog, and R. Waahlberg (eds.), *Alcohol and Drugs: The Norwegian Experience*, Oslo, National Directorate for the Prevention of Alcohol and Drug Problems, pp. 13–28.

Bruun, K. et al. (1975), *Alcohol Control Policies in Public Health Perspective*, Helsinki, Finnish Foundation for Alcohol Studies.

Christie, N. and K. Bruun (1968), The Conceptual Framework. Report to the 28th International Congress on Alcohol and Alcoholism, Sept. 15–20, Washington DC, 1968, Helsinki.

(1991), *Der nützliche Feind. Die Drogenpolitik und ihre Nutzniesser*, Bielfeldt, AJZ Druck and Verlag GmbH.

Cotts, C. (1994), "Smart money," *Rolling Stone*, May 5, 42–3.

Crabbe, J. C. and J. K. Belknap (1992), "Genetic approaches to drug dependence," *Trends in Psychopharmacological Science*.

Derks, J. and A. V. Kalmthout (1993), "Components of national drug policies and the need for comparative evaluative research," Doc. IUE 383/93, Florence, European University Institute.

Edwards, G. et al. (1994), *Alcohol Policy and the Public Good*, Oxford, UK, Oxford Medical Publishers and World Health Organization.

Elster, J. (1979), *Ulysses and the Sirens. Studies in Rationality and Irrationality*, New York, Cambridge University Press.

(1983), *Sour Grapes. Studies in the Subversion of Rationality*, New York, Cambridge University Press.

Friedman, D. P. (1993), "Introduction to the brain: A primer on stuctures and function of the brain's reward circuitry," in Christine R. Hartel (ed.),

*Biomedical Approaches to Illicit Drug Demand Reduction*, Washington, DC, National Institute for Drug Abuse, pp. 53–63.

Gibbs, J. P. (1986), "Deterrence theory and research," in Gary B. Melton, (ed.), *The Law as a Behavioural Instrument*, Lincoln and London, University of Nebraska Press, pp. 87–130.

Goldstein, A. (1994), *Addiction. From Biology to Drug Policy*, New York, W.H. Freeman and Co.

Goodwin, D. W. (1992), "Alcohol: Clinical aspects," in J. H. Lowinson, Å. Ruiz, R. B. Millman, and J. G. Langrod, *Substance Abuse. A Comprehensive Textbook*, 2d ed., Baltimore, Williams and Wilkins, pp. 144–51.

Hamaide, J. (1993), "La répression des drogues illicites en Europe occidentale: Aspects des pratiques judiciaires," Doc. IUE 385/93, Florence, European University Institute.

Husak, D. N. (1992), *Drugs and Rights*, New York, Cambridge University Press.

Inciardi, J. A. and D. C. McBride (1991), "The case against legalisation," in J. A. Inciardi (ed.), *The Drug Legalisation Debate*, Newbury Park, CA, Sage, pp. 45–79.

Jarvik, M. E. (1990), "The drug dilemma: Manipulating the demand," *Science* 250, 387–92.

Jonas, S. (1991), "The U.S. drug problem and the U.S. drug culture: A public health solution," in James A. Inciardi (ed.), *The Drug Legalisation Debate*, Newbury Park, NJ, Sage, pp. 161–82.

Karel, R. B. (1991), "A model legalisation proposal," in J. A. Inciardi (ed.), *The Drug Legalisation Debate*, Newbury Park, CA, Sage, pp. 80–102.

Kleiman, M. A. R. (1992), *Against Excess. Drug Policies for Results*, New York, Basic Books.

Knaack, F. (1993), "The common core of national strategies and legislation, nucleus of a future European strategy," Doc. IUE 402/93, Florence, European University Institute.

Koob, G. F. (1992), "Drugs of abuse: Anatomy, pharmacology and function of reward pathways," *Trends in Psychopharmacological Science*.

Kreitman, N. (1986), "Alcohol dependence and the preventive paradox," *British Journal of Addiction* 81, 365–79.

MacCoun, R. J. (1993), "Drugs and the law: A psychological analysis of drug prohibition," *Psychological Bulletin* 113, 497–512.

McKim, W. (1991), *Drugs and Behaviour*, Englewood Cliffs, NJ, Prentice-Hall.

Nadelman, E. A. (1991), "The case for legalisation," in James A. Inciardi (ed.), *The Drug Legalisation Debate*, Newbury Park, CA, Sage, pp. 17–44.

Nadelman, E. A. and J. S. Wenner (1994), "Toward a sane national drug policy," *Rolling Stone*, May 5, 24–6.

Nestler, E. J. (1992), "Molecular mechanisms of drug addiction," *Journal of Neuroscience* 12, 2439–2450.

Nestler, E. J., B. T. Hope, and K. L. Widnell (1993), "Drug addiction: A model for the molecular basis of neural plasticity," *Neuron* 11, 995–1006.

Olsson, B. (1993), "Use and misuse of narcotic drugs in the Nordic countries 1987–1991 (summary)," in B. Olsson (ed.), *Narkotikasituationen i Norden – utvecklingen 1987–1991 (Drug Use Situation in the Nordic Countries 1987–1991)*, Köbenhavn, Nordiska Ministeriet, pp. 41–49.

Pappendorf, K. (1992), "Den tyske narkotikadebatten (The German drug policy debate)," *Nordisk Tidsskrift for Kriminalvitenskap* 2, 194–9.

Pedersen, W. (1991), *Drugs in Adolescent Worlds. A Longitudinal Study of Adolescent Drug Use Socialisation*, Thesis, Oslo, Department of Psychiatry, University of Oslo.

Powers, K., D. M. Hanssens, Y.-I. Hser, and M. D. Anglin (1991), "Measuring the long-term effects of public policy: The case of narcotics use and property crime," *Management Science* 37, 627–44.

Reuband, K.-H. (1993), *Drogenkonsum und Drogenpolitik. Deutschland und die Niederlande im Vergleich*, Opladen, Germany, Leske and Budrich.

   (1995), "Drug use and drug policy in western Europe. Epidemiological findings in a comparative perspective," *European Addiction Research* 1, 32–41.

Reuter, P. (1993), "The legalisation debate: A brief survey," Doc. IUE 381/93, Florence, European University Institute.

Reuter, P., M. Falco, and R. Maccoun (1993), *Comparing Western European and North American Drug Policies*, Santa Monica, CA, Rand Corporation.

Robins, L. N. (1993), "Vietnam veterans' rapid recovery from heroin addiction: A fluke or normal expectation?" *Addiction* 88, 1041–54.

Robins, L., D. H. Davis, and D. W. Goodwin (1974), "Drug use by United States army enlisted men in Vietnam: A follow-up on their return home," *American Journal of Epidemiology* 99, 235–49.

Samson, H. H. and R. A. Harris (1992), "Neurobiology of alcohol abuse," *Trends in Psychopharmacological Science*, 13, 206–211.

Schelling, T. C. (1992), "Addictive drugs: The cigarette experience," *Science*, 255, 430–3.

Schmoke, K. (1994), "Side effects," *Rolling Stone*, May 5, 38–9.

Skog, O.-J. (1985), "The collectivity of drinking cultures: A theory of the distribution of alcohol concumption," *British Journal of Addictions* 80, 83–99.

Taradash, M. (1993), "Draft report on the legalisation of prohibited drugs," Doc EN\PR\228\228511, European Parliament. Committee on Civil Liberties and Internal Affairs.

Trebilcock, M. J. (1993), *The Limits of Freedom of Contract*, Cambridge, MA, Harvard University Press.

Vaillant, G. E. (1970), "The natural history of narcotic drug addiction," *Seminars in Psychiatry* 2, 486–498.

Vasseur, P. (1993), "Bottom up or top down?" Doc. IUE 392/93, Florence, European University Institute.

Winick, C. (1964), "The lifestyle of the narcotic addict and of addiction," *Bulletin on Narcotics* 16, 1–11.

Wisotsky, S. (1991), "Beyond the war on drugs," in James A. Inciardi (ed.), *The Drug Legalisation Debate*, Newbury Park, CA, Sage, pp. 103–29.

Woolverton, W. L. and K. M. Johnson (1992), "Neurobiology of cocaine abuse," *Trends in Psychopharmacological Science* 13, 193–200.

Zinberg, N. J. (1984), *Drug, Set and Setting*, New Haven, CT, Yale University Press.

Zinberg, N. E. and R. C. Jacobsen (1976), *American Journal of Psychiatry* 133(1), 37–40.

# Rationality, Irrationality, and Addiction – Notes on Becker and Murphy's Theory of Addiction

OLE-JØRGEN SKOG

It may seem as if addicts do not act according to their preferences. They often claim that they would like to stop doing whatever they are addicted to, but nevertheless they continue doing it. Because the minimum criterion for rationality requires that one acts according to ones preferences, this seems to imply that addicts are not rational. This question will be the main theme in this chapter. In particular, I shall introduce and critically discuss Becker and Murphy's theory of rational addiction.

I will start by giving a brief sketch of my understanding of the term "addiction" and a rough outline of Becker and Murphy's approach based on rational-choice theory (Section 1). Because the details of Becker's theory are not easily available, I try to explain the basic idea with the aid of a simplified model (Section 2) before I introduce the general model (Section 3). Section 4 provides a discussion of the nature of the phenomena captured by Becker and Murphy's model. Do they genuinely belong to the same family, or do they just superficially resemble each other – as bats and birds, sharks and whales? In Section 5, I discuss the realism of Becker and Murphy's assumptions, and in Section 6, some predictions from the theory are evaluated.

## 1. Rationality and Addiction

The hallmark of addiction is that the addicted person finds it very difficult to abstain from performing a certain sort of act. Typically, the experience of difficulty would be sensitive to the context. Under certain circumstances (say, when the addict has already performed the act and is satiated, or when the act would have intolerable consequences), abstaining would not be a problem for him. Other contexts may cause only moderate stress, whereas in still other contexts the addict may experience an irresistible urge.

The addict may or may not wish to get rid of his habit. If he wishes to quit, but feels that he cannot, or that it is extremely difficult for him, he is a dissonant addict (cf. Orford [1985]). If a person does *not* wish to quit under the prevailing circumstances, he would still be considered addicted if he found it very difficult to quit under circumstances that generated a wish to quit. This person is called a consonant addict.

Addiction is not harmful in itself. However, the behavior the person is addicted to could have direct effects (psychosis, liver damage, etc.) or indirect consequences (accidents, reduced social functioning, etc.) that are considered harmful. I am a consonant coffee addict. My addiction is not a problem as long as I can get my coffee at a reasonable price, as long as no fatal diseases are known to result from my behavior, and as long as the state does not prosecute or punish coffee users. However, the most important addictions in modern society are tied with considerable damage. Obviously, damage of one sort or another is the most important reason why the addict may wish to stop. In this chapter, I shall mainly be concerned with harmful drug addictions. The examples will largely refer to alcohol addiction because the research evidence is best for this drug. However, most of the arguments should apply to other drugs as well.

Explaining why and how rational people can become knowingly trapped in a consumption pattern is obviously not very difficult. One only has to realize that there is no one-to-one correspondence between frequency and intensity of consumption on the one hand and addiction on the other. In fact, the correlation may be only moderately strong for some substances. Thus, several heavy consumers may not be addicted, whereas several addicts may in fact consume considerably less than heavily consuming nonaddicts. For this reason, people can rationally believe that they are not at serious risk of becoming addicted, although they consume heavily. And they may consume heavily simply because life feels better that way (e.g., symptomatic consumption, without the subject necessarily realizing that he is onto a dangerous self-medication) and/or because they become socialized in a high-consumption subculture (e.g., Jellinek's [1960] delta-type alcoholism[1]).

Nor is it difficult to understand that a rational person can prefer to continue his self-destructive lifestyle after he has realized that he has become addicted, provided that he considers this to be the better alternative, all things considered. Hence, the existence of consonant addiction (the "happy addict," or the "less unhappy addict") poses no threat to rational-choice theory.

The more difficult task is to explain how and why rational actors, once they realize that their current lifestyle is actually suboptimal (i.e., not the best, all things considered), still continue to act the same way. Can a rational actor really be a dissonant addict? It follows from Becker and Murphy's theory that he can (Becker and Murphy 1988, Becker 1992).

Becker and Murphy's theory is formulated in the language of neoclassical economic utility calculus. Because the deduction of consequences is rather technical, the theory is not easily available to readers outside economics (and perhaps not even to many economists). In Section 2,

I shall present a much simplified version of the model, which may perhaps make the basic assumptions and the essential prediction more lucid. However, I will first briefly summarize the framing of the problem and the overall structure of the argument.

Becker and Murphy (1988) restrict their analysis to the simplest case, where the consumer knows everything there is to know about the consequences of different consumption careers. It is assumed that

- The instantaneous well-being (or utility) the consumer will experience from a certain consumption level now will depend on his past as well as his present consumption behavior.
- The rational consumer takes all present and future consequences of present consumption behavior into consideration. The extent to which he or she attributes weight to future consequences is measured by a separate parameter in the model, called the discount factor.
- The rational consumer chooses the consumption career that maximizes his or her overall well-being, as measured by the total sum of present and discounted future welfare levels.

These assumptions constitute the frame of reference for the rational consumer. Becker and Murphy now consider a consumption good with the following properties:

**(P1)** The more the consumer has consumed in the past, the less instantaneous welfare (pleasure) he obtains from a given present consumption level. Becker, Grossman, and Murphy (1992, p. 362) equate this to tolerance, but another possible cause could be delayed harmful effects, which reduce overall well-being later on.

**(P2)** The increase in instantaneous well-being that one obtains by increasing present consumption with one unit is larger, the more one has consumed in the past. This mechanism is related to reinforcement, which means that greater past consumption increases the desire for present consumption (Becker et al. 1992, p. 362). Other possible causal mechanisms underlying this property could be relief from withdrawal symptoms or suppression of the recognition that life has become a misery due to past consumption.

Becker and Murphy (1988) demonstrate that a rational consumer of a good with these properties could find himself in a high-consumption steady state with a lower overall welfare than a low-consumption steady state would have given him. In particular, the impatient consumer, who gives little weight to long-term consequences, is at risk of ending up in this position. The high consumption level would give a lower welfare because the long-term negative effects exceed the higher instantaneous pleasure from higher present consumption. He would not be able to leave the inferior steady state, however, because this would require more patience than he actually has: To reduce the long-term negative effects, he would have to accept a temporary setback in terms of instantaneous well-being but, since he discounts the prospects of future rewards very heavily, it does not match up with the instantaneous decline in well-being. All this will perhaps be clearer in the simplified model of Section 2.

A difficulty with Becker and Murphy's model is the fact that, strictly speaking, their rational consumer with perfect foresight will never end up at this high consumption level. Starting at consumption-level zero, their consumer will move toward a low-consumption steady state, which is not a state of addiction. Becker and Murphy suggest that this problem can be handled by assuming that the rational consumer's life may be disturbed by some unforeseen events (a life crisis), bringing him to a high consumption level. Life then becomes normalized again and he finds himself trapped at the high level. An alternative to this crisis mechanism could be to assume that the rational consumer takes a calculated risk. Initially, he may not know whether he is "vulnerable" to addiction or not, and he therefore acts according to an "expected utility" criterion. Orphanides and Zervos (1995) have developed such a model, while retaining the essential elements of Becker and Murphy's model.

## 2. A Simplified Version of Becker and Murphy's Model

Consider a situation where there are only two possible consumption alternatives during each time interval, say, consumption or abstention (or light consumption or heavy consumption). Furthermore, let us assume that the utility of present consumption behavior depends on what the consumer did during the preceding interval, in addition to his present choice. We assume that consumption gives greater instantaneous well-being than abstention if the person abstained during the preceding interval, and that the same applies if he consumed during that interval. Hence, whatever his consumption history, the consumer has an instantaneous incentive for consuming now.

Next, we shall assume that there is a delayed "punishment" for consuming, for instance due to long-term negative effects, or to tolerance. Hence, if the person consumed during the preceding interval, his well-being becomes smaller than if he had abstained during the preceding interval, whatever he chooses to do now. This is equivalent to Becker and Murphy's property $P_1$.

Moreover, we shall assume that the reduction in welfare due to past consumption is larger if the person chooses to abstain now than if he chooses to consume now. Hence, by consuming again, he may to some extent counteract the negative effect of past consumption on present welfare. Another way of putting this is to say that the choice between

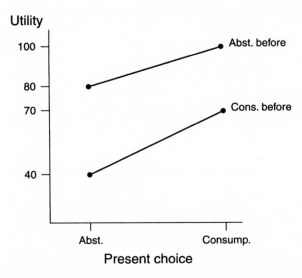

**Figure 1. Utility of present abstention and consumption when the person has either abstained or consumed in the past.**

current abstention and consumption makes a bigger difference to the experienced user than to the abstainer. This is equivalent to Becker and Murphy's property *P*2.

The welfare (or utility) levels associated with the four different combinations of successive states are displayed in Figure 1. The line corresponding to having consumed in the past is below the line corresponding to abstention in the past because of property P1, whereas the line for past consumption is steeper than the other because of property P2. The numbers along the vertical axis are suitable measures of welfare, in arbitrary units. They will be used in the examples to follow.

If the individual is completely myopic, ignoring all future consequences of present behavior, he will choose to consume now, whatever he did in the past. In the next time interval he will be on the lower branch of the welfare curve, choosing to consume again, and suffering from the consequences of his previous consumption choice.

However, if he is forward-looking, he will pay attention to the fact that the pleasures obtained from consumption now will have to be paid for later on. Two cases should be separated. If the welfare associated with continued abstention is smaller than the welfare level of continued consumption, then his choice is simple: If he has not consumed earlier, he will start to consume, and if he has already consumed, he will continue consuming. However, if the ordering of the two cases is reversed, so that it is better to abstain after previous abstention than to consume after previous consumption, the choice is not as simple. This is the situation depicted Figure 1.

Consider a person who has abstained in the past. If he continues to abstain, he will obtain a welfare level of 80, whereas, if he starts to consume and continues to do so, he will obtain a welfare level of 100 the first time and 70 on each of the following occasions. Hence, his prospective welfare levels under the two alternatives become

| Time | 1 | 2 | 3 | 4 | ... |
|---|---|---|---|---|---|
| Abstain | 80 | 80 | 80 | 80 | ... |
| Consume | 100 | 70 | 70 | 70 | ... |

If the foresight of this person is limited, he may prefer to start consuming. For instance, if his horizon is limited to the present and the next interval, he will conclude that he obtains less welfare by abstaining ($80 + 80 = 160$) than by starting to consume ($100 + 70 = 170$). However, if he looks further into the future, he may realize that, in the long run, he will be worse off by starting to consume, so he may decide to remain an abstainer.

According to the discounted utility model of standard rational-choice theory, the rational actor should take all future consequences into consideration, by calculating the overall welfare of different consumption careers. The welfare of future time intervals is discounted to a present level according to how distant they are, and these discounted welfares are added to obtain an overall measure. To secure temporally consistent plans, the discount factor decreases as a negative exponential function. Hence, if the actor values the next interval to, say, 60 percent of the present, the following interval should be valued as 60 percent of 60 percent, or 36 percent, the next as 60 percent of 36 percent, or 21.6 percent, and so forth.

When the rational consumer applies this accounting principle to the choices at hand, the temptation to consume now and to suffer the setback later is valued as

$$100 + 0.6 \times 70 + 0.36 \times 70 + 0.216 \times 70 + \cdots = 205.$$

By choosing continued abstention, he obtains an overall welfare of

$$80 + 0.6 \times 80 + 0.36 \times 80 + 0.216 \times 80 + \cdots = 200.$$

Hence, the rational consumer with a discount factor of 60 percent will decide to become a consumer because this gives him the largest overall welfare.

A person who attaches more weight to the future consequences may decide differently. For instance, this second person may value the next interval to 90 percent of the present. The weights of the following intervals then become 81 percent, 72.9 percent, and so forth. Continued consumption then becomes valued as

$$100 + 0.9 \times 70 + 0.81 \times 70 + 0.729 \times 70 + \cdots = 730,$$

which can be compared to continued abstention, valued as

$$80 + 0.9 \times 80 + 0.81 \times 80 + 0.729 \times 80 + \cdots = 800.$$

Hence, the person with significant foresight will decide that he is better off as a consistent abstainer because he pays more attention to the future losses resulting from present consumption than the myopic person, and these losses outweigh the immediate pleasures of consumption.

So far, we have considered what the two persons would do when starting off as abstainers. Let us next consider what they would do if they already had been consuming in the past. By continuing as consistent consumers, they would obtain a constant welfare level of 70. By becoming abstainers, they would suffer a temporary setback to 40 but then stabilize at 80. The myopic person would make the following comparison:

Consumption, $70 + 0.60 \times 70 + 0.36 \times 70 + 0.216 \times 70 + \cdots = 175,$

Abstention, $\quad 40 + 0.60 \times 80 + 0.36 \times 80 + 0.216 \times 80 + \cdots = 160,$

and he would decide to continue consuming. He will in effect not be able to accept the temporary setback in order to obtain the better quality of life as an abstainer later on.

The person with more foresight will make the following comparison:

Consumption, $70 + 0.90 \times 70 + 0.81 \times 70 + 0.729 \times 70 + \cdots = 700,$

Abstention, $\quad 40 + 0.90 \times 80 + 0.81 \times 80 + 0.729 \times 80 + \cdots = 760.$

This person would in effect decide to quit consuming. He is patient enough to take one step backward in order to take two steps forward later on.

The two persons both end up with consistent decisions, independent of their consumption history: The myopic person decides to consume, while the long-term planner decides to abstain, regardless of whatever they did in the past. However, there is yet another type of person to be considered: The one whose decision will depend on his consumption history.

Consider a person with the intermediate discount factor of 70%. We first consider the case where he has abstained in the past. He then faces the choice of becoming a consistent consumer or continuing as an abstainer. He will make the following comparisons:

Consumption, $100 + 0.7 \times 70 + 0.49 \times 70 + 0.343 \times 70 + \cdots = 263.3,$

Abstention, $\quad 80 + 0.7 \times 80 + 0.49 \times 80 + 0.343 \times 80 + \cdots = 266.7.$

He will consequently decide to continue to abstain. However, if he, for some reason, has consumed in the past, his calculation becomes as follows:

Consumption, $70 + 0.7 \times 70 + 0.49 \times 70 + 0.343 \times 70 + \cdots = 233.3$,

Abstention,     $40 + 0.7 \times 80 + 0.49 \times 80 + 0.343 \times 80 + \cdots = 226.7$.

Hence, in this case he will decide to continue his consumption career. This person, then, is trapped at a suboptimal level. He knows that he would have been better off as a consistent abstainer (welfare $= 266.7$), but he is unable to endure the temporary setback needed to take two steps forward and will therefore continue as a consistent consumer (welfare $= 233.3$). However, he can honestly say that if someone or something could help him to abstain for a period, then he would not relapse to consumption again. It is this latter quality that makes him different from the myopic person.

It is not difficult to verify that, with the welfare levels given in Figure 1, all persons with a discount factor between 66.7 and 75 percent will display this kind of behavior (cf. Appendix 1). Those with a discount factor less than 66.7 percent will always choose to consume, whatever they have done in the past, whereas those with a discount factor exceeding 75 percent will always choose to abstain. Hence, we obtain the following classification scheme[2]:

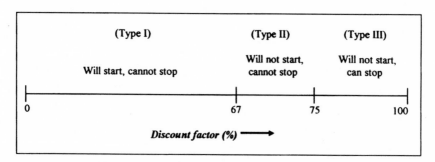

Type II persons obviously fulfill our minimum definition of addiction. When they are in the consumption state, they are dissonant addicts, knowing that consistent abstention is their global maximum state in terms of welfare. However, unless the payoff structure of the game changes, or they somehow manage to become more patient (i.e., begin to have a larger discount factor), they will be unable to quit voluntarily. But according to standard rational-choice theory, a person cannot change his discount factor at will – at least not without costs (cf. Becker and Mulligan [1993]).

Type I persons are obviously not dissonant addicts, as they do not wish to stop. As for type II addicts, they are in a suboptimal steady state. We noted above that with a discount factor of 60 percent consistent consumption gives a welfare level of 175, compared to the welfare level of 200 they could have obtained from consistent abstention. However, they are caught in a kind of intraperson prisoner's dilemma[3] because, as soon as they reach abstention (say, with the help from compulsory treatment), they cannot resist the temptation of the short-term pleasure (or relief from pain) obtained from consumption. Therefore, they immediately return to the globally suboptimal state of consistent consumption.

In fact, type I persons are consonant addicts, as they neither can nor wish to stop consuming. By definition, it should be possible to induce a wish to stop, without at the same time inducing an ability to stop in a consonant addict. This would be the case if the welfare levels associated with the different alternatives were changed so as to put his discount factor within the intermediate region. For instance, if the welfare associated with consuming after abstention is set at 90 (rather than 100), while all the other levels remain unchanged, we reduce the temptation of immediate pleasure, without changing the delayed punishment. It is easily verified that this transforms the person with a 60 percent discount factor into a dissonant addict. In fact, all persons with a discount factor in the ranging between 50 to 75 percent would be dissonant addicts under these new circumstances.

This simple model thus seems to be able to capture the two basic types of addiction described earlier. Admittedly, we have not explained how the person with intermediate foresight (i.e., the type II addict) came to become a consumer in the first place, but it is not difficult to expand the model to include such a mechanism. For instance, the person may have had an unrealistic estimate of the delayed price he has to pay for consumption, as this requires more experience than what he had initially. Thus, at the outset he may rationally believe that consistent consumption is in fact associated with a higher welfare level than consistent abstention. As was already noted, he would then rationally choose to become a consumer, whatever the value of his discount factor. When he realizes the true costs of consumption, he recalculates his choices and may either (1) stop consuming voluntarily, provided his discount factor is big enough; (2) find that he is trapped in consumption (type II addict), and perhaps realize that he may need help in one form or another, if his discount factor is in the intermediate range; or (3) continue consuming, as his myopia makes him succumb in the intraperson prisoner's dilemma.

It should be clear from this simple model that addiction does not necessarily contradict rationality. A fully rational person may find himself in a position where he is unable to stop consuming, while realizing that he would have been better off if he did not consume, and he could also honestly say that he would not start again if he were forced to stop consuming for a while. However, whether addicts *are* in fact rational is quite another issue. The argument presented here only demonstrates that this possibility is not logically excluded.

It should be noted that the type II addiction is only possible for consumer goods with property $P_2$, that is, when the choice between abstention and consumption makes more of a difference to a former consumer than to a former abstainer, say, because of the relief from withdrawal effect. It is easy to demonstrate that the parameter interval for the discount factor collapses when the difference approaches zero. Hence, property $P_2$ is a defining property of rational addiction.

## 3. Becker and Murphy's Full Model

It is not easy to find addictions that fit the simplified model outlined in the preceding section. Most potentially addictive consumption behaviors are continuous rather than discrete. And, more important, most addictions build up gradually rather than being of the "one shot and you're hooked" character described in the preceding section. Becker and Murphy's model is more realistic, being concerned with continuous rather than discrete consumption choices, and letting the effects of past consumption on present welfare be more complex than we have assumed in the preceding section. However, the added complexity does not change the basic logic, compared to the simple model.

Whereas, in the simplified model, present utility was affected by what the person did during the preceding interval only, Becker and Murphy let present utility depend on an entity they call the person's "consumption capital." This is a more general measure of past consumption of the potentially addictive good. The more a person has consumed in the past, the higher is his consumption capital. And the shorter his consumption career has been, the smaller is his consumption capital. The old consumption capital is depreciated at a constant rate, and the new consumption is added. Hence, the consumption capital may either increase or decrease over time.

The two basic properties of addictive goods described earlier are defined in terms of the person's consumption capital: ($P_1$) The higher a person's consumption capital, the less instantaneous welfare he obtains from any given level of current consumption. ($P_2$) In terms of instantaneous welfare, an extra unit of the good means more to a person, the higher his consumption capital. These properties are illustrated in Figure 2, which shows two instantaneous utility curves, corresponding to high and low consumption capital. The high-consumption-capital curve is always below the low-consumption-capital curve, according to $P_1$. In this diagram there is a consumption level offering maximum instantaneous utility. Because of $P_2$, this maximum is at a higher consumption level when the consumption capital is larger. Hence, persons with high

Utility

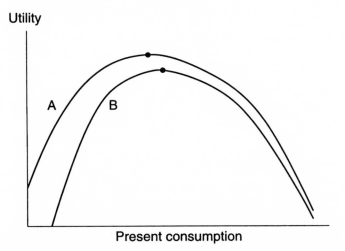

Present consumption

**Figure 2. Utility of different present levels of consumption for two different levels of consumption capital (A = low, B = high).**

consumption capital are "pushed" toward a higher current consumption because of property $P2$.[4]

On the basis of his utility function and discount factor, the rational consumer determines his optimal drinking career. For instance, given his present consumption capital, he decides what his optimum present consumption level should be, while taking the future consequences of this choice into consideration according to his discount factor. The consumption level he chooses may, or may not, change his consumption capital. If it does not change, then he has reached a steady state and he will continue at that consumption level. If his present consumption level changes his consumption capital, then he repeats the procedure, determining his next consumption level in accordance with his new consumption capital, and so on.

Becker and Murphy demonstrate that, for commodities with properties $P1$ and $P2$, the curve describing the optimal current consumption level for different values of the consumption capital may look like the S-shaped curve in Figure 3. The diagonal line in that diagram indicates the current consumption level that would leave the consumption capital unchanged. Hence, if the optimum current consumption is above this line, then the consumption capital will increase and the consumer will have moved to the right on the next round. If the optimum current consumption is below the line, his consumption capital will decrease and he will move left. Where the curve and the line intersect, there will be no change in consumption capital, and these are, in effect, equilibrium

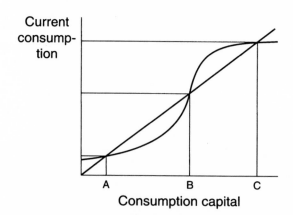

Figure 3. Optimal current consumption as a function of current consumption capital. The diagonal indicates the consumption level that will not produce a change in consumption capital.

points. Obviously, equilibrium point B in Figure 3 is unstable, as a minor deviation from this point will drive the consumer away from the point. Equilibrium points A and C are stable, however. If the person starts with a consumption capital between zero and B, he will converge toward A, whereas he will converge toward C if he starts with a consumption capital higher than B.

If the overall welfare level associated with the high equilibrium is smaller than the welfare level associated with the low equilibrium, then the high equilibrium corresponds to the type II addiction of the simple model: The starting point determines the outcome and, if the consumer for some reason should happen to accumulate a high consumption capital, he will be trapped at the high, suboptimal equilibrium consumption level.

If the consumer has more foresight than we have assumed in the construction of Figure 3, then for any given amount of consumption capital he will choose a lower present consumption level. Hence, more foresight will produce a downward displacement of the S-shaped curve, as indicated in Figure 4. This will have the effect of removing the upper equilibrium as well as the unstable equilibrium. Simultaneously, the lower equilibrium will be displaced to a somewhat lower level. Hence, the consumer with a low enough discounting of future problems will always end up with a low consumption level. He never becomes addicted.

However, if a person has even less foresight than the one in Figure 3, he will generally consume more and his curve will be displaced upward. This has the effect of removing the lower equilibrium as well as the unstable equilibrium. At the same time, the upper equilibrium is moved to a

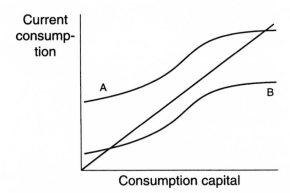

Current consump- tion

A

B

Consumption capital

**Figure 4. Optimal current consumption as a function of current consumption capital for a myopic consumer (top) and a consumer with much forsight (bottom).**

somewhat higher level. This person, then, will always end up consuming large amounts and will experience a substantial reduction in welfare, compared to what would have been the case if he had been forced to consume less. He corresponds to the type I or consonant addict, who is unable to resist the temptation of obtaining a short-term reward.

In the preceding argument, we have considered the case where the high equilibrium is suboptimal. The general model also seems to allow the high equilibrium to be the global maximum. The consumer would then be better off at the high consumption level. This case does not seem to throw light on the problem of addiction and therefore will not be considered any further.

## 4. The Nature of the Phenomena Described by the Model

As we have already pointed out, several different mechanisms seem to satisfy the axioms of Becker and Murphy's model. Both tolerance and delayed harmful consequences of consumption can support property $P_1$, whereas property $P_2$ is supported by positive reinforcement, relief from withdrawal (negative reinforcement), or suppression of the recognition that life has become a misery due to past consumption. And even more mechanisms can undoubtedly be found. This suggests that a whole series of different phenomena may be captured by Becker and Murphy's model – phenomena that do not belong to the same genuine family (e.g., the family of drug addictions). Consequently, the members of Becker and Murphy's family could just superficially resemble each other – as bats and birds, sharks and whales.

Besides all the different drug addictions, the model seems to fit other types of compulsive behavior, such as excessive gambling, overeating, and kleptomania (cf. Ainslie [1992] for an extensive list). Even more innocent-looking behaviors may fulfill the axioms. Consider the following story: Every day after work, Bob goes out with his shopmates. They normally have a beer before they go home, and Bob likes beer very much. Unfortunately, his wife is very much against his beer drinking, and she scolds him when he comes home and remains annoyed on the following day. However, his mates tease him if he abstains from drinking, but only if he drank yesterday. On the second day of abstention, they leave him alone. In this story, Bob's utility function fulfills the two requirements of Becker's model. Hence, with an appropriate event history and the right time preferences, he may get caught in a suboptimal state of drinking one beer per day. Obviously, Bob's problem is not an addiction.

This argument suggests that Becker and Murphy's criteria (as well as the minimum criteria for addiction mentioned in Section 2) are not sufficient. In particular, I would argue that it is not irrelevant *how* the properties $P1$ and $P2$ are fulfilled. These properties need to be fulfilled the right kind of way. In Bob's case they are not properties of the product he consumes but of the social context he operates in. Next, I would argue that it is not irrelevant what consumption levels we are talking about. If an individual is trapped at a suboptimal level that is not very high by "normal standards," it might not be reasonable to conceive this as a case of addiction. Empirically, these two additional criteria may converge, as it may turn out that properties $P1$ and $P2$, when fulfilled the right way, will produce local maxima only at quite high levels.

The type II person in Becker and Murphy's model is suffering from a special type of weakness of the will (WW), different from Ainslie's type, described elsewhere in this volume, and more resembling the type described by Davidson (1980). In Ainslie's case, WW is a preference reversal over time, so that the individual cannot resist a temptation as it comes close enough. In Becker and Murphy's case the individual is acting optimally in a local sense (i.e., given his consumption history) but suboptimally in a global sense (i.e., when all consumption histories are compared), at any specific point in time. He may have a desire to quit but is unable to do so. He may wish that he was more patient (i.e., had a larger discount factor) and thus could endure the temporary setback, or he may wish that the short-term punishment for abstaining was smaller, and he may regret his past consumption behavior. In fact, if he were offered a device that reduced the short-term punishment, he would accept it and become abstinent.

In real life, addiction is not simply either present or absent. Empirically oriented students of addiction typically come up with a whole range of different indicators to measure addiction, and any group of addicts would typically be distributed fairly smoothly along any scale one could construct on the basis of these items. Most probably, addiction exists in degrees. Some people have very great difficulties quitting or reducing their consumption of the addictive substance, whereas others suffer much less, but there is always someone in between. Most students of addiction would probably also argue that the scale extends all the way down to "normal" consumption and abstention. There is probably no sharp line of division between a strong habit and a mild addiction.

Although Becker and Murphy's model may allow for different degrees of addiction, it seems to imply a discontinuity between a "normal" habit and addiction. Within the frame of the model, the degrees of addiction can be measured by how much the parameters of the utility function must be changed to remove the unstable steady state. If a very small change is sufficient, one would say that the addiction is not severe. However, as Becker and Murphy tie addiction to the existence of multiple, stable equilibria, addiction seems to be qualitatively different from "normal" consumption in their model. As we shall see, this idea drives several of the predictions that Becker and Murphy derive from their model, and therefore I shall discuss it more closely.

As was pointed out earlier, only dissonant addiction is characterized by multiple equilibria. Consonant addiction is not. Now, consonant addiction is not easily separated from "normal" consumption in Becker and Murphy's full model. In fact, consonant addiction can only be separated from "normal" consumption in terms of additional criteria, for instance, the actual consumption level and/or the presence of consumption-related problems. Hence, in the case of rational consonant addiction, there is no qualitative difference between the addict and the "normal" consumer, unless this is implied by additional criteria.

However, even when there are two equilibria, the one corresponding to the highest consumption level could be located anywhere from slightly above zero to the physiological maximum, unless additional criteria are invoked. Because a low suboptimal equilibrium cannot represent addiction in any strict sense (cf. Bob), there can be no qualitative distinction between dissonant addiction and different types of dissonant "normal" consumption – it is only a matter of degree. And if – for a specific drug – such a distinction should turn out to be an empirical reality, then this must be so because there are additional mechanisms in operation, besides $P_1$ and $P_2$.

Therefore, I will argue that the qualitative difference between "normal" consumption and dissonant addiction in Becker and Murphy's model is more apparent than real. When Becker and Murphy deduce predictions from their model (bimodality and "cold turkey"; see Section 6), they implicitly assume that there is such a difference. This implies that they are making additional assumptions, which are not explicitly spelled out, to the effect that the suboptimal equilibrium is always located at a high level.

In conclusion, it seems clear that Becker and Murphy's model captures a much wider class of phenomena than the addictions – it is a theory of both bats and birds. This is not a problem for the theory if the main task has been to demonstrate that addiction can be understood within the frame of rational-choice theory. However, if the aim is to develop a full theory of addiction per se, then the theory needs to be supplemented with additional assumptions. As has already been pointed out, these assumptions need to specify "the right way" that $P1$ and $P2$ should be fulfilled, and they should also have some implications for the consumption levels where addiction can be expected.

## 5. The Realism of Becker and Murphy's Model

Rational-choice theory in general and Becker and Murphy's theory of rational addiction in particular require a series of rather strong assumptions about human actions. Below, I shall discuss the realism of some of them. The problem with assuming that the rational consumer has complete information has already been mentioned and will not be discussed in detail.

Becker and Murphy obviously have made a number of simplifications that may not be entirely realistic. When the aim is to highlight fundamentals, this is an acceptable research strategy. The discussion to follow is partly to be read as a list of suggestions as to how their theory could be developed into a more elaborate theory. However, I will also point out some problems of a more fundamental nature, which are less easily resolved.

### Consumption Capital

Becker and Murphy have not been very clear about what "consumption capital" really is and by what kind of causal mechanism it produces its effects. However, the definition implies that, inter alia, consumption capital is a kind of measure of the person's lifetime consumption of the good. It is not a simple sum of previous consumption but a weighed sum, with more weight being attributed to the close past than to the distant past. The weights are declining exponentially. This implies that the consumption capital of a person who starts drinking at a steady rate will gradually increase up to a certain level. If the person stops consuming, his consumption capital will decrease and will gradually approach zero. Becker and Murphy also suggest that the consumption capital may be influenced by other factors (so-called expenditures on endogenous depreciation or appreciation), without being very explicit about it (see below).

It is known from epidemiological evidence that the risk of long-term drinking problems such as liver cirrhosis is closely linked to a quite similar measure of drinking careers[5] (Skog 1984). Hence, it appears quite likely that the long-term reduction in welfare is causally linked to the long-term exposition to the consumption good, as measured by the consumption capital.

However, the consumption of addictive goods typically has many types of consequences, and some of them appear only after very prolonged abuse (decades), whereas other consequences show up much earlier. Tolerance typically appears after a few weeks. Hence, the temporal structure of the "punishment" is fairly complex and a realistic model would probably require a much more sophisticated measure than the one used by Becker and Murphy. A possible way out would be to include several measures of the consumption career, one for each of the major types of consequences.

Furthermore, for some drugs, the consumer has much learning to do before he can really enjoy the pleasure (recall your first cigarette, if you ever had one!). Thus the relationship between consumption capital and instantaneous utility is probably not as simple as Becker and Murphy have presumed. At low levels, welfare is probably an increasing, rather than decreasing, function of consumption capital.

Becker and Murphy attribute both $P1$ and $P2$ to the same measure of consumption capital. This may not be entirely realistic. The partial relief from "punishment" implied by $P2$ may represent relief from withdrawal symptoms or consumption as a way of forgetting that one is consuming too much and that one has damaged one's life. Property $P1$ may represent both tolerance and short- and long-term problems. It is quite obvious that all of these mechanisms cannot be modeled by the same consumption-career measure.

A symmetry is postulated in the appreciation and depreciation of consumption capital. As soon as a formerly heavy consumer stops consuming, his consumption capital starts to decrease toward zero. This may not be entirely realistic, and some would argue that it is downright wrong ("once an alcoholic, always an alcoholic"). An addict has permanently changed his life in important ways, by accumulating experiences that are not forgotten. A former addict may very well have a lifelong elevated risk of returning to the addicted state, compared to his identical (but reared-apart) twin who has never been addicted.

All of these problems can probably be handled within the general frame of the model. They would surely not destroy the main results, but the added realism might perhaps contribute additional insight into addiction. If the instantaneous utility is affected by a whole series of different mechanisms, each with its specific consumption-career measure, several interesting possibilities might emerge. As Becker and Murphy point out, with two measures, oscillation resembling binge consumption might follow.

From a substantive point of view, it is probably more important that one could also expect *temporary addiction:* The consumer might become trapped at a high level, being unable to reduce his consumption because of one particular mechanism, described by a consumption capital with a medium-range depreciation rate. However, very long term consequences, represented by the slow appreciation of a second "consumption capital" measure, would continue to accumulate. For this second measure, property $P1$ may be more pronounced than $P2$, which would imply that the wellfare level would decrease, while the temporary setback (or withdrawal symptoms) might not increase very much. This could gradually lower the threshold that prevents the addict from stopping and might ultimately allow him to reduce consumption again and get over his addiction. This scenario could correspond to the familiar "maturing out of addiction" phenomenon, as well as Alcoholics Anonymous's "hitting-the-bottom" mechanism. These possibilities remain to be studied.

As I mentioned, Becker and Murphy allow "consumption capital" to be determined by other events besides past consumption. Life crises such as becoming unemployed or divorced have been mentioned. Although these particular examples may be realistic, others may not. One is not at liberty to use the "consumption capital" as a catchall for all factors that may affect current consumption. At the very least, such factors will have to fulfill $P1$ and $P2$. If this is not the case, one would have to model their effect in the form of changes in the parameters of the person's utility function.

The factors mentioned probably satisfy this requirement: A divorce may make me less satisfied with my current consumption ($P1$) and could also be said to make my last drink more important to me ($P2$). Therefore, I start to drink more, and I may end up with a serious drinking problem. However, consider the following scenario: I am already drinking excessively, being a dissonant addict, and my wife threatens to divorce me if I do not quit. Faced with this threat, I manage to stop. If this is to be handled by a change in "consumption capital," the capital would have to be reduced below the critical threshold. But if it is reduced by my wife's threat, my pleasure from drinking at the former level must increase, which does not sound credible. In this case the change would have to be handled via the parameters of the utility function, as an extra "price" to be paid for continued high consumption. Therefore, the whole curve describing the relationship between my "consumption capital" and my optimal current consumption would change.

### Discounting

The assumptions that people take future consequences into consideration, and that they attribute less weight to these consequences the further they are into the future, are quite reasonable and uncontroversial. The assumption that these weights decline exponentially is needed in order to secure consistent planning.

However, the innocent-looking assumption that these weights decline exponentially is not at all uncontroversial. It implies that people never change their minds, unless new and unforeseen information forces them to recalculate previous plans. Ainslie (1992) claims that this is not how real people actually behave, basing his argument on experimental evidence and everyday experiences. According to Ainslie, both animals and people have discount curves that are hyperbolic (i.e., more deeply bowed than the standard exponential curves of rational-choice theory). These deeply bowed curves have the consequence that people very often change their minds and fail to stick to their plans. An example of the latter phenomenon would be the child who prefers two chocolate bars in eight days over one chocolate bar in seven days, but who seven days later prefers one chocolate bar now over two chocolate bars tomorrow. Ainslian discounting is discussed in several chapters of this volume, so I shall not go into a details about it here.

The gain–loss asymmetry represents another difficulty. People seem to discount losses less than gains, that is, they have a larger discount factor for losses (cf. Loewenstein and Prelec [1992]). Consider a certain action, producing both an immediate pleasure and a delayed pain, and assume that the immediate pleasure is larger than the delayed pain when the latter is discounted to the time of the action. Thus the rational actor would decide to perform the action. However, some time in advance the discounted utility of the pain may exceed the discounted utility of the pleasure, even if both are discounted exponentially, due to the difference in discount factors. Hence, the gain–loss asymmetry creates a weakness-of-will phenomenon very similar to Ainslie's. These and other anomalies in the standard rational-choice theory of discounting are reviewed by Loewenstein and Prelec (1992).

The positions of Becker and Ainslie with respect to discounting may at first sight appear impossible to reconcile. If people do not discount the future according to standard rational-choice theory, Becker's theory falls apart: People could very well make elaborate plans, taking all future consequences into consideration, but they could not be expected to follow these plans. In fact, in many cases they would change their minds at the last minute.

However, Ainslie's theory opens the possibility that people may gradually develop fairly consistent plans by the strategy he calls personal rules. As Ainslie points out, people operating according to deeply bowed (hyperbolic) discount curves will realize that they tend to act suboptimally. Hence, they will develop strategies to prevent this from happening. Ainslie's theory about how people obtain this can be seen as a theory of how people strive to become consistent planners. One could argue that, whereas Becker takes rationality for granted, Ainslie develops a theory about how people strive to *become* rational.

During the process that one has to go through to learn consistent planning (and perhaps also learn to become more farsighted), one may come a long way toward or into addiction. In Becker and Murphy's terminology, one may have accumulated much consumption capital before one becomes a consistent planner. Therefore, initial myopia and inconsistent planning may be an alternative way into addiction, and a realistic theory of addiction would need to handle this process. In Ainslie's theory, it is exactly when people realize that they repeatedly have fallen victim to suboptimal temptations that they learn to become consistent planners.

All things considered, it appears that exponential discounting may be empirically unrealistic and that at least some aspects of addiction are best understood in the light of dynamic inconsistencies. Relapse may be a case in point. Most addicts who try to quit their habit will typically experience numerous relapses before they succeed – if, in fact, they do succeed at all. Although relapses are hard to understand from a standard rational-choice point of view, Ainslie's position gives a rather straightforward explanation of the phenomenon.[6] Rational-choice theory would be especially hard pressed to explain why people relapse after having stayed off for a considerable period of time (long enough to reduce their "consumption capital" below the unstable steady state). It seems that Becker and Murphy would have to postulate ad hoc mechanisms that reset the "consumption capital" to a high level to deal with this problem.

### The Maximization Problem

A fundamental difficulty with Becker and Murphy's model (and with many other rational-choice models) is that it offers no attempt at explaining *how* people solve the difficult problem of finding the optimal consumption career. The mathematical complexity of the problem at hand gives a good illustration of how tough a job it is to be a rational consumer.

A standard response to this kind of objection follows Milton Friedman, who reminded us that the experienced billiard player is able to optimize his shot, without making all the complicated computations a physicist would have to perform. However, in that case there is a mechanism that allows the player to do the job, namely, learning. In other cases, for instance, optimalization in a market, the mechanism may be selection (or survival of the fittest).

But what should be the optimizing mechanism in the present case? Can one simply assume that some kind of intuition for solving such problems has developed during the evolution of *Homo sapiens?* This argument implicitly presumes that evolution has taken place in a fairly stable environment. In an unstable environment, very long term planning would be a waste of time and effort. And if one argues that learning explains the alleged ability to solve difficult optimization problems, one would have to deal with the problem of explaining the behavior that takes place before the tricks of the trade have been learned. Because the consumer may have accumulated much "consumption capital" before he has learned enough, modeling this process becomes a necessity.

A feasible approach would be to assume that the consumer applies an approximation strategy, reducing a complex problem to a problem that he can handle. Over time he would gradually learn to handle more complex problems. This solution is also a solution to the information problem, as one does not have to assume that the consumer initially has detailed knowledge of all the different short-term and long-term effects and consequences of consuming the potentially addictive drug. Hence, one does not have to assume that some exogenous shock has brought the addict to the high level; he could simply have arrived there as a result of his limited knowledge and his limited capacity for solving difficult maximization problems.

This process could be modeled by assuming that the novice may know that heavy consumption implies some risk (property $P_1$) and takes that into consideration. This could bring him to a high or low consumption level, depending on circumstances and his personal constitution. If he ends up at a high level, he may gradually experience that the drug also has property $P_2$, and he may realize that he is hooked. Gradually, other properties, as outlined earlier in this section, may also become evident, and he may enter a bingelike phase, "hit the bottom," etc.

With this approach, the ultimate fate of the consumer would depend in a continuous way on the parameters of his welfare function. The individual differences with respect to the relevant parameters(s) could be a matter of degree, rather than of an either/or nature, and his ultimate fate could be dependent on environmental circumstances. Both of these properties are realistic ones. One would not be forced to assume that the consumers are of two qualitatively different types (vulnerable and not vulnerable), as Orphanides and Zervos (1995) do.

## 6. Predictions from the Theory of Rational Addiction

Becker and Murphy deduce several implications from their theory of rational addiction. In this section, I shall discuss some of these deductions and the empirical evidence supporting them. First, however, I should point out a prediction that Becker and Murphy fail to mention. According to the theory, as soon as the consumption capital of a dissonant addict gets below the critical threshold the addict is "safe." Consequently, compulsory treatment should be a feasible strategy for society. However, the evidence seems to suggest that, in most cases, compulsory treatment is not very effective.

## Cold Turkey

Becker and Murphy (1988, p. 692) claim that their theory of rational addiction can explain

> why many severe addictions are stopped only with "cold turkey," that is, with abrupt cessation of consumption. Indeed, it implies that strong addictions end *only* with cold turkey.

This claim is based on the fact that a person who is trapped at the high equilibrium (C) in Figure 3 can reach a low level only by having his consumption capital reduced below the critical threshold B, or by the parameters of his utility function being changed in such a way that the high consumption level ceases to be an equilibrium point. The latter phenomenon could occur if the temporary setback during abstention was somehow reduced, as this would reduce the optimum current consumption for a person with a high consumption capital. The curve would in effect come to resemble the lower curve in Figure 4.

Although it is true that rational-choice theory allows for abrupt cessation of consumption, it is probably not true that a realistic version of the theory allows *only* abrupt cessation of consumption. First, the lower equilibrium point may be far from abstention. There is nothing in the theory that dictates zero, or close to zero, to be the only alternative to a high level. In fact, as was mentioned earlier, the theory itself does not even imply that the high equilibrium is really a "high" level. Second, the mechanisms that change the shape of the utility curves may very well produce a stepwise (rather than abrupt) reduction that ends within the range of "normal" consumption levels, far above zero. Such a process is illustrated in Figure 5.

As originally formulated, Becker and Murphy's theory offers no specific prediction at this point. As was pointed out earlier, one needs to make additional assumptions to restrict the shape of the curves before such predictions can be obtained. No doubt, such additional assumptions could predict "cold turkey," or they could predict a gradual "maturing out of addiction" as exemplified in Figure 5, depending on the nature of these assumptions. It would be of considerable interest to see under what circumstances one or the other would follow.

Although some schools of thought claim that "cold turkey" is the only solution to an addiction, there are good reasons for assuming that this is not always true (Davies [1962], Nordström [1988], Vaillant [1983]; but see Edwards [1985]). In fact, in a four-year follow-up of treated alcoholics (Skog and Duckert [1993]), it was found that only a small fraction of them were consistently abstaining, while a substantial proportion were drinking within moderate limits, and some were drinking excessively. Typically, changes over time were smooth and gradual at all levels,

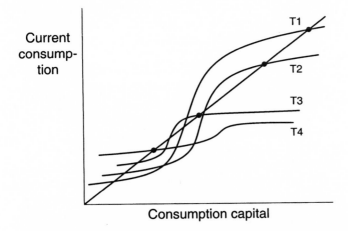

Figure 5. **Four steps in a process of gradually maturing out of addiction.**

rather than abrupt and dramatic. If Becker and Murphy's "cold turkey" argument had been correct, rational-choice theory would have been facing severe difficulties in the light of these observations. Fortunately for rational-choice theory, the argument is not correct.

### Bimodality

Becker and Murphy (1988, p. 683) predict a bimodal distribution of consumption of highly addictive drugs, with one mode located at or near abstention. Recognizing that the distribution of alcohol consumers does not fit this description, they argue that this is because alcoholic beverages are not addictive for many people.

Strictly speaking, however, bimodality does not follow logically from the theory of rational addiction. Among persons who have two stable equilibria, as suggested in Figure 3, the location of these equilibria may vary considerably, depending on the parameters of their utility curves (say, because of biological differences, differences in socialization), as well as their discount factors. Furthermore, a substantial fraction of the population may have only one equilibrium, and this may be located anywhere. No definite prediction about the shape of the distribution can be obtained from the theory without making rather strong assumptions about interindividual differences in discount factors, parameters of the utility functions, and so forth. To obtain such a prediction, one would have to assume the following property: On a scale from zero to the physiological maximum, the drug tends to "hook" people at consumption levels very much closer to zero than to the maximum. Then, one could perhaps argue that there would be very little room for "normal consumption," and those who decide to consume at all would run a substantial risk of losing control unless they monitor their actions very carefully. Under these circumstances, bimodality might follow.

However, one should not underestimate a culture's capacity to develop norms and regulations to keep people away from the dangerous consumption zone. Within a proper cultural context, it is probably possible to have controlled use of almost any drug, however narrow the safe zone should be. Moreover, addiction (as defined here and also as implied by Becker and Murphy) is not essentially a physiological concept. With the right exogenous reward-and-punishment structure (affecting the parameters of the utility function) and the right social norms on discounting, people might have little difficulty giving up consumption levels that might have hooked them if the circumstances had been different. Hence, the narrowness of the "safe" zone is clearly dependent on sociocultural context (cf. the dramatic reduction in heroin use among Vietnam veterans upon returning to the United States [Robins et al. 1980]).

The bimodality hypothesis is basically another way of expressing the idea that people who are vulnerable to addiction cannot consume at an intermediate level. Alcohol seems to offer a counterexample, even if we exclude the "normal consumers." It is an empirical fact that even alcoholics who have been to treatment (and therefore presumably are addicted) are not bimodally distributed according to consumption level (Popham and Schmidt 1976, Skog and Duckert 1993), neither before nor after treatment. The distributions are typically very skew (roughly log-normal) with the mode at a low consumption level and a fairly large dispersion parameter (coefficient of variation close to unity); see Figure 6.

Moreover, whether or not alcohol is potentially addictive to most people remains unclear. However, in many cultures, there are strict social norms regulating individual drinking, and these norms prevent a large fraction of the population from entering a consumption level that represents serious risk. In cultures that are more permissive, a larger fraction of the population are at risk. Therefore, there is a substantially larger number of excessive drinkers in "wet" cultures, such as the Mediterranean countries, than in "dry" cultures, such as some states in the United States and the Scandinavian countries (cf. Skog [1985]).

## Price Elasticities

According to Becker and Murphy, addicts should respond to price changes in much the same way as nonaddicts. Undoubtedly, the evidence points in this direction for the drugs where this kind of evidence is available (mostly alcohol and tobacco). For instance, there is no doubt

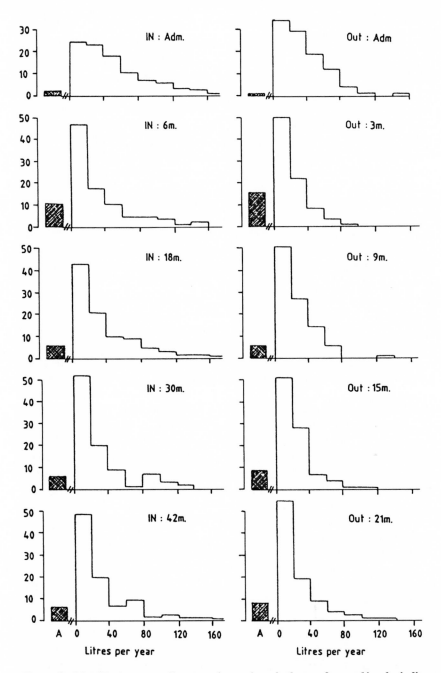

Figure 6. Distribution according to estimated equivalents of annual intake in liters of pure alcohol per year at five different points in time of two groups of patients (IN = inpatients, OUT = Outpatients) in alcoholism treatment units. The data were collected at admission to treatment and at four follow-up studies at 12- or 6- month intervals, respectively. (From Skog and Duckert [1993].)

that alcohol demand responds to prices (for a review, see Edwards et al. [1994]), and heavy drinkers and alcoholics are no exception to the rule (Babor et al. 1978, Cook and Tauchen 1982). Because addicts typically use a much larger fraction of their income on their drug than nonaddicted consumers, one could actually argue that the economic incentive to reduce consumption when prices go up is stronger for addicts.

Becker and Murphy also argue that a price change should have both immediate and delayed effects. The immediate change in consumption should produce a change in consumption capital, which should induce further changes in consumption in the same direction. The theory does not offer any suggestion as to the size of this distributed time lag – whether it is a question of weeks or years. Moreover, according to Becker and Murphy, the rational consumer who anticipates future price changes would start adjusting his consumption immediately. Hence, present consumption should be affected by both present, past, and anticipated future prices.

However, the empirical evidence for this prediction is not convincing. The prediction that future prices affect present consumption presupposes that the rational consumer is in fact able to predict future prices. No convincing evidence to this effect has been presented, as far as I know. A few econometric studies of aggregate alcohol and tobacco consumption claim to find significant effects of both past and future prices on present consumption, in addition to the simultaneous effect (Chaloupka et al. 1992; Becker, Grossman, and Murphy 1994; Keeler et al. 1993). However, the statistical methodology is unsatisfactory.

Chaloupka et al. (1992) analyze the demand for distilled beverages in a pooled cross-sectional/time-series analysis of U.S. data. They obtain significant price and income elasticities when a conventional demand model is estimated but fail to obtain any significant effects of price when a demand equation based on the rational addiction model is estimated. In fact, even the concurrent price effect is nullified. The authors suggest that this may be because much of the alcohol is consumed by people who are not addicted! This is a strange argument, as nonaddicted persons are also known to respond to price changes. Multicollinearity problems seem to be a much more likely explanation for the fact that even the simultaneous effect of price drops out of the equation.

Chaloupka et al. (1992) then try to use liver cirrhosis mortality as a proxy for the consumption level of heavy drinkers and alcoholics, and they obtain results that are in line with their hypothesis. However, the results are borderline cases in terms of statistical significance, and more importantly, their methodology is seriously flawed. Liver cirrhosis mortality has a strong distributed time lag in relation to consumption (cf. Skog [1984, 1986]), and this will automatically lead to biases in the direction reported by the authors. The authors try to deal with this problem by constructing a simple linear filter for the cirrhosis series, but they do not get it right, as they ignore what is already known about this time-lag structure from epidemiological studies (cf. Appendix 2). Consequently, they misinterpret the results.

Neither Chaloupka et al.'s alcohol study nor the study of tobacco by Becker et al. (1994) handles the problem of temporal trends in a way that produces optimal protection against spurious correlations due to collinearity.[7] Any remaining trends may induce spurious correlations between present consumption and past and future prices: If there is a causal connection between present consumption and present prices, and if there are positive autocorrelations in the consumption series (i.e., state-specific long-term or short-term trends), then one would automatically find a correlation between present consumption and past and future prices as well. It is my experience that ordinary regression techniques never handle this problem adequately. To deal with this problem in a satisfactory (but admittedly conservative) way, one would have to remove the trends in both the consumption and the price series by some filtering technique (cf. Box and Jenkins [1976]). On the basis of the results reported by the authors, it difficult to decide to what extent this problem is present in Becker, Grossman, and Murphy's study, but it is illustrating that Keeler et al. (1993) failed to obtain significant effects of future prices when the trend was included in their model.

Denmark offers a unique opportunity to test the time-lag hypothesis directly in relation to alcohol. In 1917 and 1918, the prices of alcoholic beverages increased dramatically. By March 26,1917, the taxes on "Akvavit" (the main distilled beverage) increased from 0.19 to 1.13 Danish crowns per liter. On January 1, 1918, taxes were increased again, this time to 7.69 crowns. As a result, the retail prices of distilled beverages increased by 1,200 percent in less than a year (see Table 1). Even the prices of beer increased, but to a less extent. Wine consumption was insignificant in Denmark during this period (less than 3 percent).

As can be seen from Table 1, the consumption of distilled beverages went down dramatically, from 5.1 liters in 1916 to 1.1 liters in 1918. There was an equally impressive decrease in mortality rates for delirium tremens and chronic alcoholism, confirming the well-known relationship between alcohol prices and alcohol consumption at all levels. However, neither sales figures nor mortality rates continued to decrease after 1918, as one could have expected in the light of Becker and Murphy's hypothesis. In fact, the sales figures increased again in 1919. Admittedly, most alcohol consumers are not addicted, and one could argue that per capita consumption may not be a good indicator of the addicts' response. However, 10 percent of the drinkers consume about half of all the alcohol, and the dramatic decrease in per capita consumption could not have occurred unless the addicts responded to the price change. The mortality rates, which typically display a distributed time lag in relation to per capita consumption (cf. Skog [1986]), clearly confirm this. (This time lag probably

Table 1. *Nominal prices of beer and distilled spirits (Danish crowns), sales volume of beer (liters of beer per capita) and spirits (liters of pure alcohol per capita), and number of deaths from delirium tremens (D.T.) and chronic alcoholism (C.A.) in Denmark, 1913–23*

| Year | Price of beer | Price of spirits | Volume of beer | Volume of spirits | D.T. deaths | C.A. deaths |
|------|------|------|------|------|------|------|
| 1913 | 0.13 | 0.50 | 36.7 | 6.0 | 684 | 130 |
| 1914 | 0.13 | 0.50 | 36.3 | 5.2 | 636 | 145 |
| 1915 | 0.13 | 0.50 | 32.6 | 4.5 | 634 | 117 |
| 1916 | 0.13 | 0.90 | 33.6 | 5.1 | 781 | 155 |
| 1917 | 0.15 | 2.40[a] | 33.5 | 2.5 | 250 | 65 |
| 1918 | 0.24 | 11.00 | 21.1 | 1.1 | 51 | 20 |
| 1919 | 0.27 | 12.50 | 35.3 | 1.9 | 47 | 25 |
| 1920 | 0.29 | 12.50 | 48.8 | 1.5 | 56 | 60 |
| 1921 | 0.32 | 12.50 | 45.5 | 1.5 | 51 | 63 |
| 1922 | 0.33 | 8.87 | 37.7 | 1.7 | 43 | 67 |
| 1923 | 0.30 | 8.15 | 39.9 | 1.9 | 63 | 56 |

[a]The price was 0.90 until March 25.
*Source:* Nielsen (1965).

explains why the increase in sales figures in 1919 was not matched by an increase in mortality rates.)

The absence of a clear-cut time lag in the price effect is not a serious threat to Becker and Murphy's theory. A rational addict may very well adjust his drinking fairly rapidly, as the theory does not imply any specific tempo. In fact, most real-life addicts exhibit quite substantial variations over time with respect to consumption level (e.g., Skog and Duckert [1993]), and, given this plasticity, there is no reason to believe that they may need several years to adjust to new circumstances.

However, by the same argument, one cannot obtain a critical test of the theory of rational addiction by looking for delayed effects of changes in prices. Hence, econometric analyses may simply not offer a very useful test of the theory.

And the reverse procedure (i.e., looking for forward lag correlations as signs of adjustment to anticipated future price changes) needs to be supplemented by convincing evidence to the effect that people are in fact able to anticipate future price changes. Until convincing evidence is on the table, I will remain a skeptic.

## 7. Conclusion

Becker and Murphy have obviously succeeded in proving one quite basic point: that addiction is not necessarily incompatible with rationality. No doubt, a fully rational consumer may find himself in a position where he recognizes that he would have been better off if he had been an abstainer or a light consumer, but he is unable to leave the heavy-consumption state because he cannot tolerate the temporary setback implied by quitting.

The importance of this result should not be underestimated. People suffering from different kinds of drug addiction are often treated in a highly paternalistic way, and their own preferences are not taken seriously. It is not uncommon for us, from the most learned to the man in the pub, to conceive of addicts as some kind of consumption robots who are not really able to *act* in the true sense of the term. Becker and Murphy's addicts are undoubtedly acting, but due to their impatience they have the misfortune of having to choose between "plague and cholera."

Nonetheless, it is not at all obvious that the state described by Becker and Murphy's theory is what addiction is all about. Nor is it clear that real addicts are in fact rational in the strict sense. Of course, it is far from obvious that people in general are rational in the strict sense.

I can see no good reason to doubt that people – including people suffering from an addiction – by and large try to make the best of it, given the circumstances. However, from this starting point, rational-choice theory takes a giant leap when it is presumed that the actor always has consistent preferences, both instantaneously and over time, and that he is always maximizing. In particular, strict dynamic consistency and the idea of exponential discounting may not be entirely realistic. My own experience as a former heavy cigarette smoker (I needed ten years from the first attempt to quit, before I finally made it) is best described by the term "unstable preferences." Over and over again I relapsed, giving in to short-term motives, overshadowing the long-term motives. As Ainslie implies, one has to struggle with oneself to become dynamically consistent – it is not a gift given to us at birth.

In *Confessions of an English Opium Eater*, Thomas De Quincy tells the following story, which clearly illustrates the temporal inconsistency that seems to be at the very heart of addiction:

> . . . he went so far as to hire men – porters, hackney-coachmen, and others – to oppose by force his entrance into any druggist's shop. But, as the authority for stopping him was derived simply from himself, naturally these poor men found themselves in a metaphysical fix, not provided for even by Thomas Aquinas or by the prince of Jesuitical casuists. And in this excruciating dilemma would occur such scenes as the following:
>
> "Oh, sir," would plead the suppliant porter – suppliant, yet semi-imperative (for equally if he *did*, and if he did *not*, show fight, the poor man's daily 5s. seemed endangered) – "really you must not; consider, sir, your wife and –"
>
> *Transcendental Philosopher* – "Wife! what wife? I have no wife."
>
> *Porter* – "But, really now, you must not, sir. Didn't you say no longer ago than yesterday –"

*Transcendental Philosopher* – "Pooh, pooh! Yesterday is a long time ago. Are you aware, my man, that people are known to have dropped down dead for timely want of opium?"

*Porter* – "Ay, but you tell't me not to hearken –"

*Transcendental Philosopher* - "Oh, nonsense. An emergency, a shocking emergency, has arisen – quite unlooked for. No matter what I told you in times long past. That which I *now* tell you, is – that, if you don't remove that arm of yours from the doorway of this most respectable druggist, I shall have a good ground of action against you for assault and battery" (De Quincey 1994 [1821], pp. 22–3).

My guess would be that most clinical workers will immediately recognize this particular brand of "weakness of the will", in the form of unstable preferences. Thus, one could say that Becker and Murphy's model, by ignoring it, suffers from a serious defect.

Still, one could also argue that Becker and Murphy's theory has the merit of showing that addiction may not *only* be an Ainslian type of weakness of the will, as even consistent planners may get caught. Hence, even if we could help the addict to rig his world (or rig it for him, by setting up causal mechanisms) in such a way that his planning became consistent, he might still be unable to quit.

## Appendix 1

We shall prove that the consumption careers described for different values of the discount parameter in the simple model are in fact optimal careers. The proof was suggested by Aanund Hylland.

The instantaneous utility of consuming now, given that one has abstained in the past, is denoted $U(A:C) = a$. Similarly, $U(A:A) = b$, $U(C:C) = c$, and $U(C:A) = d$. We will consider the case where $a > b > c > d$ and $a - b < c - d$.

Let $V(A)$ and $V(C)$ denote the overall utility levels of two optimal consumption careers starting with abstention and consumption, respectively, provided that such careers exist. (If not, $V(A)$ and $V(C)$ are least upper bounds.) When the optimal careers exist, we let $\{A : X_1, X_2, X_3, \ldots\}$ and $\{C : Y_1, Y_2, Y_3, \ldots\}$ denote these careers.

Let $\rho$ denote the discount factor. Because $a$ is the largest instantaneous utility, there cannot exist a consumption career with overall utility exceeding $a + a\rho + a\rho^2 + a\rho^3 + \cdots = a/(1 - \rho)$. Hence

$$a > (1 - \rho) \cdot V(C).$$

The overall utility of the career $\{A : C, Y_1, Y_2, Y_3, \ldots\}$ must be less than or equal to $V(A)$. Hence

$$V(A) \geq a + \rho \cdot V(C).$$

From these inequalities, it follows that $V(A) - V(C) > 0$.

Let us now compare consumption careers starting with $A,A$ and $A,C$, respectively. The optimal careers and their overall utility levels must be

$$U(A:A, X_1, X_2, \ldots) = b + \rho \cdot V(A),$$
$$U(A:C, Y_1, Y_2, \ldots) = a + \rho \cdot V(C).$$

Hence, starting from abstention, the rational person will abstain on the next occasion if

$$b + \rho \cdot V(A) > a + \rho \cdot V(C),$$

that is, if

$$\rho > \frac{a-b}{V(A) - V(C)}.$$

We now compare consumption careers starting with $C,A$ and $C,C$, respectively. The optimal careers and their overall utility levels must be

$$U(C:A, X_1, X_2, \ldots) = d + \rho \cdot V(A),$$
$$U(C:C, Y_1, Y_2, \ldots) = c + \rho \cdot V(C).$$

Hence, starting from consumption, the rational person will abstain on the next occasion, if

$$d + \rho \cdot V(A) > c + \rho \cdot V(C)$$

that is, if

$$\rho > \frac{c-d}{V(A) - V(C)}.$$

In accordance with $P2$, we have assumed that $c - d > a - b$, so the two inequalities reproduce the three intervals exemplified in the text. When the last inequality is fulfilled, the first one is also fulfilled, and the person will abstain regardless of past behavior (type III). When the first is fulfilled, but not the second (i.e., when $\rho$ is located within the intermediate interval), the person will abstain if he has abstained in the past and consume if he has consumed in the past (type II). And when neither of the two inequalities are fulfilled (i.e., if $\rho$ is fairly small), the person will consume on the next occasion, whatever he did in the past (type I). And because his next step in an optimal consumption career depends only on the preceding step, the entire optimal consumption career has been determined.

**TYPE I.** Starting from consumption, the person will also consume on the next occasion and will continue that way. Hence the optimum consumption career is $\{C:C, C, \ldots\}$, and $V(C) = c/(1 - \rho)$. Starting from abstention, the person will consume the next time and will obviously continue as a consumer. Hence the optimum consumption career starting with abstention is $\{A : C, C, \ldots\}$, and $V(A) = a + c\rho/(1 - \rho)$. Therefore, $V(A) - V(C) = a - c$ and type I occurs when

$$\rho < \frac{a - b}{a - c}.$$

**TYPE III.** Starting from abstention, the person will choose to abstain on the next occasion and will continue this way. Hence, the optimum consumption career is $\{A : A, A, \ldots\}$ and $V(A) = b/(1 - \rho)$. Starting from consumption, however, the person will decide to abstain on the next occasion, and he will continue abstaining in the future. Hence the optimum consumption career is $\{C : A, A, \ldots\}$, and $V(C) = d + b\rho/(1 - \rho)$. Therefore, $V(A) - V(C) = b - d$ and type III occurs when

$$\rho > \frac{c - d}{b - d}.$$

It is easily verified that $a - b < c - d$ implies that $(a - b)/(a - c) < (c - d)/(b - d)$. Therefore, type II obviously occurs when

$$\frac{a - b}{a - c} < \rho < \frac{c - d}{b - d}.$$

Starting from abstention, the person will choose to abstain on the next occasion, and so it continues. Hence the optimum consumption career is $\{A : A, A, \ldots\}$, and $V(A) = b/(1 - \rho)$. Starting from consumption, however, the person will choose to consume on the next occasion, and so it continues. Therefore, the optimum consumption career is $\{C : C, C, \ldots\}$, and $V(C) = c/(1 - \rho)$.

## Appendix 2

Annual mortality rates $(M)$ from diseases caused by chronic alcohol abuse (e.g., cirrhosis of the liver) are related to per capita alcohol consumption $(A)$, both in the same and in preceding years. Hence, one can write

$$M_t = \omega_0 A_t + \omega_1 A_{t-1} + \omega_2 A_{t-2} + \cdots$$

(ignoring curvilinearities in the relationship between the variables). Empirically, we know that $\omega_0$ is substantially larger than zero, as changes in consumption typically have immediate effects on mortality (Skog 1984). However, owing to truncation, it is probably somewhat smaller than $\omega_1$ when the time unit is one year, because the effect of consumption during the second half of a year cannot affect mortality during the first half of the year (cf. Skog [1987]). (In continuous time, the weights are probably decreasing monotonically.) Beyond a lag of one year, the weights are decreasing – rapidly at first, then somewhat more slowly. About 50 percent of the effect of a consumption change is brought out over a period of 5 years; the rest builds up over a 20- to 25-year period (Skog 1984, 1987).

Chaloupka et al. (1992) use the filtered mortality rate $\nabla M_{t+1} = M_{t+1} - (1 - \delta)M_t$ as a proxy for $A_t$. It follows from the preceding formula that

$$\nabla M_{t+1} = \omega_0 A_{t+1} + [\omega_1 - (1 - \delta)\omega_0]A_t + [\omega_2 - (1 - \delta)\omega_1]A_{t-1} + \cdots.$$

If $\omega_0 = 0$ and $\omega_i = (1 - \delta)^i$ when $i > 0$, this method could have worked. However, as we have already noted, the lag structure is much more complex. Therefore, $\nabla M_{t+1}$ will depend not only on $A_t$ but on the consumption in several years. This remains true whatever value is chosen for $\delta$. Neither of the two first terms on the right-hand side can be ignored, but presumably some of the higher-order terms may be quite small.

The variable $\nabla M_{t+1}$ will therefore be correlated with $\nabla M_{t+2}$ and $\nabla M_t$, irrespective of there being any "rational addiction" or not, that is, irrespective of any correlation among $A_t$ and $A_{t+1}$ and $A_{t-1}$. Therefore, Chaloupka et al.'s positive result when cirrhosis is used as a proxy for the consumption among heavy drinking is an artifact.

In principle, it should be possible to construct a more complex filter that does the job. However, in practice, this may not prove to be a simple task.

## Acknowledgments

I am grateful to Aanund Hylland and Karl Ove Moene who have straightened out some of my confusion along the way. Aanund Hylland also suggested the proof given in Appendix 1. I am also grateful to George Ainslie and Gary Becker for detailed written comments on an earlier version of the manuscript. Last but not least, I received useful suggestions from Ingeborg Rossow, Olav Gjelsvik, and Jon Elster. Any remaining confusion is my own responsibility.

## NOTES

1. Roughly speaking, Jellinek's delta-type (or Mediterranean) alcoholic is not a symptomatic drinker, but an habitually heavy drinker who may not realize that he is addicted unless he tries to stop drinking.
2. A formal proof that all possible outcomes are covered by this classification scheme can be found in Appendix 1.
3. When the discount factor is 0.6, the overall utility of present (and future) abstention or consumption, given past behavior, has the same structure as a

prisoner's dilemma game:

|                  | Past behavior |             |
| Present choice   | Abstention    | Consumption |
| ---------------- | ------------- | ----------- |
| Abstention       | 200           | 160         |
| Consumption      | 205           | 175         |

4. Becker and Murphy's utility function includes also the consumption of other goods as well as a budget constraint. The latter allows the elimination of other goods from the equation.
5. In fact, the risk for cirrhosis is an exponential function of a drinking-career measure quite similar to Becker and Murphy's
6. Ainslie's theory also offers a guide to understanding how people ultimately may learn to handle the problem via precommitment strategies, including personal rules.
7. Becker, Grossman, and Murphy analyze pooled cross-sectional/time-series data (51 units times 31 years) and include dummies for each year. This may not solve the trend problem unless the temporal structure is the same in all regions.

## BIBLIOGRAPHY

Ainslie, G. (1992), *Picoeconomics*, Cambridge, UK, Cambridge University Press.
Babor, T. F. et al. (1978), "Experimental analysis of the 'Happy Hour': Effects of purchase price on alcohol consumption," *Pharmacology* 58, 35–41.
Becker, G. S. (1992), "Habits, addictions, and traditions," *Kyklos* 45, 327–46.
Becker, G. S., M. Grossman, and K. M. Murphy (1992), "Rational addiction and the effect of price on consumption," in G. Loewenstein and J. Elster (eds.), *Choice over Time*, New York, Russell Sage Foundation, pp. 361–70.
    (1994), "An empirical analysis of cigarette addiction," *American Economic Review* 84, 396–418.
Becker, G. S. and C. B. Mulligan (1993), "On the endogenous determination of time preferences," Unpublished manuscript.
Becker, G. S. and K. M. Murphy (1988), "A theory of rational addiction," *Journal of Political Economy* 96, 675–700.
Box, G. E. P. and G. M. Jenkins (1976), *Time Series Analysis, Forecasting and Control*, Rev. ed., San Francisco, Holden-Day.
Chaloupka, F. J., M. Grossman, G. Becker, and K. Murphy (1992), "Alcohol addiction: An econometric analysis," Unpublished manuscript.
Cook, P. J. and G. Tauchen (1982), "The effect of liquor taxes on heavy drinking," *Bell Journal of Economics* 13, 379–90.
Davidson, D. (1980), *Essays on Actions and Events*, Oxford, UK, Oxford University Press.
Davies, D. L. (1962), "Normal drinking in recovered alcoholics," *Quarterly Journal of Studies on Alcohol* 23, 94–104.
De Quincey, T. (1994 [1821]), *Confessions of an English Opium Eater*, Hertfordshire, UK, Wordsworth Classics.

Edwards, G. (1985), "A later follow-up of a classic case series: D. L. Davies' 1962 report and its significance for the present," *Journal of Studies on Alcohol* 46, 181–90.

Edwards, G. et al. (1994), *Alcohol Policy and the Public Good*, Oxford, UK, Oxford University Press.

Herrnstein, R. J. and D. Prelec (1992a), "Melioration," in G. Loewenstein and J. Elster (eds.), *Choice over Time*, New York, Russell Sage Foundation, pp. 235–64.

———— (1992b), "A theory of addiction," in G. Loewenstein and J. Elster (eds.), *Choice over Time*, New York, Russel Sage Foundation, pp. 331–60.

Jellinek, E. M. (1960), *The Disease Concept of Alcoholism*, New Brunswick, NJ, Hillhouse Press.

Keeler, T. E., T.-W. Hu, P. G. Barnett, and W. G. Manning (1993), "Taxation, regulation, and addiction: A demand function for cigarettes based on time-series evidence," *Journal of Health Economics* 12, 1–18.

Loewenstein, G. and D. Prelec (1992), "Anomalies in intertemporal choice: Evidence and an interpretation," in G. Loewenstein and J. Elster (eds.), *Choice over Time*, New York, Russell Sage Foundation, pp. 119–46.

Nielsen, J. (1965), "Delirium tremens in Copenhagen," *Acta Psychiatrica Scandinavica*, [Suppl.] 187.

Nordström, G. (1988), *Successful Outcome in Alcoholism – A Prospective Long-Term Follow-Up Study*, Lund, Sweden, University of Lund.

Orford, J. (1985), *Excessive Appetites: A Psychological View of Addiction*, Chichester, UK, Wiley.

Orphanides, A. and D. Zervos (1995), "Rational addiction with learning and regret," *Journal of Political Economy* 103, 739–58.

Popham, R. E. and W. Schmidt (1976), "Some factors affecting the likelihood of moderate drinking by treated alcoholics," *Journal of Studies on Alcohol* 37, 868–82.

Robins, L. N., J. E. Helzer, M. Hesselbrook, and E. Wish (1980), "Vietnam veterans three years after Vietnam: How our study changed our view of heroin," in L. Brill and C. Winick (eds.), *The Yearbook of Substance Use and Abuse*, vol. 2. New York, Human Sciences.

Skog, O.-J. (1984), "The risk function for liver cirrhosis from lifetime alcohol consumption," *Journal of Studies on Alcohol* 45, 199–208.

———— (1985), "The collectivity of drinking cultures. A theory of the distribution of alcohol consumption," *British Journal of Addiction* 80, 83–99.

———— (1986), "The wetness of drinking cultures: A key variable in epidemiology of alcoholic liver cirrhosis," *Acta Medica Scandinavica Supplement* 703, 157–84.

———— (1987), "Trends in alcohol consumption and deaths from diseases," *British Journal of Addiction* 82, 1033–41.

Skog, O.-J. and F. Duckert (1993), "The development of alcoholics' and heavy drinkers' consumption: A longitudinal study," *Journal of Studies on Alcohol* 54, 178–88.

Vaillant, G. (1983), *The Natural History of Alcoholism*, Cambridge MA, Harvard University Press.

# Gambling and Addiction

JON ELSTER

## 1. Introduction

In this chapter, I discuss compulsive (excessive, pathological) gambling and whether it is usefully seen as an addiction. Compulsive gamblers are those who experience loss of self-control, by spending more than they intend (a within-episode phenomenon) or by quitting and then relapsing (a between-episode phenomenon). Following Dickerson (1984), an operational criterion is whether the gambler has sought help or treatment to control the gambling or to give it up altogether.

I shall rely on the general framework laid out in the introductory chapter and follow a similar subdivision of the topic. In Section 2, I give a brief overview of the main varieties of gambling behavior and their quantitative aspects, both in terms of the number of persons concerned and in terms of the amount of money involved. In Section 3, I discuss the phenomenology of gambling. In Section 4, I survey various explanations that have been offered of compulsive gambling. Section 5 offers a brief conclusion.

Before I proceed, let me note briefly that many of the general methodological issues raised in the introductory chapter can be illustrated by the specific case of gambling. Thus I agree fully with the following observation:

> Scientific models of compulsive or excessive gambling are relatively new. Because compulsive gambling is one of the last excesses to be included under the addictive behaviors umbrella, theories of drug and alcohol addiction provide most of the early explanations of this phenomenon. We may readily be able to generalize explanations of alcohol and substance addiction to gambling. If so, we do not have to reinvent the conceptual wheel. If not, explanations of gambling will have to be framed as an excessive behavior unlike the others. We must be ready for either outcome. (Shaffer 1989, p. 6.)

Or in the words of Lea, Tarpy, and Webley (1987, p. 270), "the issue of whether [gambling] can properly be labeled an addiction will probably not be resolved until the nature of addiction in general is better understood." Thus in exploring the nature of compulsive gambling, one should try not to be misled by superficial similarities – mistaking sharks for whales. An example of the kind of error that is important to avoid is found in the following passage:

> The more alcoholics drink, the more shame they feel; the more shame they feel, the more they drink to forget the shame, or at least make it bearable. The more compulsive overeaters eat, the fatter they grow; the fatter they grow, the more disgusting they find themselves to be, and the more they turn to food in search of comfort in the face of that self-disgust. The more compulsive gamblers gamble, the deeper into debt they go, and the more they gamble to pay off those debts. (Seeburger 1993, pp. 20–1.)

As observed in the introductory chapter, drinking may indeed be a self-sustaining activity, to the extent that people drink to escape from the awareness that they are drunks. And it has also been argued, as we shall see, that people may gamble to forget the shame associated with their gambling. In these cases, we are dealing with action motivated by the desire to reduce secondary withdrawal symptoms (see the introductory chapter). The mechanism mentioned in the last sentence of the quoted paragraph, however, is entirely different. At a superficial level, it may look like the two other phenomena identified. As with drinking and overeating, gambling "both creates the problem and is a way of resolving that problem." (Lesieur 1984, p. 16). But in alcoholism or overeating, there is no causal mechanism even remotely similar to the need to gamble in order to earn money to pay off gambling debts. The latter mechanism is more similar to what happens when an embezzler steals money from one account to put money back into another. Presumably, nobody would refer to that phenomenon as a form of addiction.

This phenomenon of the "chase" (Lesieur 1984) – gambling to win back money that one has lost – can also be used to illustrate another misleading analogy. It is often argued (see again the introductory chapter) that tolerance is a key factor in addiction. As we shall see, it is not quite clear what tolerance implies in the case of gambling, but one meaning of the term in that context might be the need to play for ever higher stakes. In a discussion of addiction as gambling, Dickerson (1984, p. 78) writes that "Loss of control, escalation of stake size and 'cold turkey' experiences following sudden cessation of high-frequency gambling have all found limited support." Presumably, escalation is taken as evidence for the presence of tolerance – the need to bet more and more in order to achieve the same level of excitement. And as we shall see, this mechanism may indeed operate. However, it is not the only mechanism that will produce escalation: The need to gamble more to repay debts will have the same effect (Lesieur 1984, p. 12 and passim). To distinguish the whales from the sharks, we need the full causal story.

It is possible to take this line of argument one step further, and ask whether the various kinds of gambling are produced by the same underlying process or processes. Thus one objective of Dickerson (1993, p. 226) "is to emphasize the difficulties in building ... general models of the addiction by illustrating that the psychological process underlying two common forms of gambling [poker machines and off-course betting] may be very different." The zombielike machine player and the dedicated racetrack bettor may be subject to entirely different motivations and, more generally, psychological processes. Although they may both, at various stages, experience craving and difficulties in giving up, these features may, as we saw in the introductory chapter, rest on a number of different mechanisms. The point will also be abundantly illustrated in the following sections.

## 2. Varieties of Gambling Behavior

On a conceptual level, forms of gambling may be classified along several dimensions. First, there is the distinction between games of pure chance and games of mixed skill and chance. In theory, and disregarding quantum-mechanical phenomena, there can be no such thing as a game relying on pure chance. Random events have to be generated by a randomizing device, with a pattern that can in principle be detected by a skillful player. Casino players are said to observe the pattern of wins in order to detect irregularities in the wheel that might give them an edge. With regard to poker machines, "players' claim that they spot sequences of reel spin results that precede a large pay out may have some validity, if recent work on the 'errors' in the random nature of the latest generation of poker machines can be replicated" (Dickerson 1993, pp. 237–8; see also Griffith 1994, pp. 290–1). In practice, these possibilities do not matter, except in feeding the self-deceptive tendencies of many gamblers.

In mixed games, skill can be attributed either to the gambler only or to both the gambler and the object on which he is betting. A good blackjack player is one who is good at remembering which cards have been played, the element of chance being provided by the random shuffling of the cards. A good horse-race gambler is one who is good at identifying good horses. In this case, elements of chance are provided not only by accidents that may prevent the best horse from winning (according to Murray [1991, p. 106], "there are a thousand ways at least to lose a horse race that have nothing to do with skill"), but also by a very large number of factors that determine which horse, on one particular day, with one particular rider, *is* the best. Whereas the former elements are irreducibly random (in the epistemic sense of being unpredictable), the latter can to some extent (the larger the better the player) be eliminated, but never completely.

A second distinction is between games in which there is a "continuous action," which allows one to be carried away by a win or a loss to place another bet immediately, and those in which games occur at preset and relatively long intervals.[1] The latter games apparently carry little potential for becoming "compulsive," "excessive," "pathological," or "addictive." They include betting on sport events such as soccer or basketball matches or on state-sponsored lotteries such as Lotto. In the claim that, in lotteries "players and the states who operate the games become afflicted with exactly the same type of addiction" (Karcher 1992, p. xiv), "addiction" is obviously not used in anything like a scientific sense. Although lotteries may give rise to problems of self-control, this is not a sufficient criterion of addiction. (Procrastination, too, may be due to lack of self-control.) The idea (suggested by Karcher [1992, p. xvi]) that lotteries are subject to a tolerance effect, so that ever-higher prizes are needed to attract players, does not seem to have any empirical support. Also, whereas the vast majority of Lotto players never win anything, "the pathological gambler invariably has a history of a big win" (Peck [1986, p. 463]; see also Lesieur [1984, p. 31]; Cornish [1978, pp. 187–8]).

Frequency of playing is one choice variable for the gambler. Others include the choice of stakes and (in horse-race betting) of odds. When gamblers escalate their playing, they may do so by playing more frequently, for larger stakes, or against higher odds. With regard to the phenomenon of tolerance, the following observation may be important. A player who increases the stakes (for given odds) stands to win more *and* to lose more. By raising the odds against him (for given stakes), he stands to win more but not to lose more. If the excitement from gambling derives mainly from the hope of winning, raising the stakes and raising the odds ought to be equally preferred by players who find that the game is turning stale. If the excitement also depends on the fear of losing, raising the stakes would be the preferred method. From the literature surveyed below, the latter appears to be the case. I return to this issue in the next section.

"Today, the poker machine, the roulette wheel and betting on horse and dog races represent the three most popular forms of gambling" (Dickerson 1984, p. 9). Other types of gambling that ought to be mentioned because of their somewhat different characteristics are blackjack (played against a dealer who behaves according to fixed rules) and card games against other competitive players. These examples suggest a distinction among games on the basis of the nature of the gambler's "opponent." In fruit-machine games, the opponent is the machine. In roulette the opponent is the relatively neutral croupier. Wins and losses among the players are entirely uncorrelated. In blackjack, the dealer is the "common enemy": If he goes bust (exceeds 21), then all the players who did not bust are automatically winners. Because of this correlation among wins, a potential is created for solidarity among the players (Ocean and Smith [1993]; see also Wagenaar [1988, p. 37]). In poker, of course, each player is opposed to the other players. Similarly, in racetrack betting each gambler is opposed to the others, because their betting behavior determines the odds. If he believes he has picked the right horse, he wouldn't want others to pick it too.

The quantitative aspect of gambling in current societies can be assessed in various ways. (For a historical survey, see France [1902].) For the United States, "the best estimate at this time is 1.1 to 4 million compulsive gamblers" (Peck 1986, p. 462), a number that may be compared to a common estimate of five million alcoholics. Also, "gambling probably ranges up to ninety billion dollars per year" (ibid.). The Rotschild report from 1978

> gave the following in £ billion for the UK: Gambling 7.1, defence 5.6, housing 4.7, health 6.5. However, if on average across all forms of gambling almost 90 per cent of this expenditure is returned in winnings, it can be seen that "turnover" figures are misleading. Despite this, the remaining 10 per cent lost or spent in 1980 terms is likely to be something over a billion pounds and is the largest single component of the total leisure industry. (Dickerson 1984, p. 20.)

An indication of the place of compulsive gambling within this total can be gleaned from the estimate that "1.5 per cent of the adult population accounted for more than half of the total stake on horse and dog races" (ibid.). Overall, Dickerson (1984, p. 21) estimates that in countries with reasonable availability of at least lotteries and off-course betting, 80–90 percent of the population gamble a few times a year; about 30 percent gamble on lotteries, football pools, or poker machines most weeks; and about 5 percent gamble regularly two to three times each week. The latter are what Dickerson (1984, p. 38) refers to as high-frequency gamblers, which include as two distinctive subsets compulsive gamblers (about 350,000 in the United Kingdom) and a small number of professional gamblers.

## 3. Phenomenology of Gambling

What is it like to be a gambler? In addressing this question, I suffer from a handicap. With respect to alcohol, nicotine, and food, personal experience and introspection help me understand how one could become addicted. I am too risk averse, however, to really understand what makes the gambler tick. Risks make me afraid, not excited. I have to rely, therefore, on other people's reports of the experience and the attractions it has for them. Especially valuable in this respect is Henri Lesieur's *The Chase*, based on in-depth interviews with fifty compulsive gamblers. I have also benefited much from three enjoyable crime novels by Walter Murray (1985, 1990, 1991) located on and around the racetrack. I did not learn much from the vastly more famous fictional accounts of gambling by Dostoyevski (1964) or Hamsun (1954). The behavior of the gamblers in these works seems as mysterious to me as it does to them.

In addressing the phenomenology of gambling I shall follow the main categories discussed in Section 2 of the introductory chapter: craving, tolerance, withdrawal, and problems of self-control.

## Craving

The following discussion concerns the craving associated with the primary rewards of gambling. Secondary rewards are considered in Section 4, in the discussion of learning and reinforcement theories of gambling. Also, I limit myself here to craving associated with nonmonetary rewards. Gambling for the sake of monetary gain is considered in Section 4, when I discuss rational-choice theories of gambling.

With regard to the motivation for gambling, there is a general dichotomy in the literature between *pull* versus *push*, excitement versus escapism, and thrill versus anesthesia (see, e.g., Rosenthal [1989, p. 123]). According to Pascal (the inventor both of roulette and of probability theory), people gamble because they seek distraction or diversion (*divertissement*) from their chronic state of *ennui* (in Pascal, a kind of anxious emptiness). Even a king, "attended with every pleasure he can feel, if he be without diversion and be left to consider and reflect on what he is, this feeble happiness will not sustain him; he will necessarily fall into forebodings of dangers, of revolutions which may happen, and, finally, of death and inevitable disease" (*Pensées* 139). People seek distraction because they cannot stand being alone with themselves, which would force them to reflect on their existence. "Thus so wretched is man that he would weary even without any cause for weariness from the peculiar state of his disposition; and so frivolous is he that, though full of a thousand reasons for weariness, the least thing, such as playing billiards or hitting a ball, is sufficient to amuse him" (ibid.).

Gambling is one of the activities that people will take up to forget about their existential or metaphysical *ennui*:

> This man spends his life without weariness in playing every day for a small stake. Give him each morning the money he can win each day, on condition he does not play; you make him miserable. It will perhaps be said that he seeks the amusement of play and not the winnings. Make him, then, play for nothing; he will not become excited over it and will feel bored. It is, then, not the amusement alone that he seeks; a languid and passionless amusement will weary him. He must get excited over it and deceive himself by the fancy that he will be happy to win what he would not have as a gift on condition of not playing; and he must make himself an object of passion, and excite over it his desire, his anger, his fear, to obtained his imagined end, as children are frightened at the face they have blackened. (Ibid.)

Along similar lines, let me reproduce two passages from Stendhal's *Le Rouge et le Noir*, the first a quotation from a sixteenth-century work describing Marguerite de Valois and the second a reflection that Stendhal imputes to her latter-day incarnation Mathilde de La Mole.

> *An itch for excitement*, such was the character of [ . . . ] Marguerite de Valois. [ . . . ] A need for hazardous sport was the whole secret of this amiable princess's character. [ . . . ] Now what can a young woman hazard? All that she has most precious: her honor, her lifelong reputation. (II.XII)
>
> He [Julien Sorel] has tremendous power over me, since he rules by terror and can inflict a frightful punishment on me if I try him too far. This idea was enough of itself to incline Mathilde to insult him, for courage was the prime quality of her character. Nothing could stir her in any way or cure her of an underlying feeling of boredom constantly springing to life again, except the idea that she was putting her whole existence at hazard. (II.XVII)

The gambler seeks excitement, but not for its own sake – only because of its ability to drive out other thoughts, something that the mere amusement in a game in which nothing is at stake could never do.[2] Thus for Pascal, gambling provides both excitement and escape, but the excitement is valued only because it provides escape (in fact, nothing else can provide it). For other writers, gambling can serve as a means of escape even when it does not generate excitement. Thus Dickerson (1993, p. 239) found that poker-machine playing does not generate much excitement (as measured by heart rates and subjective reports). Rather, "for such players, the strongly habitual person – machine interaction may represent an unthinking escape from negative emotions" (ibid., p. 240).[3]

Conversely, some writers find the main benefit of gambling is excitement sought for its own sake. There are innumerable reports about the thrills and highs experienced in high-stakes gambling. "*All* compulsive gamblers (and many non-compulsive gamblers) talk of the action aspect of gambling. It is described in terms of 'getting my rocks off,' 'adrenaline flowing,' and most often compared to sexual excitement" (Lesieur 1984, p. 44). Anderson and Brown (1984, p. 408) write that "if excitement or arousal is restored to a central role in the explanation of gambling behavior, a personally experienced and objectively verifiable state of arousal, not sexual, but probably autonomic, might be seen as being sought repeatedly by the regular gambler for its own sake." Whereas it is clear enough why gambling (as any form of risk taking) might generate arousal, it is more puzzling why the arousal would be pleasurable, especially if it is true that the fear of loss is an important condition for the excitement.

Let us return to Pascal, and his comparison among (i) genuine gambling, (ii) playing without stakes, and (iii) assurance of earning every day the maximal sum that can be won by gambling. (Remember that he refers to the gambler who plays "every day for a small stake.") To this list we might add (iv) being offered a prospect with some chance of winning but no risk of losing. (Imagine a roulette game where the players have a fixed daily number of opportunities to choose a number and on each occasion get a fixed reward if it comes up.) Pascal would claim, I believe, that the regular gambler would prefer (i), not only to (ii) and (iii), but also to (iv). I suspect he would be right – but why?

At this point, it is natural to bring up the psychoanalytical theory of gambling, according to which people gamble because they have an unconscious wish to lose (Bergler [1957]; see also Dickerson [1993, p. 239], Walters [1994, p. 176], Peck [1986, p. 463]). As gambling careers are usually triggered by an early big win rather than by an early big loss, the theory does not look very promising; yet it does at least address the apparent violation of the sure-thing principle. It does not answer, however, the important question: What's in it for the gambler? More pedantically: How can the prospect of loss of a standard reinforcer act as a reinforcer?[4] Pascal's answer would be that the feelings of hope generated by option (iv) would not be strong enough to crowd out the existential *angst*. Dr. Johnson said that nothing concentrates a man's mind so much as the knowledge that he is about to be hanged. Similarly, writers on gambling have noted that it tends to focus concentration and thereby enable the gambler to forget about his worries (Rosenthal and Rugle 1994, p. 34; Lesieur 1984, p. 14).[5] If he had nothing to lose, this effect might not obtain. These are obviously speculative remarks, but they address, I think, a real problem.

### Tolerance

Under this heading, I shall first recapitulate various observations already made above. I referred to the idea that gambling might be subject to tolerance, in the sense that ever-larger stakes and/or ever-higher odds are needed to generate the same excitement. I also mentioned the behavioral phenomenon of *escalation*, that is, the observed tendency for heavy gamblers to raise the stakes and/or the odds. I asked whether escalation in itself is evidence for tolerance and suggested two reasons for thinking that it is not. First, escalation might be produced by an alternative mechanism, for example, the need to make larger and riskier gambles in order to repay old debts. Second, I have not seen it claimed that gamblers raise the odds to sustain the thrill. When horse-race players play long shots in the last race of the day, their motive is usually to recoup losses from earlier races (Wagenaar 1988, p. 105; Cornish 1978, p. 168).

This being said, escalation of *stakes* may be caused by the need to sustain a thrill that otherwise might become jaded. According to Lesieur (1984, p. 44), the nature of "action" in gambling has "an uncanny similarity to 'tolerance' among alcohol, barbiturate, and narcotics addicts.

Once the 'high' of a five-hundred-dollar event has been reached, the two-dollar bet no longer achieves the desired effect." Cornish (1978, p. 203) similarly refers to "the possibility that habituation to certain levels of excitement may occur as a function of experience, so that it becomes necessary to raise one's stakes in order to recapture the same subjective quantity of 'thrill.'" Note the difference, though, between these two statements. Lesieur may well be right in that once the larger bets have been made, smaller bets are less satisfactory, but that does not imply that Cornish is right in that dissatisfaction with the small bets is why the gambler moves on to larger bets. The escalation might originally be caused by the need to repay debts, and then sustained by a "contrast effect" (Tversky and Griffin 1991). Before you've experienced the best, you're happy with the second best; but once you've been exposed to the best, perhaps by accident, there is little thrill to be had from the second best. Although the contrast effect and the phenomenon of tolerance are superficially similar, the underlying causal mechanisms are quite different.[6]

### Withdrawal

What happens to compulsive gamblers when they stop gambling? Some report a feeling of relief (Wray and Dickerson 1981), but most report a number of psychological and (more rarely) somatic problems. The most common symptoms are irritability, anxiety, and depression, which are also observed among abstaining alcoholics (ibid.). It is far from obvious, however, that these reports suffice to show the presence of (primary) withdrawal. Here is a description of gamblers who have *not* quit: "Compulsive gamblers are never relaxed, but the restlessness, irritability, paranoia, hypersensitivity at this stage [the final stage of "desperation"] increase to the point that sleep and eating are disturbed" (Peck 1986, p. 464). If they continue to feel this way after they quit, there is no need to explain the feeling by their quitting.

Moreover, it is quite possible that we are dealing with secondary rather than primary withdrawal (see the introductory chapter for this distinction). Rosenthal (1989, p. 104) writes that "In my experience withdrawal has been relatively insignificant both in the course of treatment and as a diagnostic criterion. There may be depression when the person stops gambling. This may be an underlying depression against which the gambling had defended. Alternatively, it may be that once the individual stops gambling he realizes how destructive his behavior had been." More recently, Rosenthal and Rugle (1994, pp. 33–4) made the following important observation:

> Some gamblers will continue to be unstable, and depending on the outcome of their last gambling episode, will be plagued by feelings of shame and guilt which will send them back into action.... Pathological gamblers frequently

believe that if they can win back what they lost, it not only erases the debt, but it is as if they had never gambled in the first place. Guilt is dealt with by the psychological defense of undoing....

Shame, on the other hand, is not something that can be undone. However, gambling offers an escape from painful awareness. The intense concentration involved in gambling, which blots out all memories of everyday life, offers a kind of primitive avoidance and a hiding out from the eyes of the world. At the same time, the social acceptance of the casino or race track denies one is disapproved of or an outcast.

The emergence of these secondary symptoms may indeed send the player "back into action," just as the painful awareness that one is an alcoholic may induce more drinking. More robust evidence for primary withdrawal comes from a report by Custer (1982) that "if gamblers had just stopped betting prior to admission to hospital it was not uncommon for staff to observe 'tremulousness, headache, abdominal pain, diarrhoea, cold sweats and nightmares to occur for a few days after admission.' He suggested that these may represent withdrawal symptoms or might be due to sleep starvation" (Dickerson 1984, p. 59). This sounds more like the real thing, that is, primary withdrawal caused by the organism adjusting to the new situation. But, in the absence of any knowledge of the neurobiology of gambling, these remarks, too, remain speculative.

### Problems of Self-Control

Gamblers, like drug addicts or overeaters, often want to quit but find it difficult.[7] Many of the difficulties are of their own making, caused by the primary or secondary cravings discussed early in this section. Other obstacles are deliberately created by those who stand to gain from their gambling. Thus, "casinos seem to be set up entirely to hinder self-monitoring cues. For instance, it is impossible to see outside from inside a casino (the few windows and doors are often blacked out), so that it is impossible to tell whether there is day or night. There are no clocks on the wall, and dealers are reluctant to tell players the time" (Baumeister, Heatherton, and Tice 1994, p. 218). That drinks are freely served also contributes to loss of self-control. "Slot machines are grouped together in sets of hundreds, so that the rattling of money is heard continuously" (Wagenaar 1988, p. 12), enabling players to obtain "vicarious reinforcement from the success of others" (Cornish 1978, p. 189). Because "betting and listening to race commentaries may result in gamblers experiencing difficulty in maintaining control of the frequency of betting and the amount staked..., the design of the off-course betting office may influence the occurrence of gambling-related ... problems" (Dickerson 1984, p. 137). The gambling arena is rigged against self-control.

Gamblers want to quit when they accumulate an intolerable combination of financial, personal, and legal problems. In one sense it is harder to stop gambling than to quit drinking or smoking. Gamblers cannot simply quit and then get on with their lives. Usually, they also have to clean up the mess they have created, notably by setting up a credible debt repayment scheme. (One of the compulsive gamblers interviewed by Lesieur [1984] had twenty-two concurrent loans.) Undoing of past wrongs is also one of the twelve steps of Alcoholics Anonymous, but in that case the purpose is to help the ex-alcoholic find peace with himself rather than to keep his victims at bay. If the gambler's life was unexciting to begin with, it is likely to be even more so when he has to live off what little income is left him by his creditors. This makes for an additional source of relapse.

As with alcohol or overeating, loss of self-control can take two forms. First, the gambler may decide not to gamble anymore and then break his resolution. Second, within any given gambling session he may spend more than he intended, notably by "chasing" or otherwise acting differently from what he had planned (e.g., by changing bet selections at the last moment). Both types of breakdown may be caused by the behavior itself. As noted, gambling may create guilt that can be relieved only by more gambling. Within a given episode, increased levels of arousal may lead first to higher concentration and then to "the irrational, confused, and superstitious thinking which results in carefully prepared plans and strategies being abandoned in the midst of the gambling session and the making of seriously damaging decisions which the gambler afterward cannot understand" (Brown 1986, p. 1008).[8]

The compulsive gambler has a counterpart that does not exist with any other addictive or excessive behaviors: the professional gambler. Some forms of gambling do in fact enable skilled players to gamble for a living. Blackjack has actually a winning strategy that, depending on the rules of the casino, allows a skilled player to have a positive expected value of between 0.5 percent and 2 percent of the stakes (Wagenaar 1988, p. 20). Because of the high variance of the outcome, however, the win may be quite delayed. With an expected value of 0.5 percent, the player would have to play 100 hands an hour, eight hours a day, for 270 days in order to be assured of a 99 percent chance of profit (ibid.). This feature of the strategy, combined with the counting skills needed, may be part of the explanation why it is so rarely used. For other explanations the reader is referred to Chapter 3 of Wagenaar (1988).

Although there seem to be few skilled "counters" who make a living by playing blackjack, there are probably more who make a living by betting on the outcome of horse races or sport events. (I disregard the living that can be made by rigging the games.) In addition to information and good judgment (see the next section), professional gamblers need considerable self-control. "'Loss of control' is ... recognised by professional gamblers as an occupational hazard against which various precautions can be taken" (Dickerson 1984, p. 58). These include, notably, prior selection of bets and avoidance of continuous betting (ibid., p. 62). Also, it is important to avoid the various modes of superstitious thinking that characterizes most gamblers. Thus in Murray (1991, p.105) the professional gambler Jay engages in the following dialogue with the main character, Shifty:

> "I'll bet him in the place hole."
> "A wimpish wager, Shifty. I'm ashamed of you. I mean, if he's good enough to be a good place bet, then he's good enough to win, isn't he?"
> "Jay, I'm just coming out of a real bad streak."
> "Suit yourself," the handicapper said. "But that's not a good betting style."

## 4. Explanations of Compulsive Gambling

The following discussion of some candidate explanations of compulsive gambling will draw both on the literature on gambling and on the wider literature on addictive behaviors. I shall not discuss theories that explain excessive gambling by personality variables such as sensation seeking (Brown 1986, Coventry and Brown 1993), chronic hypotension or hypertension (Jacobs 1989), low self-esteem (Walters 1994, p. 163), or high self-esteem (Baumeister, Heatherton, and Tice 1994, p. 222). Dickerson (1984, pp. 40–3) reviewed many of these accounts and found them generally unpersuasive. Although I am no expert on these matters, my impression is that in these studies both the dependent variable (compulsive gambling) and the independent ones (personality traits) are subject to so many measurement problems that it is hard to see the findings as very robust. Also, some of the studies are largely speculative. In any case, it is intrinsically more satisfactory to search for explanations that embody causal mechanisms of a reasonably well-understood kind. These include rational-choice theories, theories based on hyperbolic discounting, and theories based on learning and reinforcement.

### Rational Choice

It seems a priori implausible that compulsive gamblers behave in an entirely rational way. And I do not in fact think that view can be defended. Nevertheless, I believe the confrontation between rational-choice theory and gambling behavior is worthwhile, for several reasons. First, it may enable us to identify the precise kind or kinds of irrationality that are involved. Second, some aspects of gambling behavior, even among compulsive gamblers, may actually be rational. Third, if we find that rational-choice explanation does not work for gambling, and if we decide that compulsive gambling satisfies Becker's criteria for addiction, then his general theory of rational addiction may be in some trouble.

220

220                 JON ELSTER

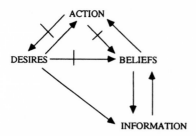

**Figure 1**

For the convenience of the reader, I reproduce Figure 6 of the introductory chapter (see Figure 1). Before I confront the rational-choice model with gambling behavior, it should be observed that the model makes sense only if the beliefs and desires are given independently of the behavior they are supposed to explain (whence the blocked arrows from action to desires and beliefs). As we shall now see, this is not always the case. With regards to beliefs, we may cite Dickerson (1993, p. 238):

> Players' expectations of payouts are not consistently associated with variations in play rate. Even when play rates suddenly fall for two minutes or so after a big win, this is not associated with a lowering of expectations for future payouts. This has led us to the proposition that it is the machine reinforcement schedule that "drives" the behaviour, and that the cognitive processes are by-products that provide the player with a verbal "explanation" of the behaviour of his or her body.... At one time or another it would seem that players may express almost any reason for continuing to play, and it is this overall perspective to the cognitive aspects of poker machine playing that leads us to consider them as the players' attempts to understand the way in which their stereotypic habit has a "life of its own." As Walker ... expressed it, "it is the gambling behavior that maintains the irrational thinking rather than the reverse."

With regard to reported desires, several findings suggest that these may also be ex post rationalizations of behavior rather than causally efficacious in their own right. They serve as *excuses*, not as motives. Thus

> subjects who had won as many times as they had lost became more conservative in their choice of a bet, whereas those that had a high win–lose ratio and those with a low win–lose ratio became relatively more risky in their choices. The authors reasoned that the successful subjects behaved as if their former good luck would continue in the future; by contrast, the least successful appeared to behave recklessly, as if they were trying to compensate for a run of bad luck (Lea, Tarpy, and Webley [1987], citing Greenberg and Weiner [1966]).

Similarly, Tversky and Shafir (1992) found that a majority of subjects assert that they will accept a second gamble both if they have won in a prior gamble *and* if they have lost in a prior gamble; however, only a minority say they will accept a second gamble if they do not know whether they will have won or lost in the first. I suggest that in both cases what we observe is the search for excuses to gamble.

Assuming now that the desires and beliefs are in fact independently given, could gambling be a rational form of behavior? The mere fact that the expected monetary value of most forms of gambling is negative does not, of course, make it irrational to gamble. Some individuals may be risk seekers rather than risk averse: They seek the thrill rather than the monetary gains (Bromiley and Curley 1992).[9] Gambling is, indeed, part of the "entertainment industry." The more complex motivations discussed previously under the heading of "Cravings" might also find rational satisfaction through gambling. Also, for most people the marginal utility is an increasing function of money through some intervals, particularly at those points where it can transfer an individual from a lower socioeconomic status to a higher one (Friedman and Savage 1948; Cornish 1978, p. 94). An analogous argument applies to compulsive gamblers who have accumulated high debts. If gambling induces a "financial and legal crisis, a person may rationally risk losing even more money on the chance of winning sufficient to retrieve the situation" (Dickerson 1984, p. 134). It is rational to choose probable disaster over certain disaster. Needless to say, the behavior that forced this choice on the gambler may not have been equally rational.[10]

Heavy involvement in gambling, however, usually indicates that rationality has been left behind. Numerous reports of loss of self-control among gamblers indicate that gambling can be a form of weakness of will. As Gjelsvik explains in his chapter, we then have to ask whether we are dealing with Davidson's or Ainslie's concept of weakness of will. Between-session loss of control is probably best explained along Ainslie's lines (see the discussion of "Hyperbolic Discounting" next). Within-session loss of control might be an instance of Davidsonian weakness of will. The arousal caused by heavy gambling may plausibly cause the kind of short-circuiting of rational choice that is at the core of Davidson's theory. However, Stein's model (see the discussion of "Hyperbolic Discounting," next) indicates that within-session loss of control, too, might be explained on Ainslie's lines.

Consider now the beliefs involved in gambling and their rationality. A general question is whether people who start out on a gambling career fully understand the prospect of disaster that they face. The original rational-choice model of addiction in Becker and Murphy (1988) assumes accurate beliefs in this regard. The modified probabilistic version in Orphanides and Zervos (1992) assumes unbiased beliefs. For my part, I find the following statement more plausible: "People's risk behaviors are ... imperfect indicators of the risks that they believe themselves to be taking. For example, investors may not realize that they are boarding an emotional rollercoaster when they assign half of their pension to an equity fund. Nor is there any guarantee that the impact of acknowledged consequences will be perceived accurately" (Fischhoff 1992, p. 137). Note that what is questioned here is not the accuracy of people's beliefs about future chance events (this is discussed below), but the accuracy of their beliefs about how these events will affect them emotionally. (See also Loewenstein's chapter in this volume.)

It is overwhelmingly clear from the literature that virtually all gamblers who reach the compulsive stage suffer from some kind of irrationality in belief formation. They believe their chances of winning are higher, even much higher, than what can be justified by the information they have. Even in games of pure chance, gamblers fervently believe that they are on winning or losing streaks.[11] Sometimes, belief formation operates by wishful thinking (illustrating the blocked arrow from desires to beliefs in Figure 1). There is evidence that "as frequency of betting increases so does the belief that one's selection involves more skill and yet the observed behaviour actually becomes less skillful, with escalating stakes, hurried bet-selection and last minute changes in selection" (Dickerson 1984, p. 134).

I suspect that "hot" mechanisms of this kind operate very frequently to shape beliefs about winning.[12] Yet, in studies of gambling, "cool" varieties of irrational belief formation figure much more prominently, perhaps because they are readily connected with the large literature on statistical fallacies. In fact, the "gambler's fallacy" is the very paradigm of erroneous statistical reasoning. This fallacy and its converse can be explained in terms of two heuristics of decision making identified by Tversky and Kahneman (1974):

> When in a game there is a 50% chance of winning, people expect that a small number of rounds will also reflect this even chance. This is only possible when runs of gains and losses are short: A run of six losses would upset the local representativeness. This mechanism may explain the well-known gamblers fallacy: The expectation that the probability of winning increases with the length of an ongoing run of losses. The *representativeness heuristic* predicts that players will increase their bet after a run of losses, and decrease it after a run of gains. This is indeed what about half the players at blackjack tables do. ... But the other half show the reverse behaviour: They increase their bets after winning, and decrease them after losing, which is predicted by the *availability heuristic*. After a run of losses, losing becomes the better available outcome, which may cause an overestimation of the probability of losing. (Wagenaar 1988, p. 13; italics added.)

Another important mechanism is the "psychology of the near-win." When the outcome of the gamble is in some sense "close" to that on which the gambler had put his money, this is perceived as a confirmation of his beliefs. Wagenaar (1988, p. 109) offers a graphic example:

> [An] example of confirmation bias is the roulette player who suddenly places a large single bet on number 24, completely out of his routine betting pattern.

His reason was that 12 is always followed by a 24. After he lost his bet I enquired what had gone wrong. He said: "It almost worked." The number that did come out was 15, which is adjacent to 24 on the number wheel. Probably he would have considered other outcomes like 5, 10 and 33 also confirmations, because they are nearby on the wheel. Also he could have taken the outcomes 22, 23, 25 and 26 as confirmations because their numerical value is close. Or the numbers 20, 21, 26 and 27, because they are adjacent on the tableau. Thus 13 out of 37 possible outcomes could be taken as confirmations of a rule that has no predictive value whatsoever. We can add to this number all the occasions on which 24 or another confirmatory number occurred, not immediately, but in the second round.

If the confirmation bias can operate in gambles of pure chance, it is obviously even more likely to be observed in gambles that involve a mix of chance and skill. At the roulette table, the concept of a near-win is pure magic or superstition. In games with handicapping, it has some evidential value, although less than what many gamblers believe. At the racetrack, choosing for a winner a horse that comes in second is seen both by the gambler himself and by others as proof that he was on to something.[13] According to Gilovich (1983, p. 1122) the "tendency to accept wins at face value but to transform losses into 'near wins' can produce overly optimistic assessments of one's gambling skill and the chances of future success" when betting on professional football games.

There are a number of distinct mechanisms that may be involved here. First, there is the idea that near-wins serve to confirm beliefs about one's ability to predict the outcome. Second, there is the idea that near-wins serve as reinforcers of gambling behavior, much in the same way as actual wins do. I return to this idea in the discussion of reinforcement theories. Third, several writers (Brown 1986, p. 1010; Griffiths 1991, p. 351) appeal to the views of Kahneman and Tversky (1982) about the "cognitive regret" produced by near-wins, and they suggest that the stronger the regret, the stronger the urge to gamble again. I am somewhat puzzled by this claim. Because regret is a negative feeling, it would seem more likely to be perceived as aversive and thus to make gambling in the future less likely. (If I miss my plane by two minutes won't this make me more careful in the future than if I miss it by half an hour?) Nonetheless, the general idea that near-wins reinforce the propensity to gamble, by cognitive or motivational mechanisms, has strong empirical and theoretical support.

In addition to the gambler's fallacy (and its converse) and the near-win fallacy, we may cite two general sources of irrational belief formation: the illusion of control (Langer 1975) and depressive realism (Alloy and Abrahamson 1988). The first mechanism refers to the tendency of subjects to believe that they can control chance events and to overestimate their control over outcomes that are partly but not wholly under their own control. The second refers to a general tendency among nondepressed subjects to view the world in a rosier light than is justified. Depressed subjects tend to be more evenhanded in their causal attribution of credit and blame, whereas nondepressives typically attribute negative events to others and positive events to their own intervention. Nondepressive subjects see themselves more positively than they do others with the same objective characteristics, whereas the depressed are not subject to this self-serving bias, nor to the opposite, self-deprecating bias. Depressed subjects have an accurate idea of how other people perceive them, whereas nondepressives exaggerate the good impressions they make on others. Finally, nondepressives exhibit the illusion of control whereas depressed subjects judge their degree of control accurately. Moreover, nondepressives show an "illusion of no control" when the outcome is associated with failure.[14]

Let us consider, finally, the third optimality requirement of the rational-choice model: optimal investment in the acquisition of new information. Whereas other forms of addiction may be characterized by a tendency to invest suboptimally in information (heavy drinkers probably do not check their liver as often as they should), some forms of gambling are characterized by an overinvestment in information. The very existence of the Monte Carlo *Revue Scientifique*, which logs successive outcomes at roulette (Cornish 1978, p. 108), is proof that gamblers are willing to spend money gathering worthless information. In games of pure chance, *any* investment in information is by definition excessive. In games of mixed skill and chance, gathering and processing of information can improve the odds. On the racetrack, "professional gambling is typified by a rational and controlled approach sustained by hours of information collection, detailed accounting and the like" (Dickerson 1984, pp. 66–7). What distinguishes the professional gambler from the compulsive gambler (and steady loser) is probably not that the former more closely approximates the optimal investment in information, but that he has better processing skills.

I take it for proven that compulsive gamblers typically – not only occasionally – behave irrationally. Does this invalidate the Becker-Murphy model of rational addiction? To answer this question, we must first ask whether compulsive gambling satisfies their properties $P_1$ and $P_2$ (see Skog, this volume). On a first approximation (see Skog for a fuller analysis), this can be rephrased as a question of whether compulsive gamblers experience tolerance and withdrawal symptoms. It is possible that tolerance does evolve, although some of the alleged evidence is open to other interpretations. There is little evidence of primary withdrawal and some evidence of secondary withdrawal. Let us assume, for the sake of argument, that properties $P_1$ and $P_2$ are satisfied. We may then expect to see some gamblers end up in the high-level equilibrium of Skog's Figure 2. As Skog observes, however, the model does not allow us to say that this high equilibrium is excessive or corresponds to compulsive gambling. There may well be some noncompulsive Becker-Murphy gamblers around.

Compulsive gamblers, however, are likely to violate some of the other assumptions of the Becker-Murphy model. They do not stick to their plans, and they do not form rational beliefs. The behavior of these gamblers cannot be predicted by the model.

### Hyperbolic Discounting

The Becker-Murphy assumptions might also be faulted on another point: because we are so constructed as to discount the future hyperbolically, as proposed by George Ainslie, rather than exponentially, as assumed by Becker and Murphy. An explanation of gambling based on Ainslie's theory would probably have to be combined with the cognitive irrationalities discussed above. If people had accurate expectations about the outcome of gambling, they might not only prefer abstention to gambling ahead of time but continue in this preference right up to the time of choice. The preference reversal that is the key to Ainslie's theory might occur only if the short-term expected benefits are blown up (and/or the long-term costs diminished) by irrational beliefs.

In the literature on gambling, there are a few explicit references to Ainslie's work. The brief reference in Walters (1994, p. 167) involves only the contrast between the short-term and long-term effects of gambling (thrill versus loss of money), with no mention of the hyperbolic shape of the discounting function. A more sustained argument that does refer to hyperbolic discounting is found in Stein (1989, pp. 77–80). It combines a straightforward application of Ainslie's theory of impulsive behavior with a Piaget-inspired account of impulse control. Stein stipulates a within-session problem: a man who starts a night of gambling, intending to leave the casino when he has 100 dollars left. This intention is highly motivated because he knows he has to pay a loan shark at least 100 dollars the next day, and he could be physically hurt if he does not pay. Yet, when he is down to his last hundred dollars, the imminent thrill he would get from betting looms larger than the risk that will only materialize later. Stein then goes on to assert that the way to overcome this problem is to move from "concrete operations" to "formal operational reasoning." In a somewhat confusing manner, this shift is related not only to Piaget's theory of developmental stages but also to the Gamblers Anonymous slogan "One day at a time" and to Ainslie's theory of bunching.[15]

In a very different application of hyperbolic discounting to compulsive gambling, Rachlin (1990) makes no reference at all to preference reversal. Rather, he demonstrates that gambling can have a positive expected value for the gambler if three conditions are satisfied. First, the gambler is not motivated by the subjective value of a single gamble but by the subjective value of a string of gambles, averaged over all strings. Second, a string ends with the first win. Thus the possible strings are Win,

Loss–Win, Loss–Loss–Win, Loss–Loss–Loss–Win, etc. Third, the subjective value of a string is the sum of the monetary values of the component
gambles (a series of losses followed by a win) discounted hyperbolically.
Summing up for all the possible strings, he finds that gambling has a
positive subjective value. He also argues that neither of two frequently
recommended ways of achieving self-control is of much help to the compulsive gambler. First, decreasing the degree of discounting (i.e., making
the future more salient) does not necessarily reduce the value of the gamble. Second, it does not help to "organize behavior over a large span of
time and to count up the benefits and subtract the losses only after very
long anticipated or experienced temporal units" (Rachlin 1990, p. 297),
because an identical argument would then apply to this increased time
period.

This last conclusion does not directly contradict Ainslie's theory that
the gambler may overcome his problem by bunching because the two
theories stipulate different principles for aggregating choices into larger
temporal units. Rachlin argues, however, that the mode of aggregation
he stipulates is more natural because "the signal indicating the end of a
unit (a win) is intrinsic to the activity itself. Count-based or time-based
restructuring would require count or time signals not typically provided
within the gambling situation" (ibid.). The only way gamblers may be
able to quit is by running out of money. In that case, relapse should
be a very common phenomenon as soon as the gambler is back on his
feet financially. Moreover, with Rachlin's theory, it is hard to see why
there are any noncompulsive gamblers. On both counts, Ainslie's theory
performs better. Relapse is prevented by successful bunching. Gambling
in moderation is made possible by the use of personal rules. (See Gjelsvik,
this volume.) This being said, Rachlin's theory is simple, powerful, and
intriguing. It would be worthwhile following it up.

### Learning and Reinforcement

The gambling setup, unlike most other addictive behaviors, is very similar
to a laboratory learning experiment. The animal (the gambler) makes a
response (places a bet) at freely chosen times. Rewards are made available as some function of the pattern of responses. The pattern of rewards, in turn, shapes the pattern of responses in the future, by the
process known as reinforcement. In gambling, the reward pattern is a
*variable-ratio* (VR) schedule, meaning that the ratio of wins to stakes
is variable in the short run. Such schedules have two relevant properties. First, it is hard to establish behavior on a VR schedule. It is a big
help to have a large win early on; in fact, as we saw, this appears to
be a precondition for becoming a compulsive gambler.[16] As casino and
racetrack managers lack the technology for sucking in novices by offering

them big wins, they have to rely on chance-generated luck. (Con-man operations, however, rely on the deliberate inducement of early wins by the mark; see, e.g., Freundlich [1995, p. 28].) Second, once the behavior is established, it can be maintained on a VR schedule even if the rewards are quite skimpy or even declining.[17]

In such explanations the function of *reward* is obviously very different from its use in rational-choice explanations. In reinforcement, the link between reward and behavior does not pass through conscious choice among alternatives that are weighed against each other for the purpose of reward maximization. Actual reward, not anticipated reward is what matters. Moreover, unlike natural selection (another mechanism by which actual rewards can shape behavior) reinforcement does not mimic maximization. It produces melioration, not maximization (see the introductory chapter for an explanation of these concepts). For these reasons, there is not full agreement on the appropriateness of using reinforcement theory to explain gambling behavior, some forms of which seem to be very much based on conscious choice and deliberation: "Human behavior will only be determined by schedules of reinforcement when people are not trying to 'solve' the problems posed by the schedule. We must therefore not expect schedules to account for the complex systems used by roulette or blackjack experts, as an example. But the repetitive, apparently mindless, paying of a simple slot machine may well yield to an analysis in terms of the schedules in operation" (Lea, Tarpy, and Webley 1987, p. 287). The description in Dickerson (1993) of poker-machine players as driven by a reinforcement schedule they do not understand also fits this picture.

Moreover, gambling differs from most reinforcement settings in one important respect:

> in gambling, unlike the case of many other types of behavior, money (a general conditioned reinforcer) is being risked for more of the same – a state of affairs which both makes the experience of non-reinforcement punishing (loss of some reinforcer) and evaluations of profit and loss easier. In many forms of behaviour which operate under VR schedules, the loss involved in making a response which is subsequently not reinforced is much more difficult to calculate (how is the effort of telling a joke set against the non-appearance of a smile?) or calculable only within wide limits. (Cornish 1978, pp. 190–1)

At the end of a day at the racetrack, you *know* that you have less money in your pocket than when you arrived. It becomes less plausible that gambling can be maintained merely by monetary reinforcers. Other, secondary rewards must take up the slack. Most obviously, the thrill of gambling may serve as a reinforcer of the behavior. Now, by all accounts the thrill is generated by betting, not by winning. This implies that the reward is forthcoming not on a VR schedule, but on a *fixed-interval* (FI) schedule (the reward is made available following a fixed interval after the response). Specifically, Dickerson (1979, 1984, p. 87 ff.) argues that stimulus events such as reels spinning or race commentaries provide intense arousal and excitement that allow them to serve as reinforcers on a FI schedule. Furthermore, it has been argued that casino betting offers reinforcement in the form of social approval by other gamblers (Ocean and Smith 1993), presumably also on a FI schedule. In addition, we have seen that near-wins may serve as reinforcers on a VR schedule. Although each of the near-wins presumably is less reinforcing than an actual win, there are more of them.[18]

## 5. Conclusion

I conclude by briefly addressing two questions. What explains compulsive gambling? Is compulsive gambling an addiction?

With regard to the explanatory question, I shall make two distinctions. On the one hand, different explanations may apply to different stages in a gambling career. On the other hand, different explanations might apply to different types of gambling. Although I shall sketch a stylized gambling career that is intended to apply to many different types of gambling, some forms may call for a different analysis. In particular, I agree with the writers who claim that fruit-machine or poker-machine playing stand apart from other games. For this type of gambling, reinforcement theory is the natural analytical approach. Reinforcers include, as we have seen, not only one's own wins, but also one's own near-wins and the wins of others. There is virtually no scope for the exercise of skill, even imaginary skills. The roulette player can at least choose a number.

With regard to most other forms of gambling. I suggest that a typical career unfolds as follows: In the first stage, moderate, occasional gambling is triggered by a desire for entertainment and a hope for monetary gain. In a second stage, often following an early big win, the gambler begins to play more frequently and for higher stakes. Secondary rewards from near-wins and social approval also begin to appear at this stage. At the third stage, an interaction between arousal, irrational belief formation, hyperbolic discounting, and manipulation by the gambling establishment eggs the player to go on. In a fourth stage, subjective tolerance and the objective need to repay debts conspire to make the players gamble for ever-higher stakes and/or on longer odds. More or less at the same time, secondary withdrawal symptoms appear that make it even more difficult to stay away from the gambling scene. In this sequence, the crucial step is the passage to the third stage. Irrational belief formation, in particular, seems to be an essential ingredient in the making of a compulsive gambler. "In order for a person to continue gambling at a regular pace, the losses *must* be rationalized in some fashion or other" (Lesieur 1984, p. 49).

Are compulsive gamblers addicts? A full answer must await more knowledge about the neurophysiology of addiction. We do not know whether gambling exhibits anything like the patterns of neuroadaptation described in the chapter by Gardner and David. If gambling turns out to exhibit primary as well as secondary withdrawal symptoms, there is a strong case for classifying it as an addiction. If not, there will nevertheless remain a number of features that gambling has in common with the core addictions.

## NOTES

1. For an early recognition of this distinction and its importance, see an observation from 1799 by a Paris judge quoted in Freundlich (1995, p. 33).
2. This observation is echoed in a study of young fruit-machine players:

   Money, paradoxically, seemed to be a fundamental factor in producing high arousal levels because none of the group said they would enjoy playing a fruit machine if they had one in their bedroom that gave free plays at the push of a button. This seems strange, considering the object of playing in these addicted players, which was to stay on the machines as long as possible using the least amount of money, that is, playing *with* money rather than *for* it. (Griffith 1991, p.125.)

3. This seems to contradict Dickerson (1984, p. 93):

   An anxiety reduction concept [analogous to that used in the explanation of compulsive behavior] does not seem to fit with the other empirical data or with the proposal in the previous section that the very process of gambling may be exciting or arousing particularly for those who bet frequently and persist when gambling. There are few observations that a session of gambling may be calming or anaesthetising.

   In his earlier work, Dickerson may have been less aware of the difference between the psychological mechanisms underlying different types of gambling. The following observation may also be relevant here:

   For those who are hyperactive (and many gamblers meet the diagnosis of Attention Deficit Hyperactivity Disorder), the intensity of gambling, at least initially, has a paradoxical effect; like cocaine or amphetamines, it slows them down, allowing them to concentrate, process affects, and feel normal. (Rosenthal and Rugle 1994, p. 30.)

4. In general, I agree with Fischhoff (1992, p. 137) in that

   When making risky choices, people may consider more than the uncertain and negative consequences of their actions. Indeed, they presumably would not voluntarily expose themselves to a risk if there were not some compensating benefit. That benefit may "just" be avoiding a more serious risk (or a certain negative consequence). Or, it may be bundled with the risk itself, such as the exhilaration of driving fast.

I am suggesting, however, that some people may have a preference for risky driving for its own sake.

5. Later in this section I discuss the possibility that some of these worries might be caused by gambling.

6. One might also ask whether tolerance could not also lead to evermore frequent play, without increasing stakes and odds. In that case, compulsive gambling would be more like smoking than like heroin addiction. I do not know any discussions of this question. My impression is that when people go from occasional gambling to regular gambling it is simply because they find the experience pleasant and want to have more of it. If tolerance to gambling exists, it sets in later and takes the form of gambling for higher stakes.

7. As I mentioned initially, Dickerson (1984, p. 38) defines compulsive gamblers as those who have sought treatment for help. In Dickerson (1993), he explicitly deals with the causes of impaired self-control, defining that concept operationally as "persistence when losing." He is aware that this measure, although reliable, might not be entirely valid. Whereas the former criterion is underinclusive (it misses gamblers who lose control but do not seek help), the latter is overinclusive (it covers those who are happy to lose their money in exchange for the fun).

8. Thus, we have seen that gambling may cause loss of control over gambling, drinking may cause loss of control over drinking, and drinking may cause loss of control over gambling. Could gambling cause loss of control over drinking?

9. Note that a person may be a risk seeker and yet have decreasing marginal utility of money throughout the relevant interval. See Bromiley and Curley (1992, p. 103 ff.) for a discussion of how to "decontaminate" utility-based measures of risk seeking by removing the contribution of the marginal utility of money.

10. Gambling with a negative expected monetary value may actually tend to increase the gambler's wealth by the following nonintentional mechanism. Because of the gambler's system of mental accounting (Thaler 1985), "spending money on lottery tickets can be expected to replace other small expenditures, while large wins may not always be returned to the spending stream, but be saved instead" (Cornish 1978, p. 43). Hence it may be that "the betting-shops' imposition of payout limits on combination bets stems not only from their desire to maximize their profits on this form of betting but also to prevent the potential 'win' from becoming large enough to tempt the winner to use it for purposes other than re-betting" (ibid., p. 178).

11. Even casino owners may be prone to such thinking. Dealers who have lost badly may be replaced (Wagenaar 1988, p. 109) or even dismissed (Dickerson 1984, p. 31).

12. A study of gamblers who root for particular teams concludes that "If bettors were able to overcome their emotional wishes for the sake of financial gain, the bets played by all groups of fans, nonfans and neutral respondents should not have differed from each other. The findings clearly showed that paid

bets reflected wishful thinking" (Babad and Katz 1991, p. 1934). Although an instance of hot cognition, this finding differs from the mechanism discussed in the text, namely wishful thinking *induced* by the desire for financial gain.

13. A gambler might exploit this mechanism to make money by selling "inside information." He might, for instance,

> tell nine different people about the inside information on nine different horses. In this way he would have at least one, and possibly two or three people come to him the next time he touted. He would have more than one person because the people who received the second and third horse that came in would think that the tout was close and 'if only' they had put the money to place or show it would have paid off. (Lesieur 1984, p. 180.)

14. There is at least a prima facie tension between these findings and the suggestion by Rosenthal (1989, p. 105) that gambling is caused by depression.

15. Stein's discussion is also complicated by opaque references to the gambler's beliefs about the chances of winning. Perhaps what she has in mind is the idea mentioned in the text: As the time of betting approaches, the prospect of imminent gain looms larger both because of the hyperbolic discounting and because of irrational belief formation.

16. It is not clear from the literature whether this is a within-episode mechanism or a between-episode mechanism. Most plausibly, it is both.

17. Lea, Tarpy, and Webley (1987, pp. 287–8) refer to experiments by Lewis and Duncan (1957, 1958) that "permitted university students to play a slot machine that was programmed to present reward on 0, 11, 33, 67, or 100% of the plays. Except for the 0 condition, the smaller the percentage of reward, the greater the persistence later when reward was discontinued." On reflection, this is not surprising. If the response has been fixed on a very low reward schedule, it *must* take longer to find out that the reward is no longer forthcoming. I cannot agree, therefore, when Lea, Tarpy, and Webley (1987, p. 288) draw the conclusion that "it is the rarity of success of gambling that induces the gambler to return to the game, not the profitable run of good luck." The laboratory setup in which rewards are first provided on a VR schedule and then withheld altogether has no analogue in real-life gambling.

18. Lea, Tarpy, and Webley ([1987, p. 287], citing Strickland and Grote [1967]) similarly report that

> subjects who saw more winning symbols on the drums that stopped spinning first or second were more likely to continue to play.... One explanation of this finding comes from traditional learning research. It is well known that the sooner a reward is delivered, the stronger the response.... Delayed rewards lead to lower rates of behavior. There seems little doubt that the winning symbol is a reward for playing the machine. If this is the case, then it makes good sense for the strength of the response, measured by the willingness to play beyond the first 100 games, to be lower when the winning symbol is consistently in the third position. This effect, that

responses closest to the onset of reward are the most strongly reinforced, would also predict that, for regular gamblers, late bets should increase and earlier bets decay.

Dickerson (1979, p. 321) confirms this prediction, but explains it by the FI schedule discussed in the text.

## REFERENCES

Alloy, L. and L. Abrahamson (1988), "Depressive realism," in L. B. Alloy (ed.), *Cognitive Processes in Depression*, New York, Guilford Press, pp. 441–85.

Anderson, G. and R. I. F. Brown (1984), "Real and laboratory gambling, sensation-seeking and arousal," *British Journal of Psychology* 75, 401–10.

Babad, E. and Y. Katz (1991), "Wishful thinking – against all odds," *Journal of Applied Social Psychology* 21, 1921–38.

Baumeister, R. F., T. F. Heatherton, and D. M. Tice (1994), *Losing Control: How and Why People Fail at Self-Regulation*, San Diego, Academic Press.

Becker, G. and K. Murphy (1988), "A theory of rational addiction," *Journal of Political Economy* 96, 675–700.

Bergler, E. (1957), *The Psychology of Gambling*, International Universities Press.

Bromiley, P. and S. P. Curley (1992), "Individual differences in risk-taking," in J. F. Yates (ed.), *Risk-Taking Behavior*, New York, Wiley, pp. 87–132.

Brown, R. I. F. (1986), "Arousal and sensation-seeking components in the general explanation of gambling and gambling addictions," *International Journal of the Addictions* 21, 1001–16.

Cornish, D. B. (1978), *Gambling: A Review of the Literature and Its Implications for Policy and Research*, London, Her Majesty's Stationery Office.

Coventry, K. R. and R. I. F. Brown (1993), "Sensation seeking, gambling and gambling addictions," *Addiction* 88, 541–54.

Custer, R. L. (1982), "Pathological gambling," in A. Whitfield (ed.), *Patients with Alcoholism and Other Drug Problems*, New York, Year Book Publishers.

Dickerson, M. G. (1979), "FI schedules and persistence at gambling in the UK betting office," *Journal of Applied Behavior Analysis* 12, 315–23.

  (1984), *Compulsive Gamblers*, London, Longman.

  (1993), "Internal and external determinants of persistent gambling: Problems in generalising from one form of gambling to another," *Journal of Gambling Studies* 9, 225–45.

Dostoeyvski, F. (1964), *The Gambler*, New York, Norton.

Fischhoff, B. (1992), "Risk taking: A developmental approach," in J. F. Yates (ed.), *Risk-Taking Behavior*, New York, Wiley, pp. 133–62.

France, C. J. (1902), "The gambling impulse," *American Journal of Psychology* 13, 364–407.

Freundlich, F. (1995), *Le Monde du Jeu à Paris (1715–1800)*, Paris, Albin Michel.

Friedman, M. and L. Savage (1948), "The utility analysis of choices involving risk," *Journal of Political Economy* 56, 279–304.

Gilovich, T. (1983), "Biased evaluation and persistence on gambling," *Journal of Personality and Social Psychology* 44, 1110–26.

Greenberg, M. E. and B. Weiner (1966), "Effects of reinforcement history on risk-taking behavior," *Journal of Experimental Psychology* 71, 587–92.

Griffith, M. (1991), "Psychobiology of the near-miss in fruit machine gambling," *The Journal of Psychology* 125, 347–57.

(1994), "Beating the fruit machine," *Journal of Gambling Studies* 10, 287–92.

Hamsun, K. (1954), "Far og sønn. En spillehistorie" ("Father and son. A gambling tale"), in K. Hamsun (ed.), *Samlede Verker*, vol. 4, Oslo, Gyldendal, pp. 73–91.

Jacobs, D. F. (1989), "A general theory of addictions," in H. J. Shaffer, S. Stein, and B. Gambino (eds.), *Compulsive Gambling*, Lexington, MA, Lexington Books, pp. 35–64.

Kahneman, D. and A. Tversky (1982), "The simulation heuristic," in D. Kahneman, P. Slovic, and A. Tversky (eds.), *Judgment Under Uncertainty*, Cambridge, UK, Cambridge University Press, pp. 201–208.

Karcher, A. J. (1992), *Lotteries*, New Brunswick, NJ, Transaction Books.

Langer, E. J. (1975), "The illusion of control," *Journal of Personality and Social Psychology* 32, 311–28.

Lea, S. E. G., R. M. Tarpy, and P. Webley (1987), *The Individual in the Economy: A Survey of Economic Psychology*, Cambridge, UK, Cambridge University Press.

Lesieur, H. R. (1984), *The Chase: The Compulsive Gambler*, Rochester, VT, Schenkman Books.

Lewis, D. J. and C. P. Duncan (1957), "Expectation and resistance to extinction of a lever pulling response as functions of percentage of reinforcement and amount of reward," *Journal of Experimental Psychology* 54, 115–20.

(1958), "Expectation and resistance to extinction of a lever pulling response as functions of percentage of reinforcement and number of acquisition trials," *Journal of Experimental Psychology* 55, 121–28.

Murray, W. (1985), *Tip on a Dead Crab*, New York, Penguin.

(1990), *The King of the Nightcap*, New York, Bantam Books.

(1991), *The Getaway Blues*, New York, Bantam Books.

Ocean, G. J. and G. J. Smith (1993), "Social reward, conflict, and commitment: A theoretical model of gambling behavior," *Journal of Gambling Studies* 9, 321–39.

Orphanides, A. and D. Zervos (1992), "Rational addiction with learning and regret," unpublished manuscript.

Peck, C. P. (1986), "Risk-taking behavior and compulsive gambling," *American Psychologist* 41, 461–65.

Rachlin, H. (1990), "Why do people gamble and keep gambling despite heavy losses?" *Psychological Science* 1, 294–7.

Rosenthal, R. J. (1989), "Pathological gambling and problem gambling," in H. J. Shaffer, S. Stein, and B. Gambino (eds.), *Compulsive Gambling*, Lexington, MA, Lexington Books, pp. 101–25.

Rosenthal, R. J. and L. J. Rugle (1994), "A psychodynamic approach to the treatment of pathological gambling: Part I. Achieving abstinence," *Journal of Gambling Studies* 10, 21–42.

Seeburger, F. F. (1993), *Addiction and Responsibility*, New York, Cross Road.

Shaffer, H. (1989), "Conceptual crises in the addictions: The role of models in the field of compulsive gambling," in H. J. Shaffer, S. Stein, and B. Gambino (eds.), *Compulsive Gambling*, Lexington, MA, Lexington Books, pp. 3–33.

Stein, S. (1989), "A developmental approach to understanding compulsive gambling behavior," in H. J. Shaffer, S. Stein, and B. Gambino (eds.), *Compulsive
Gambling*, Lexington, MA, Lexington Books, pp. 65–88.

Strickland, L. H. and F. W. Grote (1967), "Temporal presentation of winning
symbols and slot machine playing," *Journal of Experimental Psychology* 74,
10–13.

Thaler, R. (1985), "Mental accounting and consumer choice," *Marketing Science*
4, 199–214.

Tversky, A. and D. Griffin (1991), "Endowment and contrast in judgments of
well-being," in R. J. Zeckhauser (ed.), *Strategy and Choice*, Cambridge, MA,
MIT Press, pp. 297–318.

Tversky, A. and D. Kahneman (1974), "Judgment under uncertainty: Heuristics
and biases," *Science* 185, 1124–31.

Tversky, A. and E. Shafir (1992), "The disjunction effect in choice under uncertainty," *Psychological Science* 3, 305–9.

Wagenaar, W. A. (1988), *Paradoxes of Gambling Behavior*, Hove and London,
Lawrence Erlbaum.

Walters, G. (1994), "The gambling lifestyle: I. Theory," *Journal of Gambling Studies*
10, 159–82.

Wray, I. and M. G. Dickerson (1981), "Cessation of high frequency gambling and
'withdrawal symptoms'," *British Journal of Addiction* 76, 401–5.

# A Visceral Account of Addiction

GEORGE LOEWENSTEIN

In the past, addiction has been viewed as a *sui generis* phenomenon (Baker 1988). Recent theories of addiction, however, draw implicit or explicit parallels between addiction and a wide range of other behavioral phenomena. The "disease theory," for example, highlights similarities between addiction and infectious disease (e.g., Frawley [1988], Vaillant [1983]). Becker and Murphy's rational-choice model of addiction draws a parallel between drug addictions and "endogenous taste" phenomena, such as listening to classical music to attempt to acquire a taste for it, in which current consumption affects the utility of future consumption (Becker and Murphy 1988). Herrnstein and Prelec's "garden path" theory sees addiction as analogous to bad habits, such as workaholism or compulsive lying, that can be acquired gradually due to a failure to notice a deterioration in one's conduct or situation (Herrnstein and Prelec 1992).

In this chapter, I propose an alternative theoretical perspective that views addiction as one, albeit extreme, example of a wide range of behaviors that are influenced or controlled by "visceral factors" (Loewenstein 1996). Visceral factors include drive states such as hunger, thirst, and sexual desire, moods and emotions, physical pain, and, most importantly for addiction, craving for a drug. All visceral factors, including drug craving, are associated with regulatory mechanisms that are essential for survival, but all are also associated with behavior disorders (e.g., sleepiness and narcolepsy, hunger and overeating, fear and phobias, sexual desire and sexual compulsions, anger and spousal abuse, craving and addiction). At intermediate levels, most visceral factors, including drug craving, produce similar patterns of impulsivity, remorse, and self-binding. At high levels, drug craving and other visceral factors overwhelm decision making altogether, superseding volitional control of behavior.

The defining characteristics of visceral factors are, first, a direct hedonic impact (which is usually negative) and, second, an effect on the relative desirability of different goods and actions. The largely aversive experience of hunger, for example, increases the desirability of eating and also affects the desirability of other activities such as sex. Likewise, fear and pain are both aversive, and both increase the desirability of escape.

The visceral factor perspective (as outlined by Loewenstein [1996]) has two central premises that are especially relevant to addiction: First, immediately experienced visceral factors have a disproportionate effect on behavior and tend to "crowd out" virtually all goals other than that of mitigating the visceral factor. Second, people underestimate the impact on their own behavior of visceral factors they will experience in the future.

The disproportionate influence of immediately experienced visceral factors is relevant to understanding the force and persistence of addictive behavior. It helps to explain why, once addicted, people have such a difficult time quitting, despite the by-then typically obvious benefits of abstinence. Like extreme hunger, thirst, pain, anger, sleepiness, and a wide range of other visceral sensations, drug craving limits the scope for volitional control of behavior. Once the addict is "hooked," and subject to intermittent craving, the scope for volition narrows to the point where it may not be useful, either theoretically or practically, to view the addict's behavior as a matter of choice.

The underappreciation of the force of delayed visceral factors is critical to understanding why people get addicted in the first place. Underestimating the force of the craving they will experience if they try to stop taking the drug, people overestimate their own future ability to stop taking the drug. Early drug-taking behavior, therefore, results from a decision that is distorted by biased expectations.

The visceral account of addiction can be viewed as a hybrid of decision-based and disease perspectives. In the early stages of addiction, drug taking is seen as the product of largely volitional decision making. As an individual becomes addicted to a drug, however, there is a progressive loss of volitional control over drug taking.

The visceral account of early drug taking is somewhat akin to Herrnstein and Prelec's (1992) model of addiction. Both view the addict-to-be as engaged in active, but biased, decision making. The models differ, however, in their views about the source of the bias. In Herrnstein and Prelec's model, the bias results from a failure to notice the incremental detrimental effect of engaging in the addictive activity. In the visceral account, it results from a failure to appreciate the motivational force of future craving.

In its view of the later stages of addiction, the visceral account of addiction bears a closer relationship to the disease perspective. Once addicted, an individual may recognize that abstinence is the best course of action, but his ability to abstain is powerfully constrained by the force of intermittent craving.

The feature of the visceral account of addiction that most starkly separates it from other theoretical accounts is the central role played by cue-conditioned craving. Cue-conditioned craving refers to the tendency for cues that become mentally associated with an addictive drug to elicit craving for the drug. Although there is a large empirical literature on craving and its role in addiction, the insights from this literature have yet to be summarized in the form of a more general model of addiction.[1] One other theoretical account of addiction – the opponent process perspective (Solomon and Corbit 1974, Koob, Stinus, Le Moal, and Bloom 1989) – does feature conditioning and craving in a prominent role. The opponent process account of addiction, however, focuses on craving associated with withdrawal rather than cue-conditioned craving as the key feature of addiction. The visceral account's emphasis on cue-conditioned craving rather than withdrawal reflects a widespread belief among addiction researchers that craving rather than withdrawal is the critical impediment to recovery from addiction. Just as it is easier to shed weight than to keep it off (NIH Technology Assessment Conference Panel 1993), it is easier to withdraw from most drugs than it is to abstain in the long run (Goldstein 1994; Shiffman 1982, p. 72).

The remainder of the chapter, is organized as follows: Section 1 presents the basic elements of the visceral-factor perspective and discusses in detail the two regularities mentioned above: the excessive influence of immediate, and the insufficient appreciation of delayed, visceral factors. Section 2 demonstrates that drug craving exhibits the same characteristics as other visceral factors and reviews the literature on the determinants and effects of craving. Section 3 presents the rudiments of a theoretical account of addiction that incorporates cue-conditioned craving and draws out implications for who gets addicted, the effects of addiction on behavior, quitting and self-binding, relapse, treatment, and the definition of addiction.

## 1. The Visceral-Factor Perspective

Technically one can view visceral factors as short-term fluctuations in tastes. However, doing so obscures several crucial differences between visceral factors and tastes. First, visceral factors affect utility directly, even if actual consumption is held constant, and thus they resemble consumption, not tastes. The welfare effect of a change in tastes is a largely philosophical issue, but hunger, thirst, pain, etc. have straightforward effects on well-being, holding actual consumption constant.

Second, visceral factors are correlated with external circumstances (stimulation, deprivation, and such) and, as a result, they tend to fluctuate, often dramatically, over time.[2] Indeed the abruptness of such fluctuations may contribute to their potency. Changes in tastes, in contrast, are caused by slow experience and reflection, are typically not anticipated, and do imply a long-term change in behavior. Though tastes change, they tend to be stable in the short run.

Finally, tastes and visceral factors probably draw on different neurophysiological mechanisms. Tastes consist of information stored in memory about the utility conferred by different forms of consumption. Visceral factors, in contrast, result from neurochemical changes in the reward and motivation centers of the brain. "The core of the brain," Pribram (1984, p. 2) writes, "uses chemical regulations to control body functions. The configuration of concentrations of these chemicals, although fluctuating around some set point, is sufficiently stable over periods of time to constitute steady 'states.' These states apparently are experienced as hunger, thirst, sleepiness, elation, depression, effort, comfort, and so on." Their common neurochemical origins may explain why so many disorders that are associated with visceral factors (e.g., overeating, compulsive shopping, phobias, and, perhaps, some drug addictions) appear to be susceptible to moderation by a single drug – Fluoxetine (Messiha 1993).

## The Effect of Immediate Visceral Factors

Visceral factors play an important role in the regulation of behavior. They serve as "interrupts" that focus attention on specific high-priority goals. Hunger, for example, signals a current or anticipated nutritional deficit (Toates 1979). Pain (Fields 1987) and fear (Janis 1967) signal the presence of an environmental threat. Virtually all visceral factors, including drug craving, focus attention in such a fashion.

Visceral factors also motivate the individual to achieve the goals on which they focus attention. In most cases, this motivation is experienced as an aversive sensation that can be mitigated by addressing the need signaled by the visceral factor. Thus, hunger, thirst, pain, fear, and drug craving provide motivation for, respectively, eating, drinking, avoidance, flight, and drug consumption. Most visceral factors are aversive, probably because aversion provides a more reliable motivational mechanism than reward. As Damasio (1994, p. 264) argues, "suffering puts us on notice. Suffering offers us the best protection for survival, since it increases the probability that individuals will heed pain signals and act to avert their source or correct their consequences."

As the intensity of visceral factors increase, their influence on behavior tends to exhibit a characteristic pattern. At low levels, people seem capable of dealing with visceral factors in a relatively optimal fashion. For example, a person who is mildly frightened by a dog might decide to tolerate the fear and remain in the dog's proximity, or to leave. There is nothing inherently irrational about taking such visceral factors into account since they do affect well-being and generally serve important regulatory functions. It makes perfect sense to eat when hungry, drink when thirsty, and withdraw when experiencing pain or fear; to be convinced of this one only need glimpse the physical condition of people who are congenitally unable to experience pain (Fields 1987, pp. 3–5).

When visceral factors become elevated further, they tend to produce internal conflicts between behavior and perceived self-interest. Thus, as fear toward the dog increases, the individual may begin to experience a tension between how he *wants* to behave and how he thinks that he *should* behave. One can imagine an internal dialogue such as, "Get a hold on yourself. The dog is harmless; it has never bitten anyone. It can sense that you are frightened." Such efforts at "self-command" (Schelling 1984) are characteristic responses to visceral factors in the midrange of intensity.

Finally, at sufficient levels of intensity, visceral factors overwhelm volitional will altogether. Internal exhortations to do the right thing lose all effectiveness and the individual is likely to engage in self-destructive behavior such as flight (a dog can run faster than a person) or immobilization (Janis and Leventhal 1967). Decision making still occurs, in the sense of an *awareness* of the best course of action, but the individual may be unable to act on such awareness.

When visceral factors overwhelm volitional choice, deviations of behavior from perceived self-interest tend to exhibit a characteristic pattern. Not surprisingly, given their attention-focusing function, they tend to narrow an individual's perceptual and motivational focus. Hunger narrows one's focus to food, fear to options for flight, and so on. At sufficient levels of intensity, individuals make highly skewed tradeoffs between goods and activities that alleviate the visceral factor and those that do not. Sex has little appeal to a person who is starving; food has little appeal to a person in the "grip" of terror.[3]

Visceral factors also produce a second form of attention narrowing – a good-specific collapse to the present of one's time perspective. Thus, a hungry person makes shortsighted tradeoffs between immediate and delayed food, even when expecting tomorrow's hunger to be as intense as today's. This present-orientation, however, applies only to goods that are associated with the visceral factor, and only to tradeoffs between the present and some other point in time. A hungry person would probably make the same choices as a nonhungry person between immediate and delayed money (assuming that food cannot be purchased) or immediate and delayed sex. A hungry person might also make the same choices as a nonhungry person between food tomorrow versus food on the day after tomorrow. Both of these features differentiate the visceral factor perspective from models that explain addiction on the basis of generalized (across goods and activities) individual differences in time preferences.

Yet a third form of attention narrowing involves the self versus others. Intense visceral factors narrow one's focus inwardly and reduce one's concern for other people. People who are hungry, in pain, angry, or craving drugs tend to be selfish. As torturers understand well, sleep deprivation, hunger, thirst, pain, and indeed most visceral factors can cause even the most strongly willed individuals to betray comrades, friends, and family (Biderman 1960).

## Underestimation of Future Visceral Factors

The second important regularity of relevance to addiction is a tendency for people to underappreciate their own susceptibility to visceral influences. Unlike currently experienced visceral factors, which have a disproportionate impact on behavior, delayed visceral factors tend to be ignored or severely underweighted in decision making. Today's pain, hunger, anger, etc. are palpable, but the same sensations anticipated in the future receive little weight.

In a series of recent papers dealing with topics other than addiction, various coauthors and I have demonstrated what we call "cold-to-hot empathy gaps" – the tendency for an individual when cold (i.e., not experiencing an elevated visceral factor) to mispredict his or her own behavior when hot. In one paper (Loewenstein, Nagin, and Paternoster 1997), we showed sexually arousing photographs to one group of male subjects and nonarousing photographs to another; we then asked them to predict their own behavior in the context of a typical date rape scenario. Aroused subjects predicted a much higher likelihood that they would behave in a sexually aggressive manner, as if being aroused made them better able to imagine what they would do when aroused on a date.[4]

In another paper (Loewenstein, Prelec, and Shatto 1996), my coauthors and I show that people underpredict the motivational impact of curiosity on their own behavior.[5] Subjects are given a sample geography question, randomly chosen from a list of eleven such questions, and then are given the remaining ten questions. All subjects are given a choice between receiving the answers to the ten questions or receiving a candy bar, but half are given the choice before taking the quiz and the other half are given the choice after taking the quiz. A substantially larger fraction opt for the candy bar before taking the quiz, when they are not curious, than after taking the quiz, as if those in the before condition underestimate the force of their own future curiosity.

In a third paper that bears an especially close connection to the phenomenon of addiction, Daniel Adler and I studied people's predictions of how attached they would become to objects they were endowed with (Loewenstein and Adler 1995). Research on the "endowment effect" (Thaler 1980) has shown that people become attached to an object they are endowed with, even if they would not have desired the object particularly had they not been endowed with it.[6] In one study we informed some subjects that they would be endowed with an object; we then asked them to predict the price at which they would sell the object back to the experimenter once they were endowed. These subjects, and others who did not make a prediction, were then endowed with the object and given the opportunity to sell it back to the experimenter. Much in the same way that addicts-to-be seem to underestimate their own future attachment to drugs, subjects who were not endowed underpredicted substantially their own postendowment selling prices.

The cold-to-hot empathy gap may result from limitations in our ability to remember visceral states. Imagination and memory draw on similar neural resources and invoke similar cognitive processes. Human memory is well suited to remembering visual images, words, and semantic meaning, but it seems ill-suited to storing information about visceral sensations. Recalling visual images actually activates many of the brain systems that are involved in visual perception (Kosslyn et al. 1993). Thus, it appears that to imagine a visual scene in the mind is, in a very real sense to "see" the scene again in one's mind, albeit in distorted, incomplete, and less vivid form.

Recall of pain, and probably other visceral factors, however, is qualitatively different. As Morley (1993) observes in an insightful paper, we can easily recognize pain, but few can recall pain in the sense of reexperiencing it in imagination or memory. Morley (1993) distinguishes between three possible variants of memory for pain: (1) sensory reexperiencing of the pain; (2) remembering the sensory, intensity, and affective qualities of the pain without reexperiencing it; and (3) remembering the circumstances in which the pain was experienced. Most studies of memory for pain have focused on the second variant and have obtained mixed results. For example, several studies have examined the accuracy of women's memory of the pain of childbirth, most employing a so-called visual analog scale (basically a mark made on a thermometer scale) (e.g., Rofé and Algom [1985]; Norvell, Gaston-Johansson, and Fridh [1987]). These researchers have reached conflicting conclusions, with some finding accurate, some finding overestimation, and some finding underestimation of past pain.

In contrast to these contradictory findings, most studies on pain memory that have examined the issue are in agreement that subjects possess either Morley's second or third variant of pain memory, but not the first – sensory reexperiencing. For example, Morley (1993) himself, in a survey that elicited pain memories, found that 59% of his subjects were able to recall at least some aspect of the pain sensation, 41% reported that they had no recall of the pain sensation at all, and not a single subject reported actually reexperiencing the pain. Strongman and Kemp (1991) found that spontaneous accounts of pain tended to fit Morley's third variant of pain memory – remembering the circumstances in which the pain was experienced: "Overwhelmingly, the descriptions were of 'objective' details of the events rather than of the feelings of the respondents" (p. 195). Fienberg, Loftus, and Tanur (1985, p. 592) concluded their review of the research on pain up to 1985 by asking, "Is it pain that people recall or is it really the events such as injuries and severe illnesses?"

People certainly do get viscerally upset when remembering or recalling certain types of pains, particularly those that evoke vivid images (e.g., those resulting from bloody wounds or dentist drills; see Scarry [1985] and Loewenstein [1996] for a fuller discussion of this issue). These pains are likely to be exaggerated both in memory and anticipation (see, e.g., Kent 1985). Drug craving, as well as other types of pains and discomforts such as that resulting from cold (Read and Loewenstein [forthcoming]), however, are difficult to imagine and are thus unlikely to evoke a visceral reaction when recalled or anticipated. The failure to vividly recall or anticipate the discomfort of craving can help to explain the postulated underappreciation of future craving.

There is an additional factor that contributes to the underappreciation of future visceral factors: The well-documented tendency for people to overestimate their own abilities. This tendency is evident in the "above average" effect whereby well over half of survey respondents typically rate themselves in the top 50% of drivers (Svenson 1981) and with regard to their ethics (Baumhart 1968), managerial prowess (Larwood and Whittaker 1977), and a variety of other desirable skills. It is also evident in a piggyback study conducted in connection to the famous Milgram shock experiment in which subjects were informed of the methodology and of the high prevalence of shocking behavior and were asked to guess what they personally would have done if they had been subjects. Most subjects in the piggyback study did not think that they themselves would have administered powerful shocks to the confederate, as if they underestimated the effect on their own behavior of being exposed to the authoritative and relentless pressure of an experimenter (Milgram 1965; see also, Wolosin, Sherman, and Cann 1975). It seems plausible that this tendency to overestimate one's own resistance to external influences would also apply to addiction, that is, that people would have an exaggerated conceit about their own ability to resist the force of craving.

## 2. Craving as a Visceral Factor

There is a widespread, although not unanimous, belief among addiction researchers that craving plays a central role in addiction.[7] Craving refers to a "strong desire or intense longing" (Kozlowski and Wilkinson 1987, p. 31). Craving "seems to capture the essence of addiction in terms of its irresistible, compulsive, and anticipatory qualities, . . . has a strong appetitive quality, and is often used to describe intense appetites such as hunger, thirst, or lust" (Marlatt 1987, p. 42). Craving produces a powerful, often overwhelming, urge to consume a drug. Even cocaine, which at one time seemed to present the anomalous case of an addictive drug that did not produce withdrawal or craving, has been shown to produce intense craving, both in humans and other animals (Gawin 1991).

Craving is somewhat different in character from other visceral factors. Whereas most other visceral factors are present from birth, craving arises from a process of neuroadaptation to drug taking (Eikelboom and Stewart 1982, Siegel 1979). Nevertheless, like other visceral factors, craving plays an important adaptive function. Craving is the byproduct of a conditioned association mechanism that acts as an early warning and defense system to anticipate and protect the organism against the disequilibrating effect of the drug.

When a pleasure-producing drug is consumed repeatedly, internal defenses or "opponent processes" are activated to neutralize its disequilibrating effect on the organism (Solomon and Corbit 1974, Frawley 1988).[8] These processes are triggered by "feedback" mechanisms that signal the drug's presence in the body or its effects, but they can also be triggered by "feedforward," that is, conditioned anticipation of drug intake (Siegel, Krank, and Hinson 1988). The adaptive effect of feedforward is illustrated by a study in which rats who had regularly received a dosage of heroin in a specific room, overdosed when the same dosage was administered in a different room, presumably because the cues necessary for feedforward were missing (Siegel et al. 1982). Craving arises when an individual is exposed to drug-related cues that produce an adaptive response but subsequently does not consume the drug. Although the specific subjective feeling may vary from drug to drug, and perhaps between persons, craving is invariably unpleasant and powerfully increases the desire to take the drug.[9] Note that these two features – the negative hedonic effect and the enhanced desire for the drug – are the defining characteristics of a visceral factor.

Once an individual is addicted to a drug, craving appears to be the main force that keeps him taking it. Even mild craving seems to have a profound effect on behavior, an effect equivalent to that exerted by other visceral factors only at extreme levels of intensity. Indeed, a number of researchers have wondered why even mild states of craving can have such a profound influence on behavior. One explanation, offered by Berridge and Robinson (1995), is that people can crave drugs with little or no conscious awareness of doing so. Another possibility is that craving derives its incentive value not from its intensity, but from its constancy; it simply doesn't go away until the need that it signals is satisfied.

### Determinants of Craving

As endogenous taste models assume (e.g., Becker and Murphy [1988], Herrnstein and Prelec [1992], Koob et al. [1989]), craving tends to be positively related to the duration and intensity of prior drug use, and craving sometimes occurs automatically upon cessation of consumption – a phenomenon referred to as "withdrawal." However, there is a growing consensus that withdrawal itself does not constitute the major impediment to quitting, in part because highly effective therapeutic interventions exist for withdrawal from many addictive drugs.

Instead, the main impediment to quitting appears to be the problem of craving-induced relapse. As Gawin (1988, p. 12) comments, "during withdrawal, most cocaine abusers can withstand postcocaine anhedonia (withdrawal)." However, "After ... the [withdrawal] period ends, episodic craving and the risk for relapse remain because of the continued role of conditioned cues." Relapse is a constant threat because craving can be initiated by almost any environmental cue that becomes associated with the drug – for example, time of day, a particular room or even the color of the room, the presence of specific individuals or paraphernalia associated with drug taking (Siegel et al. 1988), sounds, and even positive or negative mood states (Gawin 1991, p. 1582). As Goldstein describes it,

> A typical addict smokes 10 to 50 cigarettes every day. Each one is linked to a particular time, place, and activity... For example, sitting down to the first morning cup of coffee is a conditioned cue to take out a cigarette and light it. Every meal ends with a cigarette. Sitting down at a desk to work evokes craving for a cigarette. Stepping into the lobby during intermission means light-up time. Just being near other smokers produces an automatic reaching for a cigarette. (Goldstein 1994, p. 114.)

Cue-conditioned craving is similarly important for the more intense and immediately destructive addictions, such as addiction to crack cocaine or heroin. Again Goldstein provides a vivid illustration – the behavior of a heroin addict, Charlie T., who had stabilized on methadone with a regular job, but whose urine test one day showed that he had used heroin:

> He...had suddenly been overwhelmed by an irresistible craving and had rushed out of his house to find some heroin. His description was fascinating: It was as though he were driven by some external force he was powerless to resist, even though he knew while it was happening that it was a disastrous course of action for him. (Goldstein 1994, p. 220.)

After further discussion, Goldstein and Charlie T. identified the cue that had triggered the relapse. Charlie T. had been watching a TV program about an addict:

> They showed an addict fixing, putting the needle into his vein, and suddenly I felt sick, just like needing heroin. I got that craving. I broke out in a sweat. I had that old feeling that only a fix would cure me (Goldstein 1994, p. 221.)

Theoretical models that view addiction as an endogenous taste phenomenon (e.g., Becker and Murphy [1988], Herrnstein and Prelec [1992], Orphanides and Zervos [1995]) assume that decreasing one's taste for the addictive substance is purely a matter of desisting from consumption. The visceral factor account, in contrast, places much greater importance on cues that are capable of inducing craving. Quitting involves much more than ceasing consumption for a certain interval because craving can occur at any time, even years after drug taking has ceased, if the addict becomes exposed to sufficiently evocative cues (Gawin 1988, 1991). Deconditioning – the gradual diminishment in a cue's propensity to evoke craving – can proceed so slowly that cues may retain their ability to evoke craving even after years of abstinence (Niaura et al. 1988, Shiffman 1982), which may help to explain the relatively low rates of successful long-term abstinence from drugs among drug addicts (Hser, Anglin, and Powers 1993).

Successful quitting is thus likely to require a substantial investment in change of environment and lifestyle because addiction "poisons" persons, places, and things associated with it in the sense of imparting them with the ability to induce craving. As Siegel (1982, p. 335) observes, "users will attempt to avoid all contact with cocaine, cocaine paraphernalia and cocaine users when attempting this self-initiated detoxification. Some users report that it is effective to simply avoid dealers or other social users. Others engage in destruction of paraphernalia, and still others employ physical restraint by taking a vacation or even moving to another house or city." However, regardless of such efforts, it is impossible to completely eliminate the possibility of an encounter with drug-associated cues. Hence, the AA expression "once an alcoholic, always an alcoholic," and Gawin's (1988, p. 14) pessimistic view that the third, "extinction" phase of addiction to cocaine "persists indefinitely."

### Narrowing of Attention

Craving routinely produces each of the three forms of attention narrowing that are characteristic of all visceral factors. First, it increases the value of the craved substance relative to all other forms of consumption. Frawley (1988, p. 32) refers to a "process of…increasing the behavior that facilitates drug or alcohol use and eliminating behavior that interferes with or does not lead to drug or alcohol use. This leads to a kind of 'tunnel vision' on the part of the addict." This effect is most dramatically evident in the behavior of cocaine addicts, who report that "virtually all thoughts are focused on cocaine during binges; nourishment, sleep, money, loved ones, responsibility, and survival lose all significance" (Gawin 1991, p. 1581). It is also illustrated vividly by experiments with rats that were given access to cocaine and a wide range of alternative forms of consumption. These animals lose interest in food and other forms of consumption, lose weight, and typically die in a matter of weeks (Pickens and Harris 1968).[10]

Second, craving seems to shorten the individual's time horizon, particularly when it comes to the drug itself. Addicts are notoriously short-sighted. This is usually viewed as a character trait, and, indeed, it is often seen as *the* trait that caused them to become addicts in the first place. However, myopia is as much the consequence of as the cause of addiction. Moreover, the visceral factor perspective implies that craving-induced myopia takes a very specific form: It increases the immediate desire for a specific drug but leaves time preferences for other items unchanged and should also not affect time preference for the drug in the future. Consistent with this prediction, Madden, Petry, Badger, and Bickel (1996) found that opioid-dependent individuals' time discount rates for heroin were much higher than those for money. In other words, monetary payments lost their incentive value when delayed at a much slower rate than did doses of heroin.

Third, craving is notorious for eliciting destructive behavior that belies a lack of concern for the well-being of other people. The literature on drug addiction abounds with horrifying examples of the destructive behavior of drug addicts, toward family, friends, and strangers. Subjected to the miseries of craving, severe addicts tend to classify people into two categories: Those who threaten to impede access to the drug and those who can serve as tools for obtaining it.[11]

### Imperfect Anticipation of Craving

There are many possible reasons for taking a drug one is not addicted to: Immediate pleasure, peer pressure, relief of depression, etc. These differ across drugs, situations, and people, and they undoubtedly account for much of the variance in drug-taking behavior across persons and situations. The main reason for *not* taking a drug, besides possible immediate negative consequences such as impaired driving or risk of arrest, is the possibility that one will become addicted (that is, not be able to stop), with all its associated negative consequences. Most people view addiction as a negative state of affairs; indeed, due to selective media attention to dramatic cases, stereotypes about the woes of drug addiction may well be exaggerated.

If people truly believed that they would get addicted to a drug – that they would be unable to stop taking it – addiction would almost certainly be less prevalent than it is. However, as discussed earlier, people underestimate both the aversiveness of delayed visceral factors and their influence on behavior. Lynch and Bonnie (1994), for example, report results from the University of Michigan's *Monitoring the Future* longitudinal study that suggest that high school students underestimate the likelihood of becoming addicted to cigarette smoking. Respondents were asked whether they expected to be smoking cigarettes in five years. Among respondents who were occasional smokers (less than one cigarette per day), only 15% predicted that they might be smoking in five years, but five years later 43% were in fact smoking.

There is also evidence for both forms of underestimation on the part of addicts and "dry" addicts. In the study just mentioned, for example, among those who smoked at least one pack a day, only 32% expected to still be smoking in five years, but five years later 70% still smoked one pack or more per day. More anecdotally, Seeburger (1993), in his recent book on addiction, comments that the motivation to stay off a drug...

> lasts as long as the memory of the undesirable consequences stays strong. But the more successful one is at avoiding an addictive practice on the grounds of such motivation, the less strong does that very memory become. Before long, the memory of the pain that one brought on oneself through the addiction begins to pale in comparison to the anticipation of the satisfaction that would immediately attend relapse into the addiction. Sometimes in AA it is said that the farther away one is from one's last drink, the closer one is to the next one. That is surely true for alcoholics and all other addicts whose only reason to stop "using" is to avoid negative consequences that accompany continuing usage. (p. 152.)

Wiktor Osiatynski, in a similar vein, refers to the alcoholic's tendency to underestimate the power of addiction: "After hitting bottom and achieving sobriety, many alcoholics must get drunk again, often not once but a few times, in order to come to believe and never forget about their powerlessness" (Osiatynski 1992, p. 128).

These latter illustrations of the underestimation of visceral factors are particularly disturbing because the people being discussed have had extensive experience with craving. Experience thus does not seem to be sufficient to imprint a memory for the pain of craving. This observation is consistent with research on memory for pain showing that experiencing a pain repeatedly does not go very far in terms of enhancing one's memory for the pain. For example, none of the research on the accuracy of memory for childbirth pain has revealed a significant difference in accuracy between remembered first and subsequent births (e.g., Christensen-Szalanski [1984], Norvell, Gaston-Johansson, and Fridh [1987]).

### 3. Implications of the Visceral Account of Addiction

The main features of the visceral account of addiction can be expressed in a series of simple diagrams. These resemble the diagrams often used

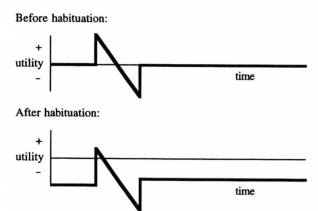

Figure 1. Opponent process account.

to illustrate the opponent process perspective, which are presented first in Figure 1 so as to highlight the difference between the two accounts.

The opponent process account of addiction is as follows: In the early stages of drug taking, the pleasure derived from consuming a drug is gradually neutralized by an opponent process that lingers after the effects of the drug cease, creating a brief period of anhedonia following drug consumption. As drug taking continues, however, the opponent process operates ever-more rapidly, reducing the initial period of pleasure associated with drug taking and intensifying and lengthening the subsequent period of anhedonia. The reduction in the drug's effectiveness due to the increasing efficiency of the opponent process produces tolerance (the need for ever-increasing amounts of the drug to achieve the same effect), and the anhedonia that follows in the wake of drug taking produces withdrawal. The opponent process account of drug addiction, therefore, views *withdrawal* following cessation of drug taking as the mechanism responsible for drug dependence.

As noted earlier, however, it is not withdrawal, but cue-conditioned craving, that appears to be the major impediment to abstinence. As Washton (1988, p. 34) notes in the context of cocaine addiction, "most cocaine addicts find it easy to stop using the drug in the short term but very difficult to avoid using it in the long term." Indeed, the very ease of stopping in the short run may exacerbate the difficulty of stopping in the long run. Washton continues: "After a few weeks or months of abstinence, the patient may have the illusion of being cured. This illusion is often the result of ignorance and/or denial about the chronic nature of addictive disease, . . .a tendency to misinterpret one's ability to refrain from drug use as proof that the addiction problem no longer exists" (Washton 1988, p. 35).

Before cue conditioning:

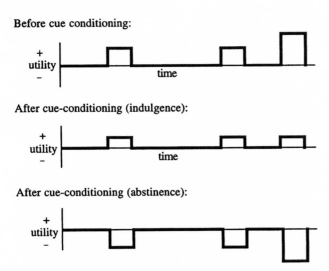

After cue-conditioning (indulgence):

After cue-conditioning (abstinence):

**Figure 2. Visceral account.**

Cue-conditioned craving is the major aspect of drug addiction that is incorporated in the visceral account of addiction. It does not play a role in most other theoretical (as opposed to empirical) treatments of addiction.

The visceral account of addiction is depicted in Figure 2, the first frame of which depicts the time course of utility of a person who is not yet addicted but who is consuming an addictive substance at three points during some relevant period of time. In the case of cigarettes, the diagram might depict cigarettes consumption during the space of an hour, for coffee or alcohol, glasses consumed during the course of a day (e.g., one at lunch and two in the evening), and for cocaine, binges occurring during the space of a week (with the largest consumption episode occurring on the weekend). It also might be the case that the timing of the episodes are dictated not by clock time, but by other regular or semi-regular events: Meals, routine tasks, or meetings with friends. As the individual continues to consume the addictive substance, either time of consumption itself, or other cues, initiate feedforward mechanisms that neutralize the effect of the drug when it is consumed (second frame of Figure 2) and produce craving when the drug is not consumed in the presence of the cues (third frame). Thus, over time, the pleasure derived from drug taking declines, and the individual experiences ever-worsening levels of craving if he fails to take the drug when in the presence of drug-related cues. Even in this cursory diagrammatic form, the visceral account of addiction provides several testable predictions as well as prescriptions for treatment and policy.

## Who Gets Addicted

Each of the major theoretical accounts of drug addiction postulates certain causal mechanisms that lead to addiction and that, in turn, suggest that particular types of people should be vulnerable to addiction. The disease model (e.g., Vaillant [1983]), for example, points to genetic susceptibilities to specific types of addictions or classes of addictions, in the same way that people differ in their genetic susceptibility to different types of diseases. There is substantial research pointing to genetic bases of addiction, although the heritability findings are at present somewhat unsatisfying at a theoretical level. It is highly unlikely that there is an "alcoholism" or "cigarette addiction" gene, so these studies inevitably raise the question of what underlying traits (e.g., impulsivity, the pleasureableness of drug use, susceptibility to peer influence) are, in fact, responsible for the observed genetic associations.

Becker's rational choice perspective focuses on low immediate or anticipated utility as the main state or trait that is predictive of drug addiction. Indeed, in his model the whole point of consuming addictive substances is to relieve low states of utility. However, although it is true that common stereotypes depict addicts as people who were miserable to begin with, the evidence is, in fact, somewhat mixed. McLellan, O'Brien, Metzger, Alterman, Cornish, and Urschel (1992, p. 232) do report that addicts suffer from a wide range of other medical disorders, family and employment problems, and psychiatric conditions, but Gawin (1988) notes that fewer than 50% of those seeking treatment for cocaine exhibit measurable psychiatric disorders, whereas only 10–15% seem to have major affective disorders. The general issue of psychiatric functioning is complicated by the relative dearth of prospective studies and the resultant lack of an obvious comparison group for evaluating the relative severity of observed symptomatology. Even if such a comparison group existed, and the comparison revealed poorer psychological functioning among addicts, however, this would not necessarily support the causal chain implied by Becker's model. It is quite possible that the pathologies observed in addicts are themselves the product of addiction or that they are unrelated causally and are simply features of the types of people who, for other reasons, tend to get addicted. Indeed, as Fischman (1988, p. 7) notes, the notion that "an organism or a person has to have some prerequisite pathology to find cocaine appealing" is challenged by "the fact that species and conditions of availability seem to be irrelevant to cocaine self-administration."

Finally, there is a class of models that view addiction as the consequence of prediction errors. Herrnstein and Prelec's (1992) "garden path" theory of addiction, for example, assumes that people fail to notice, or for some other reason ignore, the negative effects of consuming the addictive substance on satisfaction from other activities.[12] Herrnstein and Prelec's model identifies two major traits as critical for addiction: An individual's ability to "handle" the drug (in the sense that the drug has a rapid negative effect on the return from alternative activities) and the failure to notice such effects. According to this scheme, the addiction-prone are those who cannot handle the drug but are unaware of this. Becker's model assumes away the latter form of prediction error (unawareness of the drug's effect), and it predicts that the first factor – an individual's ability to "handle" the drug – will be positively rather than negatively related to addiction.

Like the garden-path perspective, the visceral factor perspective sees addiction as resulting, in part, from an imperfect anticipation of future tastes. However, whereas Herrnstein and Prelec attribute the prediction error to a failure to notice gradual change, the visceral factor perspective attributes it to an underappreciation of the force of future craving. Herrnstein and Prelec's perspective provides a useful account of some forms of addiction, specifically those in which the addiction unfolds very slowly as a result of subtle changes in tastes or in the environment, and in which the threat of addiction is not well publicized. Workaholism is such an example; every extra hour one works has an imperceptible negative effect on the quality of one's home life, and the hazards of workaholism are not well publicized. Their model applies less well to drug addictions such as smoking (where the risks are very well publicized) or crack where addiction is quite rapid and the risks are again well publicized.

Like other theoretical perspectives, the visceral factor perspective implies that people with specific character traits will be susceptible to addiction. First, the individual must consume the drug in the first place, either because the drug itself is pleasurable, because it satisfies some underlying need, or as a result of social reinforcement for drug use. Second, repeated use of the drug must, in fact, produce cue-conditioned tolerance and craving. Third, and most unique to the visceral account of addiction, the individual must underestimate the aversiveness and force of craving.[13] All three of these characteristics might be general traits that are applicable to a wide range of drugs and also to other visceral factors, or they might be specific to particular drugs and only to drug taking. One individual might find drugs generally pleasurable, tend to experience cue-conditioned craving for a number of drugs, and tend to overestimate such resistance across the board; this would correspond to the case of an "addictive personality." Another individual might exhibit these characteristics but only with respect to one or a limited subset of drugs.

## The Effects of Addiction

In many theoretical formulations, the negative effects of addiction follow from the assumption that, following repeated consumption, other activities become devalued, both absolutely and relative to consumption of the addictive substance (e.g., Becker and Murphy [1988], Herrnstein and Prelec [1992], Orphanides and Zervos [1995]). Such theories draw connections between addiction and other endogenous taste phenomena such as the enhancement in taste for classical music or haute cuisine following repeated exposure. They fail, however, to shed light on many central characteristics of addiction that are also features of other types of behaviors that are influenced by intense visceral factors.

First, addiction often does not entail continuous, or even highly regular, consumption of a drug. Consumption of many drugs is episodic, and many, if not most, addicts go through periods of abstinence, which are typically interrupted by relapse. For some alcoholics, for example, periodic binges are followed by long periods of little or no drinking. Cigarette smokers are notorious for their frequent, but rarely successful attempts to quit permanently. Even cocaine addicts alternate between binges and abstinence (Gawin 1991). Rational theories of addictions, such as Becker's, and more generally endogenous taste change theories such as Herrnstein and Prelec's, have a difficult time dealing with such episodes. This type of pattern follows naturally, however, from the visceral factor perspective, since craving, which is assumed to be the major force driving addiction, is as transient as any other type of visceral factor.

Second, the visceral factor perspective helps to shed light on why addiction is so commonly associated with inner conflict and attempts to control one's own behavior – both of which are ruled out by models such as Becker and Murphy's. Such conflicts arise because visceral factors affect behavior much more than they affect cognitive deliberations concerning self-interest (see Loewenstein [1996]). Many addicts may recognize, even at the moment of succumbing to their addiction, that they are not acting in their own self-interest. In the view of the visceral factor perspective, their inability to control their behavior is more than just a rationalization. Although other choice-based theories of addiction can explain why addicts wish, ex-post, that they were not addicted, these theories typically assume that, given the change that has occurred in their tastes, addicts view the current benefits of consuming the drug as justifying the costs.

Third, an important implication of the visceral factor perspective is that there will be a shortening of the time perspective with respect to the addictive substance (or any substance that is directly affected by the visceral factor), but not with respect to other forms of consumption. Drug addicts should make normal, or even farsighted,[14] tradeoffs between immediate and delayed food, but they will look impatient when it comes to tradeoffs between immediate and delayed consumption of the drug they are addicted to. Other theoretical accounts of addiction either predict no connection between time preference and addiction or they assume that the causality runs in the other direction (i.e., that addicts become addicted as a result of their generalized impatience).

Finally, the visceral factor perspective predicts extreme fluctuations in the addict's concern for the well-being of other persons, in direct relation to fluctuations in craving. According to the visceral factor perspective, the addict will be extremely self-centered during periods of craving but, when not experiencing craving, should be perfectly normal (or even extra self-sacrificing as a result of guilt). Such a pattern of alternating extreme selfishness and remorse is, of course, characteristic of alcoholics and other drug addicts.

## *Quitting and Self-Binding*

The underestimation of delayed visceral factors can help to explain the prevalence of self-binding behavior among addicts. The alcoholic who takes Antabuse (assuring him or herself of horrible withdrawal symptoms), the smoker who ventures off into the wilderness without cigarettes (after a final smoke at the departure point), and the dieter who signs up for a miserable, hungry vacation at a "fat farm" are all imposing extreme future misery on themselves at a point in time much more imminent than when the benefits of abstinence will be enjoyed. To those who view these behavior disorders as manifestations of myopic time preferences, such seemingly farsighted behavior must seem anomalous. Perhaps, however, the readiness to impose imminent pain on oneself does not result from farsighted preferences but from the failure to appreciate the reality of the near-future pain associated with abstinence in the face of craving. Such a tendency to underestimate craving is, according to the visceral account of addiction, exactly what causes people to become addicted in the first place.

Self-binding, however, requires a special combination of prediction errors. To bind oneself in the first place requires some appreciation for the influence of future craving on one's own behavior. Individuals who fail to recognize their own powerlessness in the face of craving will see no need to self-bind. At the same time, however, as noted in the previous paragraph, self-binding requires a lack of appreciation of the pain that one will experience as a result of being unable to mitigate the craving. This latter condition for self-binding probably explains why addicts rarely self-bind in moments when they are experiencing active craving. Self-binding requires an intellectual appreciation of one's powerlessness in the future combined with a relatively cavalier attitude toward future misery.

### Relapse

Relapse is a natural consequence of the visceral factor perspective, due to the postulated inadequate appreciation of future visceral states. Relapse results from misinformed decisions taken with an underappreciation of the impact of future craving.

The ex-addict may underestimate the risks of taking even a small quantity of the drug. There is substantial evidence that small quantities of drugs act as powerful cues that reinitiate craving for a drug that one was addicted to in the past (Gardner and Lowinson 1993). Subscribing to the myth of controlled alcohol, smoking, or drug use, the individual may find himself resuming previous consumption patterns with startling rapidity (Stewart and Wise 1992).

Furthermore, the addict is likely to underinvest in craving reduction for at least two reasons. First, if people underestimate the power of craving, as seems to be the case, they will also tend to underestimate the benefits of treatment. Second, if they underestimate the ability of environmental cues to elicit craving, they will underinvest in changing their environment. Craving reduction is an expensive proposition since it is likely to require changes in location, friendships, consumption habits, and other cues associated with drug taking, and addicts are unlikely to make such investments if they fail to understand their value. As O'Brien et al. (1988, p. 18) write, addicts "often. . .return home after a period of brief treatment feeling well and confident that they will not resume drug use. They are usually surprised to suddenly feel craving, withdrawal, or even 'high' when they encounter people or places associated with their prior drug use." That addicts are caught by surprise by their own craving is not itself particularly surprising; social scientists themselves have only recently begun to appreciate the potency of conditioned craving and its importance for addiction and relapse.

### Willpower

The concept of willpower, which played a central role in nineteenth-century accounts of the conflict between passion and reason, has yet to find its place in twentieth-century social science. Despite its prominent role in popular views of addiction, the role of willpower has been dismissed, ignored, or defined in a counterintuitive fashion in recent theoretical accounts of addiction. Disease theorists, for example, tend to view willpower as little more than a code word for the inverse of susceptibility or even to dismiss the role of willpower, as exemplified by O'Brien's comment that "addictive disorders ... are mistakenly thought to be under the control of 'willpower.'" Ainslie (1992, and this volume), in contrast,

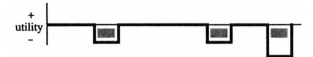

**Figure 3. After cue-conditioning (abstinence).**

while not denying the importance of willpower, tends to view it as an astute application of self-control strategies such as bunching and self-binding.

In its common usage, willpower refers to a type of inward exertion, force of concentration, and tolerance of pain or discomfort (see, e.g., Baumeister, Heatherton, and Tice [1994]). Thus, a runner's exertion of willpower reflects the pain she is able to tolerate to maintain a fast pace; likewise, the willpower that a bored seminar participant mobilizes to remain awake involves inward exertion and concentration, possibly supplemented by an overt self-infliction of pain such as biting one's tongue or stabbing one's hand with a pencil. Although cognitive strategies can also be employed, such as attempting to scare oneself into waking up, the act of will is much more closely linked with the visceral than with the cognitive.

Willpower could be introduced into the theoretical framework depicted in Figure 2 by postulating a short-term constraint in willpower, as depicted in Figure 3. The hatched area inside each episode of craving represents willpower. One might postulate that the individual is able to resist, by dint of willpower, a certain total amount (that is, intensity × duration) of craving. Thus, in the diagram, the individual could avoid taking the drug in the first and second episodes of craving but would find himself deficient in willpower, and presumably relapse, when the third, most extreme, episode occurred.

A more realistic model would permit replenishment of willpower over time, which would permit the individual to resist intermittent craving indefinitely, provided that the replenishment rate exceeded the product of frequency and intensity of experienced craving. Such a model might also permit some degree of forward-looking behavior; individuals who recognized that they would ultimately lack the requisite willpower to remain abstinent might decide there was no point in abstaining and might initiate drug use at the first sign of craving (O'Donoghue and Rabin 1996). Such a pattern of behavior has been observed in studies of dieters who, when told that they will be fed a caloric meal at some point in the future (e.g., an hour hence), tend to lose their resolve and begin eating immediately (Ruderman 1986). Other patterns of behavior are also possible. For example, one could imagine an individual who begins to exert willpower to forestall consumption, satisfies himself that he is capable of controlling his own behavior, and then proceeds to indulge, content in the belief that he is not addicted.

An additional property of willpower can shed further light on the problem of relapse: Willpower takes time to build up. Salespeople and actors need to "psych themselves up" before thrusting themselves before their customer or audience respectively. Athletes "pump themselves up" before entering the track or stepping out on the playing field. Similarly, addicts need to "gird," or "fortify," themselves to resist the urge for drug taking produced by craving. The time it takes to mobilize will power may help to explain why it is easier to withdraw from drugs in the short run than to resist craving in the long run; withdrawal upon cessation is highly predictable and can be prepared for psychologically and sometimes even pharmacologically. Craving, in contrast, typically takes one by surprise.

### Treatment

Given the preliminary state of the theoretical perspective proposed here, it would be premature to propose or advocate specific kinds of treatments for addiction. Instead I mention some existing treatments of demonstrated effectiveness, whose success can be understood in terms of the visceral account of addiction. The visceral account implies that successful treatments for drug addiction should a) alleviate craving so as to promote quitting and b) maintain a vivid memory of the motivational force and misery of craving for those who have quit to prevent relapse.

Many currently available treatments seem to operate by relieving craving. Fluoxetine (Prozac), for example, and other antidepressants, have been shown to be effective against a wide range of other behavior disorders that are associated with visceral factors, and these may have some benefits when it comes to addiction. It would be interesting to assess whether the effectiveness of antidepressants results from their capacity to mitigate craving, as some have suggested (Gawin 1991). Deconditioning craving by repeated exposure to drug-related stimuli also seems to be beneficial (O'Brien et al. 1988). Again, the effectiveness of this treatment, in an area where many treatments fail, reinforces the central role in addiction played by craving.

Treatments that don't seem to work can also be understood in these terms. For example, those that block the pleasurable effects of the drug (e.g., administration of opiate antagonists such as naltrexone) appear to be ineffective, perhaps because few people can tolerate their aversiveness. Likewise, controlled drinking by ex-alcoholics may fail because consumption of small amounts of alcohol intensifies craving for further consumption.

Keeping "alive" memories of the aversiveness and power of craving involves more subtle interventions than does reducing craving, but nevertheless seems to be possible to achieve. One method is to expose addicts who have quit to the agonies of people who are still addicted or who have recently quit and are thus engaged in an acute battle against craving. Alcoholics Anonymous currently serves this function by bringing ex-alcoholics into regular contact with people who have just quit or who are struggling with quitting, and by prescribing daily attendance for a year, followed by regular attendance for the duration of one's life.

A second method would involve exposing addicts to information that helps them to remember their own agonies while addicted. Innovative research by Gold (1993, 1994) on the sexual behavior of gay men suggests that one means of achieving this might be to persuade addicts to keep a daily diary, both while they are actively addicted and during the early, painful, stages of quitting. Much in the same way that poor memory for craving promotes relapse, according to Gold (1993, 1994), unprotected sex occurs in the heat of the moment (under the influence of a visceral factor) but people can't remember or predict what the heat felt like, and so, enter the next sexual encounter unprepared to deal with it. Based on this intuition, Gold (1994) tested an intervention designed to increase condom use. He had gay men recall as vividly as possible the last sexual encounter in which they had engaged in unprotected anal intercourse. He then compared this intervention to a no-intervention control group and to a standard intervention in which subjects were exposed to didactic posters they had not previously seen. The percentage of men in the three groups who subsequently engaged in two or more acts of unprotected anal intercourse differed dramatically between the three groups: 42% and 41% for the control and poster groups, but only 17% for the self-justification group.

### What Is an Addiction?

At present the term addiction is used to refer to a multiplicity of behavioral phenomena, to the point where the term is being applied to any compulsion or socially proscribed habit. We speak of "sex addicts," and refer to people as addicted to crossword puzzles and gambling. Should these be considered addictions? My opinion is that conditioned craving should be taken as the defining feature of addiction. In stating that the craving must be conditioned, I side with the endogenous taste theorists: The taste must be acquired in some fashion, a condition that would rule out generic sex as an addictive activity. People are born with a desire to have sex, albeit some more than others, and intense desire often precedes any actual experience. Thus, the term "sex addict" is no more appropriate than would be "food addict." Although it could be argued that some people are, in fact, food addicts, in my opinion this categorization is an error that results from confusing the general "disorder" with the more specific "addiction." I suppose, however, that one could become addicted to a particular type of food or particular type of sex due to repeated exposure, as one could to crossword puzzles. Significantly, this definition would exclude gambling from the ranks of addictions since, although once they begin they may have difficulty stopping, the best evidence seems to be that gamblers do not experience significant craving when they do not gamble (Rosenthal 1989).

### Addiction and Rationality

A critical question, with significant ramifications for social policy, is the rationality of addiction. A determination that addiction does not result from rational decision making would undercut two frequently advocated, though opposite, policies toward drug addiction: Severely sanctioning drug use and completely legalizing it. On the one hand, if addicts' drug use is not a matter of choice, then it makes no sense either practically or morally, to sanction it. On the other hand, if initial decisions to use a drug are systematically biased then legalization has the potential to produce a social catastrophe.

With the exception of Becker's straightforward position on the rationality issue, however, addiction theorists, researchers, and practitioners tend to adopt a somewhat self-contradictory stance. Although most acknowledge the powerful force of addiction on behavior, most also believe that people must be held accountable for their behavior as a matter of policy. The Alcoholics Anonymous literature, for example, exhorts alcoholics to recognize their lack of control over alcohol but at the same time counsels those who come into contact with alcoholics against coddling the alcoholic, thereby undermining his incentive to quit drinking. The belief that incentives influence behavior implicitly assumes that alcoholics do in fact have some control over their drinking behavior. A similarly ambivalent attitude on the rationality issue can be seen in Goldstein's description of relapse. Despite his self-portrayal as a disease theorist, Goldstein believes that drug users should be held personally accountable for their behavior. Consistent with this policy perspective, he describes relapse as the outcome of a decision: "Relapse is always preceded by a *decision* to use, . . . ." But the passage then continues ". . . however vague and inchoate that decision may be. It is an impulsive decision, not a rational one; and it is provoked by craving – the intense and overwhelming desire to use the drug" (Goldstein 1994, p. 220; emphasis added). Goldstein's use of adjectives such as "impulsive" and "inchoate" to describe, the decision, and his depiction of craving as "intense" and "overwhelming" point to severe limitations in the scope for volition in this "decision."

Like Becker and Murphy's perspective, the visceral factor perspective provides a straightforward answer to the rationality question. It points to important departures from rationality both in the initial decisions that lead to addiction and in the behavior of addicts. The decisions that lead to addiction reflect a systematic bias in our ability to predict our own future feelings and behavior. Once addicted, behavior is periodically driven by craving, which overwhelms rational deliberations concerning self-interest. Moreover, addiction is not alone in possessing these features; addiction is only one, albeit extreme, manifestation of the effect of visceral factors on behavior. Scientists and social scientists, however, often study extreme cases precisely because they reveal the essential features of a phenomenon. Economists focus on the great depression, neurologists on brain lesions, perceptual psychologists on optical illusions, and decision theorists on choice anomalies. The study of addiction may, therefore, shed light not only on addiction itself, but may help to illuminate an assortment of other phenomena that are influenced by visceral factors. Visceral factors are a ubiquitous aspect of everyday life and regularly undermine the rationality of decision making, both due to their underestimation in prospect and their disproportional force when they operate in the present. Whereas Becker and Murphy view addiction as one additional illustration of the universal applicability of the rational choice perspective, I view addiction as one of many types of human behaviors that are *not* usefully viewed as rational.

## Acknowledgment

I thank Colin Camerer, Donna Harsch, Kalle Moene, and Wictor Osiatynski for helpful comments.

## NOTES

1. For a more general theoretical model of preference that incorporates the role of cues, however, see Laibson (1994).
2. Although visceral factors themselves tend to fluctuate relatively dramatically, an individual's *proneness* to experiencing different types of visceral factors typically evolves more gradually.
3. In economic parlance, the marginal rate of substitution between goods and activities associated with the visceral factor (e.g., food for hunger) and all other nonassociated goods and activities diminishes.
4. We cannot, of course, rule out the possibility that sexually aroused subjects do not predict their own behavior more accurately but actually overpredict their own likelihood of behaving aggressively.
5. Curiosity is widely viewed as a type of drive or appetite that shares many properties with other drives, such as hunger and, especially, the sex drive (see Loewenstein [1994]).

6. In a typical demonstration of the effect (see, e.g., Kahneman, Knetsch, and Thaler [1990]), one group of subjects (sellers) are endowed with an object and are given the option of trading it for various amounts of cash; another group (choosers) are not given the object but are given a series of choices between getting the object or getting various amounts of cash. Although the objective wealth position of the two groups is identical, as are the choices they face, endowed subjects hold out for significantly more money than those who are not endowed.

7. In the recent past, Wise (e.g., Wise and Bozarth 1987) and others did question the importance of craving (conditioned association) for addiction. As Wise noted, animals can get virtually instantly addicted to cocaine and other substances without prior exposure. Since the animal would not seem to have had a chance to habituate to or become conditioned to the substance so quickly, these elements do not appear to be necessary for addiction. However, subsequent research by Wise and his colleagues (e.g., Gratton and Wise [1994]) shows that cocaine administration results in remarkably quick habituation and conditioned association; animals exhibit physiological signs of distress shortly preceding even the second administration of cocaine, and these distress signs rapidly escalate with subsequent administrations.

8. This is a simplification of reality. Some drugs operate specifically by producing disequilibration such that the organism responds in a pleasure-enhancing fashion – e.g., by administering its own opiates (Eikelboom and Stewart 1982). In these cases, conditioned cues will produce the opposite of craving.

9. A mild example of feedforward and its effects can be seen in the dramatic increase in hunger often experienced right before dinner, especially when one can smell, see, or hear dinner being prepared. If dinner were to be suddenly postponed or canceled after exposure to such cues, the result would be a very mild form of craving, which would provide a strong motivation for snacking.

10. It is true that cigarette smokers who quit often overeat, and drug addicts are notorious for substituting other drugs when their drug of choice is not available; craving can have spill-over effects to closely related alternative forms of consumption. But, craving favors certain forms of consumption over others. Thus, food for the ex-smoker has a slim appeal relative to that of a cigarette.

11. Wiktor Osiatynski, personal communication.

12. Herrnstein and Prelec dismiss Becker's model as depicting a process of "self-medication" (1992, p. 333), a charge that Becker probably would not deny. Becker would probably dismiss Herrnstein and Prelec's theory on the basis of its assumption of "irrationality."

13. Although such underestimation seems to be characteristic of all visceral factors (Loewenstein 1996), there may be unique contributing factors when it comes to drugs. First, people who freely consume the drug in the early stages of an addiction may forestall craving through consumption, and may, therefore, not actually experience full-blown craving until it has intensified severely. Second, people may have the wrong model of drug addiction. People who are unfamiliar with the concept of cue-conditioning may point to periods of abstinence (e.g., "I never drink before lunch," or "I'm able to go off coffee when I'm on vacation") as evidence that they are not addicted. Their model of addiction is more akin to the opponent process perspective, which

implies relatively constant consumption over time. They infer from the absence of craving or craving-driven consumption during certain time periods that they are in full volitional control of their behavior.

14. The addict may become even more patient with respect to goods that are substitutes for the drug the addict is addicted to, because drug consumption will effectively mitigate the effect of visceral factors that are increasing their immediate value. For example, cocaine addicts may be especially patient with respect to food because cocaine craving crowds out hunger.

## REFERENCES

Ainslie, G. (1992), *Picoeconomics*, Cambridge, UK, Cambridge University Press.

Baker, T. B. (1988), "Models of addiction: Introduction to the special issue," *Journal of Abnormal Psychology* 97, 115–17.

Baumeister, R. F., T. F. Heatherton, and D. M. Tice (1994), *Losing Control: How and Why People Fail at Self-Regulation*, San Diego, Academic Press.

Baumhart, R. (1968), *An Honest Profit*, New York, Prentice-Hall.

Becker, G. and K. Murphy (1988), "A theory of rational addiction," *Journal of Political Economy* 96, 675–700.

Berridge, K. C. and T. E. Robinson (1995), "The mind of an addicted brain: Neural sensitization of wanting versus liking," *Current Directions in Psychological Science* 4, 71–6.

Biderman, A. D. (1960), "Social-psychological needs and 'involuntary' behavior as illustrated by compliance in interrogation," *Sociometry* 23, 120–47.

Christensen-Szalanski, J. J. J. (1984), "Discount functions and the measurement of patients' values: Women's decisions during childbirth," *Medical Decision Making* 4, 47–58.

Damasio, A. R. (1994), *Descartes' Error: Emotion, Reason, and the Human Brain*, New York, Putnam.

Eikelboom, R. and J. Stewart (1982), "Conditioning of drug-induced physiological responses," *Psychological Review* 89, 507–28.

Fields, H. L. (1987), *Pain*, New York, McGraw-Hill.

Fienberg, S. E., E. F. Loftus, and J. M. Tanur (1985), "Recalling pain and other symptoms," *Health and Society* 63, 582–97.

Fischman, M. W. (1988), "Behavioral pharmacology of cocaine," *Journal of Clinical Psychiatry* 49, 7–10.

Frawley, P. J. (1988), "Neurobehavioral model of addiction: Addiction as a primary disease," in S. Peele (ed.), *Visions of Addiction*, Lexington, MA, Lexington Books.

Gardner, E. L. and J. H. Lowinson (1993), "Drug craving and positive/negative hedonic brain substrates activated by addicting drugs," *Seminars in the Neurosciences* 5, 359–68.

Gawin, F. H. (1988), "Chronic neuropharmacology of cocaine: Progress in pharmacotherapy," *Journal of Clinical Psychiatry* 49, 11–16.

(1991), "Cocaine addiction: Psychology and neurophysiology," *Science* 251, 1580–6.

Gold, R. (1993), "On the need to mind the gap: On-line versus off-line cognitions underlying sexual risk-taking," in D. Terry, C. Gallois, and M. McCamish (eds.), *The Theory of Reasoned Action: Its Application to AIDS Preventive Behavior*, New York, Pergamon Press.

(1994), "Why we need to rethink AIDS education for gay men," Plenary address to the Second International Conference on AIDS' Impact: Biopsychosocial aspects of HIV infection, 7–10 July, Brighton, UK.

Goldstein, A. (1994), *Addiction: From Biology to Drug Policy*, New York, Freeman.

Gratton, A. and R. A. Wise (1994), "Drug- and behavior-associated changes in dopamine-related electrochemical signals during intravenous cocaine self-administration in rats," *Journal of Neuroscience* 14, 4130–46.

Herrnstein, R. and D. Prelec (1992), "A theory of addiction," in G. Loewenstein and J. Elster (eds.), *Choice over Time*, New York, Russell Sage Foundation.

Hser, Y., M. D. Anglin, and K. Powers (1993), "A 24-year follow-up of California narcotics addicts," *Archives of General Psychiatry* 50, 577–84.

Janis, I. L. (1967), "Effects of fear arousal on attitude change," *Advances in Experimental Social Psychology* 3, 167–224.

Janis, I. L. and H. Leventhal (1967), "Human reactions to stress," in E. Borgatta and W. Lambert (eds.), *Handbook of Personality Theory and Research*, Chicago, Rand McNally.

Kahneman, D., J. Knetsch, and R. Thaler (1990), "Experimental tests of the endowment effect and the Coase theorem," *Journal of Political Economy* 98, 1325–48.

Kent, G. (1985), "Memory of dental pain," *Pain* 21, 187–94.

Koob, G. F., L. Stinus, M. Le Moal, and F. E. Bloom (1989), "Opponent process theory of motivation: Neurobiological evidence from studies of opiate dependence," *Neuroscience and Biobehavioral Reviews* 13, 135–40.

Kosslyn, S. M., N. M. Alpert, W. L. Thompson, V. Maljkovic, S. B. Weise, C. F. Chabris, S. E. Hamilton, S. L. Rauch, and F. S. Buonanno (1993), "Visual mental imagery activates topographically organized visual cortex: PET investigations," *Journal of Cognitive Neuroscience* 5, 263–87.

Kozlowski, L. T. and D. A. Wilkinson (1987), "Use and misuse of the concept of craving by alcohol, tobacco, and drug researchers," *British Journal of Addiction* 82, 31–6.

Laibson, D. I. (1994), "A cue-theory of consumption," Economics Department, Working Paper, Cambridge, MA, Harvard University.

Larwood, L. and W. Whittaker (1977), "Managerial myopia: Self-serving biases in organizational planning," *Journal of Applied Psychology* 62, 194–8.

Loewenstein, G. (1994), "The psychology of curiosity: A review and reinterpretation," *Psychological Bulletin* 116, 75–98.

(1996), "Out of control: Visceral influences on behavior," *Organizational Behavior and Human Decision Processes* 65, 272–92.

Loewenstein, G. and D. Adler (1995), "A bias in the prediction of tastes," *Economic Journal* 105, 929–37.

Loewenstein, G., D. Nagin, and R. Paternoster (1997), "The effect of sexual arousal on predictions of sexual forcefulness," *Journal of Research in Crime and Delinquency* 34, 443–73.

Loewenstein, G., D. Prelec, and C. Shatto (1996), "Hot/cold intrapersonal empathy gaps and the prediction of curiosity," Working Paper, Pittsburgh, PA, Carnegie Mellon University.

Lynch, B. S. and R. J. Bonnie (1994), "Toward a youth-centered prevention policy," in B. S. Lynch and R. J. Bonnie (eds.), *Growing Up Tobacco Free: Preventing Nicotine Addiction in Children and Youths*, Washington, DC, National Academy Press.

Madden, G. J., N. M. Petry, G. J. Badger, and W. K. Bickel (1996), "Impulsive and self-control choices in opioid-dependent subjects and non-drug using controls: Drug and monetary rewards," Human Behavioral Pharmacology Laboratory, Department of Psychiatry, Working Paper, Burlington, University of Vermont.

Marlatt, G. A. (1987), "Craving notes," *British Journal of Addiction* 82, 42–3.

McLellan, A. T., C. P. O'Brien, D. Metzger, A. E. Alternman, J. Cornish, and H. Urschel (1992), "How effective is substance abuse treatment – compared to what?" in C. P. O'Brien and J. H. Jaffe (eds.), *Addictive States*, New York, Raven.

Messiha, F. S. (1993), "Fluoxetine: A spectrum of clinical applications and postulates of underlying mechanisms," *Neuroscience and Biobehavioral Reviews* 17(4), 385–96.

Milgram, S. (1965), "Liberating effects of group pressure," *Journal of Personality and Social Psychology* 1, 127–34.

Morley, S. (1993), "Vivid memory for 'everyday' pains," *Pain* 55, 55–62.

Niaura, R. S., D. J. Rohsenow, J. A. Binkoff, P. M. Monti, M. Pedraza, and D. B. Abrams (1988), "Relevance of cue reactivity to understanding alcohol and smoking relapse," *Journal of Abnormal Psychology* 97, 133–52.

NIH Technology Assessment Conference Panel (1993), "Methods for voluntary weight loss and control," *Annals of Internal Medicine* 199, 764–70.

Norvell, K. T., F. Gaston-Johansson, and G. Fridh (1987), "Remembrance of labor pain: How valid are retrospective pain measurements?" *Pain* 31, 77–86.

O'Brien, C. P., A. R. Childress, I. O. Arndt, A. T. McLellan, G. E. Woody, and I. Maany (1988), "Pharmacological and behavioral treatments of cocaine dependence: Controlled studies," *Journal of Clinical Psychiatry* 49, 17–22.

O'Donoghue, T. and M. Rabin (1996), "Doing it now or later," Math Center Discussion Paper No. 1172, Evanston, IL, Northwestern University.

Orphanides, A. and D. Zervos (1995), "Rational addiction with learning and regret," *Journal of Political Economy* 103, 739–58.

Osiatynski, W. (1992), *Choroba Kontroli (The Disease of Control)*. Warsaw, Instytut Psychiatrii i Neurologii.

Pickens, R. and W. C. Harris (1968), "Self-administration of *d*-amphetamine by rats," *Psychopharmacologia* 12, 158–63.

Pribram, K. H. (1984), "Emotion: A neurobehavioral analysis," in K. R. Scherer and P. Ekman (eds.), *Approaches to Emotion*, Hillsdale, NJ, Erlbaum pp. 13–38.

Read, D. and G. Loewenstein (forthcoming), "Enduring pain for money: Decisions based on the perception of memory of pain," *Journal of Behavioral Decision Making*.

Rofé, Y. and D. Algom (1985), "Accuracy of remembering postdelivery pain," *Perceptual and Motor Skills* 60, 99–105.

Rosenthal, R. J. (1989), "Pathological gambling and problem gambling: Problems of definition and diagnosis," in H. Shaffer, S. Stein, B. Gambino, and

T. Cummings (eds.), *Compulsive Gambling: Theory, Research, and Practice,* Lexington, MA: Lexington Books.

Ruderman, A. J. (1986), "Dietary restraint: A theoretical and empirical review," *Psychological Bulletin* 99, 247–62.

Scarry, E. (1985), *The Body in Pain,* Oxford, UK, Oxford University Press.

Schelling, T. (1984), "Self-command in practice, in policy, and in a theory of rational choice," *American Economic Review* 74, 1–11.

Seeburger, F. F. (1993), *Addiction and Responsibility. An Inquiry into the Addictive Mind,* New York, Crossroads Press.

Shiffman, S. (1982), "Relapse following smoking cessation: A situational analysis," *Journal of Consulting and Clinical Psychology* 50, 71–86.

Siegel, S. (1979), "The role of conditioning in drug tolerance and addiction," in J. D. Keehn (ed.), *Psychopathology in Animals: Research and Treatment Implications.* New York, Academic Press.

Siegel, R. K. (1982), "Cocaine free base abuse: A new smoking disorder," *Journal of Psychoactive Drugs* 14, 321–37.

Siegel, S., R. E. Hinson, M. D. Krank, and J. McCully (1982), "Heroin "overdose" death: Contribution of drug-associated environmental cues," *Science* 23, 436–7.

Siegel, S., M. D. Krank, and R. E. Hinson (1988), "Anticipation of pharmacological and nonpharmacological events: Classical conditioning and addictive behavior," in S. Peele (ed.), *Visions of Addiction,* Lexington, MA, Lexington Books.

Solomon, R. L. and J. D. Corbit (1974), "An opponent-process theory of motivation," *Psychological Review* 81, 158–71.

Stewart, J. and R. A. Wise (1992), "Reinstatement of heroin self-administration habits: Morphine prompts and naltrexone discourages renewed responding after extinction," *Psychopharmacology* 108, 779–84.

Strongman, K. T. and S. Kemp (1991), "Autobiographical memory for emotion," *Bulletin of the Psychonomic Society* 29, 195–8.

Svenson, O. (1981), "Are we all less risky and more skillful than our fellow driver?" *Acta Psychologica* 47, 143–8.

Thaler, R. (1980), "Toward a positive theory of consumer choice," *Journal of Economic Behavior and Organization* 1, 39–60.

Toates, F. M. (1979), "Homeostasis and drinking," *Behavioral and Brain Sciences* 2, 95–139.

Vaillant, G. E. (1983), *The Natural History of Alcoholism: Causes, Patterns and Paths to Recovery,* Cambridge, MA, Harvard University Press.

Washton, A. M. (1988), "Preventing Relapse to Cocaine," *Journal of Clinical Psychiatry* 49, 34–38.

Wise, R. A. and M. A. Bozarth (1987), "A psychomotor stimulant theory of addiction," *Psychological Review* 94, 469–92.

Wolosin, R. J., S. J. Sherman, and A. Cann (1975), "Predictions of own and other's conformity," *Journal of Personality* 43, 357–78.

# Epilogue: Rationally Coping with Lapses from Rationality

THOMAS C. SCHELLING

A man gave up smoking three months ago. For the first six or eight weeks he was regularly tormented by a desire to smoke, but the last three or four weeks have been less uncomfortable and he is becoming optimistic that he has left cigarettes behind for good. One afternoon a friend drops in for a business chat. The business done, our reformed smoker sees his friend to the door; returning to the living room, he finds, on the coffee table, an opened pack of cigarettes. He snatches up the pack and hurries to the door, only to see his friend's car disappear around the corner. As he will see his friend in the morning and can return the cigarettes, he puts the pack in his jacket pocket and hangs the jacket in the closet. He settles in front of the television with a before-dinner drink to watch network news. Twenty minutes into the news, he walks to the closet where his jacket hangs and takes the cigarettes out of the pocket, studies the pack for a minute, and walks into the bathroom, where he empties the cigarettes into the toilet and flushes it. He returns to his drink and his news.

What have we witnessed? I think we can confidently guess that our subject came to anticipate that in the presence of the cigarettes something might occur that he did not want to happen; by disposing of the cigarettes he has made it not happen. Wasting a dollar's worth of his friend's cigarettes was an inexpensive safeguard. He has coped rationally with the risk that he would do something he did not want himself later to do.

I shall look in more detail at what may have been forestalled, but for the time being let us just interpret the man's act as a rational attempt to prevent some nonoptimal behavior that the presence of the cigarettes might motivate. Tentatively, we might suppose that the man would explain his behavior as anticipating some "irrational act" that he strategically precluded by acting while still "rational."

My usual interest is in how people actually exercise strategy and tactics, successfully or unsuccessfully, in constraining their own future behavior. Often the ways people try to constrain their own future behavior are like the ways they would try to constrain someone else's behavior; they appear to be treating their "future self" as if it were another individual. If our man had never smoked but his wife had, and she had recently with great discomfort foresworn cigarettes and was not yet confidently weaned, and his business friend had left cigarettes behind, he would surely dispose of the cigarettes before his wife came home. So whether we want to say that he treats his ten o'clock self as if it were "another self" or only that he treats it as he would "another's" self makes little difference.

Most literature on this subject in economics and philosophy concerns what is usually described as an apparent change in preferences. At five o'clock the man does not want to smoke; at five o'clock, he does not want to smoke at ten o'clock; at ten o'clock he may want to smoke, remembering perfectly well that five hours ago he did not want himself to smoke at ten o'clock, remembering that three months ago he did not want himself to smoke at any time. We have difficulty in just describing what the man is doing if he lights the cigarette that even a few moments ago he may have hoped he wouldn't smoke. Whether it is "rational" that he satisfies an urge to smoke, exercising his unalienable sovereignty at ten o'clock, may not be answerable within the classical paradigm of rational choice; neurologically there may be a resolution of the question, but I prefer at this point to postpone examination of whether and how that succumbing at ten might be judged rational or irrational. I'll settle for calling it *non-optimal as of five o'clock*; I'm willing to let the man refer to his anticipated lapse as "irrational" if he wants to call it that; at least, it so appears to him as of five o'clock.

These apparent changes in preference as time goes by, or as events trigger them, are important and interesting and comprise perhaps the most important and interesting of the "lapses from rationality." They can involve addiction to legal and illegal drugs: heroin, nicotine, valium, caffeine; they include thirst, sex, and appetite; they include some hard-to-manage behaviors like gambling and playing video games.

Let me clarify: I do not consider the injection of heroin or the smoking of nicotine to raise any issue of rationality. It is only when the user of heroin or nicotine makes a serious attempt to stop and has difficulty doing so, suffering occasional relapse or suffering torment on the verge of relapse, perhaps attempting to restructure his or her environment or his or her incentives, that the issue arises whether some preferences are "true" and some are interlopers, whether fulfilling one preference is rational and fulfilling an opposing or alternating preference not.

But, as I said, I shall defer treatment of those conflicting preferences. I want to introduce a number of conditions and behaviors for which a judgment about "irrationality" will be less problematic. Regardless of whether these conditions and behaviors appear less important or more important than drug addiction, binge eating, or nymphomania, they at least offer a spectrum into which the more notorious addictions and compulsive behaviors can be fitted. The latter may then be seen as members of a family not all of which are so difficult to understand.

## 1. Sleep

A good place to begin is sleep. Many people do things in their sleep that, when awake, they want not to do in their sleep. Children suck their thumbs and wet the bed; children and adults scratch lesions or tug at bandages; people lie on their bellies when their doctors recommend against it, or lie on their backs and snore. (When I was young, sleepwalking was ubiquitous; I don't know what became of it.) Probably we would not call it "irrational" to tug at our bandages, sleep being out of bounds to rationality. But a child can desperately want to stop sucking his or her thumb, and an adult may badly want not to sleep on his or her back and snore. And the child can rationally put on thick mittens at bedtime; and the snoring adult can strap a lumpy object to his back. These coping behaviors surely do not raise any question of what the person "really" wants to do.

Nightmares and bad dreams can be a problem. Having an alert partner to wake one up is a help. Certain before-bedtime activities can be avoided, as can certain foods; one also can experiment with tranquilizers.

And of course there is the problem of oversleeping. We set an alarm.

## 2. Drowsiness

Even an alarm may not solve the problem. People put the clock across the room so they cannot turn it off without getting out of bed. When getting up is important they call a friend who will call, and call repeatedly, in the morning. (In a foreign city, without an alarm, I found a waking service in the yellow pages and left a call. I got the call on time; five minutes later another call, and another five minutes after that.) Is it "irrational" not to get out of bed when the alarm goes off? People have missed important engagements; others have had to skip shaving and breakfast. Rather than say a strong preference for an extra half hour's sleep exercised a legitimate claim, we'd probably prefer to say that the barely awakened drowsy person is not quite all there; his metabolism is depressed; his brain is awash with sleep. By the standards of the night before when the alarm was set, and by the standards of the person cursing his lateness to work, staying in bed was "irrational."

Falling asleep is another problem. Actually it is two, but I defer insomnia for later. The soldier on guard may sit with his chin on his bayonet: When he droops, the pain awakens him. Truck drivers can purchase a noisemaker that is activated when a button is released; if they doze, they relax their grip and the noise startles them awake. Is it "irrational" to fall asleep even when doing so will get one in trouble? Descriptively, this may depend on whether one chooses to say a person "succumbed" to a strong temptation – as surely sometimes one does – or instead the person's brain "turned off" on its own. I don't think it matters: What matters is that people need to cope, and often can rationally cope, with undesired dozing.

Drowsiness can be caused by fatigue, lack of sleep, or using medicinal drugs or alcohol. Precautions can include drinking coffee, taking a nap, and not drinking alcohol.

Besides falling asleep when drowsy, people can be inattentive or absent-minded, failing to turn off the stove, missing telephone messages, or not hearing the baby cry. Anticipating drowsiness, one can try to avoid it, can warn others that one may be too drowsy to be responsible, or otherwise avoid responsibility that one anticipates being unable to fulfill.

## 3. Depression

When depressed, people do things, decide things, and say things they deprecate in advance and regret after. Some depression is predictable: postoperative for surgery patients, postpartum for mothers. Some medicinal drugs induce depression, as do some ilnesses, notably hepatitis (as preserved in the expression, "a jaundiced view"). Some depression is treated with dietary supplements or medicines, some (seasonal affective disorder [SAD]) with light.

Some of the behaviors associated with depression can be anticipated and guarded against. If a pregnant woman eschewed alcohol and tobacco during pregnancy, and hopes to remain nicotine free now that she has several months invested in that condition, she can be advised that the onset of depression may lead to relapse and her husband would be wise not to leave cigarettes around the house. The husband's giving up smoking is especially valuable at this time, even if he can keep it up only for a few weeks. Postsurgical depression may need to be guarded against by cardiac patients who wish, on the adamant recommendation of their physicians, to give up smoking.

Depression is a condition in which it may be important to rid the house of means of suicide (a gun, sleeping tablets, or even car keys) or to keep company on hand; a watchful friend or regular telephone calls would also help.

## 4. Euphoria

There is a euphoric counterpart to depression, although it is comparatively rare. People become impetuously generous as a result of success or good luck; gamblers who win heavily are said to become instantly spendthrift. And Jeppo in *The Informer*, newly rich and surrounded by flatterers, squandered in one evening the entire twenty pounds' reward that was to buy his steamer ticket out of Ireland.

## 5. Drunkenness

Alcohol is one of the many temptations people try to avoid, but here I refer not to abstinence but to regrettable behavior, behavior that one hopes in advance to avoid and that one regrets afterwards. The person who enjoys drinking and has no intention of giving it up may need safeguards against behaviors that, when he is under the influence, will seem perfectly rational but, when remembered the next day – if remembered – will seem foolish and unwise, or worse. The classical case is the person whom alcohol encourages to think he can actually drive a car safely; the solution is to leave the car at home and take a taxi, or to deliver the keys to the host with the request not to return them if the host thinks that best.

People who when drunk abuse their spouses or children, insult their friends or employers, fight, bet large amounts of money, or otherwise behave outrageously may have to remove their children in advance, leave their money at home, and do their drinking away from the people whose presence is conducive to bad behavior.

The same disregard of consequences that can get one into trouble after drinking can at times dispel inhibition and provide the "Dutch courage" to say what, sober, one hadn't the nerve to say, or to do what, sober, one hadn't the nerve to do, such as proposing marriage, or proposing divorce, or demanding a promotion, or quitting a job, or making up to one's children, or disowning them. Just as people rationally drink to conquer stage fright or fear of flying (or are served drinks for that purpose) they can "rationally" drink to rise to the occasion. Whether we should say, then, that they rationally drink to achieve rationality – it being irrational not to say what the occasion calls for – or to achieve irrationality – it being irrational to be insensitive to the consequences – is a choice I leave to the reader.

## 6. Extremes of Motivation

### *Pain*

American women about to give birth have been known to request that anesthesia be withheld; they want to be fully aware; they want the newborns not drugged; they want to display loving courage. An obstetrician may respond that nitrous oxide will be available for self-administration, and otherwise anesthesia will be used only in an emergency. The woman asks that nothing be available on demand for if it is available she will demand it and get it, and she wants her demands unattended; she wants not to receive relief even if she asks for it. (There are, however, evident legal and ethical issues, as well as medical ones, and if the husband is present in the delivery room there may be conflicts of interpretation.)

Advance self-denial may be formulated as not wanting to succumb "irrationally" to a level of pain that makes clear thinking and clear recall unavailable. The brain may have evolved when pain was something to be avoided, not welcomed; and a "primitive" response to pain may overwhelm any earlier resolution, taken perhaps in a more recently evolved part of the brain, to eschew relief. It may even overwhelm the very recollection of that resolution or the reason for it.

## Fear

Let me quote the first paragraph of the first chapter of my favorite book about baseball: "Fear."

That's the paragraph. The second paragraph begins, "Fear is the fundamental factor in hitting, and hitting the ball with the bat is the fundamental act of baseball" (Koppett 1967). If one has decided, fully aware of the risk, to lean into the plate, bat poised, awaiting a white object traveling ninety miles an hour toward one's face, ducking away at the last moment may be "irrational." Or maybe not doing so is the irrational choice.

Rationality may be somewhat intertwined with voluntariness. If, during the third of the three-fifths of a second the ball is traveling, one changes one's mind and backs off, doing so may be irrational – it contradicts what one earlier decided in full knowledge of the danger. If one uncontrollably, involuntarily, perhaps by reflex flinches and withdraws, maybe the act is "transrational," beyond considerations of rationality. Surely if one blinks the act does not qualify as irrational, any more than sneezing while hiding from an enemy is irrational.

A World War II movie showed an officer removing fuses from unexploded bombs in London. He wore a headset into which he described every move so that when he disappeared there would be a record. His was a calling that was very demanding: One's fingers mustn't tremble. In training, nobody trembled during practice; it was only when confronting a live bomb that anyone learned whether or not he qualified. Tranquilizers were unavailable; they reduced the sensitivity of the fingers. Possibly a fully rational person could not control his own trembling; maybe there is something "wrong" with a person so nerveless. Again we have the question of what "rationality" covers: If one knows rationally that it is safer not to tremble...?

Suppose that trembling over the bomb's fuse made detonation extremely likely, whereas a calm hand could almost surely remove the fuse safely. Should I be able rationally to persuade myself that there is no danger (unless I create it by needlessly trembling) and not tremble? I can either correctly believe the operation safe, because I am not trembling, and not tremble – a rational response – or I can correctly believe the operation extremely dangerous, because I am trembling, and tremble. We thus have two "equilibrium" pairs of belief and behavior.

When I was young I read that dogs could smell fear in me if I was afraid. (I believe it was adrenalin or some such hormone that affected the chemistry of my breath or my perspiration.) The smell was said to infuriate dogs and make them (irrationally?) aggressive. Decades later I remembered, as I jogged, pursued by dogs on occasion. I was not particularly afraid of dogs and never had been; but remembering, I realized I might well be *afraid of being afraid* of dogs. I tried to be "rational," to be unafraid because there was nothing to be afraid of. But I was subject to a sneaking "rational" recognition that if I *were* afraid there was plenty to be afraid of! Again we have two "rational"(?) equilibria.

I'll come to phobias shortly. Here the issue is whether justifiable fear may overcome one's resolve to face it, and one needs to cope in advance in order not to expose oneself later. Alcohol on the battlefield may be administered by one's superiors, or self-administered in the interest of not acting the coward. (Maybe my drinking alcohol could keep those dogs tranquil.) A sufficient level of terror may induce paralysis when action is needed; a sufficient level of terror may lead to flight, when fleeing courts disaster. That leads to our next topic.

## Panic

Many people know that when the car skids in snow the worst thing is to slam on the brakes, and yet they slam on the brakes. Technology has come to the rescue in the form of antilock brakes; before that, practice (skidding practice) helped overcome the impulse. Novice skiers can knowingly do the wrong thing when they slip; some of us could even watch ourselves helplessly doing the wrong thing.

Mountain lions have returned to Colorado and have been seen near some of the hiking trails, even near towns; signs have appeared advising appropriate behavior in the event one confronts a mountain lion. Some of the advice sounds sensible: Make continuous noise (e.g., carry a little bell that is always dingling); the lions will hear and you'll never see them. The advice that scares me is: Never turn your back and run!

## Rage and Temper

Rage is sometimes a wonderful substitute for courage and often a source of energy. But rage usually distorts judgment and triggers impulsive actions that are futile, destructive, or embarrassing. Losing one's temper is a mild sort of rage. I don't know of any programs of training for rage control, but there is the traditional prophylactic: Count to ten before speaking. If I am too enraged to mind my behavior, how can I make myself count to ten? Actually people do, and it helps. How can I simultaneously be rational enough to count to ten and at the same time not rational enough to contain my rage? Maybe the mind is not altogether singular; watching myself uncontrollably losing my temper, I count to a controlled ten and watch myself regain control.

When rage or loss of temper is predictable one can often avoid the stimulus or the occasion. There was a member of my department who was incapable of speaking, on any subject, without provoking me into bad humor and a futile argument. I eventually learned that whenever he began to speak I should simply go to the bathroom. I'd miss my chance to lose my temper and never regret the lost opportunity.

### Thirst

If a person suffers a stomach wound and must not drink for forty-eight hours, and no intravenous technology is available, it is important not to leave a glass of water nearby. Eventually, we are told, the person will drink and die. People at sea will drink salt water and die; on the desert, poisonous water and die. I think we should not conclude that the person prefers instant relief to long life, but we should infer that his central nervous system was programmed, through millions of years of biological evolution, to relieve extreme thirst at any cost. As the hours go by, the stomach-wounded person's thirst increases; his mind's capacity to think about the consequences of drinking the water steadily diminishes while his mind's preoccupation with the need to quench his thirst increases. He didn't "decide" that he would rather drink than live: He was under the control of a brain that knew that dehydration could kill and didn't know that drinking could.

Is it irrational to drink? I propose that it is neither rational to drink nor irrational. It is rational to drink only if one is capable of rational action and drinking is the right thing to do; it is irrational to drink only if one is capable of rational action and drinking is the wrong thing to do. The dehydrated nervous system is not capable of rational choice: There is no choice; there is an absolute demand for rehydration. Maybe we could identify a *primitive rationality* that takes charge. By evolutionary experience, drinking the water is the right thing to do; drinking is the wrong thing to do only at a level of mental activity that has been shut down in the interest of survival.

Most of us do not get lost in the desert or at sea, or suffer stomach wounds where intravenous liquid is unavailable. But thirst may be a useful model for the nature of choice *in extremis*, when the conscious mind cannot get our attention and when the more primitive brain kicks in and takes charge. I think this idea also applies to extreme pain.

## 7. Phobias

Dictionaries describe phobias as irrational, or at least one's behavior under their influence as irrational. They are defined as fears not based on reasoning or evidence, or fears greatly exaggerated. "Fear" may be too restrictive: Some phobias produce revulsion, and some induce nausea, fainting, or paralysis. Alfred Hitchcock's *Vertigo* revolved around Jimmy Stewart's character's reaction to heights; Howard Hughes's antiseptic withdrawal late in life was reportedly phobic.

There are many phobias; more than a hundred of them have their own Greek or Latin names: acrophobia, claustrophobia, agoraphobia, xenophobia, even phobophobia, and in a recent movie, arachnaphobia. In addition to heights, enclosures, open spaces, and things that crawl, there are fears of needles, blood, reptiles, filth, feces, viscera, leeches, and the dark. For some people it is submersion in water; for some it is the furry animals that other people love. Stage fright can reach phobic proportions. Some phobias appear to be induced by traumatic experience, whereas some are thought to be partly genetic in origin. Acrophobes get a physical sensation that sometimes attracts and repels and bears little relation to "fear." Some monkeys react to reptiles with panic; removing one of the frontal lobes of the brain, it is reported, and putting a patch over one of the monkey's eyes, sends the monkey to the ceiling in panic if there is a snake in the cage, or alternatively lets the monkey calmly pass the snake in pursuit of a banana, according to whether the unpatched eye corresponds to the intact hemisphere or the one lacking the frontal lobe.

Most phobias can be seen as abnormal or unhealthy; some agoraphobes' lives are shaped by an incapacity to leave home, and Hughes's life was reportedly devastated by his compulsive antisepsis. But acrophobes are typically normal except for their phobia. A hospitalized soldier in *M\*A\*S\*H\** who sexually harrassed a nurse was punished by her dropping his blood sample and telling him that he'd have to give blood again tomorrow; the soldier was ordinarily brave enough, but he spent the night in horror of tomorrow's needle.

Heights, needles, and even fear of the dark often yield, at least somewhat, to closing one's eyes, although if one needs to navigate a precipice closing the eyes is not an available option. Fear of flying appears phobic in some people who acknowledge that their fear is not rational; perhaps they just cannot control their imaginations, or they cannot keep their nervous systems from interpreting every slight jolt of the plane as a warning signal. Airsickness and seasickness seem to be aggravated by, if not generated by, an inability to distinguish the signals from the noise.

Some phobias have a potential to be therapeutic. "Aversive condition-ing" has been occasionally successful against nicotine addiction: People are instructed to oversmoke to induce headache, to keep wet cigarette butts in open containers to emit disgusting odors, etc. Evidently if phobias could successfully be induced, this technique would have great potential.

Not altogether unlike phobias are some more apparently "natural" or normal aversions. Some people cannot kill spiders, some cannot drown kittens, and some cannot kill the horse that broke its leg. The inability to inflict suffering may be a welcome, recent cultural evolution.

## 8. Compulsive Behaviors

One class of compulsive behaviors has been named "grooming behav-iors." These include biting fingernails, picking scabs, plucking hairs and whiskers, squeezing earlobes, chewing on lips and cheeks, and doing other things with face, head, and hands that are unsightly or painful. (The name implies efforts to remove surface imperfections.) Whereas one can avoid driving home drunk by leaving the car at home or avoid a spending binge by leaving money and credit cards at home, one cannot leave cuticles, eyebrows, and cheeks at home. The number of Americans who suffer significantly from these grooming behaviors has been esti-mated to be in excess of twenty million (Azrin and Nunn 1977). These behaviors are usually partly conscious and partly unconscious, and when conscious they may be quite irresistible.

The journal *Science* reported in 1989 (vol. 245, p. 934) that "millions of women suffer from an obsessive-compulsive disorder called trichotillo-mania. Most don't go bald, but a lot of bathroom drains can get clogged up, presumably. Now there's help: A drug called clomipramine shows promise in treating the disorder."

An interesting method of coping (interesting partly because it has application to other deprecated behaviors) is identifying precursors, be-haviors that tend to precede, as preliminaries, the unwanted actions. (Al-cohol is often a precursor to smoking relapse; if one has trouble giving up cigarettes but not alcohol, giving up the latter for a period can help to pre-vent smoking relapse.) Azrin and Nunn (1977) explain that many of the offending facial features that invite compulsive "grooming" – a whisker the razor missed, an errant eyebrow, or a small scab – are "discovered" while a hand is idly exploring the face. Once discovered, the item's de-mand for attention becomes irresistible; but if one never discovers it by hand, it doesn't offend and won't be noticed. The manual exploration is a habit that is nowhere near as compulsive as the irresistible sequel. If one can learn to keep one's hands away from one's face, eliminating the precursor activity, one may escape the irresistible invitation to groom. Keeping one's hands off the face requires only breaking a habit, not resisting a compulsion.

For cuticles and fingernails, Azrin and Nunn recommend professional manicures until the compulsive habit has subsided.

## 9. Captivation

Many of us waste time we cannot afford wasting by watching an old mystery or western, often something we had no intention of watching, something we got caught in the middle of while idly scanning the channels. For most of us there is a precursor that is not too hard to cope with: turning the set on in the first place. Like not eating the first peanut or potato chip, not getting a glimpse of the police chase can be crucial to not staying to the end. However, it is not always easy to resist looking for the late news or for something "really" worth watching; the set does get turned on, with the risk of a lost hour. I often wish the hotel would disconnect the TV in my room; I'd happily pay extra for a televisionless room.

For some of us, reading can be as bad as TV, and a cheap mystery isn't over in an hour or two. Puzzles can be captivating, and people who can't afford the time to solve them have learned they cannot easily be laid down unfinished or put out of their mind.

## 10. Nervous Interaction

Interacting with dogs was mentioned earlier, an interaction that could generate "irrational" fear in me and possibly irrational aggressiveness in dogs. More widespread is interaction among people leading to undesired feelings and behaviors. Yawning and coughing are examples, and so are giggling and embarrassment.

### Giggling

Giggling is never solitary. Two youngsters, even teenagers, can be seized with uncontrollable giggling; when scolded they may stop, but just looking at each other starts it again. To control it they must avoid catching each other's eyes. Some years ago, with a group studying the role of television in American culture, I watched an episode of the Mary Tyler Moore show, "The Death of Chuckles the Clown." A beloved clown had died when the episode opened; everybody felt the need to grieve but nobody could help laughing whenever Chuckles was mentioned. The climax was a funeral at which the entire congregation giggled uncontrollably; the minister finally assured them that Chuckles could only have been delighted at their inability to control their laughter. Fifteen minutes into the program the group I was with was laughing uncontrollably. It was nervous laughter, self-conscious laughter, participatory laughter; whenever we managed to stop, someone among us would try to stifle a giggle and, at the sound, we were rocking back and forth again, choking with uncontrollable laughter. I am sure if I had seen the show alone in my room I would have kept my poise, and I would have missed a convincing demonstration of the show's authenticity.

### Embarrassment

Embarrassment is an interactive phenomenon: It takes two to make somebody embarrassed, and usually both are. A lone astronaut stranded on the Moon can do nothing to embarrass himself.

I had poignant experience while driving with a friend. He began to complain about the treatment he had received from an anonymous referee. As he enumerated the errors and fallacies of the referee's report I recognized the manuscript: I was the referee. The author's name had been removed and it had not occurred to me that my friend might be the author. He assumed my complete sympathy because this manuscript was in the style and methodology of an earlier manuscript that I had told him I admired.

I had a choice. I could confess at once, guaranteeing mutual embarrassment, or I could feign sympathy and risk a worse embarrassment if he discovered that I not only was the referee but had deceived him during his diatribe. I took the chance; he never knew; we were not embarrassed.

Suppose he had caught on. He might, for example, have been quoting something from the referee's report that he had not thought to associate with me, and with me beside him the attribution to me became inescapable. He might have turned to me in shock as he discovered my dirty secret; my treachery would have been the greater because of my earlier claim to have admired the earlier manuscript. As we looked in each other's faces, and he knew that I knew that he knew that I knew that he knew I was the referee, our "common knowledge" of my role would have allowed no escape from an embarrassment that might have afflicted us both forever.

Suppose instead (and conceivably this is what happened) that he had caught on, just while complaining to me, to who the referee was and appreciated the mutual embarrassment that would ensue if he let on; he might have kept secret that he knew my secret and spared us both. If it had become apparent to me that he had caught on and was not letting on that he had caught on, I should have cooperated in disguising my awareness of his awareness. The important thing was to avoid "ratification," mutual acknowledgment of the mortifying fact that I was the referee. "Ratification" is Erving Goffman's (1955) term. "Poise" is Goffman's term for skill in disguising or hiding one's own embarrassment to cut the positive feedback between one's own and the other's embarrassment or the talent to be casual in dismissing the occasion for embarrassment.

So, there are rational ways to reduce the likelihood or the intensity of embarrassment, but whether embarrassment itself is rational or irrational, or neither of the two, is not easy to assess. Usually, embarrassment is a mutual awareness of something that causes an unpleasantness that is due entirely to the awareness. If we could agree that there is nothing unpleasant except the mutual awareness, we might rationally agree to ignore whatever it is that is making us uncomfortable. Knowing that if I do not become embarrassed, the mutual embarrassment will be aborted, should I rationally be able to make myself unembarrassed? Just as there were two equilibria in the fear-of-dogs cycle (rationally fearing them and providing grounds for fear or rationally not fearing them and giving no grounds), there appear to be two possible equilibria for mutual embarrassment: being embarrassed and providing each other grounds for embarrassment or not being embarrassed and providing no grounds. Whether this makes embarrassment "irrational" I do not know.

## 11. Misbehaving Minds

It is an interesting question whether rationality should be construed as including command over one's mind or how much command might be demanded. Guilt and regret, bad memories, apprehension of painful experiences to come, or even a tune playing over and over in the mind are hard to expunge by a rational act. One can sometimes "forget" by becoming absorbed (the student worried about tomorrow's exam can go to an exciting movie to displace the anxiety), but it is hard to teach one's mind the principle of sunk costs.

Being able to fall asleep at appropriate times is a help and a comfort that many of us miss, regularly or occasionally. Insomnia is a perverse phenomenon: Awareness of it, remembering that one is insomniac, aggravates the insomnia. Some people report that they become so sensitive to their own sleeplessness that, as they finally begin to drift off, they notice it and jolt themselves awake. The best antidote to insomnia is to forget that one is afflicted.

I love sashimi. I read some years ago that there is a rare occurrence of a live worm in raw fish, a worm that is not destroyed either by the chewing or the digesting of the fish. There are two such worms, one of which is serious because it can do harm to the intestine; the other is less serious but uglier: It can be regurgitated, after growing large, and come out of one's mouth. I know the odds of this happening, and there is no reason to think that suffering such trauma is more likely than dying in an automobile crash on the way to a Japanese restaurant. But I could not, for a long time, keep myself from thinking about that dreadful worm, the one that might come out of my mouth, and wondered whether I could ever eat sashimi again.

Daydreaming, also known as fantasizing, is ambivalently irrational. Imagine an adult playing out a scenario in his or her mind, finding large amounts of money, heroically saving a child, making passionate love, or delivering a lecture to an enraptured audience: What is the person *doing*? There are two interesting possibilities: The person is wasting good time unawares, idly letting his or her mind play at his or her expense, or the person is enjoying a good enough facsimile of the real thing to be getting genuine pleasure at little material cost. Either way there is some form of self-deception; both the wayward enjoyment of the autonomous fantasy and the counterfeit pleasure of the "authored" fantasy depend on a somewhat convincing pretense that what is being imagined is real.

What could be more irrational than caring what happens in the final chapter of a book that someone has written? You tell me that someone is finishing a poignant novel and hasn't decided whether the heroine's kidnapped daughter will survive the final chapter; you ask me whether I care how it turns out. The final chapter consists merely of binary digits on a diskette that will become letters on a page; change the letters and the daughter is murdered; change them again and the daughter is rescued. It's all letters on a page: There is no such daughter! But if I read the book, I care; I may weep if the daughter doesn't survive. Weeping is part of my enjoyment of the book, my utterly irrational participation. It is fantasy, but fantasy that I do not control; the author does. And here's what is so wonderful: If I could discipline myself to think rationally, and reduce the daughter to digits on a diskette, I would lose some of the best of life in a world of art and civilization. My ungovernable and irrational mind gives me nightmares, worms in the sashimi, embarrassment at things past, and fears of things to come; but it lets me identify with characters in a play or novel and lets me experience, at least momentarily, feelings that money cannot buy.

And then there is absentmindedness and forgetfulness, for which we learn tricks to cope. Forgetting, or having faulty memory, may be thought of as a sort of intellectual irrationality, a little like computing wrong or reasoning faultily. If one knows that one forgets, or knows that one remembers certain things wrong, one can try to cope, for example don't ask about someone's spouse by name if you know you are likely to get the name wrong, and write down where you parked the car.

## 12. Temptations

The reader will probably acknowledge that most, or at least some, of the conditions I have described can reasonably be called "lapses from rationality," perhaps "normal, justifiable lapses from rationality." Turning around and running from the mountain lion, or yanking back the hand that needs its wound cauterized with a hot iron, is an act that I know is wrong, which somehow I cannot help at the time, an act for which I may seek some coping strategy or device, and an act for which I need not apologize.

By "temptations" I mean the kind of circumstance or phenomenon that I illustrated at the beginning of this essay with the cigarettes flushed down the toilet. I have in mind the temptations that people wish to resist but find hard to resist but those they often resolve to resist but fail to resist, sometimes with serious consequences. The distinguishing characteristic is that, notwithstanding the cliché of the "drug-crazed" addict, the person succumbing to what I call temptation is usually quite aware, while succumbing, that he or she is violating an earlier resolve to abstain and will eventually regret the momentary lapse and any ensuing longer lasting relapses. (Remember, I am interested only in the "temptations" that people wish to resist; the contented overeater, addict, or nymphomaniac dwell outside my subject.)

I have been particularly interested in the ways that people try to govern their behavior in relation to temptations by avoiding the opportunities or the stimuli, by manipulating their own incentives or capabilities, or by affecting the functioning of their nervous systems. (The cigarette example represented one or more of these; we'll explore it further.) Some of these strategies may require an understanding of the nature of the lapse; some just require understanding how to prevent it. I can know that, if there are peanuts on the coffee table, I'll eventually start eating them and that I can avoid eating them by having them removed; that doesn't mean I can describe how my mind will be working when I reach the point of putting a peanut in my mouth fully aware that I didn't want to do it and didn't intend to do it and will shortly wish (or am already wishing) that I hadn't done it.

There are many behaviors that display the paradox that a person who is quite uncrazed and fully conscious apparently "voluntarily" does what the person is simultaneously fully aware one shouldn't do. Scratching hives, poison ivy, or chicken pox almost always aggravates the burning and itching; the person scratching knows that it does and even while scratching can be amazed at what he or she is doing. The boy who believes masturbation is evil, harmful, or contrary to God's command continues to believe it as he watches himself masturbate. The man or woman who is persuaded that sexual infidelity is fraught not just with risk but with the near certainty of awful consequences continues with the persuasion while engaging in the act. This phenomenon, altogether different from that of the thirst-crazed water drinker, the pain-crazed evader of the cauterizing iron, or the panicked confronter of the mountain lion, is utterly tantalizing. One sees oneself doing what one knows one should not be doing; there is no loss of awareness of consequences, only (this is one way to say it) loss of command from one part of the brain to another.

## 13. Addiction

A central role in what I call "temptations" is played by addictive substances. I appreciate the different needs of different groups – psychiatrists, lawyers, pharmacologists, legislators, psychologists, and neurologists – for their own specialized definitions of addiction; but I believe understanding the nature of the lapse from rationality that occurs when someone succumbs to temptation can be advanced by comparing a wide range of behaviors: gambling, eating, drinking, smoking, sniffing, inhaling, injecting, masturbating, or watching television. What is happening when the reformed alcoholic accepts the drink, the reformed smoker rushes to the store before it closes to buy cigarettes, the conferee reaches for the Danish on the table, or the boy convinced that masturbation is evil masturbates is not yet susceptible, as far as I can tell, to scientific description. I believe too little attention is paid to introspective reports.

To illustrate what I have in mind I return now to our friend who flushed his friend's cigarettes away at the beginning of this paper. I averred, and expected no dispute, that the man's action was interpretable as a rational act, probably taken in anticipation of some lapse in his later rationality. This anticipatory preemption is easy to describe. Harder to describe is what that later action, the one he wanted to avert, would represent, what the state of his "rationality" would have been, at the later time, had he later engaged in smoking, or perhaps what the state of his rationality is still going to be at that later time when he might have engaged in smoking but does not. (Actually, maybe he will; his preclusive act may not have been decisive.)

An interesting question is whether he, at the time he disposed of the remaining cigarettes, had a good understanding of what his later state of mind was going to be. Might he, if we could ask him, be able to tell us just what the mental or emotional circumstances were going to be that he wanted to guard against?

There are a number of possibilities.

## 14. Alternative Scenarios

One possibility is that our toilet flusher anticipates drinking alcohol and knows by experience that drinking interferes with his reasoning so that he succumbs to the temptation of cigarettes if cigarettes are readily available. If the individual believes that what alcohol does is to distort or to anesthetize some of the functions or characteristics that go under the name of rationality, we can call this situation "anticipated irrationality." We discussed it earlier.

This drinking contingency can be divided into two parts. The simpler case is that the drinker enjoys relaxing in the evening with a few drinks even though it impairs somewhat his "rationality," because nothing he plans for the evening places demands on that part of his rationality that is subverted by alcohol. He could keep his smoking under control by going without alcohol, but for the price of a pack of cigarettes he can eliminate the danger and have his drink, and that is what he has chosen.

The second case is that he wishes not only not to smoke but also not to drink, but he has a drinking problem, which he knows he may not be able to control this evening: To be on the safe side (with respect to smoking, not to drinking) he destroys the cigarettes. We need here some reason why he doesn't pour the liquor down the toilet too. Maybe he is going out for the evening where he will be confronted by an opportunity to drink, expects to succumb against his (currently) better judgment or expects to feel obliged to drink among his friends, and fears coming home with impaired rationality to find cigarettes on the coffee table. (Our story might have been more tantalizing if, upon discovering the cigarettes his friend left behind, he had studied the pack momentarily, had then put it back on the coffee table, and had gone to the pantry and poured his whiskey down the sink!)

Counting the alcohol contingencies as the first two, another set of possibilities is that cigarettes by their physical presence – the sight of them, perhaps the smell of them, or the mere unforgettable knowledge of their presence – stimulate a craving, a craving that is a serious discomfort and distraction unless satisfied by the smoking of a cigarette. There are at least three cases here.

One is that the craving is such a discomfort and distraction that it will produce an unproductive and disagreeable evening; at the risk of complete relapse it would be rational to avoid such a dismal and unproductive evening by going ahead and smoking. The presence of the cigarettes is an irritant that if not removed will make it rational to smoke. (An alcoholic might be considered rational to drink before undergoing some exceedingly painful procedure, the risk of relapse being a lesser evil than the pain.)

A fourth possibility, the second of these craving contingencies, is that he knows he will *not* succumb – will not suffer a lapse from rationality – but will be sufficiently distracted by the presence of cigarettes to make it worthwhile to dispose of them. In the same way he may, when it is time to leave to work, turn off the TV, not because he expects to succumb to it but just because the flickering screen continually disturbs his concentration.

The third craving contingency (the one I find hardest to understand, though not to recognize) is that he expects to succumb "irrationally," not merely to be distracted, and not to be so distracted that it would be better to go ahead and smoke, but simply to be unable to maintain his resolve not to smoke. He wants now not to smoke later, no matter how strong the craving, and he cannot trust his brain to function "rationally" under the stimulus of available cigarettes. (The case of extreme thirst mentioned earlier may be an exemplar.) He would rather handcuff himself to the radiator across the room than be free to succumb. He doesn't need to; it is the presence of the cigarettes, or the knowledge of their presence, that will influence his brain chemistry, and *that* he can take care of in the toilet. Less poignantly, people often remove the peanuts, or the Danish, from the conference table or the nearby buffet, either in fear of succumbing or just to remove the distraction. (Clinicians have told me that recovering heroin addicts suffer much less craving when in a "clean" place where they know there is no chance to obtain heroin than when they believe, rightly or wrongly, that there is some possibility of obtaining the stuff.)

A sixth possibility is that the craving is independent of the presence of cigarettes. He knows that late-night fatigue (or late-night awakening) or some circadian change in brain chemistry (he needn't know what) will produce an irresistible craving for tobacco. It is the same whether the cigarettes are in open view, stowed in a cupboard, or five miles away in a vending machine. Destroying the cigarettes has no effect on his choice to smoke, only on his ability.

Here, too, we can distinguish two cases. One is that there will be no other cigarettes available at reasonable cost. No stores will be open, no one will be on the street from whom to bum a cigarette, or perhaps the man lives out of town without a car and no buses will be running. Tossing the cigarettes effectively denies the wayward choice.

The other (seventh) case is that the craving is the same whether or not cigarettes are present, but their absence affects his ability to avoid surrender. I can think of two reasons. One is that an impetuous urge might control his behavior for a minute or two, but not for an hour, and if he grabbed his car keys and drove away his better judgment would overtake him within the time it would take to get to the store and park the car, and he'd be safe. (Maybe knowing that he'd return without cigarettes suffices to keep him from getting in the car.) Alternatively, in self-discipline some lines are harder to cross than others: He might allow himself "just one cigarette" if this act of God offers the opportunity, whereas getting in the car and driving in search of cigarettes would be a flagrant violation of the regime he has imposed on himself, and the prospective loss of self-respect would suffice to deter him.

An eighth case is that the individual simply believes that if the cigarettes are there he will smoke. It may not matter where his belief came from. If instead his problem were alcohol, it is easy to believe he may have been authoritatively told that if there is liquor in the house he will drink it or is

likely to. Therapies to cope with cigarette addiction have not institution-
alized any such lore about the inexorable consequences of spending an
evening in the company of cigarettes, but our man could have received
strong advice to that effect and taken it seriously even without a theory of
his own of how the breakdown occurs in the presence of cigarettes. If his
belief is based on his own experience with earlier attempts to quit, it may
be a belief in behavioral phenomena that he can analyze in retrospect.

His belief could be true, and it serves his purpose that he destroyed
the cigarettes. His belief could be false, and he has wasted a dollar for his
friend. And there is a third possibility: The proposition that if cigarettes
are available he will ineluctably smoke before the evening is over may
be the kind that is true of anyone who believes it and false of people
who do not. Anyone who "knows" that with cigarettes around he will
smoke before midnight knows that as midnight approaches he will have
an irrefutable argument for going ahead and not waiting for midnight.

Somewhat akin to belief is suspense. Suspense produces discomfort
and anxiety. If one spends an evening watching oneself, wondering
whether one is going to succumb to temptation, two things can happen. One is that the evening can be exceedingly disagreeable; the second is that the suspense goes away once a cigarette is smoked. Until the
cigarette is lit one is uncomfortably apprehensive that he may light a
cigarette; lighting the cigarette provides an escape. Is there something
irrational here? There is a painful uncertainty whether I shall survive the
night without smoking, an uncertainty that is dispelled upon smoking.
Can the certainty that failure has occurred bring relief from uncertainty
whether it will occur? (Again, if it were alcohol, the anesthesia might
enhance the relief.)

We have so far, I believe, somewhere from nine to eleven distinct scenarios, depending on how we count subcases. But they are all scenarios
of what the person has in mind when he "rationally" disposes of the
cigarettes. That is an important part of our subject, and in several of the
cases it may be an adequate diagnosis of just what later would happen if
the cigarettes were not made to disappear.

## 15. Recapitulation

Drinking contingencies:

1. Wants *to drink*; knows he may smoke.
2. Wants *not to drink*; knows he may drink, may smoke, so pours away the alcohol.

Craving *induced by presence* of cigarettes:

3. Discomfort so great it would be *rational* to smoke.

4. Disomfort enough to be *worth the dollar*.
5. Craving so great he will *lose control* and smoke. Analogy to thirst.

Craving *independent of presence* of cigarettes:

6. If available will smoke; if not, can't.
7. Local absence affects *ability to resist.*
    a. Loses control only *briefly*, not long enough to acquire cigarettes.
    b. Act of God versus flagrant violation.

Belief in *inevitability*:

8. Belief is *true*; good to dispose of the cigarettes.
9. Belief is *false*; he wasted the cigarettes.
10. Belief is true *if (and only if)* he believes it.

Suspense

11. Not craving, not belief, but *suspense* so disagreeable he will succumb to the need to dispel it.

## 16. Postscript

The tantalizing case, in terms of sheer description, is the third "craving" contingency: With no alcohol or other exogenous chemical influence, no brainwashing about inevitability, just the anticipation that, either gradually or impetuously, the resolve not to smoke will be, or may be, replaced or overwhelmed by the desire to smoke, and in full consciousness that he badly wanted (wants?) not to, he will voluntarily smoke. This is often a correct anticipation; it is the anticipation of something that actually occurs. But exactly what it is that actually occurs continues to defy description.

## REFERENCES

Azrin, N. H. and R. G. Nunn (1977), *Habit Control in a Day*, New York, Simon and Schuster.
Goffman, E. (1955), "On face-work," *Psychiatry: Journal for the Study of Interpersonal Processes* 18, 224.
Koppett, L. (1967), *A Thinking Man's Guide to Baseball*, New York, Dutton.

# Index